BURNED

BURNED

THE INSIDE STORY OF THE 'CASH-FOR-ASH' SCANDAL AND NORTHERN IRELAND'S SECRETIVE NEW ELITE

SAM McBRIDE

MERRION
PRESS

First published in 2019 by
Merrion Press
An imprint of Irish Academic Press
10 George's Street
Newbridge
Co. Kildare
Ireland
www.merrionpress.ie

9781785372698 (Paper)
9781785372704 (Kindle)
9781785372711 (Epub)
9781785372728 (PDF)

British Library Cataloguing in Publication Data
An entry can be found on request

Library of Congress Cataloging in Publication Data
An entry can be found on request

Typeset in Minion Pro 11/15 pt

CONTENTS

For Anna, Kate and Patrick, without whose generous patience this would not exist, and for my parents whose labours freed me to dig with a pen, rather than the spade of my forebears.

AUTHOR'S NOTE

Some of the facts in this book will seem so lavishly far-fetched that I feel it necessary to assure the reader that none of this is fictitious. I have sought to lay out the evidence so that the reader can form their own view of not just what really happened but, crucially, why. While much of what happened is factual, the reason that it happened is less straightforward. I have attempted to leave it to readers to decide why events turned out as they did and in order to do so I have sought to incorporate the views of all the key individuals in an effort to explain – even if it does not excuse – why they acted as they did.

What follows draws heavily on the tens of thousands of pages of evidence published by Sir Patrick Coghlin's public inquiry into the scandal, which involved remarkable work by a small team without whose work this book would be missing multiple key sections. Much of that evidence has never before been reported. Frequently, I have specified that a piece of evidence emerged in written or oral evidence to the inquiry. For stylistic reasons, on other occasions I have not made this explicit even where I am reporting what transpired at the inquiry or in its voluminous evidence bundles.

Unless otherwise referred to, all references to RHI refer to the non-domestic Northern Ireland RHI.

For simplicity, I have referred to the Department of Finance throughout even though its name was the Department of Finance and Personnel until May 2016.

My gratitude goes to the scores of sources who have fed through information on an unattributable basis, some of whom continue to hold senior positions and whose actions are at some risk to their own positions. Without them, this book would be shorter and far less complete.

PREFACE

It was a Tuesday night three weeks before Christmas in 2016 and I was tired after a long day covering Stormont for the *News Letter*. That afternoon there had been a debate in which almost half of Assembly members from the opposition parties were incredulous that public cash was going to an alleged UDA (Ulster Defence Assocation) boss, while the rest of MLAs (Members of the Legislative Party), from the DUP (Democratic Unionist Party) and Sinn Féin, were incredulous that the issue was even being raised. But all of that – along with the Stormont edifice within which Northern Ireland's politics had been contained for almost a decade – was to be blown away by a scandal triggered that night by a BBC *Spotlight* documentary on something called the Renewable Heat Incentive (RHI).

For about a fortnight there had been rumours within political and media circles that *Spotlight* was investigating a significant story about one of First Minister Arlene Foster's special advisers, Stephen Brimstone, who had suddenly quit his £92,000 role and was said to have had an RHI boiler which was being investigated by the police.

In fact, Brimstone did not feature in the programme. But the story *Spotlight* told – of extreme incompetence by civil servants and of a bungled subsidy which was to cost taxpayers hundreds of millions of pounds despite a whistleblower personally having warned Foster – was shocking, even by Stormont's standards of ineptitude.

In almost a decade reporting Stormont, I had seen at close quarters both the individuals and the flawed system central to the scandal. Yet for some reason, there was something about the scale and nature of this squander which meant that as a taxpayer I was angry watching BBC reporter Conor Spackman casually tossing bundles of cash into a fire as he set out the perversity of what had happened.

But there was a particular reason why that night I was less dispassionate than might otherwise have been the case. Just weeks earlier, my mother-in-law had been given a fatal diagnosis: a doctor told her that she had motor neurone disease. Despite having spent much of her life voluntarily helping others as a nurse in Africa, she was now a victim of the NHS's vast neurological waiting list and had to pay to be diagnosed by a doctor at a private hospital. (The diagnosis, made by a doctor whose work has led to the recall of 3,500 patients and a Department of Health inquiry, would later turn out to be wrong.)

It was the juxtaposition of what seemed like the feckless profligacy – or worse – of senior figures in Stormont with the consequences of that money not being available to the health service which drew me into the story.

In the weeks that followed, the more that I examined what had gone on, the more suspicious it seemed. The weekend before Christmas I used comparison software to contrast the 2011 RHI legislation in Great Britain and the Stormont legislation signed off by Arlene Foster the following year. Having done so, it was difficult to give credence to the official explanation for the absence of cost controls in the Northern Ireland scheme – that putting in cost controls would have been complex and time-consuming.

Scrolling through page after page of the two pieces of legislation, it was clear that Stormont had copied and pasted about 98% of the GB law, with minor changes. The vast majority of what changes there were involved technical changes to reflect Northern Ireland legislation, such as changing 'authority' to 'department'.

And yet, when I got to Part 5 of Section 37 of the GB regulations, the copy and paste stopped. There were 107 missing words and it was those missing words which at that point were estimated to cost taxpayers about £500 million. It was clearly someone's conscious decision to stop copying at that point, before resuming the process for the remainder of the bill.

This book is the culmination of my desire to establish who made that decision, and why. Since then, the scandal has led to the collapse of devolved government in Northern Ireland, which at the time of writing some two and a half years later has not been re-established. It has led to a public inquiry which has exposed long-hidden incompetence and misbehaviour not just among Stormont's political class but within the Northern Ireland Civil Service, the institution which more than any other has shaped Northern Ireland since its creation in 1921.

And the scandal has also exposed the disproportionate influence of a vast, monopsonistic company which received preferential treatment from government – simply because of its size. The preferential treatment helped it grow still bigger, thus increasing its influence and creating an inescapable circle antithetical not only to capitalistic theory but to basic principles of fairness.

****

What follows will make uncomfortable reading for some DUP members who never expected their actions to be exposed. Few of us, even if not engaged in nefarious activity, would relish our candid text messages, emails, phone records and flaws being pored over in public as has happened to them. But with the power, prestige and handsome salaries which those individuals enjoyed as public servants comes the requirement to be accountable. Their personal discomfort has to be weighed against the wider public interest, as some of them have come to accept.

I have never set out to traduce the DUP or any other party but have followed the evidence where it has led – from the DUP, to the civil service, to boiler owners, to Sinn Féin, private consultants and elsewhere. The truth is too important to be the plaything of those who either want to cover up the DUP's role in this affair or to use RHI as a stick with which to beat the party.

To those who have formed a negative view of the DUP based on the actions of some of its members who feature in this story, consider this: key pieces of information in this book have come from DUP members. Some of them spoke publicly at the RHI Inquiry; many others spoke privately to the author. Without them, some of what we now know would have forever remained hidden. All parties are a mixture of those driven by high principle and those who have baser motives.

This book should be read with the knowledge that we all make mistakes – and there will be too many in what I have written. Therefore, I hope that this is not perceived as a puritanical denunciation of those who have erred honestly, but as an attempt to understand how and why RHI fell apart. It is only by frankly addressing each individual's role that we can piece together why what now seems obvious did not seem that way to at least some of those most closely associated with the scheme at the time.

To anyone adversely affected by any of my errors, I apologise in advance. If any book was to wait for perfection, it would never be published. I trust you will accept that I have made an honest – if imperfect – effort to understand what transpired.

****

There is one final important context in which this book should be read. Northern Ireland is not a society riven with gross corruption of the sort which daily afflicts hundreds of millions of people's lives around the world. Driving from Belfast to Dungannon, one is not stopped by police eager for bribes, as would happen on the road from Lagos to Abuja, nor do companies have entire divisions devoted to paying political bribes, as has been the case in Brazil.

Therefore, some of the worst behaviour set out in this book – which will to many readers appear morally corrupt, even if it is not in breach of the law – is in my experience the exception, rather than the norm. It is inaccurate to take the worst practices revealed by RHI and extrapolate that all politicians and civil servants are inept or worse. That is patently not the case – it was politicians and civil servants who ultimately played key roles in exposing RHI. In Stormont there are capable and honourable public servants. As one of many examples, Aine Gaughran, the Department for the Economy's senior press officer at the time of the crisis in 2016 and 2017, was unerringly professional as chaos unfolded. Over scores of phone calls, emails and other queries, she responded politely and promptly, never once seeking to suppress the truth or apply inappropriate pressure.

But when bad behaviour is discovered, it should be shocking. It is only by expressing outrage at serious malpractice that we can deter its recurrence. Once a society becomes endemically corrupt, it is a cancer which is almost irreversible. One of the most dangerous, but now widespread, public views about politicians is that 'they're all the same – they're all in it for themselves'. They aren't – but if we assume that they are, then it is barely newsworthy to report on bad behaviour and we are unwittingly hastening the fulfilment of our bleak analysis.

The work of the inquiry, along with other material now being published for the first time, allows the truth about RHI to be known in considerable part. But even after the multi-million-pound inquiry – and the modest efforts of the author and other journalists – there are elements of this story which defy explanation or which hint at darker truths than those which can for now be proven. Now we know in part, but some of this story remains unknowable and that is one of the reasons why it is so compelling.

CHAPTER 1
ON HIS KNEES

Deep in the belly of Broadcasting House, Jonathan Bell's silver-white head was bowed in prayer. On his knees, the man, who just seven months earlier had been part of the DUP's powerful team of Stormont ministers, was being prayed for by two elderly associates who laid their hands on the politician's shoulders as the television cameras rolled.

BBC staff looked on bemused as one of the men – who despite being under hot studio lights was still wearing an overcoat necessary on a cold Belfast night – prayed: 'We ask for the power of thy Holy Spirit to come upon Jonathan and those who interview him, that you will direct them in all that they think and say, that at the end of the day we all will have been done [sic] for the glory of Christ. Father, hear our prayer, for Christ's sake. Amen.'

As Bell rose, the two allies who had joined him – the politician's father, Pastor Fergus Bell, and an intriguing business character called Ken Cleland – slapped him on the back. But while the scene added a layer of spiritual intrigue, which even for Northern Ireland's religiously infused political landscape was rare, the two protagonists in the studio knew that a brutal political defenestration was about to begin. Bell, a self-confident character who had always been disliked by many of his colleagues, had been around politics for long enough to understand that his words would critically destabilise his party leader, already embroiled in a financial scandal that had been leading news bulletins for more than a week.

Seated opposite the Strangford MLA was a big beast of broadcasting: Stephen Nolan, BBC Northern Ireland's aggressive and populist presenter, whose daily radio programme reached more people than any other outlet.

For an audience who had been given teasers about the dramatic nature of what was to be said in the interview recorded a day earlier, the first image they saw of the politician – kneeling in a television studio – was compelling. A few moments later, seated languidly across a studio desk from Nolan, Bell's opening words were dramatic:

I have undertaken before God that I will tell you the truth and yes hundreds of millions of pounds has been committed and significant amounts of money has [sic] been spent. I am authorising every detail, every document, every civil service document that I signed, every submission that I signed to be made publicly available and to be examined exactly as the truth I now give you.

By Wednesday, 14 December 2016, the day the interview was recorded ahead of broadcast the following night, Bell had been talking to Nolan for a full week. When he arrived at the BBC's Ormeau Avenue headquarters that afternoon, it was amid unusual secrecy. Rather than coming through the front entrance, he drove into the internal car park and was brought into the building through a side entrance. From there, it was a short distance to Studio 1 – a rarely used windowless studio, which had been commandeered for what would be one of the most dramatic political interviews in the history of Northern Ireland.

Inside the studio, one of BBC NI's most senior editors, Kathleen Carragher, was crouched behind a screen, unseen by the cameras, following what was being said. A few yards away, BBC NI's veteran political editor, Mark Devenport, and a handful of senior production staff were crammed into a tiny nearby room under a staircase, which had been hastily rigged to receive a live feed of the interview as it was recorded.

Bell was a willing interviewee and quickly got to the point. He was there to unburden his soul about his role in keeping open a disastrous green energy subsidy – the Renewable Heat Incentive (RHI) – when it could have been reined in or shut. By now, much of Northern Ireland was aware that the decision to keep the flawed scheme open was projected to cost taxpayers about £500 million.

Pressed by Nolan on why he, as the minister in Stormont's Department for Enterprise, Trade and Investment (DETI), did not close RHI at the first opportunity, Bell replied: 'Other DUP spads involved themselves in the process … I was then informed by my special adviser in the department that other DUP spads were not allowing this scheme to be closed.'

The word spad, an abbreviation for ministerial special adviser, would have meant little to most viewers. But to anyone familiar with Stormont it was instantly clear what Bell was doing: he was accusing some of the DUP's most powerful figures of deliberately wasting vast sums of taxpayers' money. Within the DUP's ultra-centralised structure, spads were people of immense power.

Bell went on to name the two spads as Timothy Johnston, the DUP's most senior backroom figure, and Andrew Crawford, the long-standing adviser to Arlene Foster. Foster had been Bell's predecessor as DETI minister and had set up the scheme. By now she was both DUP leader and First Minister.

It was a clever move by Bell to seize the initiative. He was putting himself up against one of the most aggressive interviewers in Northern Ireland. However, as much of the information was new, Nolan did not yet have the full picture as to what had gone on. Bell's story was particularly compelling because he was committing to full publication of every document and demanding a judge-led public inquiry – the most rigourous investigation possible under British law. Why would he be doing that if he had any doubts as to the accuracy of what he was saying?

The constant references to God gave Bell's interview a confessional quality, which attempted to elevate it above the dirty world of politics. By underpinning the drama with theology, Bell was making it harder for the DUP to make him the scapegoat for what had happened. Some people – even some Christians – viewed the prayer scene at the start of the broadcast as a gimmick that undermined Bell. Standing in the studio, Bell had asked Nolan if he could pray before they began and the broadcaster agreed. It is unclear whether Bell knew at that point the cameras were rolling; he soon did because producers were concerned that a decision to air that scene could appear to be intrusive. At the conclusion of the interview Bell was asked if he wanted that segment to be broadcast. The politician gave his consent and that was the first image a quarter of a million viewers saw the following evening.

The interview was littered with the insistence that he was telling the truth; the late Ian Paisley had exhorted him to tell the truth, his wife that morning had told him to tell the truth, even God had told him to tell the truth.

The broadcast contained a slew of remarkable allegations, including the claim that the second-most senior civil servant in his department had come to him to whistleblow about Bell's spad. According to Bell, the civil servant had been asked 'behind my back' to 'cleanse the [departmental] record' by removing Foster's name and a reference to the Department of Finance from a departmental submission about RHI.

He then spoke of the period just after cost controls were introduced, where Stormont received confirmation from the Treasury that it would have to bear the full bill for the overspend – a colossal sum for a devolved administration. At that point, in January 2016, Bell said that he had been advised by the civil service to shut RHI immediately, which he wanted to do, but he was 'ordered' by a 'highly agitated and angry' Foster to keep the scheme open. He said: 'She walked in and shouted at me that I would keep this scheme open. She shouted so much that then Timothy Johnston came into the room.' Breaking down, he said he had tears in his eyes because 'children are dying' as a result of the NHS losing money: 'The regret that I ultimately have now, when we're seeing terminally ill children being sent home from hospital, is that I didn't resign ... I think we all should hang our heads in shame for what has occurred.'

It was an explosive, gripping performance. But although some of what Bell was revealing was accurate, sceptical viewers might have wondered why he had not thought to tell the public about this for almost a year – until the point where he thought he was going to be blamed. Nolan asked the 46-year-old politician: 'Are you involved in a coup to take Arlene Foster down?' Bell replied: 'Nothing, as God is my judge, could be further from the truth.'

But all was not quite as it seemed. What Bell presented as a straightforward case of political corruption was more complicated. The public inquiry Bell demanded would ultimately dissect his ministerial career and expose an unflattering portrait of a minister who took limited interest in the work of his department, while acting in ways which did not sit easily with the devoutly religious image he had cultivated.

****

Almost a year later, at the opening of the public inquiry into the cash for ash scandal, a section of the Bell interview was played on video screens in Stormont's old Senate Chamber – where for 111 days witnesses would give evidence about the scandal. Counsel for the inquiry David Scoffield QC described it as 'gripping television' that had an 'explosive' impact. The lawyer said: 'It's probably unprecedented in contemporary Northern Ireland politics as an example of a former minister turning on senior party colleagues, including his party leader, the then First Minister.' But until now the story behind that theatrical – and bitter – split with his party has never been told.

It began a full week before he recorded the interview. Bell rang Nolan, who on his morning radio show had picked up on the scandal after the broadcast of an exposé by colleagues in BBC NI's *Spotlight* team the previous night. Nolan had a sharp eye for spotting the significance of a story but his instinct was reinforced by quantitative evidence. Whereas a good Nolan show would involve about 150 calls from the public, in the days after *Spotlight*, the programme was getting upwards of 300 calls a day, with most of the callers – unionist and nationalist alike – expressing fury. Responding to the sense of anger and interest in the story, the programme would break multiple revelations about the scandal for weeks.

Bell was eager to talk, and he had gone to the man who could deliver his words to a bigger audience than anyone else in Northern Ireland. Nolan invited Bell to his salubrious home on the shores of Strangford Lough that day. That in itself was indicative of the story's significance because Nolan valued his privacy. Although an ebullient media personality, only one politician – Martin McGuinness – had ever been to his rural home.

Bell did not hold back. What he had would blow the government wide open, he claimed, and the former minister spoke candidly about what he knew. What Nolan did not know was that the man in front of him was secretly recording him, something he would admit to several days later.

The following night, Bell returned to Nolan's home. This time the broadcaster was joined by his senior backroom team, composed of his editor, David O'Dornan; producer, David Thompson; and BBC's Ireland correspondent, Chris Buckler, an old friend of Nolan's from their days at the Belfast's Citybeat radio station.

Bell, who agreed for the meeting to be recorded so that the journalists could fact-check his claims, positioned himself at the end of the dining room table. With a tape recorder in front of him, the MLA opened up. At points, he would veer off to relate tales that were irrelevant to RHI but revealed the level of distrust that now existed between himself and DUP colleagues. He had brought tape recordings and bulky paper files from his old department to back up his riveting tale. Some of what he said has never been broadcast for legal reasons and because it is not clear whether it is accurate. He referred to allegations that one senior DUP politician had been having an affair with another politician and that another senior DUP member had taken drugs. Seamlessly, he would shift from those lurid tales of alleged iniquity to impressing upon his listeners the fervency of his faith. Over coming days, Bell would repeatedly tell Nolan that God had told him to come to him with the story.

Demonstrating the vanity which had not endeared Bell to many of his party colleagues, he spoke about himself in the third person, with the journalists attempting to steer him back to the topic in hand. Showing remarkable trust in the journalists, at Bell's own suggestion he handed over the password for his personal email account, which he had used for government business, and gave them permission to search through it for any relevant material.

Over the coming days, the small team moved into the office of a BBC executive who was on holiday and began going through Bell's paperwork and recordings. Nolan, who flew to Manchester every weekend to present phone-ins on BBC Radio 5 Live, withdrew from those programmes and worked round the clock to get the story on air.

But the MLA still had not committed to going in front of a camera. He wanted the BBC to do the story – but he did not necessarily want to be seen to be their source. Bell told them that if they did the story he would then come out after it to confirm that what had been said was accurate. Several days into the contact with Bell, he arranged for Nolan to meet him in an isolated spot near his County Down home. Nolan parked beside Bell's car and the MLA got into the passenger seat. After a brief conversation, he handed over another audio recorder containing a secret recording of a senior civil servant.

As Nolan drove back to Belfast he listened to what he had been given. Whether deliberately or inadvertently, the recording finished and another conversation played. This time it was a conversation between Bell and former First Minister Peter Robinson. They were discussing what Bell was doing and whether he should go to *The Times* or to Nolan with his story. Robinson sounded cautious in what he said, with Bell driving the conversation. Nevertheless, the involvement of Robinson – just a year after he had stepped down as DUP leader – added a new layer of intrigue to what was unfolding.

By Monday evening, it seemed that Bell would not do an interview, though he had given enough material for a one-off TV programme. Nolan and Buckler went to meet Peter Johnston, BBC NI's controller, to make their case for bringing the story to air. Now less than a fortnight to Christmas, Johnston asked: 'Can this hold until after Christmas?' Convinced by the journalists' arguments for urgency, Johnston gave them the green light. He now sent for Carragher. As the most senior editor in the BBC's Belfast newsroom, Carragher had frequently clashed with Nolan – who operated within a silo and was as fiercely competitive with BBC colleagues as he was with rival organisations. One senior BBC source said that there were 'massive tensions' between them but they quickly agreed to work together professionally and agreed that they could press ahead without Bell speaking on the record.

The following night there would be a furtive meeting between the journalists and Bell, which would be decisive. The BBC had booked a room in the Holiday Inn, a mid-market hotel across the road from Broadcasting House. Arriving separately, the politician, Cleland and the BBC men – Nolan, Buckler and Thompson – gradually entered the bedroom. Cleland, an adviser and religious companion, was a figure whose role has not been fully understood and who would crop up again in the story. It was clear to the journalists that Cleland was very influential in Bell's decisions. One BBC source described him as 'the strategist' who referred throughout to himself and Bell as 'we', and it appeared to the journalists that Cleland was the key figure who had to be convinced if Bell was to talk.

During the half-hour meeting, a deal was struck, with Bell giving his word that if *The Nolan Show* revealed parts of the story the following morning, then he would do a TV interview. The next morning *The Nolan Show* made a series of revelations based on Bell's conversation, his secret recordings and the paperwork he had turned over to the BBC. The story threw the Executive into a tailspin. Stormont Castle released a statement to the programme, which said that no one from the DUP or the Office of the First Minister and deputy First Minister had sought to delay closure of the scheme. But within an hour, Stormont Castle had contacted *The Nolan Show* to retract its own statement, which then only came from the DUP – not the joint office shared with Sinn Féin. Cleland was delighted with the coverage and Bell agreed to now come and be interviewed.

****

On the night the Bell interview was broadcast, what viewers did not know was that his allegations were heavily reliant on a secret recording of one of Stormont's most senior civil servants just two days earlier.

Four days before the interview was broadcast, Andrew McCormick, the permanent secretary of Bell's old department, was at home on a Sunday afternoon when he received a phone call from his former minister. Now five days after the *Spotlight* programme and amid a fevered political atmosphere, Bell wanted to exercise his right to view ministerial papers about the scheme, which had come to him as minister. Unknown to McCormick, Bell was taping the exchange.

In a lengthy conversation, the politician said that the attempts to rein in RHI when it had been out of control the previous year had been delayed by Johnston, the DUP's most powerful backroom figure. When Bell asked if there was documentation that would show that, McCormick said it was unlikely because 'people know when to use emails and when not to', and went on to admit that 'the actual to-and-fro of what's really going on very rarely goes down on paper, you know'.

During the conversation, McCormick inadvertently – perhaps out of nothing more than politely attempting to hurry the conversation along – agreed to Bell's suggestion that delays were the responsibility of the First Minister's spads. That bolstered Bell's belief that there had been a hidden hand interfering in his department – and he was now potentially going to be thrown to the wolves to protect that unseen individual or individuals. In fact, McCormick had at that point no evidence that the First Minister's advisers were involved and instead believed the delays to have been primarily the work of Foster's spad, Andrew Crawford.

Parts of the conversation revealed Bell to be hopelessly confused about the key timeline of the delays. At one point he suggested that the spike in applications – where claimants piled in before cost controls – had come after cost controls. McCormick agreed to meet him the following day and Bell said he would bring 'one of my researchers' with him.

By this stage, the DUP was suspicious of what Bell might do. Prior to McCormick allowing Bell to view documentation in his office, the mandarin spent more than an hour with Timothy Johnston and Richard Bullick, the First Minister's two key lieutenants, who had asked to go through the material with him in advance.

In that meeting, McCormick told Foster's closest advisers that he had understood that Crawford had worked in the background to delay cost controls. The civil servant felt exasperation at what seemed to be a reluctance by the DUP spads to accept the evidence of delay from someone in their party. By the time McCormick left that meeting and travelled a mile across the Stormont Estate to his department's Netherleigh House headquarters, Bell was already waiting to see him.

But alongside the former minister that evening, Bell was accompanied by someone familiar to McCormick – Ken Cleland. Cleland was a somewhat mysterious figure, known to many at Stormont and an associate of some senior DUP figures. He and his wife had been extremely close to Peter Robinson, the former First Minister, and his wife Iris. After the revelation of her affair with a young man and subsequent financial transactions with property developers, Mrs Cleland stood by her friend, taking her shopping and looking after her at a point when some of the former DUP MP's erstwhile friends forsook her.

Peter Robinson had trusted Cleland with a sensitive Stormont appointment, putting him on the board of the Maze Long Kesh Development Corporation, a body with responsibility for developing the economically significant and potentially lucrative site of the former Maze Prison, but whose work was riven with political arguments. In that role, Cleland had travelled with the then DUP Health Minister Edwin Poots and McCormick, Poots's then permanent secretary, to Germany three years earlier for a study trip. The three men had discussed their shared Christian faith, meaning that when Cleland arrived with Bell he was a figure known to the civil servant.

On entering Room Two in Netherleigh House with Bell, Cleland said to McCormick that he was probably wondering what had brought them together. Answering his own question, Cleland told him that they had become close companions in Christian fellowship. McCormick recollected that they presented themselves as 'seekers after truth, indeed potentially as "agents of righteousness"'. Cleland proceeded to inform the mandarin that he had arrived bearing a prophecy about Bell. The self-proclaimed prophet went on to predict that Bell would be vindicated over RHI. The agent of righteousness then admonished the civil servant: 'We've got to be very careful what our motivations are here ... and we're not going to allow any motivation, which is a wrong motivation, because God will not bless that.' Later, McCormick would ponder whether Bell had engineered the encounter to appear motivated by high religious principle so that he would lower his guard.

With the politician's spiritual adviser having prepared the path, the MLA then turned to more pressing temporal matters. Bell, who was prone to exaggerated earnestness, even if answering Assembly questions on mundane matters, did not undersell the significance of his mission. He told McCormick that he was determined to make public the truth of what had happened even if it cost him his career. He assured McCormick that he would strongly protect the interests of officials and not allow them to be blamed for the failures of others.

McCormick, one of Stormont's most experienced senior civil servants and someone who was respected across the political spectrum for his integrity, handed over a file of documents to Bell and left the room for him to study it.

Prior to contacting McCormick, Bell had spoken to Robinson who advised him that as a former minister he could go and ask for documentation from the department. Bell's closeness to Robinson and the fact that there was some contact between the two men about the issue in this period led to speculation within the DUP as to whether Bell was acting as part of some wider plan.

During a whispered conversation while McCormick was out of the room, Cleland asked Bell: 'Why did you decide to go to the fount of all knowledge or of all wisdom?' A source familiar with Bell's thinking in this period said that this was a coded reference used by the two men to refer to Nolan. But before Bell could answer, McCormick reappeared in the room.

On his return, Bell asked McCormick what he would say if he was asked why there had been a delay in reining in the scheme. Speaking bluntly, McCormick replied: 'Well to be totally honest with you, I'd be saying I was aware that there were discussions within the party and the ministers and the special advisors had been asked by others within the party to keep it open – that's the truth.'

After more than an hour at Netherleigh, and with the alarm for closing time ringing, Bell and Cleland bade their farewells and disappeared off into the night.

Throughout the encounter, Bell had made a series of references to preparing himself for some future occasion on which he might have to answer for what had happened on his watch. For three months, the Assembly's Public Accounts Committee had been holding hearings to investigate the scandal, and McCormick assumed that was what Bell had in mind. He never considered that he might have a more immediate and more public plan. But the day after his meeting with the former minister, the DUP spad in McCormick's department, John Robinson, informed him that his meeting with Bell and Cleland had been recorded.

It is still not clear how Robinson had knowledge of the recording, but within the DUP it was known that Bell had a habit of covertly recording conversations. McCormick was profoundly disturbed. For a former minister to secretly record his most senior civil servant was not just outside of his experience; it was unprecedented. Over coming days, it became clear that Bell had given the recording to the BBC and was threatening to give permission for it to be broadcast.

It was a period of intense personal turmoil for McCormick. After a long career in the civil service, just three weeks earlier he had been interviewed by the First and deputy First Ministers in what was the final stage of the competition to be Head of the Civil Service. At that point he did not know whether he had got the £180,000-a-year job, but he knew that the rules had recently been changed to allow the DUP and Sinn Féin ministers to conduct the final interviews for the appointment – a level of political control over the politically neutral post which does not exist anywhere else in the UK. In the days to come, DUP minister Simon Hamilton said in a message to senior DUP spad Richard Bullick: 'His concerned reaction suggests he has said things he knows he shouldn't have. This could be very bad for him. And us.'

Bell had told the public in his Nolan interview that McCormick was 'a man of the utmost integrity and one of the finest servants of the civil service that the public could ask for'. Yet he had secretly recorded him on at least two occasions and was holding over this 'man of the utmost integrity' the threat of releasing those conversations if he did not act in a certain way. Almost two years later at the public inquiry, Bell would be pressed repeatedly to explain why he had felt it necessary to act with subterfuge. He told the inquiry that 'all I wanted to do was have a valid record of what my concerns were'. But when David Scoffield QC asked him why he had not chosen to use 'more transparent ways' of securing that objective, Bell did not answer the question but gave a rambling reply, which included everything from the scale of the RHI overspend to the fact that he had been a premature baby and a comment on his political career.

Eventually, inquiry chairman Sir Patrick Coghlin interjected:

> You have told us already that you regarded him as a man of integrity. All I'm trying to find out … is why, given that assumption on your part, your acceptance of his integrity, you found it necessary to carry out a concealed recording. Now one possible inference is that you did not consider him to be a man of integrity.

Bell paused for several seconds before saying: 'My answer to that is that I do believe him to be a man of integrity. I also believe I needed a contemporaneous, accurate account and … the permanent secretary had to act to [the wishes of] his current minister, who may or may not want information released.'

****

The interview with Bell had been recorded on the afternoon of Wednesday, 14 December and clips from it were trailed on Nolan's radio show the following morning. It was clear that Bell had spoken out in a way which was sufficiently significant for the BBC to immediately bring it to air, inserting it into the schedule so late that it did not even feature in that morning's newspaper TV listings. The DUP top brass consulted David Gordon, who as Executive Press Secretary was just three months into his job as Stormont's top spin doctor.

As a former editor of *The Nolan Show* and one of Northern Ireland's sharpest journalistic minds, he could see the scale of the unfolding crisis. Knowing Nolan inside out, Gordon had a cunning plan for how to manage the growing mess. That afternoon he phoned Buckler – who was covering the story for the *News At Ten* – and asked him if he was to interview Foster could he guarantee that the interview would also be played as part of the special programme in which Bell was speaking out. It was a shrewd move, which attempted to not only save Foster from Nolan's aggressive interview style but also potentially split the BBC team by offering the major opportunity to one of Nolan's closest friends. But when Buckler relayed the call to Nolan and Carragher it was Carragher who – despite her years of clashes with Nolan – ruled out the idea, saying firmly that Stormont would not be dictating who could conduct a BBC interview.

Having attempted to circumvent Nolan, the DUP now accepted that it was better for Foster to face his questions rather than allow Bell's allegations to go out unchallenged. The news was relayed to the BBC at about 5.30pm, with the interview scheduled for 8pm – a rapid turnaround for such a major broadcast – and a satellite truck was despatched to the Stormont Estate.

During the negotiations about whether to do the interview, Foster had spent that day in Stormont Castle being briefed by Johnston and Bullick. McCormick was also present in the baronial castle which served as the Office of the First Minister and deputy First Minister. McCormick's DUP minister had asked him to personally attest to the accuracy of a fact sheet which was being drawn up for the BBC.

Although Nolan was Stormont's most feared journalistic inquisitor, the BBC personality had a reputation for being somewhat chaotic, and he was late arriving at Stormont for the interview with Foster. As the DUP and civil servants waited for the BBC crew to arrive, someone produced fish suppers which they ate while making final preparations for what would be a career-defining moment for Foster.

It was after 8pm – just over two and a half hours before the Bell interview was to be aired – when the presenter finally arrived at the castle's security barrier. With him was a senior BBC editor, Kevin Kelly, and producer, David Thompson, as well as the technical team. At the front door of the castle, they were met by Gordon.

As they walked down a corridor in the castle, one of the journalists saw a group of elderly men in a dimly lit room. It appeared to him that they were praying.

As equipment was set up in the First Minister's ground floor office, the atmosphere was frosty. The delay in Nolan's arrival meant that McCormick had just 30 seconds to quickly speak to him as he passed through the castle entrance. A pale McCormick, who was described by one of those present as having seemed 'petrified', was asked to confirm that an RHI fact sheet was accurate. 'Yes, I can confirm that,' he said. Having been kept waiting by the DUP so that he would have a conversation with Nolan, the mandarin later recalled how he was 'very frustrated' that he had only seconds to converse with him and as a result he left the castle immediately to go home. That small detail would become significant much later.

But despite the fact that Nolan had been late, Foster now took her time in appearing. Nolan sat and waited as the clock ticked down on what he knew was already a tight timetable until the interview aired. When Foster did arrive, she just said: 'Stephen. You have been a busy boy', and sat down. As her microphone was fitted and technicians checked the lighting and sound, the First Minister said nothing to Nolan and kept her head to the side, choosing not to look at the broadcaster.

Unseen by viewers at home, Foster's two key spads, as well as Gordon and DUP Press Officer Clive McFarland, had positioned themselves at the back of the room in Nolan's eyeline. But, just minutes into the exchange, it was Foster who was visibly uncomfortable, breathing heavily and speaking over the interviewer's questions. With cables running out of the castle to a satellite truck, footage of the interview was being viewed live in the BBC newsroom in central Belfast where Buckler was communicating directly to Nolan via an earpiece.

Foster presented a simple version of events in which officials had failed to ever raise problems with the scheme during her tenure and she had made no mistakes. As Nolan probed her about the fact that on her watch the scheme was launched without cost controls and then a proposal to put in cost controls was abandoned, Foster facetiously said: 'Yes, Stephen, so I'm supposed to have a crystal ball in relation to these issues?'

Nolan went on to ask her: 'Do you know why there were these delays [in introducing cost controls], then?' Foster shot back: 'I've no idea.' An incredulous Nolan said: 'You haven't asked?' Laughing nervously as she replied, Foster said: 'No, that's a matter for Jonathan. Why would I ask? I was Finance Minister at the time.' Pressed on how she could not have enquired, given the scale of the overspend, Foster pinned the blame on her colleague, saying: 'I am bemused as to why he would leave it open for such a period of time.'

Under acute pressure from the interviewer, Foster was asked: 'So let me get this right – we are hearing now of people who have been putting boilers into sheds and blasting heat into the sky. We know that these delays were a factor. And as our First Minister you still haven't asked what the delays were about. You still haven't briefed yourself.' Again with a smile on her face, Foster replied: 'No, because Jonathan signed off on a submission on the 4th of September ...'

Nolan cut across her: 'Do you not want to know?' Again shifting the focus to Bell, she replied: 'Well, I'm sure you've asked him the reason why he's left the scheme open for that period of time. I'd be very interested to hear why he has said that ...' Foster went on to deny Bell's allegation that she had shouted at him to keep the scheme open, and counter-alleged that it was Bell who had 'used his physical bulk to stand over me in quite an aggressive way ... he is a very aggressive individual'.

Foster presented the final two-week delay in closing the scheme – a point after cost controls were in place but which led to a multi-million pound increase to the bill for taxpayers – as being down to civil service and legal concerns. It would later emerge that in reality that delay had been a political price extracted by Sinn Féin. Even at this stage, when fighting for her political career, Foster was still trying to cover the full story to protect the DUP's relationship with Sinn Féin – a fact republicans would soon forget as they rewrote history and presented her as someone with whom it was impossible to work.

As soon as the interview finished, Foster took off her microphone and left the room, without saying goodbye. Johnston immediately got to his feet and approached Nolan, threatening legal action over Bell's allegation about his role in the scandal.

After the interview aired, the broadcast returned live to Nolan in the studio with BBC NI's political editor, Mark Devenport. Devenport, a hugely experienced journalist not given to exaggeration, began by saying: 'Words are almost failing me.' The programme ended with a flurry of rights of reply from those named by Bell, all of whom denied wrongdoing.

****

Later at the public inquiry, Foster was grilled on why she had told Nolan she had 'no idea' why cost controls were delayed. By then it was clear that her closest aides – who spent hours preparing her for the major interview –

had been aware of the allegation that it was her spad who was responsible. She told the inquiry that McCormick had not spoken directly to her about that prior to the interview, but she 'became aware of his belief after the recording of *The Nolan Show* … once the recording was over, I went into the junior minister's office … and Andrew sheepishly said it was his belief that Andrew Crawford had delayed the scheme'. She went on to say that it was 'certainly … after *The Nolan Show* that I spoke directly to Andrew about the issue'. Hamilton, who was also there that night, gave similar evidence to the inquiry about a conversation with McCormick 'definitely after the interview'.

However, McCormick said that if that conversation did occur it could not have been after the recording – and therefore would have to have been before Foster told the public she had 'no idea' why cost controls were delayed. The civil servant – who, like Foster, was giving evidence under oath – said that Foster and Hamilton's version of events 'could not possibly have happened'. Speaking gravely, he told the inquiry: 'I'm very concerned by what I've had to say this morning.'

The credibility of McCormick's explanation was strengthened by what had been his immediate reaction to Foster's interview when it went out that night. After watching her 'no idea' answer, he texted DUP spads in shock to say: 'Difficult to understand why she said she had no idea … when I have said I would have to tell [a Stormont committee] that.'

****

On the day after the *Spotlight* programme went out, Bell discussed the issue by phone with North Antrim DUP MP Ian Paisley – a figure removed from the party leadership, and perhaps an indication that by this stage Bell was looking beyond the party hierarchy for advice. According to Paisley, they discussed the situation on 7, 8 and 9 December with the contact taking the form of a phone call, a conversation in Parliament Buildings and then a personal visit to Bell's home.

Paisley found a 'troubled' party colleague who 'was concerned about his future' but insisted they never discussed an appearance on *The Nolan Show*. During a 'rambling' discussion over tea in Bell's home the MLA advised with characteristic self-importance that he had 'a team of the greatest legal minds in Britain working on the case for him', Paisley later told the inquiry. In Paisley's evidence to the inquiry – by which point he knew that his former colleague's DUP career was over – he said he had listened in 'amusement' to Bell's claim that he had 'recordings and documents' that proved corruption. Naming senior DUP colleagues, Bell claimed that some of them were making vast sums of money out of RHI, Paisley said. The MP said that 'frankly it was quite sad' but they 'parted on good terms'. Paisley went on to discredit his former colleague's version of events, saying: 'I was aware I had just met Walter Mitty in the flesh.' However, the fact that Paisley had such extensive contact with Bell at the point where he was about to go public with his allegations was in itself striking. For years, there had been enmity between Paisley and the DUP leadership.

By contrast, Bell was closer to Robinson than any other DUP MLA and was reverential towards him. Bell employed Robinson's son, Jonathan, as his constituency office manager and Robinson's daughter-in-law as his part-time secretary. At a time when, as DUP leader Robinson felt under internal threat, he rewarded his friend's loyalty, promoting him to junior minister in 2011 and then a full Stormont minister in 2015 – a decision which inadvertently led to Bell taking responsibility for RHI at the point where it was about to fall apart. There were also sensitive personal circumstances which meant that Bell had a unique bond with the Robinsons, which went beyond simple transactional politics.

One Stormont source who observed the DUP at the closest of quarters over more than a decade said: 'Peter could ask Johnny to murder someone and he'd do it.' That metaphor could not have been used for many of the others around Robinson. He had always been feared and respected within the DUP rather than loved.

Robinson did not have many close friends and was wary of several senior colleagues whose loyalty he suspected. But Bell's devotion to the DUP leader was such that while still a minister – and around the time that RHI was falling apart – he began work on a PhD about his party leader and told colleagues that Robinson had agreed to turn over some of his personal papers to him for the academic study.

Although Robinson had stood down as DUP leader by 2016, given Bell's closeness to Robinson, his contact with Paisley – who was from a rival internal faction – stands out.

The picture is further complicated by comments Cleland and Bell made to the BBC journalists as they discussed the story in that period. Both men gave the impression that they were concerned about Foster's leadership, seeing it as an attempt to liberalise the party and move it away from its religious roots.

If that was a significant motive for what Bell did, it does not sit easily with the idea that Robinson was in any way orchestrating what was going on. Robinson was the man who had spent years gradually modernising and moderating the DUP. He had a vision of the party replacing the Ulster Unionist Party as the dominant party of unionism, and knew that to do so meant reaching beyond the narrow world of Protestant evangelicalism.

When contacted for this book, Robinson was reluctant to explain why he had discussed with Bell whether to go to The Times or Nolan and whether he was encouraging him to speak out as he did.

Instead, he responded – along with other DUP figures to whom separate questions were asked – with a solicitor's letter which claimed that what had been put to him was 'replete with inaccuracies and defamatory content'. The letter did not specify anything which was actually inaccurate but threatened that 'in the event that publication of inaccurate and defamatory material occurs our clients are fully prepared to issue appropriate legal proceedings'. Further attempts to secure answers to the questions drew no response.

****

After the BBC *Spotlight* exposé on 6 December, the foundations of the Stormont Executive – which with the DUP and Sinn Féin jointly at the helm had ruled Northern Ireland for almost a decade – were rocking. By the time the Bell interview went out, they were crumbling. A massive audience had watched the extraordinary programme. When it was broadcast on BBC One NI, 56% of everyone watching TV in Northern Ireland at the time was tuned in. The average for that 10.40pm slot was for BBC One to have 18% of all viewers. The following day, the Sinn Féin deputy First Minister Martin McGuinness phoned Foster to ask her to step aside as First Minister while an investigation took place into the allegations. She instinctively refused, and from that point devolved government in Northern Ireland was on a path to implosion. But to understand why the revelations of December 2016 shook Northern Ireland, we have to go back in time.

CHAPTER 2

IN THE BEGINNING

Fiona Hepper, who had nothing to contribute as an energy specialist, arrived in June 2010 to head up the team of Stormont civil servants responsible for energy policy. In a textbook move for the Northern Ireland Civil Service, Hepper was a 'generalist' who shifted from department to department, learning on the job, before climbing the career ladder in an entirely different area.

The psychology graduate began life in the civil service as a statistician, and over a 30-year career had worked on everything from cross-border economic cooperation to labour market policy, communications, telecoms and emergency planning.

This was how Northern Ireland had been ruled from its creation in 1921. While the ministers in charge of departments had shifted from the Official Unionist Party during the first half-century of the fledgling state's existence, to direct rule ministers flying in and out from London, to power-sharing ministers appointed after the 1998 Good Friday Agreement, there had been one constant: the Northern Ireland Civil Service.

The energy team, which Hepper now headed, sat within the Department of Enterprise, Trade and Investment (DETI), a relatively small department of about 600 officials but with sprawling responsibilities for tourism, company law, economic development, consumer protection, health and safety law, cross-border trade and telecoms. When Hepper arrived in her new post, she had four hours with her predecessor to be briefed on the new role and was given a bundle of documentation. It was a huge job. Energy policy was in flux. There was a push for renewable energy systems, about which there was limited understanding, alongside proposals to extend the piped natural gas network in Northern Ireland and moves to harmonise the electricity markets between Northern Ireland and the Irish Republic. On top of that, DETI's small energy team found itself responsible for transposing EU energy directives into law – a responsibility the devolved Scottish or Welsh administrations did not have to do because energy policy was only devolved in Northern Ireland.

Not long into the post, Hepper decided to create a renewable heat branch within the wider division. But while that might have implied that there was now a significant team working on the issue, it was the equivalent of one and a half full-time staff, with the official in charge of the branch working part time. But no one at the time viewed this as a Father Ted approach to public administration – it was just how things had always been done in Stormont.

Although Northern Ireland had a huge public sector compared to anywhere else in the UK, the reality was that a region of 1.8 million people was always going to be doing things on a shoestring by comparison to Whitehall, the throbbing administrative centre of the British State from which an empire had once been administered and wars directed. But despite Stormont's small size, there was a culture of civil servants doing whatever it took to please their ministers and a reluctance to hand back power to Westminster.

By the time Hepper arrived at DETI, it had for some time been under pressure to set up a Renewable Heat Incentive (RHI) as part of an EU-wide endeavour to financially induce businesses to move from fossil fuel heating systems to sustainable green alternatives. There were two main reasons: an EU directive had set challenging targets for renewable heat. If those were not met by 2020, there would be huge fines from Brussels. The second imperative to launch RHI came from business. The rest of the UK had been moving ahead with a scheme that would launch in late 2011. Without that subsidy being extended by Stormont, Northern Ireland firms would be at a competitive disadvantage. In the aftermath of a major recession, that was a potent argument in favour of action.

The Whitehall department responsible for the GB heat subsidy had in 2008 offered Stormont the chance to piggyback on its scheme, something which would have meant Stormont agreeing for Westminster to legislate for it. Hepper's predecessor, in consultation with Arlene Foster, the DUP minister who would spend seven years in the department, decided not to avail of that opportunity. They believed that Westminster was rushing unnecessarily and were aware of a wider political concern in Northern Ireland, which at that point was just a year into the restoration of devolved government. The unionists and nationalists who made up the Stormont Executive were agreed that the whole point of devolution was to allow them to decide their own policies. In that context, simply handing back power to Westminster was counterintuitive.

Regardless of that benign logic, which might explain what happened in 2008, from this moment of divergence suspicion would subsequently arise as to why a handful of civil servants and politicians in Belfast had decided to do their own thing and whether someone somewhere in Stormont had spied an opportunity to exploit a funding stream from London.

Civil servants and politicians often consciously chose not to record controversial information, which makes it difficult to be certain what happened in the early years of the scheme. And the fact that the department had a deliberate policy of not recording important information means that if there was any inappropriate decision to deliberately exploit the RHI funding it would almost certainly not be recorded.

After deciding to run its own subsidy for renewable heat, Stormont then took its time about deciding what that should be. Staffing shortages contributed to it taking a year for DETI to hire – largely with EU money – consultants AECOM Pöyry to produce a report on the local potential for renewable heat.

But many years later, at the public inquiry which would dissect the inner workings of Stormont like never before, the independence of that report came under scrutiny. There has long been a suspicion that civil servants sometimes hire consultants because they want an apparently independent voice to advise them to do what the officials wanted to do anyway. The inquiry revealed a level of departmental involvement in writing the report, which was not publicly apparent at the time.

Initially, the consultants sent DETI a draft version of their report. But after discussions with DETI officials they made changes to that document. In response to that changed version of the report, civil servant Alison Clydesdale, head of DETI's sustainable energy branch, emailed the consultants in May 2010 to say that the report was now 'closer to what we need'. But she went on to make a series of suggestions for further changes. One of the requests was to alter what the consultants were recommending should be done to incentivise renewable heat. Clydesdale wrote: 'We would need something stronger than "some form of incentive".' She went on to make a series of suggestions and told the specialist engineering consultancy: 'I'm not sure about saying that geothermal energy should be prioritised and supported over other resources – perhaps you could think about some rewording here … this wording could present difficulties going forward.'

Four days later, senior AECOM consultant Andrew Turton replied to say: 'Please find attached the latest version of the report with the changes as requested — I hope these are now as desired!'

Having at the request of the department scored out 'some form of incentive will be required', the consultants then replaced it with what would be the report's key recommendation: 'The GB scheme appears to be inefficient for Northern Ireland ... Northern Ireland needs to develop a NI specific incentive scheme.' It seems clear that the department influenced that key recommendation, even though it had already assured the Assembly that the report would be an entirely 'independent assessment'. However, the report presented that as a means of being less generous – not more generous – than what was being planned in GB.

Intriguingly, Turton's initial report had contained a recommendation to review the GB RHI scheme once it started, and to 'monitor the cost-effectiveness of the incentives through applications supported'. That was also scored out. The failure to either monitor what was going on in GB or to keep a close watch on the cost of the scheme would be two crucial areas which would make it possible for the costs of Stormont's scheme to escalate rapidly. Why had someone chosen to remove that part of the report?

Rather than have the confidence to take the experts' advice and then make its own decisions, DETI appeared to be wanting to steer the consultants towards telling it what it wanted to hear in certain areas. At the inquiry, Clydesdale defended her actions, insisting that much of what she had done was 'correcting the report and correcting inaccuracies'. At the time, Foster presented the report to the Assembly as being based on 'reliable data' and that it had 'considered appropriate methods of incentivisation', something she said was 'absolutely vital to ensure that future policy decisions regarding the incentivisation of renewable heat are based on sound evidence'.

In a September 2010 letter to the Assembly committee which scrutinised her department, Foster said: 'I can assure you that I am committed to developing the renewable heat market in Northern Ireland and see many benefits in doing so.' That personal commitment to RHI and a desire to be associated with it would mark many of Foster's pronouncements when she thought the policy was popular. Once it began to implode, the minister suddenly became very keen to stress how limited her involvement had been.

Once the report was agreed between the consultants and the department, one of Hepper's first tasks was to get her team to summarise it for the minister. On Hepper's advice, Foster issued a press release in September 2010 to reassure those pressing for a renewable heat subsidy that Stormont was planning to follow what had happened in the rest of the UK by setting up its own incentive scheme.

By the time Hepper arrived, the need to get a renewable heat subsidy launched was also being driven by the fact that Westminster had made available to Northern Ireland a pot of £25 million for four years from 2011, which could only be spent once a Stormont scheme was launched. That was unusual in government spending. Generally, a need would be identified which would have a certain cost and then the budget would be found. But here the cart came before the horse, with money being made available and Stormont finding itself under pressure to spend it. From the outset, the central concern for some in Stormont was that the money might not be spent in Northern Ireland.

Two years after her arrival, by which time the scheme was still six months from being launched, Hepper emailed her minister's special adviser (spad), Andrew Crawford, a figure who from early on appeared to have taken a particular interest in the scheme. In that email she referred to the 'exceptional circumstances' as a result of 'the pressure to spend the Treasury money or lose it'.

As decisions were being taken about how the scheme would operate, one central preoccupation of those designing the scheme was that it would see as much of the available money spent as possible. Even if there was no deliberate desire to overspend because of a belief that it was all Treasury money, the ambition to spend as much of the available budget as possible was always going to conflict with what taxpayers might assume would be a desire to spend as little of their money as possible in order to achieve the desired goal.

****

Under devolution, senior members of the Northern Ireland Civil Service were unusually keen to satisfy their political masters. Having for decades operated under direct rule ministers from Westminster, many of whom spent limited time in Northern Ireland, suddenly civil servants found themselves reporting to ministers who had firm ideas about what should be done.

Looking at the political landscape, even civil servants with stunted political antennae would have realised that the DUP and Sinn Féin were likely to be in charge for a very long time. In that context, many civil servants bent over backwards to please their ministers. Some officials were reluctant to give their minister bad news. But in some cases, this was not necessarily in the politician's interest.

In November 2008, four years before RHI would be launched, Hepper's predecessor as head of energy division, Jenny Pyper, was sent a memo by a subordinate. In it, Pyper was reminded that when they had opted out of the UK-wide RHI scheme, she had sent a submission to the minister on the issue but they had taken out a paragraph saying that DETI 'cannot hope to develop this area of work with current resources'. Years later, when they were asked to explain how the debacle had started, civil servants would claim that they had inadequate resources to set up the RHI scheme Foster asked them to create – and Foster would say that she had never been told of the extent of the staffing difficulties in energy division.

Just five days before that memo, Pyper – who would go on to become the Northern Ireland Utility Regulator – received another memo from an official who alluded to the glacial pace of Stormont's own thinking on incentivising renewable heat. Referring to a Whitehall document to which DETI had been invited to contribute, they said: 'I am finding it hard to find something positive to say on heat, so it is not mentioned specifically.'

****

By her own admission, Hepper was 'not an energy expert'. Nor were those around her in the team designing the RHI scheme. Joanne McCutcheon, the part-time official who headed up the renewable heat branch, came from a telecoms background. Completing the tiny team was Peter Hutchinson, a relatively junior official who had joined the civil service five years earlier, graduating with an arts degree before grappling with the complexities of biomass boilers, air source heat pumps, photovoltaic panels and tariff methodologies. Like the others, Hutchinson was a generalist, who had come straight into DETI from university. But Hepper had no qualms about the team, taking the view that they would 'learn on the job'. After all, it was how the Northern Ireland Civil Service – and to a large extent, its Whitehall equivalent – had operated for longer than anyone could recall.

However, with it clear that none of those designing the policy were experts, the department acted as it invariably did in these situations – it turned to private consultants. Hepper and her boss authorised a contract that would ultimately see £100,000 paid to Cambridge Economic Policy Associates (CEPA) for recommendations about incentivising renewable heat. If the RHI scandal resulted from a series of genuine mistakes from the outset, rather than a calculated attempt to fleece money from the Treasury, then that decision was critical to all that followed.

The situation exposed a fundamental weakness for government departments largely staffed by generalists: they were hiring in outside consultants because officials lacked expertise to do the work, yet those same civil servants would be the ones scrutinising the work for deficiencies. The absence of internal specialists meant that there was always the potential that the consultants would bamboozle the client with apparently detailed analysis, with the department lacking the cognitive clout to query the report.

Later, CEPA would claim that when it was given the contract it had less expertise in renewable heat than the department that hired it. The global consultancy firm's director, Mark Cockburn, said: 'we were learning a new area as we went along', and as a result it had sub-contracted part of the work to another consultancy, AEA. It was the partially sighted leading the partially sighted and ultimately both would see their reputations damaged as a result of the arrangement.

Seven years later, Cockburn told the public inquiry that 'I don't think we had many conversations' about the risk of the subsidy being overly generous. At that point, he said, the emphasis was to design a scheme, which was sufficiently attractive to encourage uptake, with the idea that it would be giving claimants too much money regarded as 'a very remote possibility'. The desire to make a green energy scheme generous, rather than Stormont using its powers to pare back Westminster's approach, was at first glance curious. The DUP – which held the energy portfolio for the unbroken decade in which devolution operated from 2007 to 2017 – was at best sceptical about green energy.

Prominent DUP politicians were firmly opposed to any environmental subsidies. Their reasons ranged from opposition to overburdening taxpayers to a belief that global warming was not caused by human activity.

The most outspoken critic was Sammy Wilson, the Finance Minister at the time when RHI was set up. In one of his frequent forays against environmentalists, the East Antrim representative denounced 'the high priests of the new global warming religion' for foisting high energy prices on the public.

But while Wilson was steeped in the DUP, with enough outspoken comments to fill an encyclopaedia, Foster was a very different figure. The epitome of the New DUP, she had spent years in the Ulster Unionist Party before defecting to the DUP in 2004 as the balance of power within unionism decisively shifted in favour of the party founded by Ian Paisley. Largely eschewing the heady rhetoric of the likes of Wilson, she became a Stormont minister in 2007 and cultivated a reputation for tough pragmatism with a desire to be seen to be attentive to the business community.

That circumspection meant that she was never given to the sort of controversial pronouncements on climate change, which the Finance Minister relished. But she had not endeared herself to environmental groups either. They were furious when in 2008 Foster, the then Environment Minister, rejected the case for an independent environmental protection agency, leaving Northern Ireland the only part of the UK and Ireland without such a body. So any decision to create a green energy subsidy more generous in Northern Ireland than in the rest of the UK would not have been expected under a DUP minister – unless there was some secondary benefit which they could see. Given the scale of the catastrophe that was to follow, some people would look back at what had happened during the design of the RHI scheme and wonder if someone in the DUP had not been primarily thinking about the environment at that point but had spotted the potential to supplement Stormont's budget by the back door.

CHAPTER 3
LET'S SPEND BIG

In late June 2011, consultants CEPA delivered their verdict on how Stormont should incentivise renewable heat. Except, bafflingly, they didn't. The company, which would be paid about £100,000 to advise DETI on how to encourage green heating systems, delivered a report which did not fulfil their central contractual obligation.

Key sections of the lengthy technical document focussed on a comparison between setting up a Stormont-run RHI scheme, or a grant-based scheme, called a challenge fund. The challenge fund would competitively allocate the available funding from the Treasury each year, allowing the market to provide the most cost-effective means of using the money. Once the funding ran out each year, it would shut, making it impossible to overspend. The alternative, an RHI scheme, would by contrast provide ongoing payments over 20 years to each boiler owner, with the payments linked to how much heat they produced. Having examined the numbers, it was clear to CEPA that the challenge fund provided vastly superior value for money.

On three separate occasions throughout the 145-page report, CEPA said: 'the challenge fund delivers the most renewable heat, at the lowest cost'. The report did say that an RHI scheme would have other benefits – such as providing a long-term signal to the renewables industry and encouraging people to use their boilers, rather than simply install them and revert to fossil fuels – but was clear that such a scheme would be 'significantly more expensive over the long term'. CEPA calculated that an RHI scheme would cost about £200 million more than the challenge fund. It wasn't even close.

But then, having said that, the report made no recommendation. To anyone who might have studied the report, it was a strange outcome – but all was not as it seemed. Behind the scenes, CEPA felt that the department had steered it away from saying what it really thought.

Private emails from six years later – by which point CEPA was preparing to face the public inquiry into a scandal in which it had played a crucial role – helped unravel the mystery of how the consultants delivered a report, which did not meet their contractual obligations. Yet, the civil servants seemed happy with it and agreed to pay them £100,000 without quibble.

In one email, Iain Morrow, a former CEPA employee who had been heavily involved in writing the report, told the consultancy's director, Mark Cockburn, that in 2011 it had been 'clear that DETI wanted an RHI' – a 20-year expensive scheme – rather than any other proposal. In the email, which the inquiry compelled the company to release, he went on:

> They would have liked us to recommend an RHI, but we felt, I think, that we couldn't make the judgement for them about whether their internal issues made a challenge fund unworkable. So, we agreed with them that the report would not make a firm recommendation. I seem to remember that this wasn't something they accepted easily. They wanted us to make a recommendation, but we said that it could only be to do a challenge fund, which they didn't want.

Sitting before the public inquiry in 2017, Cockburn admitted that 'there probably was some negotiation over what the final position would be'. He was pressed by inquiry chairman Sir Patrick Coghlin as to why CEPA had not directly recommended what it believed was the best option. The consultant replied that because of DETI's views 'we might have had to be a bit more nuanced about it'. Coghlin asked: 'Why would you have to be more nuanced if you have integrity about your reputation?' The middle-aged Cambridge economics graduate implied that his view of the independence of CEPA was rather different to how the company had originally described it. Readers of CEPA's 2011 report were informed that it had carried out an 'independent economic appraisal'. Cockburn suggested that he did not think CEPA should overly rock the boat by recommending something which might be awkward for the client 'if they didn't feel comfortable with it'.

The image, which emerged from the inquiry, was of a ventriloquist consultant who – in exchange for a large sum of money – was essentially echoing back to DETI elements of what it wanted to hear. Although it was perhaps not prepared to do whatever the client wanted – and did not recommend an RHI scheme – CEPA was willing to substantially fudge its professional opinion purely because those paying it wanted that to happen.

Arlene Foster's spad, Andrew Crawford, told the inquiry that when he looked back on the period he was baffled as to the apparent predisposition of officials towards an RHI. He insisted that both he and Foster were 'agnostic' as to what form the incentive should take.

On CEPA's evidence, the non-experts in DETI were successfully leaning on the expert consultants to alter their findings for the future of a scheme worth many hundreds of millions of pounds over two decades. And yet civil servant after civil servant – who, whether in DETI or the Department of Finance, were asked to sign off on the scheme – would go on to tell the inquiry that they had put faith in the recommendation for an RHI scheme because of the credibility of CEPA. Rachel McAfee, an economist in the Department of Finance, was one of many officials to scrutinise the RHI proposal, said that due to her lack of energy expertise 'I would have relied so much on the consultants'.

The civil servants in DETI's energy division, who worked with CEPA on the report, denied to the inquiry that there had been any attempt to substantially change it. Energy division boss Fiona Hepper said indignantly: 'We were certainly not pushing them in one direction or another. That is not what we were paying for.' Peter Hutchinson, the mid-ranking official beneath her who was the main point of contact with CEPA, was less emphatic, but said that he did not remember attempts to get CEPA to support an RHI scheme. 'Not that I can recall,' he told the inquiry. 'We went back to them and said "those recommendations [in a draft report] don't stack up" … I don't recall having a, you know, that kind of negotiation or anything like that. I don't think that's right.' But despite the civil servants' denials, CEPA's evidence was compelling because it reflected badly on the company. The idea that a major global economic consultancy was something of a gun for hire, willing to alter key recommendations of its reports to suit a paying client, was an argument that undermined the firm's credibility – and that of both Morrow and Cockburn. It was difficult to see what motive they could have had for concocting it.

****

CEPA's draft report had arrived with DETI at the end of May 2011, prompting a series of DETI comments and questions to the consultants, one of which said that CEPA needed to 'be very clear why RHI is [the] preferred option over [a] challenge fund.' In a telling response, CEPA replied on 15 June to say: 'Our recommendation is based on the assumption that DETI wants to do an RHI. The challenge fund option is for comparison purposes to show what could be achievable.' That comment suggested that DETI's mind was all but made up and the challenge fund was simply being put into the report so that – on paper at least – there could be some comparator.

There was further evidence that the department seemed to have made up its mind before the consultants had reported or the minister had formally taken a decision. In a document sent to Whitehall to justify what Stormont was doing, Peter Hutchinson in DETI's energy division set out that a decision had been reached that 'the most appropriate method ... has been assessed with consideration given to several options ... the Northern Ireland RHI option is consistent to the GB position and provides long-term, stable support for those wishing to invest.' The document is dated 19 May 2010, but Hepper told the inquiry that she believed it was from 2011. Even if it was May 2011, it was still a month before Foster had as minister decided that there should be an RHI as opposed to some other solution.

But, as baffling as it might initially seem that the department appeared determined to go with the far more expensive option, there was method in the apparent madness. Firstly, the renewable heat money coming from the Treasury could only be spent on the subsidy itself – not on the administration necessary to get the money to claimants. The cost of running the scheme would come out of DETI's own budget. CEPA believed that the challenge fund would be expensive to run – with administration costing perhaps 10% of the total funding. At that point, Stormont was facing belt-tightening and it would not have been easy to argue for the money to take on staff.

Some in DETI were still smarting from the unhappy experience of another green energy grant scheme just a few years earlier. The scheme, Reconnect, had seen 1,295 biomass boilers installed against an expectation of only 375 – with the costs of administering the scheme ending up being 14% of the total funds handed out. DETI thought that administering an RHI scheme would cost £1.5 million but the challenge fund would involve £5 million of administrative costs. That was partly because they could 'piggyback' on the existing GB RHI scheme by using its administrator, Ofgem, and the IT systems it had already designed for Whitehall.

Shane Murphy, who was DETI's senior principal economist, later told the public inquiry that he was clear that the officials designing RHI favoured it over the far cheaper alternative largely because it would save DETI a relatively small sum – even though they knew that overall the RHI would cost taxpayers far more. Murphy said that he had quizzed colleagues about the decision at the time. He said that it essentially did not matter that the challenge fund might be far better value in the long run because public sector budgets tend to be short term, and if the money was not available to DETI at that point there was nothing that it could do. He admitted that such reasoning would however look 'pretty strange' to the public. But there was no evidence that the civil servants had even tried to secure the money, nor that they had informed their minister of what was a fundamentally political decision.

Speaking frankly, Murphy said that civil servants 'relatively regularly' make decisions that would seem nonsensical to the person in the street. But Murphy – one of the few to internally challenge as the scheme was being designed – said that civil servants operated on the basis of a belief that there is a much bigger picture; even though the rules may seem absurd to them, they trust that there is a grand plan they cannot see, and that the rules by which they operate have been put in place for good reason. The manner in which he spoke about the civil service operation was akin to how a religious person may explain why God allows bad things to happen in the world – essentially faith fills the gap between what seems to be wrong and a wider belief that it must be right.

But there was arguably another reason to disregard the challenge fund: the very fact that it was cheaper. If Stormont set up a grant scheme, it could fund it using £25 million from the Treasury to cover the first four years. But there was no guarantee that Northern Ireland would get any money beyond that point. By contrast, an RHI scheme meant that Northern Ireland would receive £25 million and an ongoing high level of funding for the next 20 years – even if there wasn't a single boiler installed beyond that point. By choosing an RHI, Stormont was committing the Treasury to keep pumping money into Northern Ireland for two decades after the last boiler went in. That was politically attractive to both the DUP and Sinn Féin. Although the parties were diametrically opposed on many issues, they wholeheartedly agreed on a form of economic nationalism. As Irish republicans, it was obvious that Sinn Féin – a party grown out of a terrorist organisation, which only a few years earlier had explicitly waged economic, as well as human, war on the UK – would seek to get every possible penny out of London.

But in that mission they found willing allies in the DUP. Under Ian Paisley, and then Peter Robinson and Arlene Foster, the DUP's unionism was infused with Ulster nationalism. The party prided itself on extracting what it could from London – or anywhere else – for its constituents, and was not afraid to boast about it. At election time, the party would trumpet that Northern Ireland had the lowest household rates in the UK – and then would press for more Treasury money. Although popular with voters, who financially benefited from that hard bargaining, the DUP's stance sometimes led to criticism from other unionists that its populist approach could be damaging to the Union in the long term, with resentment building up in other parts of the UK.

Cockburn told the inquiry that even at the very early stage at which his firm had been involved, on several occasions DETI was asking if it could increase subsidies, leading the consultants to think that the main concern was around the payments being too low – not too generous. He said that DETI 'were asking are there grounds to increase the tariff … they were going in one way'.

CEPA consultant, Iain Morrow, the main author of the report, later told the inquiry that although it was clear that RHI was a more expensive option, the cost was not the only criteria, with 'political acceptability' being another issue.

When, under enormous pressure and after the collapse of Stormont, Foster was asked at the public inquiry whether she had wanted to deliberately maximise the amount of Treasury money coming to Northern Ireland by choosing the most expensive scheme, she strongly denied that had been the case. Foster, by then the DUP leader, said: 'At the end of the day it's still public money and it has to come from somewhere.' However, evidence would emerge proving that her closest handpicked adviser in the department, DUP colleague Andrew Crawford, had just such a crude philosophy of shipping money from London to Belfast.

****

By June 2011, the horse-trading between DETI officials and CEPA about what the report would recommend had delayed the delivery of the final document. But, with the Assembly about to rise for the summer, pressure was on to start the process of setting up RHI. The department wanted to launch a public consultation – a necessary first step before bringing legislation to the Assembly – before the summer holidays. That would see the consultation completed by the autumn and allow DETI to press ahead with launching the scheme quickly.

But in its haste to do so, some officials began to cut corners. Although the final report had not been received, Hepper was sufficiently confident about what it would say that she sent a submission to Foster. In the submission, which purported to summarise the key CEPA findings, Hepper told Foster that 'the NI RHI option is the preferred approach and offers the highest potential renewable heat output at the best value.' For a single 20-word sentence, that was astonishingly inaccurate and misleading.

Firstly, CEPA had not said that a Northern Ireland RHI was the preferred approach – on the contrary, the consultants preferred a challenge fund. Secondly, the RHI did not provide the highest potential renewable heat output. Stormont had set a target that 10% of all heat should come from renewable sources by 2020. CEPA's initial calculation was that if the government did nothing, almost 5% of heat would come from renewables by that date anyway. It believed that that an RHI scheme would deliver 7.5% but the challenge fund would secure 8.75%. Thirdly, the RHI was far from the best value – in fact, it was the costliest option. With the consultants believing that they had been steered in a certain direction by Hepper and her team, were the civil servants now attempting to do the same to their minister?

Hepper later attempted to explain the sentence as meaning that a Northern Ireland RHI was the best option when compared to the alternative of simply replicating the GB RHI. But if that was her intent, her choice of language was grossly inadequate and misleading. The natural meaning of the words represented a far more sweeping statement – and that is how Foster said she read them. But Hepper's submission to Foster was not just inaccurate – it was unusual in that it did not give the minister a recommendation. The various options were set out without a clear preference from the team of civil servants, who had been working on the policy for more than a year. A few days later, Hepper met Foster and Crawford in person to discuss the submission. It was at or immediately after this meeting, on 14 June, that the minister would decide to press ahead with the more expensive RHI scheme.

Hepper later told the inquiry that there had been 'a fulsome discussion around the detail of the figure-work and the two different options'. Foster disputed that that was likely to have been the case – but said that she had no clear recollection of the discussion. Foster's limited recall of events would prove to be a recurrent feature of her evidence to the inquiry. Foster said that going against her officials' advice 'would not have been my natural course', and so she is likely to have gone along with at least a verbal steer from Hepper, even though the official's submission had not made a recommendation. However, what transpired in that meeting will forever remain elusive because no records were kept of what was said. That would be particularly suspicious were it not for the fact that under the DUP and Sinn Féin Stormont had developed a widespread practice of deliberately not recording many meetings – and sometimes even important multi-million-pound decisions.

The man who was then the most senior civil servant in Foster's department, David Sterling, told the inquiry that officials had consciously not recorded many internal discussions which ought to have been minuted because the DUP and Sinn Féin were 'sensitive to criticism'. Sterling said that as a result of the desire for the public not to hear about what was going on it had become 'common' not to keep records because 'it is safer sometimes not to have a record that might, for example, be released under Freedom of Information, which shows that things that might have been considered unpopular were being considered'.

In acquiescing in politicians' desire for secrecy, civil servants broke their own rules which were clear that significant internal or external meetings must be minuted. In response to Sterling's comments, both the DUP and Sinn Féin insisted that they had never asked for records not to be kept, something Sterling accepted. That suggested that canny officials did not need to be ordered to break their own rules but instead willingly did so after picking up on the desires of ministers and their advisers.

By the time the final CEPA report arrived on 28 June, the costs of RHI had risen further. Hepper admitted that the minister had not been told that the costs had changed after she made her decision, either evidence of sloppiness or an implied understanding from the officials that a leap in costs was not the sort of issue which would cause themselves or the minister to re-think – perhaps because of the belief, spoken or unspoken, that as much Treasury money should be secured for Northern Ireland. But two other critical errors had been made, one of which would wrongly lead at least one senior DUP figure to later work to keep RHI open when it was out of control, based on an erroneous belief that London was paying the full bill.

CHAPTER 4
TWO FATAL ERRORS

When Fiona Hepper's June 2011 submission went to Arlene Foster, it contained three letters which would have meant nothing to most people – but to some within Stormont it made their eyes light up. The letters were AME, and to some politicians and civil servants they signalled that the funding was effectively 'free money'.

As with all ministerial submissions, the document followed an established format whereby Hepper and her team filled in answers to a series of questions, one of which was on the nature of the funding. In that section, Hepper simply said it was 'AME' – the acronym for Annually Managed Expenditure, which mandarins and politicians pronounced 'Amy'.

What Hepper had sent to Foster was a significantly inaccurate simplification of the true nature of how the scheme was to be paid for and one which years into the future would haunt Foster and her spad, Andrew Crawford. Two months earlier one of Hepper's subordinates, Alison Clydesdale, had established that this was far from the full story and there was a major risk to the department if it spent beyond what the Treasury had allocated. Clydesdale had sought to clarify how the funding arrangements would work and had been told that the money would be coming directly to Stormont under AME arrangements. That is the form of spending used for government schemes where a budget is difficult or impossible to predict, such as for welfare claims.

Most devolved government spending is very different and involves the block grant – the annual lump sum the Treasury sends to Stormont – being divided up into multiple finite budgets, department by department, project by project. Each department is headed by a permanent secretary whose formal title of 'accounting officer' alludes to the significance of accounting for the department's spending. It is a major crisis if a department spends beyond the budget democratically authorised for it by Parliament or the Assembly. But the amount required for demand-led expenditure, such as pensions, student loans or unemployment benefits, is difficult to predict, and there is a principle that the money should be paid if the individual meets the criteria set by Parliament. Therefore the funding is 'managed' and predictions are made as to the likely demand, but no budget is set.

Where RHI would break with long-established public sector accounting principles was that it would be described as AME – that is, demand-led and without a budget – but it would also have a budget. It would be on that rock of confusion – allied with the cynicism of some senior figures who saw the chance to squeeze more money out of the Treasury – that Stormont would perish.

In April 2011, Clydesdale spoke by phone to Jon Parker, the joint head of the Treasury's energy branch. She followed that up with an email in which she asked him to set out in writing how the department could commit to 20-year payments based on funding, which was only for four years, as well as a request to set out the practicalities around how the money would come to DETI. Parker made clear that any commitments entered into during the initial years of the scheme would be honoured over a 20-year period and that Stormont's funding would be based on a share – roughly proportionate to Northern Ireland's size – of the GB scheme, with 2.98% of the GB RHI budget being made available to Stormont. He then went on to set out a critical warning, which ought to have disabused anyone in Stormont who read it, of the notion that RHI was a bottomless cash pit. Parker said:

> The other key point it is necessary to let you know about is that the [Whitehall department] DECC RHI spending is not being treated as standard AME, where the Exchequer takes on all risks of overspend. Instead, there is a risk-sharing arrangement whereby should RHI spending in one year exceed the SR [spending review] profile, then DECC would need to repay this in future years.

Parker went on to say that not only would any overspend have to be recouped in future years – something which assumed the overspend was small enough to be recovered from the budget remaining for future years – but that on top of that there would be a penalty 'likely to be of the order of 5%' taken out of the department's budget if it overspent. He said that 'again, these rules would be applied in equivalent fashion to NI'.

The following month, Clydesdale received a second email warning in clear terms that the funding was not unlimited. Bernie Brankin, an experienced official in DETI's finance division, told her that she had spoken to Stormont's Department of Finance and 'RHI spending is not being treated as standard AME'. Instead, she said, it was being treated as if it was allocated to the department out of the block grant, with a strict budget. She explained: 'If you underspend in any year, that part of your budget is lost to the department and, if you overspend in any year, DETI's budget will be reduced by the amount of overspend in future years.' The email – which referred to a verbal discussion between the two officials – went on to say: 'You will need to take this treatment of AME into consideration when drawing up your proposals on how you will spend this allocation ...' Crucially, the email was copied to Hepper.

Hepper was copied into another email later that day from Clydesdale in which she said to another DETI official that she had spoken 'at length' to Brankin about the situation and that it 'presents a significant challenge'. Stormont's finance department would require evidence of DETI's ability to control the number of RHI applications. Perhaps influenced by the problems with the recent Reconnect grant scheme, she said that grants would be 'the riskiest route financially as it is hard to control the number of applications especially at the end of the programme'. Clydesdale went on to say that CEPA would have to be asked 'to factor this in as a risk factor' because 'I didn't see any evidence of this in the draft that we have already received ... it will need to be fully addressed'.

Almost seven years later, Clydesdale told the public inquiry that in May 2011 'I recognised the need for cost controls to control over/under spending and the associated risk'. That claim is supported by her emails from the time. Yet almost immediately after her engagement with Parker, Clydesdale was moved to another role as part of the constant churn of civil servants moving around the system.

The following month, just days before Hepper's crucial June meeting with Foster, another Whitehall civil servant, Akhil Patel in DECC, the department running the GB scheme, gave DETI another warning about overspending. Patel emailed Peter Hutchinson – the main individual under Hepper who was working on designing RHI – and told him explicitly that if they overspent, the money had to come out of DETI's budget. If that wasn't sufficiently explicit, Patel added: 'Clearly, this represents a large financial risk on the department so the policy team is currently looking to develop a system of tariff degressions [further cost controls] ... to ensure (among other things) that we manage the risk of overspending against our budget.'

Essentially, Patel was telling DETI that although the GB scheme had been set up with a basic cost control of tiering, that was not enough, and so it was looking to add an additional cost control of degression.

Tiering was a simple mechanism whereby there were two tariffs which every boiler owner could claim. The first high tariff was only available for 1,314 hours each year – allowing high payments for 15% of the year. After that, the second-tier tariff was all that could be claimed and it was far less lucrative. The intention was to encourage energy efficiency, discourage fraud and shield taxpayers from having to pay huge sums to those who legitimately needed to run their boilers for most of the year.

Patel's message did nothing to prompt a sudden change of course within DETI. Days later, Hepper, who was aware of the nature of the funding, gave Foster the first of many submissions which simply described the funding as being AME. Hepper later told the inquiry that she was 'pretty sure' she had verbally explained to Foster that the funding could threaten the department's budget if it overspent. Whatever was said in conversation between Hepper and Foster, the civil servants would go on to continually misrepresent the funding as simply 'AME' for years, with one civil servant suggesting that the inaccurate information was simply copied and pasted from one ministerial submission to the next.

Foster herself would tell the inquiry that her belief that the bill was being paid by London influenced how she viewed the issue of cost controls. David Scoffield QC for the inquiry put it to her that in a later 2013 submission to her from Hepper there was 'a pretty stark warning', because it referred to a 'finite budget' which 'can't be breached', and explained that therefore 'we must have this facility [an emergency brake of cost controls] available to us.' Tellingly, Foster replied: 'Yes, but I was also aware that the AME budget [meaning the Treasury would pay the bill, rather than Stormont] was there [in the submission].'

At the inquiry, Hepper played down the significance of the point, arguing that the department never intended to overspend anyway and would 'try our best to make sure that that did not happen'. Although she knew that limits on the scheme were necessary to prevent overspending, she thought that 'we'd plenty of time to do [cost controls]'.

Sam Connolly, the DETI economist assigned to assist energy division, accepted at the inquiry that Foster had made her decision based on 'untrue' information in the submission from Hepper. Connolly would himself admit to the inquiry that he had failed to follow the rules for public sector economists and argued that RHI was a policy 'involving concepts and sums of money that were beyond me'.

****

Days before Foster had even formally decided that there should be an RHI scheme and before the final CEPA report had been received, Hepper took a decision of her own which indicated that she was confident the minister would back that option. Hepper authorised the spending of public money on an outside law firm, Arthur Cox, to write the legislation that would set up RHI. It was a remarkably bold act which further suggested Hepper was convinced that she knew the minister's mind. But what was to follow was more baffling.

Alan Bissett, a partner at Arthur Cox, was a specialist energy lawyer whose services did not come cheaply. When DETI asked him to work on drafting the RHI legislation, he expected a substantive assignment. But it gradually became clear that something else was going on. Bissett was ultimately paid to largely copy and paste the Westminster legislation, and in doing so he replicated the GB scheme's system of tiered tariffs. But that was stripped out by DETI officials – not once, but on multiple occasions. Having hired lawyers to draft the regulations, civil servants now disregarded Bissett's work and produced their own draft of the regulations.

Speaking of the bulk of the work, which he was asked to undertake, Bissett told the inquiry: 'It didn't seem clear to me why it couldn't have been done by the Departmental Solicitor's Office. We weren't advising anything to do with policy; we were just drafting and were changing references and correcting terminology from GB to NI terminology.' One DETI official suggested Bisset capitalise some letters and queried his use of semicolons. Meanwhile, cost controls were being stripped out without alarm. Ultimately, it became clear to Bissett that his company was one of three sets of lawyers involved in drafting the legislation, with Stormont's own lawyers and those from Ofgem also contributing. 'Objectively it seems odd,' he told the inquiry.

Bissett also told how DETI later commissioned his firm to advise it on what ought to have been a basic function of the civil service – asking their

Whitehall counterparts what they were planning to do in future with their RHI scheme. Inquiry counsel David Scoffield QC asked him: 'Why on earth were lawyers being paid to do that?' Bissett replied:

> That did seem odd ... I had assumed that relationships between DECC and DETI were not good and we were being asked to do that ... I would have felt that DETI would have been in a better position to tell me what DECC was doing. We had no contact with DECC – they wouldn't speak to us. One of my colleagues tried to find out timelines and what was happening and they wouldn't speak to us.

But while Bissett wasn't kept in the loop, Hepper and her team believed they had good reason to disregard the regulations drafted by him and instead draw up their own legislation without tiering.

The explanation lay with CEPA. In its report, the consultancy had set out proposed tariffs for a host of green technologies – from ground source heat pumps to solar thermal units. It drew attention to the fact that the subsidies proposed included two tiers for some technologies, in line with the situation in GB. The consultants explained how tiering operated and went on to say: 'However, when setting the NI recommended levels for this report, the incremental fuel cost was higher than the subsidy rates in all cases. Therefore no tiering is provided in the rates in this report.' With that decision, the consultants were taking an enormous risk. If the cost of fuel was ever less than the rate of subsidy, the scheme would be fundamentally flawed. Even at that point, it should have been obvious that the cost of fuel was constantly fluctuating while the proposal was for the tariffs to remain set in stone for 20 years, with guaranteed inflationary increases.

But the problem was to get much worse. DETI launched a public consultation on its proposals and received responses which complained that the tariffs proposed for Northern Ireland were lower than for GB. At a glance, the Northern Ireland scheme did indeed seem far less generous. Not only were the initial tariffs for the smallest biomass boilers lower – 4.5 p/ kWh in Northern Ireland as opposed to 7.9p in GB – but the most lucrative GB tariff was available for far larger boilers. In GB, it was possible to install a 199 kW boiler, capable of pumping out more than four times the heat of the 45 kW boilers which were to get Stormont's top subsidy.

But the small print showed that unlike the situation in GB, where tiering meant that after running the most lucrative boiler for 1,314 hours in the year the subsidy dropped to 2p, Stormont proposed to pay the top rate for the entire year – with no heat limit.

Although it is hard to pin down who precisely decided not to include tiering, it is clear that its absence was the result of a conscious decision. In early April 2011, the issue was explicitly raised by Connolly, the DETI economist. Having read CEPA's first draft report, he asked Hutchinson why the scheme was more generous than GB's. Connolly asked specifically: 'Why has tiering not been used as per the GB RHI?'

DECC had the previous year – in publicly available documentation which DETI might have been expected to be studying – recognised that the biomass tariffs could lead to a 'perverse incentive to over generate heat'. That was, it explained, because the subsidy was higher than the cost of fuel. It said that 'this perverse incentive is expected to be significant for non-domestic biomass space heating installations that are less than 1MWth' – that is, every type of biomass boiler eligible under the Stormont scheme. DECC went on to explain in simple language why, as a result of this obvious danger, it was implementing tiered tariffs. At the rates being proposed for Stormont's scheme, the problem might have been modest, but it was about to be amplified.

In response to the consultation, the department asked CEPA to carry out a second piece of work – what would become known as the CEPA addendum report – to consider some of the responses and make final recommendations before the scheme was launched. Throughout this entire period, the evidence points to DETI repeatedly attempting to make RHI more generous and more widely available. On one such occasion, Hutchinson, after seeing a draft of the addendum, wrote in the margin to query why the consultants were not proposing to allow claims for large industrial biomass installations. CEPA had already made clear to the department that the reason for doing so was that there was no need to subsidise such large biomass heating systems – they were already economical without any subsidy. But Hutchinson told CEPA he was 'still concerned about not having a tariff for this sector given [the] possible disadvantage in comparison to GB market [which was subsidising such boilers] ... some calculation attached for your consideration'.

Hutchinson, a young civil servant being asked to deal with a complex area in which he had little expertise, was under considerable pressure. The softly spoken official was working so hard that he was recommended for bonuses by his superiors in this period, with the citations referring to him having 'performed exceptionally well' and having 'worked largely on his own' managing CEPA.

The final 47-page CEPA report was delivered in February 2012 and agreed to hike the level of tariffs for every one of the technologies being subsidised. Even an outsider could have seen that the obvious effect was that Stormont was going to draw down more of the Treasury money than if the tariffs were less generous – higher rates were more likely to encourage people to join the scheme, so there would be more participants, and each of them would also receive more.

CEPA now recommended more than doubling the size of biomass boilers getting the most lucrative subsidy from 45 kW to 99 kW. And the tariff for that boiler was also increased by 31%, rising from 4.5 p/kWh to 5.9 p/kWh. Aside from the growing overall cost, there was a clear problem: the same report gave the price of biomass fuel as being massively lower. Research for the report had found that biomass fuel in Northern Ireland could be as cheap as 2.85 p/kWh for those buying wood chip in bulk – one of several places in the report where it was clear to a casual reader that there was now a big gap between the cost of running a boiler and the subsidy rate. On CEPA's own figures, that meant that the subsidy was more than double the cost of fuel. But the consultants, whose main report had said there was no need for tiering, did not point out the obvious difficulty.

At the inquiry, Hepper was grilled as to how she and her colleagues could not have spotted the problem. Audibly exasperated, chairman Sir Patrick Coghlin put it to her that 'you didn't need to be an expert to see this differential … you wouldn't need to be an expert in economics or, indeed, energy to see that if you have a tariff that is paying you more than the [cost of] fuel you're using to burn and to achieve that tariff, there's a problem.' Setting out a complicated logic for how she and her team had justified the situation to themselves, Hepper replied that 'in our thinking about how that came to be, we took the price of the fuel, we took it …' Sir Patrick interjected to say that 'any common-sense person would've seen that difference, and if they didn't appreciate the significance of it, they would've asked'. Hepper said she 'had a narrative in my head', which rationalised the apparently illogical proposal. She suggested that because RHI was meant to include payments for the 'hassle costs' of installing green technology as well as a rate of return to cover borrowings, there was an explanation for the gap. There were other costs involved with biomass boilers, such as increased electricity costs, which slightly complicated the calculation.

The picture which emerged from the inquiry was that Hepper – and the multiple civil servants who saw the proposal – had been bamboozled by the 'experts', leading them to miss a basic fact staring them in the face. Although the biomass tariff was the most glaring mistake in CEPA's work, the consultants had been responsible for a series of other basic errors with numbers in tables which did not add up. The inquiry's technical assessor, energy expert Dr Keith MacLean, put it to Hepper that 'if you looked at almost any of the numbers in the tables in that report, they would not allow you to calculate any of the tariffs … it seems to me nobody actually just got a calculator out and checked, "does this make sense?"' Hepper said she 'assumed' that her colleagues had done some checks, 'but I also would've assumed that the expertise that we were buying in would've checked their basic figure work, too'. The blind were now leading the blind, with each believing that the other could see.

****

More than four years later, as CEPA prepared to come before the Assembly's Public Accounts Committee – the precursor to Coghlin's later public inquiry – its top brass attempted to understand how things had gone so disastrously wrong.

Internal emails, which the public inquiry compelled them to release, show that senior figures in the company – which has worked for governments all over the world – knew that it was responsible for a huge error.

In November 2016, CEPA director Kirby Owen emailed fellow director Ian Alexander to inform him that it 'turns out that the first report in 2011 wasn't all that bad at all but whomever did the redo in 2012 [addendum] … missed completely (or skated over) the fact that in the 2012 recommendations the subsidy value per kwh was greater than the fuel cost per kwh.' He went on: 'The result … people were heating empty barns because you could make a financial profit on the whole thing even if you just vented all the heat …

it's a true problem, a truly bad recommendation on subsidy design … ouch'. Speaking frankly in the expectation that his email would never emerge publicly, Owen went on to say: 'Happily, the 2011 report says a lot of words about "monitoring is necessary", although I don't think it meant watching out to correct the mistakes we made is necessary and the tariff design error … was indeed an error. But we won't call it that.'

Owen commissioned an internal analysis of how RHI operated. One graph showed that if boilers were run for about 55% of the year, 'the whole thing turns into a money-making machine' – even if there was no use for the heat. In the event, it was clear that most of those using RHI had a use for the heat and would have had to otherwise pay for it themselves, so it was even more lucrative for them than for those who may have been just generating heat to receive the payments. And in some cases boilers were running for far longer than 55%, with nearly round-the-clock usage. CEPA had based all of its calculations on the assumption that boilers would run for an average of just 17% of the time.

In another candid internal email, Owen – who was not involved in the scheme's design – marvelled at the 'super profits' available to those running boilers for long periods. In one email, he concluded by saying: 'So the folks who heated empty barns were evil villains indeed, but they needed a poor tariff design to abet them … Sure, we're not on the hook for fraud. But – assuming I'm right – our tariff design … encouraged it.'

There was another problem with the proposed tariffs – the huge gulf between the various bands encouraged any savvy businessman to install multiple 99 kW boilers, which would earn 5.9p for every unit of heat produced. But if he installed a 100 kW boiler – or any other boiler up to 1,000 kW – the rate did not fall slightly, but collapsed to a paltry 1.5p.

Some legitimate scheme participants would later feel aggrieved that there were accused of 'exploitation' for doing what was lawful and what they believed the designers of the scheme must have realised when they set the tariff bands as they did. It is to the credit of some businesses – including several Sainsbury's supermarkets in Northern Ireland – that they installed a single large boiler and received a relatively modest payment by contrast to what was on offer.

There was a particular contradiction in setting up a Northern Ireland RHI, which was more lucrative than its GB counterpart. The whole justification for Stormont departing from what was happening in the rest of the UK was that the GB scheme was too generous for Northern Ireland. In GB, the tariffs were based on the assumption that they were incentivising people to move from gas. But in Northern Ireland, where piped natural gas was still only being established, the assumption was that people would be moving from oil. With oil more expensive than gas, it required less incentive to switch to renewables. And yet, having said that Northern Ireland required less incentive than GB, what DETI ultimately did was create a scheme which was more generous.

But there is an intriguing footnote to this. In December 2016, as the political scandal raged, Mark Anderson, an academic expert in biomass, wrote an article for the *Slugger O'Toole* political blog. Anderson, who was a close friend of Crawford's, appeared to hint at that argument around oil being almost a cover story for why Northern Ireland was setting up its own scheme. Writing at a point where it was not publicly known that he was linked to Crawford, he set out the argument about Northern Ireland having a greater dependence on oil heating. However, he went on: 'The real reason to provide a different structure was that the GB scheme was significantly under-subscribed. The economic consultants, CEPA and AEA Technology, from the beginning, proposed a non-tiered tariff to achieve the required interest in the incentive.' Was that purely supposition on Anderson's part or did he have some inside insight into what had really gone on in 2012?

****

As DETI moved ahead to launch RHI, the scheme was being set up in a way which would see it shovel taxpayers' money to those lucky enough – or well-connected enough – to get in at the right time.

Two huge errors had been made. One – the misdescription of the funding – was unquestionably an error. There was no conceivable reason for the civil servants to describe the funding as pure Treasury cash other than due to sloppiness or a culture whereby they thought that such small but fundamental clarifications were unimportant.

But while the second disastrous decision – to strip out the limited cost controls present in the GB scheme – may also have been accidental, it is possible that it was not a mistake and was a conscious reaction to the first error. If there was a belief that consequence-free spending was possible, and if the political philosophy was to maximise the Treasury funding for Northern Ireland, it would be quite logical to remove any impediments to making the scheme as expensive as possible.

Foster accepted at the inquiry that 'the last thing a Northern Ireland Executive wants to do ... is to hand money back to the Treasury' and said that 'there would have been pressure to spend that money'. She said that the 'pressure would have been on to find a scheme to spend that money ... there would be an awareness that if money is coming in ... then we have to make sure we find a way of spending it'. But she denied that the logic of that position was that the more expensive the scheme the better.

No piece of paper has ever turned up to show that there was a deliberate decision to exploit the funding and all of those who were involved have said that it was a genuine mistake. But Foster, Crawford and the civil servants are here hoist by their own petard of not recording many of their key meetings and decisions.

It is true that when a government records what it is doing, it can lead to embarrassing leaks. But a written record is also a protection for those in power – if a decision is not recorded as having been taken, then there is a strong argument that there was no such decision. By not having such a culture of recording what was going on, those in DETI at the time were later shorn of the protection that it would offer. The mere absence of a record is not in itself proof that something did not happen. And, aside from a general culture of oral government, if the motivation here was to consciously and wrongly exploit the Treasury, there is a specific reason why that thinking would not have been recorded.

But despite the fact that the scheme was now heading towards its launch with fatal shortcomings, all was not yet lost. A forceful warning was just around the corner, one which would mean that Foster's department was going into the disaster with its eyes open. That message would heighten the suspicions of those who would later look back and wonder if someone had consciously chosen to create a scheme which would enrich claimants – and at least one major multinational corporation.

CHAPTER 5
LICENCE TO BILL

On 13 April 2012, Arlene Foster did something which defied rational explanation: she signed what was close to a blank cheque. Of course, ministers do not literally sign cheques, blank or otherwise, and government payments are handled by officials far beneath them. But the document to which Foster put her name consented to the idea that setting up an RHI scheme was value for money without knowing how much it would cost. Even if she had no other direct role in the RHI scandal, Foster's signature that day undermined her boast of being someone who was forensic with detail and by implication could be trusted to handle the complex business of government.

Known as a regulatory impact assessment, the document was part of the democratic checks and balances within the world of government. The bureaucratic title belied its intent: this was a piece of paper meant to be a protection for the minister – and, by extension, the public – ensuring that their express consent was required before an expensive policy could get to an advanced stage. Fiona Hepper sent the document to Foster and Crawford alongside a submission recommending that she sign it. By doing so, Hepper said, she was signing to 'approve the final NI RHI' policy and to confirm that she was content for the scheme to proceed. Foster took her official's advice and signed a declaration which said: 'I have read the Regulatory Impact Assessment and I am satisfied that the benefits justify the costs.' There was one problem: the document did not set out the scheme's costs. Hepper had simply referred to the £25 million available for the first four years of the 20-year scheme. Primary school arithmetic would have established that a scheme, which cost £25 million for the first four years but ran for 20 years in total, was going to cost far more than £25 million. But it was the figure for the first four years which only really seemed to exercise the department. It was the only figure put in the submission – a form of short-termism driven by the fact that budgets were allocated on a short-term basis and that commitments over a period of 20 years were almost incomprehensible. Whether it factored in the officials' thinking or not, it was also the case that whatever happened in 10 or 20 years' time they would almost certainly have long gone.

During probing exchanges at the public inquiry, Foster and Crawford faced ferocious scrutiny of that decision. The inquiry's technical assessor, Dr Keith MacLean, asked Crawford if there was any point in the officials' going to the minister 'if all you're going to do is tick a box' to say that if the civil servants were happy with it, then the minister was happy. Crawford candidly admitted that Foster's signature had been little more than a 'box-ticking exercise'. In withering comments which implied that Crawford had failed the minister, MacLean – who had worked at the top of the UK energy industry – said: 'She was also relying on you to give her the advice. I just find it inconceivable in my career that I would ever have put a paper to somebody to sign that they were saying that the costs are justified without having those costs.' Crawford replied tamely: 'Well, unfortunately, it was signed off, and I didn't flag it up at the time.' When asked if he had considered how much the department was committing itself to in total, Crawford said that he did not think that he had considered a figure for the total cost of the scheme, although he was aware that it was more than the £25 million in the documentation. It wasn't even the first time that Foster had signed what MacLean referred to as a 'blank cheque' for RHI. Earlier in the process, she had signed another document, which stated that the scheme represented good value for taxpayers – yet without any figure for how much it would cost over its lifetime.

When Foster appeared at the inquiry two days after Crawford, senior counsel to the inquiry David Scoffield QC pressed her: 'But when you're signing the declaration, which says that you're satisfied that the benefits justify the costs, you're putting your signature to that – should you not have thought to yourself, "I need to understand what the costs are?"' Foster replied: 'But I did; at that time, I understood that the costs were £25m and the tail [the remainder of the 20 years] was going to be paid so there was no issue for me in terms of was this [money] going to come.' Perceptively, MacLean jumped in to ask: 'Is what you're saying there that whatever the extra cost was, it was going to be covered by the Treasury [so] it didn't matter?' Foster responded: 'Well, it's not that it didn't matter; it's just that we had had the assurance … that [it] was going to be covered by Treasury.'

Foster challenged MacLean's suggestion that she had signed a blank cheque, arguing that she was aware of the £25 million cost over its first four years. MacLean said: 'Let's be generous then, and say it was a cheque for £25 million and not an indeterminate figure; it was not a cheque with the bottom right hand corner number of £445 million which at that time was the best estimate of what that cost was going to be.' Foster said: 'I go back to the point that I made in relation to the tail – that we had been assured that this was happening in GB, that it would happen here in a similar fashion.' MacLean highlighted that 'the fact that it's covered doesn't mean that it's good value'. He highlighted that Foster was being given 'precision and detail' about relatively small figures for the administration costs of the scheme – one figure mentioned was £136,000 – 'yet not about the total cost'.

But that wasn't the only problem for Foster at that point. In the submission, which asked her to sign the 'blank cheque', Foster was given more misleading information. In a prominent table, the submission set out the proposed tariffs for Stormont's scheme and the equivalent situation in GB. From that it was obvious that GB had tiering – but tiering was absent from DETI's proposals. In a small-print footnote on that page, Hepper explained that tiering was used to ensure that a boiler was not 'over-used just to receive an incentive'. But she copied the consultants' erroneous claim that 'tiering is not included in the NI scheme because in each instance the subsidy rate is lower than the incremental fuel cost'.

The scale of the scheme would have been obvious to the minister. She was told that the plan was to keep the scheme open until 2020 but that the last payments would not be made until 2040. Foster was being asked to commit her successors to potentially huge spending on this policy – and spending out of which they would find it exceptionally difficult to wriggle because she was told that tariffs were being 'grandfathered'. That legal term signified that they were locked in and effectively exempt from a future government rethink where they could be slashed. She was given some comfort that there would be 'scheduled reviews built-in … to allow DETI to ensure that the scheme remains fit for purpose and value for money for the duration.' However, the officials' errors were not picked up by the minister or her adviser – and the apparent view of the 'box-ticking' nature of the process does not suggest that she deeply pondered the extent to which the officials' claims about value for money could possibly be right. That now undermines one of her later boasts. In October 2016 – just over a month before cash for ash would become a vast public scandal and imperil her career – Foster wrote an article for the *Slugger O'Toole* political blog. It began: 'Detail is important. For someone from a legal background like

myself this is a given.' The article, which also claimed that the DUP had
helped to secure a 'durable' system of devolution, now seems like Foster's
point of peak hubris. Despite knowing how she had operated as a Stormont
minister, she wrote: 'Our ascent to the natural party of government doesn't
mean overseeing the paper shuffling'.

Foster would later attempt to blame her civil servants for the entirety of
the RHI disaster and not accept that she had made any errors which could
have been seen at the time.

But whatever Foster's failings, it is clear that she was failed by her
officials. Hepper's March 2012 submission, seeking approval for the scheme
to proceed, told Foster that 'under RHI only "useful heat" is deemed eligible;
this is defined as heat that would otherwise be met by fossil fuels'. The
submission – on the cover of which Foster wrote by hand 'content' – added:
'This excludes deliberately wasting or dumping heat with the sole purpose
of claiming incentive payments.'

Missing the 'blank cheque' wasn't the only occasion on which Crawford
failed to spot bear pits for his minister. Despite the handpicked spad being
paid around £80,000 in the expectation that he would be digging through
detail to protect his minister, Crawford admitted that he had not read either
of the two CEPA reports for which DETI had paid £100,000 and which
formed the basis of the scheme. The spad denied even having been sent
the second report – CEPA's addendum. If that is the case, he did not insist
on seeing it. Foster said she believed that Crawford was reading at least
the executive summary of reports, such as CEPA's, but seemed reluctant to
criticise the man who had been at her side for most of her ministerial career.
When Crawford was asked if he had let the minister down by not reading
the reports, he said:

> Look, I let; I believe I let; I'm very sorry that I didn't read it in detail
> to flag this up ... I do not think that there was an expectation there
> that I should be analysing technical reports and bringing things to her
> attention which are at odds of [sic] the submission that she is signing.
> However, look – it is a regret of mine that I didn't identify this and flag
> it up.

****

But although it might seem that Crawford was neglecting to scrutinise the scheme, there is other evidence of him taking an interest in RHI in this early period. The full picture of how Foster's spad – who is perhaps the single most significant figure in the entire RHI story – acted in this period is complex. To understand Crawford's significance to this story, it is necessary to understand the immense power wielded by spads within the devolved Executive. Personal appointees of their ministers, spads were handpicked outside employment law and given generous salaries far above those of MLAs and sometimes higher even than those of ministers.

Some spads were exceptionally capable and some of them were widely respected for their abilities to oil the wheels of power, sitting between ministers and mandarins. But the Stormont system saw spads become more and more powerful, while lacking the constraints of accountability to which ministers – at least on paper – were subject. And Stormont was awash with them. The Office of the First Minister and deputy First Minister alone had eight spads: four for the DUP and four for Sinn Féin. That department fought a long and determined rear-guard action in an attempt not to reveal how much its eight spads were paid (up to £92,000, it later admitted). Salaries for many of the spad roles had more than doubled since devolved government returned to Northern Ireland after the 1998 Good Friday Agreement, and by 2015 a total of 19 spads were costing taxpayers almost £2 million a year. There was a sense at Stormont that spads were attractive to ministers because they could act in ways which carried the implied authority of the minister while allowing the minister plausible deniability if their actions became politically problematic.

In an interview for this book, Alan Clarke, who was the longest-serving chief executive of the Northern Ireland Tourist Board, said that he always viewed Crawford and Foster as inseparable. Clarke, whose role saw him ultimately reporting to Foster because the tourist board was under her department, said that Crawford 'almost became quasi-permanent secretary [the most senior departmental official] of the department in terms of what you might say are difficult things: Irish language, difficult grant applications, whatever else'. He said that senior civil servants had made clear to him that 'you cannot put a line between him and Arlene – they speak with one voice'.

Crawford told the inquiry that 'from the very start of the RHI I was aware of budgetary implications' and was asking questions about how the scheme was being funded and where the money was coming from. Significantly, the powerful young DUP adviser also told the inquiry that 'I always likened the RHI scheme to the NIRO ... That was always my view when the RHI was being set up and through the various iterations or the various papers coming forward: that there was a parallel in the two schemes moving forward'.

The NIRO (Northern Ireland Renewables Obligation) was being overseen by the same Stormont department and the way in which it was set up was lucrative for Northern Ireland. It was close to 'free money' in that the money for the scheme – much of which funded wind turbines – came from the public across the UK in the form of a charge on their energy bills. However, it was set up in a way that was doubly beneficial to Northern Ireland. Firstly, the amount, which the Northern Ireland public had added to their bills, was less than elsewhere in the UK. And secondly, the subsidy paid to developers was higher in Northern Ireland. That led to an explosion of wind farms across Northern Ireland – some of which had significant political connections – and pulled huge sums across the Irish Sea, far beyond the 3% share of the UK pot, which Northern Ireland would have received on a basic pro-rata share.

If Crawford's understanding of RHI was, as he said, always viewed through the prism of the NIRO, and if he was being constantly told that RHI was being fully paid for by the Treasury, which he was, then it is easy to see how he would have come to the view that Stormont could spend as much as it wanted on RHI without consequences. In effect, RHI could be a backdoor addition to the block grant, particularly benefiting the rural community in which the DUP had a significant support base and especially agriculture, with which Crawford had long-standing high-level ties.

Foster told the inquiry that with NIRO some people viewed it as a good thing that Northern Ireland was getting more than its proportionate share of the UK budget. She said: 'We were aware that NIRO was being funded and there wasn't any difficulty if Northern Ireland went over its share as it were. And in fact for some people it would be seen as a good thing because we were taking more out of the pot as it were and bringing it into the Northern Ireland economy.' Then, referring to how RHI was set up, she went on:

> But if I had known there was a DEL consequence [Stormont might have to pay some of the bill], I would have been alerting the Executive to that

... I think if I had known that it was AME with a DEL consequence, then I'd have had more of an alarm bell ringing as to degression [a cost control] and things like that.

However, when pressed about the implications of that logic, she insisted that although Stormont wanted to get as much Treasury money as possible into Northern Ireland it would never have deliberately chosen an expensive scheme, which was poor value for money in order to do so.

★★★★★★★★★★★

Having engaged two firms of consultants and a specialist lawyer to make up for the lack of expertise within DETI as it tried to design its scheme, Hepper turned to a fourth outside body for advice. But, as with the previous three sets of advisers, DETI would not be happy with some of the feedback and would simply ignore some of it.

There was no tendering in August 2011 before DETI decided that it would appoint the GB energy regulator Ofgem – a section of which ran schemes on behalf of Whitehall departments – to explore how RHI might operate. In what the civil service described as a 'Direct Award Contract', no one else was able to bid for the work. Hepper justified the request – which was approved by Foster – by arguing that the way in which Westminster legislation had been drafted meant that Ofgem had to administer the scheme because it was described in law as 'the authority' responsible for the GB scheme. Her submission to Foster described Ofgem as 'experts in the design of the scheme' and added: 'In addition, Ofgem legal advisors and development staff will carry out one full review of the draft regulations, and will advise DETI on Ofgem's ability to implement the regulations as drafted, what changes may be needed to enable us to implement them in practice, and what changes may be required to streamline or improve implementation.' But, having told the minister that one of the terms for Ofgem getting the contract was that it was to undertake to give expert advice on how to best set up the scheme, DETI would go on to consciously ignore explicit warnings which it was paying Ofgem to give.

The scheme was to be set up under regulations, a form of secondary legislation, which would receive less scrutiny in the Assembly than primary legislation. After awarding the contract to Ofgem, the regulations – which the department had drafted after rejecting the work of Bissett – were sent to Ofgem's lawyers for line-by-line scrutiny. The response came back to Hutchinson and Joanne McCutheon – two key staff working under Hepper to design the scheme – on 7 November 2011 and it was brutal.

The 26-page memo, which was drawn up by an Ofgem lawyer, set out 'a considerable number of concerns' with the regulations and said 'it is critical that these concerns are addressed by DETI'. Many of the problems had already been highlighted in relation to the GB legislation on which Stormont was basing its scheme, and DECC, the Whitehall department responsible, was working on amending it. Ofgem suggested that DETI could either wait until the GB scheme was amended and change its scheme, or it could choose to 'be proactive in addressing the issues'. Ofgem highlighted problems with preventing heat being used just to make money from RHI and warned about the potential for installing multiple small boilers to milk the most lucrative subsidy rate, rather than a single large boiler, which may otherwise be more logical. It also raised the potential for 'parasitic' burning of wood – where a boiler existed solely to dry wood, which was then fed into the boiler which dried more wood to be fed to the boiler and so on – simply to claim subsidy. It warned about the difficulties of deciding how to deal with domestic houses being heated under a non-domestic RHI. The document also explained that the regulations were so loosely drafted that 'perverse' outcomes could be lawful. Every one of those areas would become problems for Stormont's scheme. But DETI decided to press ahead with its scheme largely unchanged, with the explanation that it would later follow whatever happened in GB.

Ofgem did not give up, coming back again and again to warn DETI that there were serious problems with what it was doing. In June 2012 – five months before the scheme would be launched – Ofgem suggested to Hutchinson and McCutcheon that they should speak to Whitehall about the changes being made in the GB scheme. Ofgem even passed on details of a contact who could explain the situation. Years later, Hutchinson spent five days giving evidence to the public inquiry but McCutcheon, his immediate boss, was the only major figure directly involved in the scheme not to give evidence at all, for reasons not made public at the inquiry. In May 2011, as it seemed that DETI was determined to press ahead with legislation, which it had been told was profoundly deficient, Ofgem lawyer Marcus Porter emailed a colleague to express alarm at what was unfolding. He concluded by observing that 'taking the easy course now may well lead to problems later'.

Porter, a former flight lieutenant in the RAF's legal branch who in that role undertook courts martial, was so alarmed at what DETI was doing that on several occasions he recorded in writing to Ofgem colleagues that the body should consider refusing to take on the administration of the scheme until DETI agreed to address the deficiencies.

In June 2012, a further Ofgem legal review of the regulations reminded DETI of the GB cost controls. That same month a crucial teleconference took place involving six Ofgem staff and two DETI officials – Hutchinson and McCutcheon. Ofgem emphasised again the problem of DETI pressing ahead with implementing a scheme known to have multiple deficiencies. But minutes of the meeting show that DETI said it was their intention to do so and then alter it the following summer. Ofgem's minutes recorded:

> Ofgem's advice was to wait until the GB regulations are amended as the amendments will serve to negate any risk that the regulations currently pose. However, DETI were clear that they have a commitment with their minister to bring the regulations into force by the end of September … It was also felt that to do otherwise would also put financial arrangements in jeopardy.

Porter, the experienced Ofgem lawyer who was on the call, later told the inquiry that the concerns he raised at that meeting 'seemingly made no impression on DETI'. He was dismayed.

The officials, who were already behind schedule on getting the scheme launched, appear to have believed that they could not delay any further. Hepper said that the timetable for launching RHI had been set by Foster. Foster accepted that she had told the officials to get the scheme launched 'as soon as possible' but said the 'as possible' was crucial in that context and added: 'I certainly don't have any recollection of saying "This has to happen by September."'

The impression of officials feeling under ministerial pressure to move rapidly is reinforced by an email sent just minutes after the June 2012 meeting

by senior Ofgem manager Luis Castro. Castro, who had been present, said
to a colleague that DETI officials had told them that 'NI ministers want the
scheme to go ahead as soon as possible … and will not wait for amended
GB regs'. Ofgem manager Keith Avis, who chaired the teleconference, was
'nervous' about the minutes of the meeting containing criticism of the GB
regulations, something which would be implicitly critical of DECC, a major
client of Ofgem. But Porter felt strongly that the minutes should reflect what
had been said. Two days later, after being shown draft minutes, which did
not fully convey what had gone on, he emailed Avis to ask for the minutes
to be changed. After Avis expressed reluctance to do so, Porter said: 'I
think it important that there is an official record that, at our first "meeting"
with DETI we hammered home the fact that we had significant concerns
regarding the course they are proposing to adopt.'

The following day Castro emailed to back up what Porter was saying:
'I think that what is important is that we capture the fact that our clear
recommendation to DETI was to wait until regs are amended due to the risk
the current ones pose.' Hutchinson – the only DETI official on the conference
call who gave evidence to the inquiry – did not dispute that Porter had
made clear the risks of pressing ahead. However, he suggested that once it
was made clear that DETI intended to do so the Ofgem figures accepted that
and moved on to discuss other issues. It was a hugely significant moment.
Months earlier, DECC had decided that tiering on the GB scheme was
insufficient to protect public money, and moved to urgently implement an
interim cost-control measure ahead of a longer-term sophisticated system
to prevent an overspend. DETI, meanwhile, was moving in the opposite
direction – stripping out the limited cost control of tiering and making no
concrete plans to implement the changes happening in London.

The absence of tiered tariffs concerned many of those who viewed
DETI's proposals. Ofgem's Oliver Moore noted internally in July 2012 that
the increased biomass tariffs had jumped out at him, as well as the fact that
there was no tiering. He highlighted that tiering had proved a good way of
reducing the incentive to waste heat, adding pointedly that 'taking it out
increases the likelihood of abuse and heat wastage'. But, determined to get
RHI launched soon, DETI's mind was made up.

The inquiry heard illuminating evidence from two Ofgem figures who
worked closely with DETI officials in the design of the scheme. Both of them

separately said that they believed the civil servants were under pressure from someone higher up in Foster's department to get the scheme opened quickly even though they knew it was flawed. Both Catherine McArthur, a former senior policy adviser to the Energy Minister in New South Wales, and Keith Avis were clear that the urgency did not originate with the officials they dealt with. When asked for her sense of where the time pressure was coming from, McArthur said:

> My sense, having worked with [DETI officials] Peter and Joanne, is that there was somebody – a layer removed perhaps from them; I don't know how many layers removed – who was putting on the time pressure and was making the decisions. It seemed that they were unable to give guidance or a steer of any kind which to me suggested that they didn't have a great deal of control necessarily and that it was in somebody else's hands.

Avis had a similar sense:

> My overall view is that it [the time pressure] was coming from high, high up in the organisation – that it really was something that they were very much committed to and if, throughout this process, you mentioned about timing or any sort of delay it was very much 'we hear what you're saying; however we have got a commitment to push forwards'. I think there were stages where there was direction right at the top, at ministerial level, where there was a need to move forward quickly.

That impression is clear from a contemporaneous email from Ofgem's Matthew Harnack to colleagues in August 2012. Relaying a phone conversation with Hepper, he said: 'They noted that the minister is adamant that the scheme <u>must</u> go live in October, and I had to give them an assurance that there is no risk to this happening ...' Foster told the inquiry that if officials took her desire for haste to mean that they should press ahead with a defective scheme, they were wrong and they did so without ever properly informing her.

The final point at which it is alleged there was still a chance for DETI to pull back from the brink towards which it was rushing came just days after the June 2012 teleconference call with Ofgem. Hepper, who said that those on the call had fed the Ofgem warning through to her, insists that she spoke to her superior, David Thomson, and then to Foster herself. Thomson said that he recalled Hepper having brought the issue to him and that at that point she was going to bring the issue to Foster for a decision. But that critical conversation is now disputed – and with no written record of what actually transpired, it is Hepper's word against Foster's. Hepper told the inquiry that she had a 'clear recollection of the conversation with the minister' about the warning and that 'I don't believe that this was downplayed in any way'.

When asked if the minister was told specifically that Ofgem's recommendation was not to proceed without cost controls, she said: 'Yes, and I did not downplay that; I said that's the advice from their lawyers.' Hepper admitted that there had been no formal written ministerial submission on the issue, and accepted that with hindsight that ought to have happened but blamed time pressure for not having done so.

The DUP is a party which is exceptionally precise in its use of language – even when lawyers are not involved. For that reason, Foster's evidence to the inquiry on this point was striking for what it did not say. In her written evidence to the inquiry – evidence which would have been carefully put together – Foster, who by then was DUP leader, said: 'I have no recollection of being clearly informed about the risks of proceeding without cost controls.' Because of what it does not say, the comment leaves open the possibility that Foster was informed clearly but has forgotten it, or even if that was not the case that she was informed in some way of Ofgem's warning – but not in explicit terms. Whatever happened in that conversation – if, as seems to be the case, it took place – nothing was done to halt the launch of a scheme which many, if not all, of those launching it had been told was seriously flawed.

****

The die had now been cast and only the formalities – and at Stormont they often tended to be formalities – of passing the legislation through the Assembly chamber stood between the hapless scheme being opened to those who would enrich themselves from it. On 18 October the scheme was brought before the Enterprise, Trade and Investment Committee – the cross-party Assembly committee which scrutinised Foster's department – and sailed through without its fundamental flaws being spotted. The minutes of that meeting indicate little of what transpired, but it would later be claimed that, as with the minister, the committee was not given the full picture by officials.

Four days later, the regulations came before the entire Assembly where any one of the 108 MLAs had the chance to question what was happening. In a brief 460-word speech, Foster gave little of the key detail about how the scheme would operate. But she did talk about 'my department', 'my commitment to the sector' and 'my desire to see levels of renewable heating increase'. Her comments were typical of how many Stormont ministers – but particularly Foster – liked to operate. The minister was eager to be associated with a scheme, which she thought would be politically popular, rather than modestly pointing out – as she would later claim – that most of the significant work was done by her officials.

Speaking on behalf of the scrutiny committee, Patsy McGlone, its Social Democratic and Labour Party (SDLP) chairman, welcomed the scheme but said that 'some concerns have been expressed that the tariffs for the renewable heat incentive are lower than those in Britain'. He claimed that the committee's scrutiny of the proposal had been 'considerable and reflects the importance and long-term nature of the proposals'. And he went on to pledge that the committee 'will pay particular attention to the reviews, and it will scrutinise the implementation of the scheme', something it would fail to do.

However, although those comments turned out to be an embarrassing overstatement of the committee's largely acquiescent role in the process, McGlone did raise the fact that the green energy charity Action Renewables had expressed concerns that the 'rates and bands for biomass could create a distortion in the market and lead to applicants installing boilers with a smaller than required capacity'. McGlone's support for Foster's scheme was surpassed by one of the DUP members of his committee, who was positively gushing about RHI. Robin Newton, who would go on to become a highly controversial Speaker of the Assembly, told the chamber that it was 'a good news story' in 'an area where, I believe, we are often maligned, and I do not believe that that maligning is justified'. In remarks which are now excruciating to read, Newton said: 'This project is leading us down a road, and I believe that, when we reach the final stage, the economy of Northern Ireland will have benefited significantly from the steps that the minister has taken.'

Sandra Overend for the Ulster Unionist Party referred to CEPA's report – sections of which were dangerous garbage and with tables where the numbers did not add up – and enthused that it had 'undoubtedly been invaluable in informing decision-makers on the best way forward'. The only other speakers in what could not accurately be described as a debate were Alliance MLA Chris Lyttle, Green MLA Steven Agnew and Sinn Féin's Phil Flanagan, each of whom also welcomed the scheme. Without a single dissenting voice, The Renewable Heat Incentive Scheme Regulations (Northern Ireland) 2012 passed their final legislative hurdle and became law. But there was a remarkable fact which went unrealised by everyone in the Assembly chamber that day: Foster had not even read the legislation which she was asking MLAs to vote into law. The minister made the admission almost six years later when being grilled by the public inquiry. In a revelation which left some of her DUP colleagues slack-jawed in disbelief, Foster casually said that she had 'definitely not' read the regulations.

Under questioning about a deficiency in the regulations whereby they did not adequately define 'useful heat' eligible for subsidy, making it more difficult to crack down on potentially fraudulent claims, Foster said that she 'imagined it would have been defined in the legislation'. When asked if she had at any stage read the regulations, Mrs Foster said: 'No. No, I didn't. So there's … absolutely not. I didn't read the regulations.' David Scoffield QC for the inquiry asked Foster if she would have read the regulations when she brought them to the Assembly for approval. She said: 'No, I don't believe I would have read them at that stage. I probably would have only read the explanatory note, but not the regulations involved.'

The clarity of Foster's recollection about not reading the legislation was striking because that day at the inquiry she had repeatedly used phrases such as 'I don't remember', 'I can't recall' and 'I don't think I have any clear recollection' about key meetings from 2012 which went unrecorded. The tone with which she spoke and her body language conveyed no embarrassment at the admission that as a government minister she had not read a piece of legislation tabled in her name and which she was asking MLAs to endorse.

****

Given the centrality of Crawford to this story, there is an intriguing footnote about this period. Before joining the DUP staff team in 2004, Crawford had worked for two years as a policy officer for the Ulster Farmers' Union (UFU).

His time at the UFU – a body with major political clout in Northern Ireland – coincided with the two-year tenure of a Londonderry farmer, John Gilliland, who had been elected as the union's youngest-ever president at the age of 36. Gilliland was a green energy pioneer who specialised in biomass, running boilers on his farm long before RHI and growing willow, which was turned into wood chip to be burned in biomass heating systems. He was no stranger to politicians, having stood as a unique independent candidate in the 2004 European elections with the backing of the Alliance Party, the Workers' Party and a rainbow coalition of other smaller parties. Foster told the inquiry that she knew that Crawford and Gilliland 'would have known each other for quite some time'.

In spring 2011, Gilliand wrote to Foster about his 'favourite bug bear, a Northern Ireland Renewable Heat Incentive'. He relayed how David Dobbin, the chief executive of major Northern Ireland milk processor, Dale Farm, had said that the delay in launching RHI 'was severely undermining the Northern Ireland dairy industry's competitiveness against his GB competitors'. The correspondence shows that Foster was being personally contacted about RHI and therefore presumably was asking internal questions about it in order to be able to respond. Gilliland met Foster and Crawford at DETI's Belfast headquarters in August 2011 to discuss RHI. Without a minute of the meeting, it is unclear what exactly was said. But it is clear that Gilliland was pushing the minister to get the scheme launched.

Although a committed environmentalist, Gilliland had more pressing personal reasons to secure the subsidy. In 1996 he had set up Rural Generation Limited, a research and development company exploring uses for wood chip, and the company had gone on to sell biomass boilers. In 2009, the firm had installed a biomass boiler at Stormont Castle.

But as the long-delayed RHI remained uncertain, the firm struggled to stay afloat and cashflow dried up in late 2012. On 2 November the company was wound up. Gilliland was interviewed by the *Irish Farmers Journal* and that day the journalist contacted DETI to ask for a comment from Foster. None arrived. However, he was advised to look for a public statement from the minister the next day. On the morning of 3 November, Foster announced that Stormont's RHI scheme was finally opening. Crawford phoned Gilliland that night and commiserated with him over the demise of Rural Generation Ltd. Gilliland later recalled that the spad had 'encouraged me to get back up on my feet and said pioneers such as myself would be required to deliver this new policy on renewable heat'. What the public did not know was that even though Foster was inviting applications to her shiny new scheme, there was no one to accept those applications. In DETI's haste to open RHI, it had done so before finalising terms with Ofgem to administer the scheme. Hepper told the inquiry that the department had a 'line in the sand' date for launch and was determined to do so. The small matter of not having anyone to run the scheme was not going to stand in DETI's way.

DETI was now in a weak position to negotiate Ofgem's fees. A huge increase in the administration costs left Hepper furious, but there was no one else to run RHI and it had already been opened. Eventually, they settled on a compromise figure. But there were a series of unresolved issues which would lead to disputes down the line. It would later also become clear that Ofgem was planning to inspect only a tiny handful of RHI installations – something which meant that fraudsters were unlikely to get caught.

But even though the scheme was profoundly defective from the outset, the damage did not have to be fatal. If the tariffs were reviewed regularly and the scheme was monitored, it would quickly become apparent that there was a problem. Even in that optimistic scenario, the first claimants to get into the scheme would benefit from a grossly over-generous subsidy. But the problem would be halted before it became insurmountable. However, what was to follow would make it much harder to believe that what had happened in setting up the scheme so disastrously had been entirely accidental.

CHAPTER 6
CASH FOR ASH BEGINS

From the very first biomass boiler he installed, Neil Elliott knew that RHI facilitated a simple practice: burn to earn. The plain-spoken Fermanagh businessman had hired an installer, who had worked on the GB RHI, to assist his small renewables firm with its first contract for an RHI boiler. Elliott recalled the installer's question: 'What's tier one? And what's tier two?' The baffled businessman replied: 'What's a tier?' The installer changed the question: 'When do you fall off?' Elliott replied: 'No, there is none in Northern Ireland. It's open.' Bewildered, the installer asked: 'What? What do you mean it's open? There's no cap?' Elliott later recalled:

> We're [saying to him]: 'No. It's just as much as you ...' And suddenly, everyone then realised, you know, 'I'm paying 4p a kilowatt-hour for fuel here, and I'm getting possibly 6p at that stage or whatever, so I'm making a third here. And that's it. And I can just use it as much as I want'. So, energy efficiency just went out the window and it was just essentially: 'Use it as much as you can. You can't lose.'

Elliott, an adventurer who in 2006 had led a small team of climbers to the top of Mount Everest, had been in the renewables business for a few years when RHI launched. Speaking with candour to the RHI Inquiry in 2018, Elliott recalled: 'It just grew and grew and grew, to the point [that] we would have had ten times the staff we had initially – just on the RHI alone. It just became so big. It was incredible.' But even though he could quickly see the fatal flaw at the heart of the scheme, prospective customers were not always easy to convince that it was a sound investment:

> People weren't aware of it, I suppose, initially. They didn't understand it. And maybe, somewhat, they didn't believe it either ... one of the first ones we would've quoted for was a hotelier, and all his mates were in a hotelier association. They kinda laughed at him and said: 'Ach sure, that — you couldn't believe that that's true'. But whenever the money started flowing from the RHI, they [saw] 'this thing's real'. And just the word of mouth got out and it just grew and grew from there.

Elliott said that he took no action to alert DETI to the flaws he could see 'as we thought that DETI would cap the scheme or amend the scheme to the same scheme as the UK mainland … we did not communicate any potential flaws in the scheme to anyone, but it was widespread knowledge within the renewable industry that the incentive was too good to be true.' Elliott said that he could not see how the department – or anyone else – was unaware of what was going on in open view. And yet that is what the civil servants and politicians would later claim.

When DETI later attempted at the inquiry to explain how it had failed to understand the biomass gold rush, it initially claimed that there had been a 'conspiracy of silence' from the industry. However, Andrew McCormick, who would go on to become the most senior civil servant in DETI, then contradicted that allegation and said that based on what he had come to see he realised there were warnings, but 'if people aren't listening, then it's not much good people trying to speak to them.' Elliott said that 'not unless you were blind and deaf' could anyone have remained unaware of the problem. 'Any event you went to, all installers were advertising the same thing: cash for ash, earn as you burn. Everyone knew, in the renewable industry, including the customers. The more energy you used, the more you got paid. I can't understand how anyone could say they couldn't see that.' He went on: 'I can't understand how anyone could say they didn't understand, because I'm not superintelligent, so it wasn't that I knew something that others didn't. You know, everybody knew that the RHI was what it was.'

Elliott said that at Department of Agriculture events, to promote green energy to farmers, there were so many renewable installers that the organisers had to erect a marquee to fit them all in. The regular events – at which DETI officials were present and met installers – lasted for a large part of a day. Elliott said that installers were openly flogging their wares based on the ultra-lucrative RHI, with slogans such as 'cash for ash' prominently displayed. DETI's Peter Hutchinson, who gave talks at some of the events, said that he did not recall ever seeing such lurid marketing.

The then Sinn Féin minister at the Department of Agriculture was Michelle O'Neill – who would go on to become deputy leader of her party. O'Neill defended her department's role in advertising the subsidy, telling the inquiry that it had a responsibility to raise awareness of government initiatives relevant to farmers but 'it was for the DETI minister and department to ensure the scheme was fit for purpose and value for money. It is not the role of a minister or department to scrutinise the work of another minister or department.' Despite the widespread take-up of the scheme among farmers in particular, O'Neill said: 'I did not know of any flaws in the scheme and no concerns were brought to my attention before February 2016 [when it was shut].'

Although Elliott was quick to see how attractively open-ended the subsidy was for claimants, he was not the first to do so. Just weeks after the scheme launched in November 2012, Brian Hood of BSH Holdings was openly marketing the scheme as one from which a handsome profit could be made – and marketing it in those terms to Stormont itself. RHI had been open for just over three weeks when Hood wrote to Stormont's Department of Justice to propose that it use RHI boilers to heat a new police and fire service training facility outside Cookstown.

At that point, the design of the college proposed using two huge one-megawatt boilers to heat the entire site. Hood suggested that instead he could install multiple 99 kW boilers – the maximum size permissible for the most lucrative RHI tariff. As well as the massive financial incentive from RHI, he believed there were valid engineering reasons why multiple boilers would be more efficient, such as reducing the amount of heat lost in underground pipework travelling from two central boilers to multiple buildings around the large site. He told the Department of Justice that the running costs of the heating 'could be turned into a profit rather than cost' and calculated that the 'profit' would be £44,740 a year. In contrast to the normal heating costs proposed for the training centre, a 20-year heating bill of £2.3 million would be turned into a profit of almost £900,000. The figures were eye-watering.

Hood later said that he had simply read the RHI regulations and then double-checked his interpretation of them with DETI officials who had confirmed that he could do what he thought the law permitted. But those planning the college were sceptical, questioning whether multiple boilers could be installed and qualify for RHI when the heat demand was so great that the planned pair of 1MW boilers would have been too large to qualify. But even if that was technically possible under the RHI regulations, they wrote back to Hood and questioned whether it was 'appropriate for a Government-funded facility to attempt to exploit possible loopholes in the RHI and recover the benefit'. Hood double-checked with DETI, who said it was fine, but the team responsible for the college came back to again reject his proposal, describing it as 'manipulation'. Shortly after, one of Hood's colleagues emailed DUP Finance Minister Sammy Wilson to set out RHI's benefits and suggest that it could be used in government buildings and schools. In his own hand, Wilson scrawled on the correspondence a message to his officials: 'Double dutch [sic] to me, but has DoJ [Department of Justice] checked this out. They are notorious for choosing expensive options.'

Hood had difficulty convincing prospective clients that the scheme was as good as his marketing brochures claimed. He recalled that people would say to him: 'The Government doesn't pay you to heat buildings … why would they be doing this?' Hood put his money where his mouth was, becoming the first person to be accredited on the scheme. That milestone would see him stand beside a beaming Arlene Foster while she did something which until the RHI scandal would be most associated with her ministerial career – posing for a public relations photo. In an accompanying press release, Foster said: 'I hope this installation is the first of many.' It certainly would be.

Rapidly BS Holdings developed a marketing slogan: '20 years of free heat'. Far from being hidden away, the slogan was on all its literature, on its website, across social media and emblazoned on the side of its fleet of vehicles. Based on Hood's calculations at that point, if a 99 kW boiler ran 24 hours a day, seven days a week, 365 days per year, the owner would need to pay about £35,000 for fuel – but would receive RHI funding of about £51,000, leaving a profit of more than £16,000 on top of the free heat. That crude calculation did not include payments for electricity to the boiler or servicing – but even with those costs built in, it was a lucrative proposition.

Hood's earliest marketing material – sent out en masse across Northern Ireland to any business he thought might have a significant heat need – included a heading called 'profit' and said: 'The more efficient we can make the plant the greater the opportunity for you to obtain profit on the heating you use. Theoretical profit could be 157% of the fuel cost – but inevitable losses in the system have an affect [sic] on that.' In layman's terms, for every £1 of fuel, Hood's crude calculation was that claimants at that point could make £1.57. In reality, the figure would have been somewhat lower, given the additional costs associated with biomass boilers – particularly electricity and maintenance of a boiler which was working hard. But as the scheme went on, the profits would rise considerably because not only did the cost of fuel fall but the tariff increased significantly for people entering it in subsequent years.

And Hood's figures were based on those using wood pellets. Claimants using wood chip, which was far cheaper, were in some cases receiving more than £2 for every £1 of fuel before electricity and others costs were taken into consideration.

Hood said that it was quickly clear to him that abuse was possible on the simple basis that 'you'd open the windows but don't turn the heating off'. However, he said that his clients were reputable companies who would not do such a thing. There was, though, an underlying assumption that the scheme was wildly generous because that was how the government wanted it to be, the middle-aged businessman told the inquiry. 'They'd set the tariff, they'd done their due diligence and who are we, as a mere company, to question the Government? They'd got it right, as far I was concerned.' Hood expected the tariff to start off high to stimulate interest and then gradually be cut – perhaps to as little as 2p. In fact, the opposite happened. 'The problem is they didn't turn the tap off. They turned the bath tap on and left it running.' But even at this point, the only way that the bath could overflow would be if no one ever came back to check on it. With hundreds of millions of pounds of taxpayers' money being committed for two decades into the future, it was reasonable to assume that the scheme was not being left unattended.

****

The widespread concern that RHI was too good to be true meant that just two months into the scheme Foster decided to write to Northern Ireland's main banks. In what was a personal, cast-iron guarantee to stand over the scheme, which Foster would later abandon, she urged them to look favourably on those wanting to borrow in order to buy equipment to get on to RHI. The two-page letter could have hardly been more reassuring. In language of sparkling certitude, it set out a commitment which must have brought smiles to the faces of the bank executives who could now lend – and profit – because of RHI. The letter, which was drafted by Hepper, said that the unalterable level of payments over 20 years provided 'certainty for investors by setting a guaranteed support level for projects for their lifetime in a scheme, regardless of future reviews'.

Then, in a key section, which provided a seemingly unbreakable promise that subsidy rates would be locked in for 20 years, Foster said: 'Tariffs are "grandfathered" providing certainty for investors by setting a guaranteed support level for projects for their lifetime in a scheme, regardless of future reviews.' Foster said that her department believed that RHI was 'a real opportunity' for investors and concluded: 'I am therefore writing to encourage you to look favourably on approaches from businesses that are seeking finance to install renewable technologies. The government support on offer through the incentive schemes is reliable, long-term and offers a good return on investment.'

The letters had actually been conceived some four months earlier at a meeting of a cross-departmental group promoting sustainable energy, which Foster chaired. At a meeting in September 2012, Foster's spad, Andrew Crawford, had raised a query about how RHI would interact with a different biomass subsidy aimed at farmers. In response, a civil servant said that there were problems persuading banks to lend for renewable energy equipment. The minutes of the meeting show that Foster then 'advised that she would write to the main banks to explain how the incentive mechanisms operate'. For four years, copies of her letter lay largely unknown in filing cabinets at DETI and in the plush offices of bank chief executives in Belfast. Then, at the height of the RHI scandal in December 2016, the letter suddenly re-emerged – and in a way which caused backbiting among senior DUP figures.

The *Sunday World* newspaper had reported on the existence of the letter after seeing reference to it in emails from a DETI official. But DETI refused to release the letter itself, so the contents were unclear. At the time, Foster was seeking to distance herself from the scandal and was heaping blame on both her civil servants and her successor as minister, Jonathan Bell. *Belfast News Letter* reporter Adam Kula asked the DUP for a copy of the letter and was surprised when within a few hours it was emailed to him by DUP Press Officer Clive McFarland. McFarland, a former DUP councillor from Omagh, was respected by the media for his honesty and lack of guile. One veteran Belfast journalist described him as 'a proper human being' whose conduct was in contrast to that of some other party figures who were regarded as slippery. But McFarland's actions that night did not impress some of the DUP top brass.

The story of how Foster had personally given the banks a cast-iron guarantee about the generous RHI funding was published online that night and immediately picked up by other media outlets.

That evening John Robinson, the DUP spad to Simon Hamilton – the minister who had succeeded Jonathan Bell – sent a text message to fellow DUP spad Richard Bullick: 'Did you know that Clive sent all the bank letters to Sam McBride [*sic*] earlier? All over Twitter. Unbelievable.' Bullick replied that the key issue for the DUP had been to highlight one line from the letter – that the rate of return which Foster quoted was the relatively modest 12%. That, Bullick argued, showed that Foster had been unaware of how wildly over-generous the scheme had been, and that it was 'not a licence to print money'. Robinson replied: 'Exactly but just bucked out without any briefing. Mad.' Hamilton then texted to say: 'Just seeing this all now. What on earth did he do that for?' Robinson responded: 'Never mind that, he assumed every letter was the same and hadn't read them all to see if there was anything nasty in any of them. Must have been on the drink.'

As DUP director of communications – the party's chief spin doctor – before becoming a spad, Robinson had for years been McFarland's boss and within months would be back in the role. The exchanges – only brought to light by the public inquiry's sweeping powers of compulsion which gathered up DUP text messages – were an example of the tensions at the top of an outwardly united party and evidence of how decisions made in 2012 would come back to haunt the DUP.

****

Just two months into the scheme, a letter landed on the desk of Stormont's SDLP Environment Minister, Alex Attwood. The correspondence, from a firm called Renewable Energy Manufacturing (REM) Ltd, set out how it had a technology which turned poultry manure into fuel. That would have caused ears to prick up in Stormont for multiple reasons. Northern Ireland's biggest employer was the poultry-processing giant Moy Park. Stormont policy was to facilitate its expansion but this intensive agriculture created huge quantities of nitrate-rich manure which was difficult to dispose of without damaging the environment.

The firm set out how 'the current Northern Ireland RHI tariffs act as a deterrent for farmers to employ our Poultry Manure to Energy [product]'. The letter argued that Northern Ireland's RHI meant that a farmer who installed two 99 kW biomass boilers would receive nearly four times more in incentives than a farmer who installed one 200 kW heat from poultry waste system – even though both systems produced almost identical heat. It went on: 'The result is a "perverse incentive" for farmers needing more heat than a 198kw unit will produce to install a number of small wood chip boilers rather than one larger [poultry manure to energy] system.' Attwood forwarded the letter to Foster, his ministerial colleague. The letter went to energy division where Peter Hutchinson and Joanne McCutheon drafted a response to be issued by Foster's private secretary on behalf of the minister. It dismissively told the company that whereas it had claimed that two smaller boilers could be used to 'game' the system by attracting a higher subsidy than a single larger boiler, 'I can assure you that this is not the case'.

In fact, it very much was the case. The warning was to be the first of many, which might have been a prompt for civil servants to read the regulations and investigate whether what they were being told was happening was in fact possible. Instead, the consistent response was an implicitly arrogant dismissal based on the premise that the department knew best.

The accompanying submission to Foster was even more strident. It said that the firm's concerns 'relate to a perceived flaw in the RHI whereby installers are incentivised to install multiple smaller boilers instead of a single large boiler – this is not the case'. Intriguingly, Andrew Crawford again took an interest in a specific detail of the scheme at this point. After reading the submission, he sent a query back to energy division to ask: 'If two boilers are installed at different times will they not attract greater support than a single boiler?'

It had taken the industry weeks to work out something officials would never work out for themselves. It was not until after the scheme had closed that civil servants realised – after it was pointed out to them by the Audit Office – that an uncapped scheme where the subsidy is higher than the cost of the fuel was a perverse incentive for claimants to run their boilers as long as possible. Although focus would later turn to the fact that the tariff was set higher than the cost of the fuel, that in itself was not the problem. The intent was to pay off the cost of buying and installing the boiler – in the region of £45,000 – the fact the tariff was above the cost of fuel was a means of doing that.

The core problem was the lack of either tiering, to cut rates as the boiler ran for longer periods, or a simple cap on how much could be paid in subsidy for each piece of equipment. The combination of the fuel being cheaper than the subsidy and the absence of a cap meant that if someone had already splashed out on the costs of installing a boiler they were being financially incentivised to recoup those costs as quickly as possible – and then make pure profit – by running it for long periods. The fact that many boiler owners ran their boilers for long periods was not in itself proof of fraudulent intent. Some, such as poultry farmers, had huge heat requirements and it just so happened that RHI turned that otherwise expensive outlay into a profitable activity of its own. But there have been far too many stories of calculated abuse of the scheme – boilers running for long periods with windows open or in areas which were barely insulated – to believe that everyone who made huge claims did so in good faith.

Though a depressing example of flawed human nature, it is hardly surprising that if a scheme is set up so that it is easy to fraudulently claim – and very difficult to get caught – then some people are going to exploit it. In doing so, not only were they stealing money, which could have been spent on worthwhile causes such as hospitals or schools, but they were corrupting the very essence of the scheme. Having intended to improve the environment by moving people from finite and heavily polluting fossil fuels to sustainable and cleaner sources of energy, RHI led to the opposite: public money was incentivising the public to damage the environment.

In April 2013 – some five months into Stormont's scheme – Westminster legislation was passed to give greater powers to DECC, the Whitehall department running the GB scheme, to ensure that its budget was not exceeded. Although at that point there was no immediate budgetary concern, the department publicly explained that it thought it was prudent to put in place measures which would allow it to quickly step in if there was a sudden increase in demand. It was a recognition of the unpredictable nature of RHI. Unlike most government grants, which involve getting approval from officials before making an investment, RHI involved people installing boilers themselves and then applying to enter the scheme. So long as they met the criteria for the scheme, there was no legal means whereby they could be rejected at that point. That meant that the department could never be sure how many people had installed boilers and were just about to apply to enter the scheme – a fundamental weakness in being able to predict the required budget.

The GB 'degression' changes allowed DECC to 'degress' the tariffs according to how much of its budget had been committed. It meant that the more people who applied to the scheme, the less lucrative it became for those who joined after them. The ability for DECC to reduce its tariffs had only been on the statute book for a month when it was used for the first time. DECC minister Greg Barker wrote to Foster to say that the uptake for small and medium-sized biomass boilers was 'a real success, even beyond our initial expectations'. But that meant, he said, that DECC had considered the likely cost to taxpayers of that success. As a result, Barker said that it had decided to cut the most popular biomass tariff. It was an indication that the level of tariffs in GB were now judged unsustainable and was in line with how many green energy schemes had operated in the past. With new technologies, subsidies often started high, but as it either became apparent that they were too generous or as the cost of the technology dropped, then the subsidy was reduced.

On the same day that Barker's letter went to Foster, DECC issued a press release setting out how the tariff was being reduced. DETI officials certainly saw the press release and judged it relevant to their work because that day they saved it into the Northern Ireland Civil Service's TRIM data management system.

Just six months into Stormont's RHI scheme, there had now been a barrage of prompts to look at the issue of cost controls and some of the key assumptions behind the scheme. At this stage the number of claimants was in single figures, and although those who had entered the scheme would have locked in lucrative uncapped subsidies for 20 years, action at that point would have contained the problem. But, for whatever reason, nothing was done.

The following month, there was another moment that might have jolted DETI to spot 'cash for ash'. On 3 June, Ofgem sent Hutchinson a spreadsheet with the Northern Ireland RHI data for that week. It gave considerable detail about the applicants' behaviour. It set out the size of the boilers, showing that they were generally far bigger than the 50 kW boilers which CEPA's modelling had expected and on which it had based the tariffs. Aside from any other problem with the scheme, if CEPA's assumptions were wildly wrong then the tariffs were going to be wildly wrong. One number in the data gave away that something potentially problematic was going on. The spreadsheet showed that several of the early biomass installations were running for 168 hours per week. There are only 168 hours in a week so that meant that the boilers were running round the clock. A simple calculation would have shown how much money they were making.

That same month, senior Ofgem figure Edmund Ward attended an event organised by the green energy charity Action Renewables. Promotional material for the event to explain RHI to potential claimants included the strapline: 'Find out how to generate heat and get paid for it!' Subsequently, the organisers circulated some of the speakers' presentations to those who had attended. Ward was sent a presentation by the chief executive of the Renewable Heat Association in which attention was drawn to perverse incentives. Under the heading 'lessons for DETI', it said: 'Don't let there be perverse incentives' and argued for tiered tariffs. DETI was not present at the event – and was criticised by some attendees for not being there. However, the energy division team were regularly going to similar events to promote RHI. Their evidence to the inquiry was that they never picked up on the flaws of the scheme at such events, despite what multiple witnesses described as participants' open discussion about the extremely lucrative nature of the subsidy.

Solmatix, a firm which attended such events, had a leaflet that literally marketed RHI as 'cash for ash'. Its literature said: 'When you factor in your guaranteed quarterly RHI grant income, you're effectively benefiting from FREE heat plus a significant financial reward. It's cash … for ash.'

Hutchinson, who most regularly attended such events for the department, was over-worked by his superiors who effectively left him to single-handedly keep a day-to-day eye on a novel and complex incentive scheme which DETI's own risk analysis had shown was vulnerable to fraud. But he was also being asked to expand RHI.

The non-domestic RHI had always been intended as the first stage of a larger scheme, which would allow domestic applications and also include further technologies. With pressure to spend the RHI money on offer from the Treasury – and to hit the EU targets – Hepper again turned to CEPA for advice. Having paid £100,000 for the flawed initial advice, DETI now agreed to spend about the same again for advice on how to get more people into the scheme. CEPA delivered its 131-page report in June 2013 and for those who read it there were a series of warning signs. The consultants raised one of the most flagrant abuses of the non-domestic RHI. The warning, on page 66 of the detailed report, came as CEPA set out several risks. Among them are problems with metering which 'broadly relate to the range of issues encountered by the non-domestic RHI to date'. Under the heading 'useful heat', it went on to say: 'With direct metering, properties may be heated to higher than best practice levels, windows opened, etc., if the tariff is tied to heat generated. In this case, the tariff could exceed operating costs.' It was an unvarnished articulation of the sort of practices the industry had immediately spotted were being incentivised by DETI.

Throughout the report, the consultants also warned that the department could not afford the payments, which would be necessary if it was to reach its target of securing 10% of renewable heat by 2020: 'In short, if DETI is spending more than 4.2p/kWh, it is not going to be able to afford the 10% target with its assumed budget. In that regard, we note that many of the tariffs in this report are above 4.2p.'

The report also reiterated the cost of wood chip and wood pellets – the two main biomass fuel sources – and said that the prices collated in its initial report had been substantiated by a Northern Ireland stakeholder group with which it had discussions. Not only was this in itself another chance for DETI to be reminded of the gulf between the cost of fuel and the level of its subsidy, but the report recommended that, as part of what were meant to be regular reviews of the non-domestic RHI, DETI specifically review the cost of biomass fuel.

****

By December 2013, RHI had been open for a year in Northern Ireland. But despite the riches on offer, just 85 applications had been made to the scheme. Some in DETI were disappointed, and there was an understandable sense that RHI was underperforming. At least, that's what the story was when the scandal erupted in 2016. It was the explanation offered by both Foster and her civil servants for why cost controls had not been prioritised. However, had the numbers been examined in more depth, they would have realised that was not quite the full story. The department was not comparing like with like. They were comparing Northern Ireland's fledgling scheme with the more established GB scheme at that point. Had they compared their scheme with the GB scheme at the same stage, a year after it had been set up, they would have seen that Northern Ireland had a higher pro-rata take-up than GB.

On one reading, Stormont was lulled into a false sense of security by the mistaken belief that there was limited demand for its scheme and, whether consciously or subliminally, this contributed to cost controls being delayed. But was that really what happened? Several pieces of evidence suggest that DETI may have known that RHI was performing well.

In December 2013, Foster wrote in reply to another letter from Barker, the Whitehall minister. She told him: 'The Northern Ireland RHI has only been in operation for 12 months, yet there has been an encouraging level of uptake, with the number of applications for the Northern Ireland scheme being around 7% of the number received by the GB scheme during its first year of operation.' Given what Foster would later claim about low uptake helping to explain the inaction over implementing cost controls, that is a remarkable sentence. The 7% quoted is far above Northern Ireland's 2.8% share of the UK population. Foster was now clearly aware that the uptake on her scheme was more than double what had been experienced in GB at the same stage of that scheme's life. Perhaps that was in her mind – or in the mind of the civil servant who drafted the letter for Foster – when she also assured Barker that among the issues being considered by DETI was 'cost control'.

The following month, Foster was asked in the Assembly to provide an update on the scheme. Oozing confidence, she gave no hint of alarm or disappointment. Foster told MLAs that the performance of her scheme was better than that in GB, and said that while Northern Ireland accounted for less than 3% of the UK heat demand, the number of Northern Ireland applications equated to 6.8% of GB applications. That, Foster said with the sort of clarity that gave many observers the idea that she was a competent minister, 'demonstrates that the Northern Ireland scheme is punching above its weight'. Four months later, in a briefing which went to Foster, the then head of DETI's energy division, John Mills, told her:

> The current NI uptake compares favourably with the GB uptake at the same point in time on a pro-rata basis. The NI scheme is currently tracking at 7.2% of GB applications, 7.2% of accreditations and 4.1% of heat capacity, despite the NI heat market being only 3% of the UK market. This suggests that the NI RHI could experience a higher volume of applications but for smaller installations.

He was certainly right about that. As 2013 ended, the first year of RHI had seen multiple explicit warnings about the fledgling scheme or moments that ought to have prompted reflection by DETI. Rather than move to address the myriad problems with the subsidy, the department was putting all of its energy into expanding the scheme. But already there had been another seismic warning – a warning so significant that it would help to topple the future First Minister.

CHAPTER 7
WHISTLING IN THE WIND

It was a Monday morning and Janette O'Hagan was in the office of Okotech, her small technology company, in Antrim. The business had been set up the previous year and was centred around the development of energy - efficient heating controls called heatboss. The product enabled heating to be wirelessly controlled, switching the heat on and off in individual rooms remotely, rather than heating an entire property when much of it may be empty. Her pitch to businesses was simple: buy my product and expect to pay 30% less for heat. But on the morning of 26 August 2013, O'Hagan was not marketing her fledgling company's product to potential customers. She had stumbled across something hard to believe, but because it was impacting her business she quickly came to see that it was true.

While most businesses were interested in discovering how they could save money on their heating bill, companies with biomass boilers seemed to have no interest. Baffled, O'Hagan dug into the issue. She had picked up in conversations at industry events that these businesses were receiving the RHI subsidy. She recalled:

> The more I was hearing, the more I was getting more convinced, so I looked online, and I went onto the DETI website and looked at the tariffs that were set, and immediately I thought — and I mean immediately — thought that, 'That can't be right. You know, that can't be right. Where is the limit? How do you ensure people are being efficient there?'

> And then, whenever I compared it to the GB tariffs and their tiers, and they just seemed to have got it. They got it that, 'Yes, we have to incentivise people to take up this technology' … but they knew that there had to be a limit, you know: 'We have to not incentivise waste'.

This epiphany immediately explained why when she contacted businesses with RHI boilers they were not interested in being efficient because the more that they burned, the more they earned. With scant knowledge of politics, she was unsure what to do. But she was clear that she had to try to alert the authorities to what was happening. Not only was her business suffering as a result of the RHI but she was angry at the thought of such waste being incentivised by government. That Monday morning she decided to go right to the top – to Arlene Foster. O'Hagan sent an email to DETI's generic email address, marking it for the attention of Arlene Foster. It was a general email setting out her company's attempts to facilitate energy efficiency and asked for a meeting with Foster to discuss the issue. Moments after hitting 'send', she had second thoughts. Would an email to a generic email inbox get picked up? And, if it did, would it ever make its way to the minister?

O'Hagan decided to try another route. Searching the DUP website, she found an email address where Foster could be emailed about constituency issues. Five minutes after sending the initial email, she sent a second to Foster but added the line: 'Given the benefits of RHI, we find that many of our potential customers are no longer worried about becoming more efficient, because they are now more sustainable.' It was a cryptic reference to the problem, but her intention was to secure a meeting at which she could explain RHI's central flaw. Eight days later, there had been no response to either email.

Undeterred, O'Hagan sat down again and emailed *arlene@arlenefoster. org.uk*. This time she was more direct, telling the minister: 'Given the benefits of RHI, we find that many of our potential customers are no longer worried about becoming more efficient, in fact it pays them to use as much as they can – in fact the incentive to use more is leading to misuse in some cases.' Now, just ten months after the launch of RHI, Foster had been warned explicitly that it was in itself a perverse incentive to waste heat and was being actively abused. O'Hagan never received a reply to that email and there is no electronic record of it ever having been passed on to DETI – unlike the initial email, which Foster had forwarded to her private office. However, two days later O'Hagan was contacted by a DETI official who said that Foster could not meet her but a meeting would be arranged with officials. The businesswoman was in no doubt that it was her second and more direct email to Foster that led to the response.

O'Hagan had not known what to expect and was pleasantly surprised to be told that she was being offered a meeting. A month later, she was sitting around a table in DETI's Netherleigh House headquarters with the triumvirate of civil servants who knew more about RHI than anyone else – Fiona Hepper, Joanne McCuthcon and Peter Hutchinson. The fact that all three met her for an hour at a time when the civil servants say they were overworked suggests that this was thought to be more important than simply a businesswoman with a commercial complaint.

But their disposition in the meeting left O'Hagan despondent. On leaving the rambling DETI headquarters, she felt that she had wasted her time. As in her email to Foster, O'Hagan had warned them of the perverse incentive to run boilers around the clock with windows open. With lurid language, she told the civil servants that she was surprised people weren't mounting radiators on the outside walls of buildings, such was the financial incentive to waste heat. The response – she thinks it was from McCutheon, but certainly from one of the three – never left her: 'We don't think people will do that.' O'Hagan shot back: 'Well, they can, and they will, and I'm surprised they're not mounting them on the outside.' She was certain of her facts because she had compared Stormont's scheme to the one in GB and she also had first-hand experience of how those with biomass boilers reacted to the offer of cutting their fuel bill, as well as what others in the energy industry were saying. But she also had something else.

Just two months earlier, O'Hagan had approached BS Holdings, the biomass installer which had within weeks worked out that the scheme was a money-maker, with a proposal to work together – the heatboss system would be installed along with the biomass boiler, thus saving money on two fronts. But ahead of the meeting, the boiler installer sent her an email to caution that for its RHI customers 'the more heat generated, the more funding'. The implication was clear: a product which cut their heating bill was going to reduce their income, so it wasn't going to be attractive. At the meeting, it was suggested to her that if BS Holdings was to trial some of her promotional literature with its customers then the leaflets should be rewritten to remove the references to savings. Instead, the suggestion was that she should market her product to RHI users as a means of ensuring 'control' and 'comfort'. But at the meeting with DETI officials, O'Hagan was told that it was their 'assumption' that if a business was going to invest in an expensive biomass boiler it would be the last stage of an attempt to become more environmentally friendly and would have been preceded by efforts to become more energy efficient.

Based on what they told O'Hagan, the civil servants don't seem to have been able to comprehend that a business might be more interested in making easy money than cutting its carbon emissions. Yet the explanation which they gave to O'Hagan did not fully add up because in their own paperwork for the RHI scheme they had identified the risk of fraud and overcompensation. And it is harder still to understand why they were so dismissive of her central claim because by now Hutchinson, at least, had firm evidence about how the early claimants were using their boilers far more than had been anticipated. Although DETI's small RHI team was not monitoring it in the hands-on way that Whitehall was examining trends in the GB scheme, they were receiving sufficient information in RHI's first year to raise eyebrows.

As early as seven months into the scheme, Hutchinson was estimating that boilers could be used for as much as 35% of the year – more than double the 17% CEPA had estimated. It was also clear from the data coming through to DETI by then that the only real interest was in biomass. That in itself ought to have been a red flag because the scheme had been set up to incentivise a host of green technologies, and the subsidies were meant to have been calculated so that there would be no predominance of a single technology.

Hepper later told the public inquiry that O'Hagan had only raised 'anecdotal' evidence. She said that the businesswoman had been encouraged to contribute to a consultation on the expansion of the scheme. But when O'Hagan looked at the consultation, most of it related to the domestic scheme and she felt that she had already explicitly told the key DETI figures about the central problem. If they wouldn't believe her when she told them in person, why would they react differently if she filled in a consultation response form? O'Hagan later told the inquiry: 'I just keep thinking a blind man on a galloping horse would have seen it. You know, how could they not?'

It would be the emergence of O'Hagan's email to Foster, three and a half years after it was sent, that would trigger former DUP minister Jonathan Bell to speak out and then the process of Foster's toppling as First Minister, the collapse of Stormont and the public inquiry.

O'Hagan, who stressed that she had no political motive for what she did and who was not involved in the leaking of her email in December 2016, could never have imagined where her attempt to raise the alarm would lead. Although she later came to be referred to as a whistleblower – and at various points had later referred to herself as such – she told the inquiry that she did not think that she was in truth a whistleblower, because she was not blowing the whistle from the inside but was rather a 'concerned citizen' who could see there was a problem. For that reason, she did not seek anonymity when she approached the department. Her 2013 attempt to alert those in authority to the problem was the first of multiple efforts to get DETI to open its eyes to what was going on. The dismissive response from officialdom shook her confidence in the machinery of government. She later reflected: 'It seems to me that the effective route is probably to go to the media.'

****

The civil servants' refusal to believe that RHI was open to widespread abuse makes even less sense because of something which had happened just three months before they met O'Hagan.

After receiving CEPA's report on expanding RHI, DETI opened a public consultation about doing so. Yet, one section of the July 2013 document – some eight months after the scheme had opened – proved that there was an awareness of the need for cost controls and that Foster was personally aware of this. In a foreword to the 45-page document, Foster made clear that she knew about the potential costs of RHI ballooning out of control, and therefore her department was proposing measures to prevent that. She wrote: 'I am conscious that whilst this is a sector that requires significant support, budget levels are finite and cannot be breached.' The document dedicated an entire section to cost controls, saying that 'a method of cost control is to be introduced that will ensure budgets are not overspent and will hopefully remove the need for emergency reviews'. It went on to set out in detail – an indication of how officials had engaged in considerable work on the subject – just how the various cost controls would operate.

The department proposed to follow GB's system of degression 'in the future' but said that 'in the interim it is proposed that a simpler system is put in place'. Setting out the precise situation, which would develop two years later, the department said:

Whilst tariffs are designed to ensure that the budget is adhered to there is always a risk that renewable heat technologies might be deployed in greater numbers than what is forecast and payments exceed expectations. The risk of this increases as tariffs become available for larger technologies such as biomass over 1MW, biomass/bioliquids, CHP and deep geothermal. Therefore DETI must retain the right to suspend the scheme if budget limits could be breached; however this will only happen at a last resort and, at this stage, is not envisioned to happen.

The 2013 consultation document led to the existing non-domestic RHI regulations being amended in several areas – each of which was far less important than the need for cost controls. The fact that this happened shows it would have been straightforward to amend the scheme at that point if the issue had been prioritised. It also proves that the need for cost controls was not somehow overlooked by a team of busy officials. They had not only understood the issue, but had put proposals to the public, which were then consciously not implemented. Stemming from that is an obvious question: given that the problem had been identified and a proposed solution worked out in great detail, why – and on whose instructions – was that proposal abandoned?

Two years later, the then head of DETI's energy division, John Mills, found himself having to explain to Stormont's Department of Finance how he had allowed RHI to run out of control with calamitous financial consequences. In the behind-closed-doors meeting – in which minutes were kept, perhaps because by that stage civil servants were now worried about where the blame would fall – he was asked why the 2013 recommendation for budgetary controls was never implemented. Mills claimed that it had been down to a conscious decision by Foster – an explosive allegation, given what was to follow.

Minutes of the meeting recorded him saying that 'it was a ministerial decision to look at [opening] the domestic scheme rather than pushing through the trigger points [cost controls] on non-domestic which would have significantly delayed the implementation of the domestic scheme'. Mills, a veteran senior civil servant, then repeated that claim in public to an Assembly committee in February 2016, saying that 'the minister decided that the priority should be on the introduction of the domestic RHI scheme. So resources were devoted to that'. But Foster always robustly disputed that she had ever been presented with a choice about either implementing cost controls or expanding the scheme.

Then, two and a half years after Mills made that potentially career-ending claim about Foster, he retracted it. When called before the public inquiry, which by that stage had uncovered hundreds of thousands of pages of documentation, shedding much more light on the situation than would have been apparent to Mills at the time, he said that there was no evidence to support what had been his belief at the time. His claim about Foster, he said, had been 'completely incorrect'. Explaining his original comments, Mills said that when he arrived in DETI at the start of 2014 he felt that 'the course was set' to expand RHI rather than work on cost controls and he 'assumed there was some ministerial authority for it'. However, he went on: 'As part of the inquiry, as I gradually went hunting for what I imagined to be a submission for ministerial approval, I didn't find one'. He said that in his view 'there is no evidence of the minister being asked to make that decision'. Mills accepted that he was 'at fault' for not asking to either see a piece of paper in early 2014 showing that the minister had agreed to what was happening or, if that had not happened, then putting a submission to Foster. However, even if Foster never explicitly asked to delay cost controls, her actions may still have – even inadvertently – had that effect. Just as her impatience to get the scheme launched in 2012 appears to have influenced officials to press ahead with what they knew was a flawed scheme, so now the minister's eagerness to expand the scheme led to her officials believing that it was this which she was keenest to see done first.

Mills said that he made the expansion of the scheme the top priority for those under him in response to Foster's desire for expansion. During meetings with Foster every six weeks, he recalled that 'my impression during those discussions was the minister's disappointment that the domestic RHI scheme was not ready'. Foster and Crawford's frustration at the delay in launching the domestic RHI is recorded in their own handwriting in this period. On the face of a submission sent to them by Stuart Wightman in September 2014, which proposed that the scheme would launch in November, Crawford wrote: 'Can we not open the scheme before November 2014?' On another submission later that month, Crawford wrote by hand:

'Need to get this launched.' Two days later, Foster wrote by hand on the same submission: 'Get this launched ASAP.' There was unmistakable ministerial urgency to expand RHI – yet no urgency about introducing cost controls. While officials should have done far more to put before Foster the critical need for an emergency brake for the scheme, it is possible to see how they came to believe that her overwhelming priority was expansion in an attempt to increase expenditure – not doing something which might dampen demand.

Mills also said that when he joined the department at the start of 2014:

The concern was that [RHI] take-up was very slow and we were handing money back to Treasury and certainly in early January, February, in the 'lines to take' [for Foster] that I remember – the question that we didn't want to be asked was 'how much money are you giving back to Treasury' and there were a lot of lines about trying to defend why [that was the case].

He said he had a 'general recollection, across a number of meetings, of being asked [by Foster] about timelines and the need for progress' on expanding RHI and that 'the predominant tenor of that time was: We're underspending, or we're giving back money to Treasury and the risk of overspend is not high up the risk profile.' One explanation for how cost controls came to be abandoned – and apparently without any express ministerial authority to do so – was that the department was chaotic in this period after the entire team working on RHI was replaced within a few months.

In December 2013, Hepper – despite having presided over the creation of such a disastrous scheme – was promoted to become a deputy secretary in the Department of Education, one rung beneath the most senior civil servant in the department responsible for Northern Ireland's schools. The following month she was succeeded by Mills, a history graduate who, like her, was not an energy expert and had been in charge of water policy prior to joining DETI. Four months after Hepper's departure, Joanne McCutheon, who had been directly beneath her, left on a career break. For 12 weeks after her departure she was replaced by Davina McCay, a mid-ranking civil servant within energy division who acted up until a replacement could be found. That replacement ultimately arrived in June 2014 in the form of

Stuart Wightman, someone who had worked as an engineer in the Roads Service before working in public transport policy and then water policy. Just a month after McCutheon left, Hutchinson – who was immediately beneath her – also left, moving to Stormont Castle. He would not be replaced for about six weeks. At the end of June his successor arrived. Seamus Hughes, an experienced official who over the course of more than 30 years had slowly worked his way up from the lowest grade of administrative assistant to the mid-ranking deputy principal, was now the man who would be overseeing the scheme on a daily basis as it slid into chaos the following year. He candidly told the public inquiry that he had 'close to zero' knowledge of energy policy when he arrived in DETI.

On his first day, Hughes was given electronic links to hundreds of pages of complex background material on the RHI policy, including CEPA's bulky reports. Having just arrived from the Department of Agriculture's farm policy branch, Hughes said: 'They didn't make a lot of sense to me, to be honest, on an initial reading of them.' With the exception of the minister and her spad, who would also soon be moving on, all those who had designed the scheme had now gone. It was the trio of Mills, Wightman and Hughes who would be left holding the parcel when the music stopped the following year.

But there had been another change. DETI's top official, Permanent Secretary David Sterling, had also moved in June 2014 to be replaced by Dr Andrew McCormick, a cerebral Oxford-educated geologist who had spent nine years as permanent secretary of the Department of Health, the Stormont department with the biggest budget and constant challenges. Sterling's deputy, David Thomson, left at the same time as him, with a brief gap before he was replaced by Chris Stewart. On his first day, the experienced McCormick received a detailed briefing about his new department. It contained 53 issues, 17 of which were energy issues. RHI was in final place on the energy list. It would be more than a year later before RHI was brought to him for a substantive discussion.

In the space of six months, almost the entire spine of DETI, which was handling RHI, had been moved to be replaced by individuals who had no expertise in energy. In most cases there seems to be have been little – if any – contact between the old and new teams. The problem was exacerbated by the failure to recognise that RHI was a vast financial commitment over a 20-year period, and therefore it needed formal structures to ensure that all of those who would be running the scheme would know what had gone before. Both in Whitehall and Stormont, the civil service had been emphasising the use of formal project or programme management to ensure continuity and clear lines of accountability for the implementation of policies involving the expenditure of huge sums of public money. Prior to RHI's launch, McCutcheon had asked Hepper if it should be reviewed to see if project management was appropriate. Hepper said that she did not think it was necessary and that they were 'too late in any case', as the scheme was about to be launched. But, although allowing so many key staff to leave at once was almost certain to create problems, and the absence of project management exacerbated that risk, there was some effort made to warn the incoming team of potential problems.

Before he left, Hutchinson put together a 14-page handover note – initially for McCay and then for the permanent replacements, Hughes and Wightman. Alongside it, he printed out voluminous documentation about the scheme's background, leaving it for his successors in two large lever-arch files. The 14-page handover note contained basic information, such as who to speak to in Ofgem and where to find documents in the TRIM record management system. But it also gave his successors critical information about pressing issues. Hutchinson wrote:

> Tariffs – it is becoming apparent that the payments made to installations are higher than would have been expected ... many installations had a higher demand (time of operation) than had been assumed in the tariff calculations; this is especially true of certain sectors. As the demand is higher than what has been assumed, the tariffs can become over-generous. This issue would need to be considered as a matter of urgency. The email from Janette O'Hagan [in brackets he included the TRIM reference so they could find the email] is also relevant to this point, where applicants could over-use technologies for financial gain ... the solution would be to 'tier' tariffs ... certainly this should be considered for biomass under 100 kw as a matter of urgency. This has been discussed with Edmund Ward and he advised that Ofgem would be able to implement without too many changes to existing systems.

That paragraph demonstrated remarkable understanding of most of the central flaws in the scheme. Hutchinson was passing this to his successors, and his use in two places of 'urgency' indicates an attempt to impress upon them the gravity of the situation. It is clear that Hutchinson – particularly in light of some of the later conspiracy theories, which surrounded the RHI – was not someone who was deliberately attempting to keep a money-making scheme open when it should have been reined in. But why had it taken him so long to realise this and how could it be that on his departure the issue would be abandoned?

It appears that in Hutchinson's final weeks in post in spring 2014 the problems with the scheme were crystallising in his mind and it was becoming clear to him that too much public money was going to claimants. In his final week, Hutchinson received from Ofgem's Ward an eyebrow-raising case study of a timber manufacturer claiming RHI which he said would help DETI with 'any considerations on tiered tariffs'. He did not name the company but it subsequently emerged that it was Eglinton (Timber Products) Ltd in County Londonderry.

Hutchinson did not even have to do the calculations himself, but was told that the firm's RHI boiler 'operates for 153 hours a week, which is 7,956 hours of operation in a year'. The payments, Hutchinson was told, were £100,484 a year. The case study was all the more striking because the company had installed a single 990 kW boiler rather than ten 99 kW boilers, meaning that it was getting a subsidy level which was almost a quarter of what would have been on offer.

Hutchinson later told the inquiry that the figures, along with O'Hagan's email and a presentation by a boiler installer at a biomass event he had attended, had gradually concerned him. But there was no sense of panic in DETI or an urgent submission to Foster. On his final day at DETI, Hutchinson drew up an update for the Assembly committee, which scrutinised the department. The update, which was copied to Foster and Sterling, highlighted that the majority of biomass boilers on the scheme were getting the most lucrative subsidy available and 'it may be appropriate to review' the tariff.

Central to his belated appreciation of the problems with RHI was a renewed contact from O'Hagan. In Hutchinson's final week, as he was preparing the handover note, he received an email from O'Hagan, which was typically forthright about what was going on. The businesswoman told him:

Buildings are using more energy than before because it pays them to do so. The flat rate means that there is no incentive at all to be efficient so the heat in buildings in [*sic*] all year round with the windows open everywhere. When we had spoken, you did not believe that people would do this, but please believe me that it's happening with almost everyone that we approach. It's making it impossible for us to sell energy efficiency equipment to these buildings, even when that's exactly what should be happening as the first step and indeed what is happening in GB. The building owners there know that it's in their interests to be efficient, in Northern Ireland it is not – it's in their interests to be wasteful with what's strictly not a renewable energy source.

The blistering email went on: 'We've been told by a well established biomass company here to remove the saving detail on our product's literature because their clients were no longer interested in making any savings. I think that you'd agree that there is something inherently wrong with that approach to funding and it's going to put companies like ours out of business.' O'Hagan concluded her email in explicit terms: 'If you need proof of what's happening on the ground, I'd be happy to provide information. It's got to a stage now where it simply cannot be ignored any longer.'

Hutchinson did not reply to the email and instead passed it to McCay, who was succeeding him. However, it seems to have been the moment at which various pieces of evidence came together in his mind and he realised that there was a potentially serious problem. Having received no response, the following month O'Hagan emailed Hepper's secretary who replied to say that both Hepper and Hutchinson had left. McCay then replied to say that DETI intended to review RHI tariffs over the coming months and that 'the issues you have raised are on our radar'. A relieved O'Hagan replied that the news was 'most comforting'. Several months after leaving, Hutchinson returned to DETI to brief Hughes, his replacement, about the plans for expanding RHI. But during more than an hour the focus of the questions was on making RHI bigger – not reining it in. Hughes did not ask about the 'urgent' need to review the existing scheme and Hutchinson did not raise the issue.

****

In late 2013 an issue arose which brought an RHI problem right to Foster's ministerial desk and contained a huge clue as to the lucrative nature of the subsidy. Ofgem had initially advised that those with loans from the Carbon Trust – a green energy body, which funded environmental investments by businesses – could apply to the scheme. But a few months later Ofgem changed its mind, believing that such loans would be unlawful because the money being lent came from the government and therefore claimants would be getting a double incentive from public funds – a *prima facie* breach of EU state aid law. However, EU law allows a *de minimis* exemption for low-level state aid that does not exceed €200,000 over three years.

DETI was unhappy at what Ofgem was doing – not least because it was embarrassed at having passed on Ofgem's initial advice to claimants who now were complaining that they had been turned down for RHI. DETI decided that it would attempt to allow the individuals to enter the scheme under the *de minimis* rule. But in order to prove that the arrangement would not breach the €200,000 over three years, it needed to do some detailed calculations as to how much each individual would receive from RHI. To do so, DETI obtained the application forms for those who already had Carbon Trust loans for biomass boilers – some of which showed eye-wateringly high payments.

Each form asked the applicant to estimate the proportion of the year the boiler would be in use. On one claimant's form, 8,640 hours was typed – meaning that it would be running for all but 120 hours in the year. But this was scored out by hand and 6,000 hours was written in – equating to the boiler running for almost 70% of the hours in a year. Based on 6,000 hours, the individual had then calculated that the 99 kW boiler would secure an annual RHI payment of £36,234, amounting to £108,702 over a three-year period. A simple calculation would have shown that this would be almost three quarters of a million pounds over the 20 years of the scheme.

By July 2014, the scheme had been open for almost two years and there had been 216 applications. But within six months that figure had almost doubled, and by the end of December 409 applications had been received. Hughes, now the main person overseeing the scheme, said that as applications poured in and it is now known that firms were openly marketing the scheme as 'cash for ash', he and his colleagues believed that the growing interest in RHI showed 'this was starting to work the way it was meant to work'. It may have been that the consultation on cost controls had actually contributed to that increased demand. Although few claimants would have read the consultation, it would have been read by many in the green energy industry, and they were now aware that the 'too good to be true' tariffs could soon be coming to an end. Waving that consultation document under the nose of a dithering potential customer would have would have been a potent marketing tool.

Now less than two years into the scheme, DETI had a huge body of evidence about the problems with how RHI was running. A paper prepared for a heads of branch meeting within DETI in May 2014 referred to the 'potential need for [a] review of tariffs (particularly for biomass less than 99kw) ... a system of tiered tariffs might be appropriate'. It added that uptake of the scheme 'remains positive in comparison to GB figures', again contradicting the defence later offered by Foster and her officials for not acting sooner.

Yet that same month a submission from Mills to Foster referred to cost controls not as an urgent priority to prevent financial disaster but as 'technical changes to the scheme', which he now said were to be addressed after RHI had been expanded.

The previous year DETI had received correspondence from the representative body for the biomass industry in Northern Ireland in which it specifically warned about the problems with the tariffs, with people deliberately installing multiple 99 kW boilers to get the most lucrative subsidy.

Throughout this period DETI was continuing to heavily market the scheme and was cannily using EU funding to do so, meaning that the money for the scheme itself was coming from the Treasury while the marketing of it was being funded from Brussels. The advertising blitz included TV ads, promotions emblazoned on the side of buses, billboards, newspaper adverts and online advertising. But if the marketing was to suddenly get through to the public, there was going to be a problem. The way in which the legislation had been drafted made it almost impossible to turn down a valid application. At the point when the scandal erupted in December 2016, just 12 of the 1,958 applications had been rejected – a 99.4% success rate. That made it difficult to predict future applications. People simply installed a boiler, filled in the application form and waited for the money to arrive. There was no need to give DETI warning or seek pre-approval. If cost controls were not going to be introduced to allow for an emergency brake then the only other defence against a run on the scheme was vigilant monitoring of what was happening.

DETI was receiving weekly updates from Ofgem on projected usage, based on applicants' application forms. Had these been monitored to any extent they would have shown that by mid-2014 some 63% of all applications were for a 99 kW biomass boiler, which was expected to run for 45% of the year – double the average boiler size anticipated by CEPA and running for more than two and a half times longer than expected. Basic calculations would have shown that these people were in line to get annual payments of £22,900 when CEPA had expected that the average claimant would be getting £4,500.

In November 2014, Wightman emailed senior Ofgem manager Teri Clifton to warn her that there was renewed pressure to cut budgets at DETI and scrutiny was turning to the £211,000 a year paid to Ofgem to run the scheme. In a remarkable false economy, DETI was haggling with Ofgem over a relatively small sum while well over a hundred million pounds was being committed for expenditure. DETI was consistently exercised about comparatively small amounts coming from its budget but relatively relaxed about huge sums, which it thought were being funded directly by the Treasury.

Clifton's response shows that DETI was by this stage well aware of the fact that its scheme was taking off in a way which the GB scheme had not. Defending Ofgem's fees, she said that 'applications are coming in above the expected 3% [Northern Ireland's share of the UK population] as you know'. But DETI still seemed to be fixated on spending the money available from the Treasury for the first four years of the scheme, and there was still an underspend. From ministerial level down, the underspend was viewed as the key problem and therefore the focus was on expanding and marketing a scheme, which even a few hours of concerted thought would have revealed to be a disaster waiting to happen.

CHAPTER 8
BURNING FOOD

Though it would have startled the small number of MLAs in the largely empty Stormont Assembly chamber on 8 December 2014, what they were about to do would stand out as one of the starkest examples of their inability to perform their legislative roles.

It was the penultimate Assembly sitting before the Christmas recess – RHI had been going for just over two years – when they gathered in Parliament Buildings that Monday. Unusually for an Assembly which often struggled to fill its order paper with serious business, there were seven pieces of legislation on the order paper when the Speaker called MLAs to order at noon. But items such as the Food Hygiene Rating Bill and the Modern Slavery Bill weren't the sort of topics that filled the Assembly chamber or excited the passions of many MLAs. Nor was the legislation being brought by Arlene Foster. Stormont was good at having sectarian rows and the chamber would be filled for arguments over tribal disputes. But there were only a few MLAs who showed either aptitude or interest in the boring business of being a legislator – scrutinising tedious legislation line by dreary line. To many MLAs, the Domestic Renewable Heat Incentive Scheme Regulations (Northern Ireland) 2014 looked like another dry and uncontroversial piece of legislation, which extended the existing non-domestic scheme to private homes. There was no time limit on speaking about legislation and any one of the 108 MLAs could ask anything they liked about the scheme. But there was limited interest. Between Foster getting to her feet to open the debate and sitting down again some 40 minutes later at its close, no MLA had come close to raising the fundamental flaw with a scheme that had already committed vast sums of taxpayers' money some 20 years into the future – and, even as they spoke, was running out of control.

Reading from a speech in front of her on the ministerial lectern, Foster extolled her department's record, telling MLAs that 'we already have a very successful non-domestic RHI', with applications 'currently running at 4% of all UK applications, well ahead of the expected 3%'. That was a significant figure because the GB scheme was a year older than Stormont's. The information available to Foster showed that her scheme was not only well ahead of the GB scheme – at a comparable point in each scheme's life

– but Northern Ireland's scheme, which was supposed to be less generous, had now overtaken the level of applications to a larger and more established scheme.

As well as extending RHI to domestic homes, Foster also asked the Assembly to amend the rules of the existing non-domestic scheme to clarify that those in receipt of Carbon Trust loans could enter the scheme by paying back their loans. Responding to Foster's speech, the DUP arch-sceptic of green energy, Sammy Wilson, spoke from the back benches. Although he reminded the Assembly of his general opposition to green incentives, he welcomed what Foster was doing. In what is now an example of how political arguments can wither with age, he said:

> In closing, I will mention that many people ask what use the Assembly is and what is done. The minutiae of government, which can have a huge impact on businesses, individuals and employment, can often be easily overlooked when it comes to the kind of reporting that goes on. I would like to congratulate the minister. The issue was brought to her attention … she has responded quickly. That is the kind of fleet-footedness that we want to see in government here … that has illustrated, once again, the value of having this place.

Unnoticed by everyone that day was the fact that this was the moment where, according to the department's own consultation document, cost controls were meant to be introduced.

Wilson is not the only one who may now wish they had chosen their words more carefully. Patsy McGlone, the SDLP chairman of the cross-party committee charged with scrutinising DETI, assured the Assembly that since the launch of RHI in 2012 'the committee has closely scrutinised the development of the renewable heat incentive … and has requested and received regular updates from the department'.

When he appeared before the public inquiry, McGlone said that the department had not been candid with his committee. On that, he had a point. However, the impression he gave was that unless a department admitted to problems it was unlikely that a committee could do much to uncover them. That sense of docility was more widely reflected across the Stormont system where the legislature was generally tame in scrutinising the executive. The fact that in an Assembly of 108 MLAs the number of Assembly members who were not in governing parties could be counted on one hand added to the blurred lines between the role of government ministers and legislators.

MLAs often did not seem to realise the powers at their disposal. Assembly committees had sweeping statutory authority to compel witnesses and documents. At Westminster, near-identical powers had been used to force the appearance of media tycoon Rupert Murdoch over the phone-hacking scandal at the *News of the World* in 2011 – a dramatic example of how even a powerful mogul was accountable to the representatives of the public. But in almost a decade of devolution since 2007, Stormont committees never once used those powers – despite MLAs at points beating their chests and threatening to do so when facing uncooperative individuals or institutions.

McGlone was one of Stormont's more independently minded and capable MLAs. Rigorous scrutiny by his committee – facilitated by a backbench DUP rebellion against the party leadership – helped to prevent a decision by Foster's successor, Jonathan Bell, being slipped through at huge cost to energy users. Gareth Robinson, son of the then First Minister Peter Robinson, was working for two major renewables companies, which seemed set to gain from that decision. At the time, the First Minister's son declined to say if he was lobbying the DUP-run department to pursue a policy favourable to his clients. The former DUP councillor's lobbying activities were attracting increasing scrutiny in that period. In response to questions from the author at the time, Robinson had threatened to take legal action due to 'your unhealthy fixation with me', and he could count on some senior DUP figures to preferentially facilitate his business activities.

After the brief Assembly debate on 8 December, MLAs once more unanimously nodded through Foster's legislation with not even a solitary voice of opposition. RHI was now being expanded at the very point where it was about to run over budget and there wasn't any political debate about the issue.

****

Politicians weren't the only ones ignoring the growing problem. Invest NI was the biggest public body for which Foster's department was responsible.

The inward investment agency had an annual budget of about £100 million, much of which was handed out in grants to either indigenous Northern Ireland firms or used to entice foreign companies to set up in the province. Although the quango was an 'arms' length body' and Foster was not responsible for its day-to-day management, she was the minister who was democratically accountable for what went on within its Belfast city centre headquarters.

In autumn 2014 – just a couple of months before Foster expanded the scheme – Invest NI employee Jim Clarke became aware of the central problem with RHI. Clarke, an experienced official who was nearing the end of his career, had learned of the scheme through an Invest NI programme, which funded energy efficiency advice for companies. He was effectively a middleman between each company and the expert consultant who would analyse and make energy efficiency suggestions.

But a pattern began to emerge when the consultants' figures showed that RHI incentivised firms to install multiple small boilers, with no cap on their earnings. With a brief to give each business candid advice, they honestly set out the reality of the scheme – it was burn to earn – and submitted their reports to Invest NI.

Around October 2014 Clarke said that he was also 'aware through conversations, anecdote and rumour that some unnamed RHI accredited businesses had adopted inefficient practices to maximise RHI tariff returns'. When asked at the inquiry why he did not alert DETI, he said that he was new to the job and had significant responsibilities. But he later added: 'To be honest about it now on reflection, that isn't an excuse; I should have been aware of that and I should have flagged it up with the relevant people in DETI.' When asked if officials talked about the RHI issues among themselves, he said: 'Yes ... we were aware of issues ... we were all aware ... to be frank, everybody in our team was aware of these issues.' He said that he discussed it with his manager, Peter Larmour, but 'his opinion was it was DETI policy; so why would we question DETI policy?' In written evidence to the inquiry, Larmour denied that he was ever aware of the problems with RHI. But when that was put to Clarke he said: 'I was aware, and I told him, and he knew.'

Clarke was one of a handful of witnesses to the inquiry who stood out because although he clearly had not done enough to raise the alarm, he later faced up to what he had done, rather than seeking to pass the blame to others or deny the obvious. For that he was commended by inquiry chairman Sir Patrick Coghlin, who said to him: 'Can I just say that it is enormously refreshing to have someone like you approach the questions which we ask – which I recognise may be difficult – with an impressive degree of honesty.'

One of those who prepared the reports, which went to people like Clarke, was Alastair Nicol, an experienced energy expert. Within two months of RHI launching, he had seen the potential for major problems. He attempted to alert Ofgem that it was 'rumoured in the marketplace' that by altering the density of the liquid in heating systems, scheme applicants could achieve higher meter readings and therefore increase the payments they received.

In January 2015, just over two years into the scheme, Nicol emailed Invest NI official John Batch about a report he had written about a hotel that wanted to install four smaller RHI boilers rather than one or two larger units, 'so as to generate the maximum' RHI income'. Nicol felt that in engineering terms the idea was 'ludicrous' – but that it was what RHI was pushing people towards. Nicol said that he expected to get 'real stick' from the hotel owner because his report advised that the hotel should install a 'technically appropriate solution rather than an RHI-driven solution'. Showing extraordinary awareness within Invest NI of how RHI was operating, Batch replied: 'As you know sometimes the hotels just see the cash cow called pellets!!'

Nicol later told the public inquiry that he discussed the issue with the hotel owner and found him 'absolutely adamant [that he] wanted to go after this RHI money' even though it meant that a large part of the car park would have to be lost to accommodate so many boilers.

That was not the first time the issue had been raised explicitly with Invest NI. In a 2014 report on a commercial wood-drying business, Nicol told it that what was being proposed would give 'absolutely no incentive to dry the wood efficiently'. In another report, he said: 'Unfortunately the RHI payments are so large in Northern Ireland that it pays to waste heat – in other words the RHI payment is larger than the fuel cost. Economically and environmentally this is a very undesirable situation.' During years of doing reports about biomass installations, Invest NI never queried anything Nicol said about RHI. However, he knew they were reading his reports because they would correct his grammatical errors.

****

Most of those involved in setting up RHI – including CEPA, Hepper and Foster – later argued that they believed they had a key defence against the tariffs being set at the wrong level in that the scheme was meant to be regularly reviewed. Such reviews were expected to entail detailed analysis of how the scheme was operating and in particular would focus on how much was being paid to each claimant. That in itself was a remarkably relaxed approach for someone like Hepper to take and – if Hepper's account of having passed on to the minister Ofgem's warnings about tiering is accurate – for Foster to explicitly approve.

Hepper, who had been warned that the scheme was flawed from the outset, would have known that even if a review, after a year or two, realised that the scheme was wildly over-generous and the review rectified that, it would make no difference to those already claiming. Each claimant who got in while RHI was flawed was guaranteed to not only keep their current levels of subsidy for 20 years, but to see those payments rise with inflation each year. However, even that limited safeguard was soon forsaken. Although the reviews were mentioned in the internal departmental documentation when the scheme was set up, and also referred to publicly by Foster at that time, there was no timetabled date when the first review was set to begin. That meant that the reviews – if indeed they would ever have happened, given the dysfunctionality of the department – became much less likely once the wholesale changeover of the key RHI staff was allowed to take place over the first half of 2014.

The failure to review the scheme meant that civil servants were in breach not only of the conditional authorisation, which RHI had been given by the Department of Finance, but also in breach of the assurance they had given to their minister. For all that Foster would later unfairly blame her civil servants for, some of what had transpired, this was one of the clear areas in which she had reason for righteous anger. Her officials had on multiple occasions given her – and others – written assurances that reviews would take place and explained that this was not some administrative nuisance, but a crucial mechanism to protect public money. The minister had a right to expect that such a review was going to be done. But John Mills, who took over from Hepper, questioned the later assumption that a review would have led to the perverse incentive being ended. Mills – whose evidence to the inquiry has to be seen in the context of him defending the failure of his team to instigate such a review – questioned the view that it would have been transformative. That belief, he said, 'ignores the "political saleability" of such action'. He said in 2014 the scheme 'appeared to be experiencing low uptake, money was being returned to Treasury and the tariff levels were lower than the GB scheme' – as the previous chapters have demonstrated, at least two of those assertions are incorrect. He said that in 2014 the priority was to expand and advertise RHI. He added: 'In this context, it may be wondered how likely that the following message would have been embraced: "This scheme is under-performing and we're returning money to Treasury so what we really need to do is introduce urgent legislation for cost control measures to dampen down demand."'

Mills's argument suggests that Stormont's political climate was such that even if there was a perverse incentive it was unlikely that there would be much urgency about ending it. Others who worked with Mills are sceptical about that claim, seeing it as an attempt to shift the blame for what was a basic bureaucratic failure.

However, there is an intriguing caveat to the idea that the review was 'missed' and that this was an accident by a chaotic department. In February 2013, just three months after RHI launched, the Assembly debated sustainable energy. During a fairly low-key debate, the DUP MLA Gordon Dunne made an intriguing comment about green energy schemes. Dunne was a member of the Assembly committee that scrutinised DETI, and for that reason Foster and Andrew Crawford were in regular contact with him and the three other DUP MLAs on the committee. During his speech, Dunne, a backbench MLA who had only been in the Assembly for two years at that point, said renewable energy was 'by far one of Northern Ireland's biggest economic opportunities'. He cautioned that 'if we are to secure major investment … the Executive must address a number of issues'. He said that DETI had to ensure 'that the incentives offered remain at a level that will continue to make renewable energy schemes financially viable and attractive for would-be investors'. He then explicitly opposed the idea of regular reviews of such lucrative subsidies: 'Long-term stability around policies and avoiding regular reviews of the level of incentives offered will strengthen investor confidence and encourage investments in the types of scheme required to reach the 2020 targets, such as small-scale single wind turbines.' Was this view of a junior DUP MLA entirely his own, or did it reflect the views of others within the party? When approached about the issue for this book, Dunne did not respond.

Dunne's was not the only intriguing DUP move during the early years of RHI. Foster's spad was involved in planting a public question to his own minister about whether RHI was likely to become less lucrative.

Late on the night of 19 September 2014, Andrew Crawford emailed DUP MLA William Irwin. His terse email – perhaps suggesting that they had discussed the issue by phone – had the subject 'Written question'. The email said: 'Question for deti [*sic*] … Does DETI have any plans to reduce the level of Renewable Heat Incentive (RHI) for new commercial biomass boilers?' Crawford's email to the MLA came a day after the spad had sought assurance from Mills about the level of tariffs and Mills had assured him that biomass tariffs had not been cut, but had in fact risen with inflation. Three days after Crawford's request, Irwin tabled the written Assembly question – and requested a priority response. The answer, prepared by officials and issued by Foster, came back to say that 'there are no proposals in the [then recent] consultation to reduce incentives.' When the scandal emerged publicly, the DUP eventually clarified that Irwin's son-in-law was an RHI claimant. Irwin said that he had never lobbied on his behalf.

That was not the last time Irwin was involved in RHI. In February 2015 – just as the scheme was running out of control – Irwin's assistant emailed Crawford. The email by Lavelle McIlwrath, a former DUP councillor, was sent from Irwin's email address. McIlrath sought confirmation on behalf of an unnamed constituent that DETI 'has no immediate plans to change the Biomass Boiler scheme for agriculture users? (heating poultry houses etc)'. Crawford did not reply by email, so his response was not recorded. However, he phoned McIlrath because in a second email a week later the DUP man referred to their phone conversation and then alluded to what they had discussed by adding: 'Saw another piece scaremongering about the biomass scheme in the paper last week.' As so often in his evidence to the inquiry, Crawford said that he could not remember what had transpired.

The planted Assembly question was one of several curious examples of how hands-on Crawford was at various points in RHI, sometimes over seemingly small details. Why had he been keen to get the minister to publicly clarify that RHI rates would not be cut, and did Foster know the question she was answering was planted? We have an answer to at least the first of those questions and it is potentially significant, given what was to follow. Crawford told the inquiry in writing that he wanted Irwin to ask the question because he knew the answer would reveal that RHI cost controls were being delayed, and he wanted that publicised – especially to farmers. But when he appeared before the inquiry, Crawford said that he had limited recollection of what had gone on and sought to slightly row back on his initial written explanation. He instead said he wanted to publicise that tariffs would not be cut. The spad said that he felt it was simpler for the information to emerge through a written question rather than by Foster issuing a press release to explain that they had abandoned the original plan to introduce cost controls. But even that answer does not fully explain his actions. If he simply wanted to inform the public that cost controls on RHI as a whole – a scheme that encompassed all sorts of technologies, from air source heat pumps to solar panels – were being delayed, why did the question he drafted single out commercial biomass boilers? Did Foster's spad at this point know more than he was letting on about a particular issue with biomass boilers – the very boilers that, on his watch, were running on a 'burn to earn' basis?

Crawford's interest in the level of the RHI subsidy for biomass later contributed to a belief from Andrew McCormick that the spad might have been acting in ways which were not clear to him at the time, and which on reflection caused him concern. McCormick told the inquiry that when looking back on events it appeared to him that 'well before the problems with the scheme began to emerge (in March 2015), Crawford appeared to be interested specifically in the tariff. While the origin of the flaw with the tariff still appears to have been a genuine mistake, it is possible that, like many in the private sector, he became aware of the issue relatively quickly.' He said that Crawford's 'early interest' in the level of subsidy was evident on a number of occasions, including his planted question to Foster.

Just over a month after his planted question was answered, Crawford sent a fascinating email to the huge poultry processor Moy Park, Northern Ireland's biggest private sector employer and a major RHI beneficiary.

Crawford, who had multiple links to the huge company, told it in November 2014 that the 'changes (likely to apply from summer 2015) are not likely to have a negative impact on Moy Park growers'. McCormick later told the inquiry that he found that noteworthy because he did not believe there was any hint of retrospective changes to the scheme, which would have meant Moy Park required such reassurance. When asked at the inquiry if there was any reason why people should be suspicious of what he was doing in that period, and whether he may have known by late 2014 that the scheme was far too generous, Crawford said: 'At this stage, I remain [*sic*] that I wasn't clear about the tariff rate – the attractiveness, as you describe it, of the tariff. I can't say more than that.'

****

By spring 2015, the riches available under RHI were widely known across Northern Ireland – especially in rural areas. Foster's evidence to the inquiry was that although she represented one of Northern Ireland's most rural constituencies, Fermanagh and South Tyrone, and although she had been the minister who was responsible for the scheme, she never became aware of just how financially rewarding RHI was. Whatever Foster knew, it is clear that many farmers were by now well acquainted with the nature of what something being openly marketed as 'cash for ash' entailed. But among vast evidence about what was known about the burn-to-earn nature of RHI, there is one situation which stands out.

In an extreme example of the perverse incentive at the heart of the scheme, a meeting of the Ulster Farmers' Union (UFU) Rural Enterprise Committee on 26 March 2015 recorded: 'Ton of oats example – £130/ton at the market [value] and £300 to burn it. This obscures the market return when compared with conventional end use. The benefit to the poultry industry is apparent.' When the document emerged at the inquiry, barrister Donal Lunny said: 'That seems to be suggesting that you can sell a ton of oats to the market for use as food or feed at £130 a ton, but if you burn it you'll earn £300, presumably under the RHI, and that is a potential illustration of the perverse incentive where the tariff income greatly exceeds the cost of the fuel. Is that what was being discussed at that point?' Christopher Osborne, the UFU's senior policy adviser, replied: 'Yes it was.' He went on to say that 'obviously I don't think oats can be used to basically fuel a boiler as such'. However, Lunny said that while oats would be 'an unusual biomass fuel, it probably qualifies as biomass under the regulations from 2012'. Not only was Lunny right, but there is reason to believe that the practice set out in those minutes may have been more than hypothetical.

Biomass was not defined in the regulations, meaning that oats were a legal fuel and corn was far cheaper at that point than wood pellets. There is less energy in oats, but not much less – about 4,800 kWh per ton in wood to about 4,000 kWh in oats. Biomass boilers, which were specifically designed to burn grain, were available on the market. For a hard-pressed farmer whose crop was fetching poor prices due to the global market, it was clear why it would be attractive to put it through an RHI boiler and substantially increase its value.

The issue was explicitly discussed on an online agricultural forum in the month before the UFU meeting. Under the title 'Wheat in a wood pellet boiler', a farmer from Merseyside wrote on *The Farming Forum*: 'Has any one try this with wheat been half what wood pellets are at the moment would it work or would 14% wheat be to damp or are there any other problems from trying this [sic]'. Another farmer replied to say: 'Very intrigued by this, you could always dry below 14% and it'd still be cheaper than pellets'. A Warwickshire farmer said: 'I was looking at mixing oats 50/50 with the wood pellets'. Another user said that there were boilers that specifically burned grains but that burning wheat in a standard boiler was unlikely to work because of heavy deposits, which would build up in the equipment. However, he added: 'Oats works the best I am lead to belive [sic]'.

Although there is no evidence that this practice was going on within Northern Ireland on a large scale – and perhaps was not happening at all – the fact that it would be profitable was a measure of how wildly overgenerous RHI was. A scheme that had been set up with the intention of improving the environment was now so lavish and unregulated that it had become a perverse incentive to burn food.

****

On 26 February 2015, Seamus Hughes, an experienced civil servant with weathered features who would now be central to the unfolding disarray, despatched a series of proposals to Ofgem. One A4 sheet he sent to London was startling. DETI was proposing to double the size of boilers which could claim the most lucrative biomass tariff – but consciously not introduce tiering. It was the worst of both worlds. DETI was going to take the more generous part of the GB scheme – the fact that boilers up to 199 kW could avail of its top tariff – but not copy across the crude cost control that came with it. At best, this pointed to ineptitude within DETI; at worst, this was a conscious attempt to make an already lucrative scheme – and one Stormont thought was being paid for by 'free money' – far more generous.

The document also made clear that DETI was not only aware of tiering in the GB scheme but was deliberately and explicitly choosing not to incorporate it into its own scheme – despite the mountain of evidence it had been given that its scheme was already overly generous. DETI set out a limp logic for what it was planning. The department said that the original policy intent had been for larger installations to receive lower tariffs. But that was not happening, it said, and multiple smaller boilers were being installed to get the most lucrative rate. However, what was being proposed would have directly contradicted what the department claimed was its policy – smaller subsidies for larger installations. The proposal was the opposite of that – extending the highest subsidy rate to much bigger boilers. Hughes, whose brow was often wrinkled in apparent bafflement as he tried to explain to the inquiry what had been going on in this period, was unable to provide any coherent explanation for what he had put to Ofgem. Asked to explain another part of the proposal, Hughes gave the sort of vague answer which peppered his evidence: 'Yes. No, I honestly can't recall what would've been behind that.'

The entire episode undermines DETI's claim that its staff were over-worked or overly focussed on launching the domestic RHI scheme to prioritise cost controls, which then innocently kept getting pushed back. Here was a proposal that had never been in the 2013 public consultation on phase two of the scheme, yet energy division staff had spent time drawing it up and putting it to Ofgem – which had repeatedly recommended existing cost control measures as the priority. Yet at the same time the cost control proposal on which DETI had consulted in 2013 was simply abandoned.

DETI was also working on opening the scheme up to air source heat pumps, an extremely generous 'district heating' tariff for installations serving multiple properties, deep geothermal and large biomass over 1MW – a category CEPA originally said was economically viable in Northern Ireland without any subsidy. From the outset, phase two of RHI had meant to correct the failure to introduce cost controls at the outset. Now phase two was being presented by Hughes as nothing more than further expansion of the scheme – with a conscious decision to yet again remove cost controls from the equation.

Just a fortnight later, having waited and waited for something to be done about the perverse incentive she could see all around her, Janette O'Hagan again contacted DETI. Emailing Davina McCay, who by then was temporarily looking after RHI, she warned that 'potential clients which have moved to biomass are no longer interested in making any efficiencies' and referred to an installer who had told her of an installation, which would see payback in two years 'if he kept the heat on 24/7' versus a three-year payback 'if he kept the heat on the hours that it was needed (8 hours a day five days a week). In anyone's eyes this is completely wrong and motivates further waste'. McCay replied to say that she no longer dealt with RHI but had copied the email to Hughes, who was now responsible. Hughes replied to tell O'Hagan that RHI was being expanded. But, in what was a dismaying message for O'Hagan to read, he told her that tiering now was not being proposed in the immediate future.

O'Hagan was 'raging' when she read his email. Having spent almost two years repeatedly explaining to the various people running RHI how it was fundamentally broken, she seemed to have gotten nowhere. The entrepreneur forthrightly wrote back that night to say:

> I believe that the tiered funding in NI needs to ensure that people who avail of non-domestic RHI don't just waste fuel for the sake of earning money on the RHI repayments. I had spoken to Fiona Hepper and her team about this two years ago. She'd advised me then that they didn't think that businesses would abuse the system, but we see it time and time again when out on client sites. To assume that this isn't happening is not acceptable in my view. This doesn't happen in GB as the higher rate RHI repayment only covers a certain amount (~around 75% of a 40 hr week) of their usage and the remainder of usage is at a lower rate – thus encouraging efficiencies.

The email became plaintive:

> I've tried to speak to each person who has subsequently taken on the RHI role and Davina had acknowledged that when she was looking after Renewable Heat she intended to review elements of the non-domestic RHI, including tariffs. She had said that the issues that I was raising were on the RHI team's radar and would be dealt with. It's really disappointing to hear that that's not the case any more, other than possibly in the future for budgetary controls. The rest of us, who are actually trying to save energy, money and the environment have an uphill struggle against such legislation. I understand that it is a renewable resource, if replanted, but really should it be being wasted for profit?

It was a blistering description of the need for urgent action. If Hughes claimed to have been unaware before now, that defence was no longer sustainable. Here was a plainspoken explanation of the problem. More than that, her emails contained beneath them the blunt messages she had sent the previous year, in which she had set out widespread abuse of RHI. But her pleas fell on deaf ears. Now Hughes did not bother to even reply. At this point, O'Hagan took the view that DETI simply was not interested in addressing the problems with RHI, even though it had been clearly and repeatedly made aware of them. It was not an unreasonable assumption to make. But just five hours after he had replied to O'Hagan's initial email, Hughes sent another email – to the Treasury in London. Outside the Department of Finance, contact between officials in any Stormont department and the Treasury was rare – and largely against the rules – but for someone at Hughes's relatively lowly grade it would have been exceedingly unusual.

It was clear from his email that Hughes was doing so after having read a message which ought to have caused him alarm. The deputy principal grade civil servant had found Treasury official Jon Parker's 2011 email in which he had warned DETI that RHI was not really being fully funded by the Treasury and set out how overspends would cost DETI. Now Hughes replied to Parker, asking for clarity around the funding. He noted that 'uptake has been good and is increasing'. Parker had by then left the Treasury and the email was returned undelivered, so Hughes then turned to DECC, the Whitehall department running the GB scheme. Officials there put him in touch with a new Treasury contact but he refused to deal with it, advising Hughes that all contact should be through Stormont's Department of Finance.

A week after O'Hagan's email, a note from DETI's heads of branch meeting indicated the first flicker of concern about the shrinking RHI budget. It informed those present that uptake had 'increased over the last few months' and that 'for budgetary control, consideration is now being given to including a tariff reduction in April 2017 for the biomass tariff'. But even the warning of increasing numbers did not jolt officials into considering how they would handle a sudden stampede. The proposal – and it was only being thought about, rather than decided, at this stage – was to cut the subsidy level in two years' time. Not only was there no panic, but new promotional activity was being approved, with posters being produced to encourage more applications.

Four days later, Hughes's boss, Stuart Wightman, said to a colleague that the level of uptake 'has increased significantly over the last few months and we're expecting uptake to remain high with over 200 new applications for biomass heating systems from the poultry industry (linked to Moy Park's expansion) expected over the coming 12 months'.

In fleeting evidence of fiscal prudence, Wightman observed: 'With RHI payments for accredited non-domestic heating installations committed for 20 years, it is important we manage our budget carefully.' He calculated that RHI expenditure had risen to about £800,000 a month and was going up by about £60,000 each month. Using those figures, he calculated that there would be an annual bill of £14.28 million – but he was concerned that his figures might be conservative, given the looming applications from the farmers who supplied Moy Park. By then both Wightman and Hughes had spoken to Moy Park manager David Mark – a figure who was promoting RHI to the farmers contracted to supply the company's abattoir with about five million chickens every week. Mark had informed Hughes that the company had 782 poultry sheds and at that point just 36% had converted to biomass. His expectation was that they would get 60% into the scheme by the end of the year as well as building 45 new poultry sheds in the same period, each of which would have a biomass boiler.

After speaking to Wightman at the end of February, Mark emailed senior Moy Park figures to alert them to the commercial significance of what he had been told. He said that he had been informed that no changes to RHI were envisaged until October of that year and that the most lucrative tariff would be available to larger boilers, which would be 'helpful' to Moy Park. He warned his colleagues that Wightman had said that the October legislation would allow for the subsidy to be cut and said: 'I think we have a firm basis for RHI investment going forward until at least October 2015 with a positive look forward after that.'

****

Given that it was Wightman, Hughes and Mills who were left running the scheme at the point where it ran out of control, assessing what they knew is crucial to judging their culpability for what happened. When the scandal began to erupt, Wightman initially claimed that he only recalled being given three pages of Peter Hutchinson's detailed 14-page handover note – the document that set out key areas of concern with the scheme and highlighted O'Hagan's emails. However, with the emergence of emails at the inquiry, he eventually accepted that he had been given the entire document when he arrived at DETI in summer 2014. He made the admission after the inquiry obtained an email, which showed that the document was emailed to him and he forwarded it to himself at that time – a year before the disastrous surge in applications.

But Wightman said that he did not recall reading beyond the first three pages. The civil servant came under pressure from the inquiry to explain why he had not handed over to it the entire document when it was in his possession. He insisted that he had not sought to hide the material, despite having obtained it in full in 2016 for a second time when, in preparing for a Stormont Public Accounts Committee inquiry into RHI, he had found a paper copy. He initially only gave the inquiry three pages, something he said that he did consciously because he believed that he had only read three pages in 2014 – an illogical explanation because the inquiry required individuals to hand over all material in their possession relevant to RHI. Whether or not they had read it was irrelevant. Regardless of the reasons for his initial non-disclosure of the full document, on Wightman's own evidence he never bothered to read the 14 pages – something that would have taken about 20 minutes – despite just having arrived in energy division with no energy expertise. Even without knowledge of the disaster that was to follow, that fact suggests a blasé approach to his role.

When Wightman's name first emerged publicly in early 2017, the author was contacted by someone who had observed his work in the Department for Regional Development (DRD) where he had been prior to joining DETI. Rodney McCune, who was special adviser to the DRD's Ulster Unionist minister, but by 2017 had left politics and was a lawyer in Singapore, said that in his experience of Wightman 'his self belief was not matched by his ability'. Wightman told the inquiry he was more focussed on the 'divisional plan' because it contained objectives that had his name against them: 'Coming into a new job, obviously you want to impress as well, you've got things that have got your name against it. You know, that was my number one priority.'

In Wightman's defence, he was not being given the resources necessary to adequately monitor or develop a complex and novel scheme involving relatively new technologies. His own time was split between RHI and energy efficiency, while Hughes – and especially Mills, his boss – also had other responsibilities. That meant that in Northern Ireland there wasn't a single full-time civil servant working on RHI. At the same time in Whitehall some 77 officials were working on the GB RHI. Some of that is explained by the scale of the larger scheme, but much of the work needed to be done regardless of its size.

Mills was unhappy at the lack of staff being given to him to run what he had been led to believe was a ministerial priority. He felt 'betrayed' because he had been given the expectation that he would get additional staff to run the domestic scheme but then had not been given them. He said that his inability to even get two or three extra junior staff for the domestic scheme left him assuming that any further staffing request would be turned down. Speaking sardonically in his evidence to the inquiry in 2018, Mills said: 'I mean, there are 30 people on RHI now and it's closed. So there was [in 2015, when it was open] 2% of me, a third of Stuart Wightman and half of Seamus on the non-domestic.'

In an interview with consultants PwC – who were called in by DETI in 2016 to investigate what had happened but whose work was superseded by the public inquiry – Wightman said that he believed the funding was coming from London. Answering candidly – in a process where he did not expect the report to ever be made public – he said: 'In spring 2015 if I had of known it was DEL [Stormont's budget] we would have probably been jumping over backwards to try to get it turned off quicker.' For his part, Hughes believed that there was effectively a bottomless pit of RHI money from London and that all DETI needed to do was to 'ask for it from Treasury to be able to get it'. However, in autumn 2014, six months before it began to dawn on Wightman and Hughes that the budget might not be limitless, Wightman had emailed a colleague and attached a copy of the 2011 Treasury email warning that the scheme had a finite budget and overspends would be penalised. That is one of several pieces of evidence that question how much care they were taking over the 20-year spending commitments beginning on their watch.

It is clear that by March at the latest Wightman was well aware of the problem. On 19 May 2015 Jeff Partridge, in DETI's finance division, emailed Wightman and Hughes to draw attention to the 2011 Treasury email and advised that energy division 'should take steps to curtail spending' to 'keep within the likely ceiling of £12.8m' until there was further clarification. Wightman responded with the alarming news that 'we're already committed to an annual spend of £17m (an overspend of £4.2m) even if we were to close both schemes today'. But that alarm was tempered by his belief that the budget was not really a budget but merely an indicative figure for expected expenditure. Wightman told his colleague that 'we should surely be making the case for more RHI AME money from HMT/DECC rather than curtailing the scheme'. But far from taking Partridge's obvious advice to rein in the scheme in any limited ways available to them, energy division continued to promote RHI over coming months. Setting aside the political pressure, which was to come to delay cost controls, it is impossible to see any rational explanation for the lack of basic measures to discourage further installations after this point.

With DETI's finance division alarmed that the message was not getting through to Wightman, the issue was escalated to Bernie Brankin, a veteran finance official. She sent him a curt one-sentence email the following day: 'Stuart, please stop entering into commitments immediately to ensure that monthly cumulative expenditure does not increase.' That message ought to have prompted panic because energy division knew that there was no way to stop making payments – by choosing not to implement cost controls, they were at the mercy of the market. Whatever number of people installed boilers, they had to subsidise them for the unlimited heat which they produced over the next two decades.

An hour later Wightman replied to his colleague to point out the reality – there was no means of doing what she was requesting. He told her that a decision to close RHI 'will have to be taken by the minister rather than you or I' and could only happen once there was absolute clarity about whether London or Stormont was paying the bill. He said that if it was clear that Stormont was paying the bill then it 'might' be necessary to close RHI. Then, in a section now farcical to read, Wightman cautioned that such a move would lead to problems so 'cannot be taken lightly'. He added: 'This will create a great deal of negative press and correspondence.' The negative press from keeping open a scheme that was haemorrhaging taxpayers' money did not seem to feature as a consideration in his thinking.

However, at some level Wightman became convinced of the need to rein in the scheme. Within two days, he was referring in emails to a decision to introduce tiering from October of that year – some five months away at that stage. In his interview with PwC, Wightman initially claimed not to have been aware in spring 2015 of the threat to DETI's budget. In fact, he claimed that this was not known until sometime between October and December of that year. But documentary evidence shows that he had been made aware of the issue by spring at the latest – and should have been aware of it from the previous year.

On Saturday, 23 May – less than two months into the financial year – Wightman emailed senior Ofgem manager Teri Clifton to say that 'due to the unprecedented increase in RHI applications over recent months it has become clear that we are currently overspent on our proposed budget this year'. He said that DETI was seeking clarity on its budget but that until that came 'DETI requests that Ofgem queues all new applications for a period pending budget confirmation'. Such a request demonstrated Wightman's lack of basic knowledge of the regulations which his own department had got the Assembly to pass to set up the scheme. A quick scan through the legislation would have shown that there was no emergency brake if the budget began to be threatened.

The email caused consternation within Ofgem, which was not only alarmed at being asked to operate outside the law but was worried that if there was now no budget it might not be paid. By looking at the regulations, Ofgem's lawyers immediately clarified that there was no power for it to fulfil DETI's request. Four days later, during a teleconference between DETI and Ofgem, it was made clear to Stormont that its instruction was legally impossible. Just after the meeting Hughes emailed Ofgem to formally advise it to 'disregard' what his boss, Wightman, had asked.

Despite his undeniable understanding at this point that the budget had been blown, cost controls would not implemented for another six and a half months. In late spring of 2015, as the department lurched deeper into crisis, things were chaotic in DETI with disagreement among officials as to the gravity of the situation and a belief among some of them that London was paying the bill – which they say made them act with less urgency. All the while, the biomass industry was picking up signals – and getting privately informed by some Stormont insiders – that the scheme was soon going to be less lucrative. Things were about to get much worse.

CHAPTER 9
OUT OF CONTROL

Just as officials began to finally realise that the scheme was running out of control, Arlene Foster left the scene. The timing of her departure at a point where RHI was starting to fall apart appears to have been entirely coincidental. The DUP Health Minister, Jim Wells, had resigned suddenly after a backlash over controversial comments which linked child abuse and homosexual relationships, prompting a mini-reshuffle of the DUP's ministerial team. The Finance Minister, Simon Hamilton, was on 11 May moved to replace Wells and Foster was promoted to replace Hamilton as Finance Minister – the most powerful ministerial post after the First and deputy First Ministers. It was both a reward for her loyalty to Peter Robinson, the DUP leader, over many difficult years, and a recognition of what was then believed to have been a successful period as DETI minister. It was also a move that placed Foster in prime position to succeed Robinson when he retired as DUP leader just six months later.

Foster was replaced at DETI by Jonathan Bell, who until then had been junior minister to Robinson. Bell had demonstrated unique loyalty to the DUP leader, and his appointment ensured that no one less enthusiastic in their support for a leader who was regularly under internal pressure entered the DUP's ministerial team. Foster was leaving at a point where RHI was about to envelop not only the department, but the entire Executive. From her point of view, the timing of her departure was fortuitous. As someone whose tenure in the department was of unprecedented length, and who had been responsible for the scheme from its inception, she left just weeks before the first ministerial submission setting out its impending implosion.

And when Foster began to hear about the problems with RHI, she may have had reason to believe that although she had set up the scheme it might be difficult to detect her fingerprints at key stages in the scheme's development. Under her tenure, record-keeping at DETI had been abysmal. On the one hand, the inability to produce documentation which conclusively proves the extent of the minister's involvement in key decisions makes it harder to blame her for what went wrong. But, as with the design of the scheme, Foster is now the victim of those shoddy practices within the department during her time at its helm. If she did act properly, the absence of key written records now leaves her in the position of only being able to ask the public to accept her word for swathes of what went on during her seven years in DETI.

It is hard to believe that, in such a lengthy tenure, Foster was entirely ignorant of her officials routinely not minuting meetings in which she was a key participant. Andrew Crawford, who was at Foster's side for her seven years at DETI, told the inquiry that during his entire time at the heart of Stormont he never once saw minutes of a meeting involving his minister. If that is true, it is astonishing. Ministers frequently have to chase officials about a decision that has not been implemented, or they find themselves in dispute about what was agreed in meetings. The spad or the private secretary would be the first individual to dig through paperwork to establish the recorded factual position. It is difficult to accept that not once in his lengthy Stormont career did Crawford have to go searching for such a record. He made his claim in the context of insisting that the DUP had never asked for inconvenient facts not to be written down in order to avoid them becoming public under the Freedom of Information Act (FoI) – a law which the DUP, a party which valued secrecy, hated.

Crawford was asked if Foster's private secretary should have been saying to him, or to the minister, that other officials were failing to send minutes of meetings with the minister, despite being obligated to do so by civil service rules. In a typically disjointed response, Crawford said:

> It would be wrong for me to say that in this situation because I never seen [*sic*] any minutes from any meeting in any department so in this particular case, should [the private secretary] have came [*sic*] to me … and said 'Andrew, I need a minute of that meeting', bearing in mind that I didn't do it before, it would be wrong for me to have said I should have done it in this case.

Crawford and Foster both defended the department's appalling record keeping by saying that officials always appeared to be scribbling down notes during meetings. It had to be pointed out to them that a series of jotted thoughts in the notebooks of multiple civil servants is not an agreed minute of a meeting, something which members of churches, golf clubs or residents' associations would immediately comprehend. At a basic level, Foster, her private secretary or her spad needed to see the minutes of meetings in which she was present to ensure that they were accurate. Otherwise, if a set of minutes did exist – which might be released under FoI or emerge in court proceedings – the minister was being left vulnerable by a spad who was in this area failing to be her eyes and ears within the department.

The power of the holder of government minutes is so obviously significant that it has been a subject satirised in political comedy, most memorably in *Yes, Prime Minister*. Famously, when a dispute arose in cabinet about something raised at the preceding cabinet meeting, the wily Cabinet Secretary, Sir Humphrey Appleby, drew to the cabinet's attention that the minutes of the last meeting did not record such a discussion. After protests from the minister, who knew that he had raised the issue, Sir Humphrey embarked upon a breathless explanation of the importance of minutes in government:

> It is characteristic of all committee discussions and decisions that every member has a vivid recollection of them and that every member's recollection of them differs violently from every other member's recollection. Consequently, we accept the convention that the official decisions are those and only those which have been officially recorded in the minutes by the officials … so in this particular case, if the decision had been officially reached it would have been officially recorded in the minutes by the officials, and it isn't, so it wasn't.

As would later become apparent, Crawford was not some wide-eyed innocent who lacked Sir Humphrey's guile, and he would surely have appreciated the elemental importance of what was recorded. Indeed, it is instructive in this regard to observe that rather than using his government email address Crawford chose to use his own personal Hotmail email account for government business, meaning that the contents could not be searched by departmental officials and would not emerge under FoI unless Crawford decided to hand over emails.

When during his evidence to the inquiry Crawford was pressed about the absence of minutes, he sought to blame civil servants, saying: 'I cannot answer how, if neither [official] was doing their responsibility or duty, I don't know where that happened or where that originated or where that started.' But it is not just an absence of minutes which hampers a full understanding of what Foster and Crawford were getting up to in this period. The DUP pair developed a second system, which for them had the happy benefit of ensuring that the public would never get to see the most sensitive messages passed between them.

Foster and her spad developed a system of making political comments on Post-it notes, which were immediately destroyed – something which had begun in their days together at the Department of the Environment. In what RHI Inquiry barrister Joseph Aiken described as 'politics by Post-it', the inquiry uncovered a practice that means we now cannot know if some messages about the RHI scheme were immediately destroyed. The secretive system also meant that the messages were never able to be evaluated for release under FoI – despite the law stating that significant government decisions, even if they are written on a napkin or a paper plate, ought to be retained.

It was a beautiful system for a party which hated scrutiny. Crawford acknowledged that these notes 'wouldn't have been formally recorded in the system' and 'there would be no record of it'. But, after news reports about the Post-it note communication following its emergence at the inquiry, Foster sought to play down the scale of the practice. Foster said usually what was written on notes was 'things like "speak to me about this" … it may have been something that he wanted to raise with me about the submission orally, rather than write it down, that perhaps wouldn't have been appropriate to put on a submission'. When asked why that would be, she said: 'I don't think it's appropriate to put on a submission that's going back into the civil service "speak to me".' Foster then suggested that there was not much room to write comments on ministerial submissions. Describing the notes system as 'a very innocuous thing to do', she added: 'There was nothing on any Post-it notes, from my memory, that would have caused any concern.'

The advantage of that system is that Foster and Crawford are now the sole arbiters of what 'would have caused any concern'. Inquiry chairman Sir Patrick Coghlin described it as 'a sophistication of the lack of a record system because although you have a record here, you have another tier that is a removable record – it's a removable record if it is about politics.' There did, however, come a point when Foster suddenly took a keen interest in what had been recorded about RHI. After the scandal began to emerge, Foster contacted her former private secretary, Glynis Aiken, in person and asked her to check whether she had any recollection of discussions about cost controls. Aiken said that she advised Foster that in her personal notebooks she did not find 'anything that was considered important' – and then dumped the notebooks.

****

In late May, just a fortnight after Bell's arrival at the department, its most senior civil servant, Andrew McCormick, met DECC. On 28 May, just after meeting the Whitehall officials, he emailed the new minister's spad, Timothy Cairns, Mills and others, to inform them of what had transpired. DECC, he said, felt that Stormont should not be limited by the Barnett Formula – the mechanism whereby Northern Ireland gets a population-based share of public spending in GB. Rather, he said, DECC's view was that 'the key was to give HMT early warning of the increased demand'. This message, which implied that the funding might be open-ended after all, confused what ought otherwise to have been a clear picture by this stage.

There was however a huge caveat, which McCormick did not mention. DECC was not in a position to decide on what funding Stormont would get. That job was for the Treasury alone and it was precisely this sort of confusion which meant that Stormont officials were meant to channel all their funding queries through the Department of Finance. However, in McCormick's defence, the Department of Finance had broken its own protocols by telling DETI that it should engage directly with DECC to ascertain the funding position. Rules were now being jettisoned with gay abandon. Wightman – who by this stage had on several occasions seen the 2011 Treasury email making clear that the funding was not standard AME – does not seem to have informed McCormick of this critical detail.

Although it was now clear to DETI's top brass that RHI was far beyond its budget and there was at best uncertainty about how that spending would be paid for, there is little evidence of any panic. Certainly within Energy Division the issue was viewed as a budgetary problem – they needed to persuade London to give the scheme more money – rather than a more fundamental deficiency in the entire scheme. Shane Murphy, DETI's head of analytical services, remembered that in this period Energy Division were defensive and did not accept that the problem was a 'financial crisis' but rather a 'function of policy success'. Chris Stewart, the second in command in DETI's hierarchy of mandarins, said that Energy Division 'thought well it's not a great problem – you know it's AME, we'll just ask for more money, we'll get more money and that'll be that. They weren't hugely worried at that stage. They ought to have been'. But there were at least two senior DETI figures who were uneasy about that approach.

The day after travelling to London, McCormick was back in Belfast for the fortnightly stocktake meeting of DETI senior management. Unusually, it was to be an explosive affair. Trevor Cooper, DETI's forthright and experienced director of finance, clashed bitterly with Mills, the similarly frank energy director. The meeting – attended by about a dozen senior officials – descended into a 'shouting match' between the two men, McCormick later recalled. Mills, a veteran official with grey hair and a sonorous English voice, asserted that Finance Division was not doing enough to secure additional budget. Cooper retorted that the scheme was already over budget and that there were more significant issues with it than simply getting more money. He was alarmed that his colleagues' projected figures were moving around wildly in a short space of time, something that suggested they had limited understanding of how it was operating. McCormick, a diplomatic and consensual figure, closed down the discussion to allow for a specific meeting on RHI. But before that meeting could take place, it became clear that the department was now facing a second huge problem. Not only was expenditure beyond budget, but officials had missed the need to seek formal re-approval for RHI from the Department of Finance in April – a condition that department had set when it approved the scheme at the outset. It now meant that as claimants continued to sign up to RHI all of the new expenditure was irregular – the gravest situation within public sector accounting because it meant that there was no democratic authorisation for the spending of public money.

The situation was not just an administrative error. Had DETI gone back to the Department of Finance in late 2014 to begin the process of seeking re-approval, it would have entailed a review of RHI which probably would have led to at least some of the fundamental issues in RHI being spotted. However, given the dysfunctionality and incompetence, it is impossible to say with certainty that this would have prevented the looming disaster. When multiple explicit warnings had already been missed or ignored, it is possible that such a review would also have led to the scheme continuing on its way with little change. At about 4.30pm on 3 June, five days after the 'shouting match', five senior DETI officials gathered in Netherleigh House.

Cooper informed those present that the previous day he had reviewed the scheme paperwork and realised its approval had expired two months earlier and all increased spending was now irregular. The hole was deepening.

★★★★★★★★★★★

Amidst this bureaucratic bedlam sits a remarkable allegation: civil servants in one Stormont department consciously set out to mislead their colleagues in another department. Confronted at the 3 June meeting by news of the deepening RHI difficulties, senior figures were informed of one means of mitigation. Cooper, a heavy-set official with an unembellished manner, told the inquiry that the tone of the meeting was that 'we're not in a great place here, you know – we need to put our best foot forward'. He said Wightman suggested that although the Department of Finance approval made clear that there had to be a thorough review of the scheme – and although no such review had been conducted – they could pass off another lesser piece of work as having been the review.

During a captivating afternoon of evidence to the public inquiry, Cooper spoke frankly about what he said was a plan from which not one of DETI's senior figures present at the meeting – including McCormick – demurred. The finance director's claim had particular weight because he was in the room and was one of those who on his own evidence did not raise their voices against the attempt to mislead fellow civil servants.

Inquiry barrister Joseph Aiken put it to Cooper that a briefing note prepared after the meeting suggested he tell the Department of Finance that a review of RHI had been conducted in 2013 'when everyone knows that's just not what happened'. The civil servant replied: 'Correct.' Cooper recalled: 'This fig leaf was raised at the 3rd of June meeting. We hadn't done a review. So, you know, "Could it — could it be [said we did the review]?" Stuart [said] 'look, we haven't done a review, but we have done this, etc. etc.' Inquiry panel member Dame Una O'Brien asked: 'But nobody said: "You can't do that because that's not a review?"' Cooper replied: 'No, including me … everyone knew that there hadn't been a review done.' Grasping the significance of what the witness was saying, Aiken asked: 'What was going on with the culture in DETI … that meant communications that are inaccurate seem to be acceptable?' Cooper paused for a long time before eventually saying: 'I'm not sure what the answer to that question actually is. It's a very difficult one to answer, because there's actually no defence.' When asked if it was a human mistake or a cultural problem within the civil service, Cooper said: 'It's potentially cultural.'

The day after the meeting, Wightman gave effect to the 'fig leaf' plan and drafted a document, which masked the full gory picture of what had happened. A week later he had a five-page briefing note to inform Cooper's discussions with the Department of Finance. It misleadingly said: 'In October 2013, DETI commenced a Phase 2 review of the domestic and non-domestic RHI schemes.' Wightman's rosy presentation of the situation extended to presenting DETI as having done more than it said it would do, implying that the review had been conducted even earlier than necessary. Then, showing either extreme naivety about the scheme he was running or else immense confidence in his powers of persuasion, Wightman actually claimed credit for the vast overspend, writing in the document that 'despite the drop in oil prices over the winter months, we have successfully increased uptake of the Non-domestic RHI scheme over the last 12 months.' He also claimed that a second review – this time of the tariffs – was 'ongoing'. But the truth was that there was nothing that could be characterised in civil service terms as a review – an in-depth analysis of the tariffs – at that point. Had there been such a project, it would almost certainly have uncovered the perverse incentive.

Cooper said he was 'not defending' what had happened. Aiken put it to him that even though some people at the 'fig leaf' meeting may not have fully understood the implications of what they were discussing, as the summer progressed 'these type of characterisations are known to be untrue' – but kept being used. O'Brien observed: 'Things might have turned out differently if you had been honest with each other at the time.'

Stormont's culture of departments, often operating as ministerial fiefdoms rather than as part of a coherent government, may have contributed to the culture whereby civil servants sought to protect their department rather than the wider public interest. Ministers were wary of problems being communicated outside the department for fear that it would end up with ministers from rival parties who might leak the news. In this case, however, it is difficult to see what happened as anything other than an example of the human temptation to shift the blame. That is because not only was the finance ministry, like DETI, in DUP hands, but it was headed up by one

Arlene Foster who had no motive whatsoever to draw attention to calamity in a scheme of her making.

One of the alarming elements of Cooper's evidence was that he said that he went along with the plan – despite it being clear that he was often a voice of challenge within the department and was known for asking difficult questions of colleagues. The senior DETI official's evidence suggested a department that was more focussed on protecting itself from criticism than on presenting the full truth – even to other civil servants.

Wightman did not deny that he had suggested the 'fig leaf', telling the inquiry that he had 'very little recollection at all' of the 3 June meeting. He admitted that the documentation indicated that he had wrongly suggested a review had already taken place, but insisted: 'I would not have set out to mislead other officials'.

McCormick told the inquiry in writing: 'I have no recollection of anyone making the point that Trevor Cooper has highlighted, and if there had been an explicit suggestion that we should misrepresent the position to [the Department of Finance] I am sure that I would remember that.' He added: 'In summary, I was not in any way aware of, or party to, a decision to seek to pretend … that the 2013 consultation had been in fulfilment of the condition of approval in 2012.'

The significance of what happened after the 3 June meeting was that the language then adopted carried through into multiple other documents, misrepresenting the position to more and more civil servants.

But Cooper himself was aware of something else which should not have happened in this period – but which suited him because it removed a criticism of his division. In May, Mills had been highly critical of Cooper's team. In an internal 'assurance statement' – a document meant to provide the permanent secretary and the department's audit committee with assurance that all was well across DETI – Mills had recorded that 'despite the repeated requests for information from the finance division and [the Department of Finance], the division has yet to receive any clarity around the maximum available RHI budget going forward … Without this clarification, both schemes may need to be closed to prevent overspends.' At the inquiry, Cooper accepted that the criticism had been a fairly accurate portrayal of the situation. However, when the final version of the document was circulated to members of the departmental board, references to the RHI situation were far more anodyne and criticism of the finance division was removed altogether. Cooper said that there had been a series of internal conversations with senior officials about the issue before the changes were made. He conceded: 'It looks bad. I totally accept that.' Mills told the inquiry that within the civil service 'it's not done to say things like that [criticisms of colleagues in formal documents]'. The incident was a demonstration of how mechanisms to prevent problems arising could be circumvented with the knowledge of multiple senior civil servants.

****

Alarmed at what was going on, Cooper sent an email to fellow senior official Shane Murphy which tore apart Energy Division's proposals to address the RHI problems. The 12 June message noted that there was 'nothing on how they're going to constrain spend'. Cooper said that he felt there was 'a fair bit of naivety' on the part of Wightman and his division, with them having 'glossed over' the issue of reviews. Getting to the kernel of the soaring RHI bill, he said: 'There's no self-awareness that the reason they may be delivering greater renewables than GB counterparts is the simple fact that we may be overcompensating – so it's not actually over-performing; indeed, potentially quite the contrary.' While O'Hagan had been trying to raise the alarm from without, Cooper was now trying to raise the alarm from within. In Murphy he had an ally who was sceptical about Energy Division's increasingly far-fetched claims about the success of RHI. But their attempts at forcing critical thinking on Mills, Wightman and Hughes would be undermined by what was to happen five days later.

On 17 June McCormick called another meeting of his top team to take a decision as to how they would address the difficulty. Energy Division advised those present that they had legal advice that said that closing RHI at that point was not an option – a claim which was incorrect, as RHI would later be closed within the space of about two months. Energy Division advised the meeting that it could take up to a year to cut the tariffs. As kindred spirits alarmed at what was unfolding, Murphy and Cooper had for several days been discussing tactics to pressure Energy Division at the meeting. Murphy later recalled Cooper bluntly asking them – he believed it was Wightman who was asked – whether 'you can make money just by running these things' and receiving 'clear assurances from Energy Division that this was not the case'. He said that Wightman and Mills simply offered the explanation that it was a demand-led scheme, which was experiencing higher than expected demand. A series of proposals from Cooper and Murphy aimed at cutting expenditure were rejected by Energy Division as either impossible or unfeasible. Eventually in frustration Murphy asked: 'Could you at least stop promoting the thing?' That line would soon become of great significance.

Having been told by Energy Division that the only option was to take a less radical path – the implementation of tiered tariffs – McCormick and the others decided to pursue that route. From this point, the department was embarked upon a course of action that did not fully address the problem. But once that course had been set and significant work had gone into moving towards tiering, it would become increasingly difficult to alter the position. However, the facts were not quite as they were understood by DETI's senior management on that day. In fact, Wightman and Hughes had only asked for legal advice on whether they could unilaterally move to suspend the scheme – and the advice confirmed that they could not because there was no such power in the legislation. However, they had not even asked the equally significant question of whether they could now move to introduce legislation to give them the power to suspend RHI.

Wightman's concern was that Stormont had lost a series of court challenges where it had failed to engage in public consultation or give adequate notice to the public of a sudden change in course. Wightman said that he 'knew from my experience' that legislation would require a slow process of consultation and Assembly scrutiny. Although they were going to require legislation anyway to introduce tiering, Wightman calculated that this could be done more swiftly because there had been a public consultation on cost controls in 2013 – the one which DETI had subsequently quietly abandoned. There was one huge flaw in that explanation: the 2013 consultation had never been about tiering. Instead, it had involved a more complex mechanism, which had been drawn up by Peter Hutchinson. Therefore, the entire justification for proceeding to only tier the tariffs – rather than close the scheme or implement a power for DETI to close the scheme – was based on a false premise and one which could easily have been seen if they had gone back and read the 2013 consultation. It was a hopelessly confused situation where, yet again in DETI, the blind were leading the blind.

Yet the idea that the scheme might have been too generous ought to have been apparent to Energy Division for another reason. By the beginning of March, DETI had been told by Ofgem that more than 12% of boilers were being run round the clock, seven days a week, 365 days a year. One RHI boiler owner told the author that some people in his situation had just written down the highest number of hours available but were not actually intending to run their boiler flat out. This is backed up by usage figures later published by the Northern Ireland Audit Office which found that just ten boilers were running between 90–100% of the year. Beneath that, 65 boilers were running for between 80–90% of the year, a further 129 were running for 70–80% of the year and another 213 were running for 60–70% of the year. Regardless of whether the figures were accurate, they were what the department was being told at the time and were startling. But, as with myriad other warning signs, no alarm bell rang in DETI.

Referring to earlier data from Ofgem in late 2014, which also showed far higher boiler usage than expected, Wightman told the inquiry: 'I can confirm that through these checks I was aware of actual average weekly operating hours in the order of 91 (54% load factor), but regrettably this did not alert me to the issue of potential overcompensation.' It is not the case that all those running at such high levels were fraudsters. Some businesses have extremely high heat demands, and with no cap on usage it was lawful to claim for all their heat. The usage figures also dispel the erroneous perception, which would later develop among some of the public, that everyone on the scheme was a crook. The Audit Office figures show that there were 81 boilers running for less than 10% of the year and another 192 boilers running for between 10–20% of the year. Self-evidently, those individuals were not milking the subsidy for all that they could get.

An early June communication between two of the Stormont officials who had the greatest knowledge of RHI indicates that DETI was aware of extreme usage. On 9 June, Hughes emailed Cathal Ellis, the Department of Agriculture's renewable energy technologist – a position which meant that he knew how valuable RHI was to farmers. Even before RHI launched, the Department of Agriculture had worked out that a boiler costing £36,000 could receive a £35,000 subsidy in its first year – meaning that during the second year the farmer would move into profit and continue there for another 18 years. The department – headed up by Sinn Féin minister Michelle

O'Neill – promoted RHI at 58 events during the lifetime of the scheme. Referring to poultry farmers' use of RHI, Hughes told him: 'Anecdotally we are led to believe that some houses are running 24/7 and if this is the case we are seeking an understanding of why this is happening.' Ellis replied to Hughes to tell him what would probably have been self-evident to the man or woman in the street. Repeating some of Hughes's words back to him, he said: 'There are rumours of houses running 24/7 (I don't think in NI yet!) – the reason to maximise the output from the boiler for RHI.'

Wightman, to whom Hughes's email was copied, said that he could not recall what Hughes was referring to, and he thought it was 'much later' around September that 'I certainly remember hearing anecdotal claims of basically empty buildings being heated'. However, in his earlier interview with PwC – which he never expected to be public, so may have been less guarded, but which was based on not seeing very much of the material, so equally may have been confused – Wightman had said something different. Referring to a meeting with Ofgem around October 2014, he said: 'I remember raising the issues … in passing [that] there [were] anecdotal claims that people were heating empty sheds.'

By spring 2015, it was clear to DETI's senior civil servants that there was a significant problem. There had been a sudden increase in the number of applications, those who got into the scheme were running their boilers far more than had been anticipated – and as a result they were claiming huge sums. And, almost uniquely in government spending, the commitments were for 20 years, meaning that the total bill was going to be vast – even if the scheme could be shut immediately, which it could not. And yet, it took until 8 June before the minister – the individual who was the titular head of the department – was verbally alerted to the situation and a further month before he was given a written submission about the crisis. By involving the political side of the department, an entirely new problem was to emerge. For all that DETI was a dysfunctional department in this period, it was a paradigm of order and civility when compared to what was going on within the DUP. The ineptitude of the civil service and the scheming of some in the DUP was about to be united and would give birth to the monster that would topple the entire Stormont edifice.

CHAPTER 10
BELL AND THE BIG BALLS

It was meant to be a relaxed evening largely away from the immediate pressure of politics. Bell, not yet a month into his first full ministerial role, was in London for a meeting with his Westminster counterpart, DECC Secretary of State Amber Rudd. Sitting in an unassuming London curry house on the evening of Tuesday, 9 June, Bell and his spad, Tim Cairns, along with the minister's private secretary, Sean Kerr, were fortifying themselves ahead of the next day's business. Dinner was not intended to be all work and the trio each relaxed over three pints of Cobra beer. Cairns believed that Bell rarely read his ministerial submissions and the best way to keep him informed, and to get him to take decisions, was through oral briefing. Therefore, as Bell and Kerr sat on one side of the table in Paradise Restaurant in Pimlico and Cairns sat on the other side, the spad took his minister through what he should say to Rudd. As that work element of the dinner came to an end and the starters were arriving, Cairns raised something that had been on his mind for more than 24 hours – RHI.

Bell and Cairns had first been told of the emerging RHI problem the previous day. During a routine departmental meeting between DETI's top team and the minister, RHI was item six on the agenda. Bell was told the projected spend for that financial year was now £23 million and that the tariffs had not been reviewed as had been meant to happen. Cairns recalled that the tone from the permanent secretary, Andrew McCormick, was that officials had 'dropped the ball' but were working to put things right, and would soon be bringing proposals to the minister in an urgent submission. As was common in meetings, Bell said little but noted the position and asked to be kept informed.

As Cairns was leaving Parliament Buildings that day he decided to take the issue further. The Assembly office used by Bell and Cairns was adjacent to the one used by Foster and Andrew Crawford. After being told about the RHI problem and separate escalating issues with another green energy scheme, the NIRO, Cairns's natural inclination was to talk to his colleagues who until a month earlier had been in charge of both schemes. Cairns's political antenna had gone up when the civil servants had told him that the scheme's approvals from the Department of Finance had lapsed.

Knowing that Foster was now the Finance Minister, he asked her if she knew what was going on. Cairns later recalled that Foster had said: 'I know nothing about that,' before turning to Crawford to ask: 'Andrew, do you know anything about that?' Crawford similarly said that he was unaware of the issue. Cairns suggested that it would be helpful if Bell and himself met Foster and Crawford more formally to discuss RHI because they would know more about it as the team which had developed the scheme. Foster readily assented to the proposition.

Cairns, a trained lawyer in his early 40s whose family was steeped in the DUP, had been employed as a DUP policy officer for two years from 2002 before abandoning politics for nine years – a period in which he went to Canada to study theology and then work as a religious minister. Returning to Belfast in 2011, Cairns had returned to his old policy officer role at the DUP's Dundela Avenue headquarters, but within a year had been asked to become Bell's spad while he was a junior minister.

After his brief discussion with Foster and Crawford that Monday evening, Cairns had not discussed the issue with Bell. Now, relaxing over beer and bhajis, Cairns raised the subject. The adviser informed Bell that he had talked about RHI with Foster and Crawford who were keen to meet a proposal, which Cairns advised his minister to accept. Bell immediately took offence at the suggestion that anyone else should be involved in how he ran DETI. Cairns said that he 'very quickly and aggressively' made clear that 'he ran the department, not Arlene'. Cairns tried again, telling him that while that was true it might still be best for them to meet and hear what their predecessors thought. Bell shut down the conversation, which moved on to other matters. Although Bell had been sharp with his spad to the point that Kerr had felt uncomfortable, it was a brief flash of steel and did not spoil the night. After the meal the three men walked along the embankment and Bell pointed across to the Palace of Westminster, telling his companions that he would be an MP by 2020. The trio knew each other pretty well by now, having worked together in Stormont Castle, where for the last two years Bell had been a junior minister – in effect an aide to the First Minister.

In the bar of the trendy Park Plaza Westminster Bridge Hotel they continued the conversation. Over more beers, Bell outlined his plan to become an MP and claimed that a senior DUP strategist was managing his parliamentary assault for 2020. When they headed to bed that night, there was little hint of what was to come. At breakfast the following morning, the curry house trio were joined by McCormick and energy division boss John Mills, both of whom began pressing Bell to take a decision that day over the future of the NIRO, another lucrative green energy scheme, which had seen vast subsidies travelling from GB to Northern Ireland but was now under threat from a Tory policy shift. Touching a nerve, which had been pricked the previous evening, Cairns got involved to tell the civil servants that Bell could not take such a decision by himself, and it would have to be referred to others in the DUP. The civil servants continued to press for an urgent decision, leading to Cairns re-emphasising to his minister that the decision was not his alone to take. At this stage Bell erupted. Furious, he saw his spad's conduct as an attempt to undermine his authority in front of his most senior civil servant. Bell made clear that he would be making his own decisions. By now Cairns was talking over the minister who was his boss – all in the presence of officials and in the midst of a busy central London hotel room.

Bell later recalled that Cairns 'frequently spoke over me and stated the department would take a different perspective [to] the one that I was considering … it was inappropriate and led to tension'. Cairns's intervention 'jarred' with McCormick because it was 'a sharper intervention with a minister than I had seen before' and 'right at the borderline of normal conversation, if not over it'. Eventually Cairns – in an attempt to defuse the situation, he later said – left the table and checked out of his room. But when he came back down some time later, Bell was still at the table and wanted to speak to him. By now the officials had gone. Cairns later told the public inquiry that Bell became 'enraged'.

Cairns was waving – whether consciously or not – his finger in the direction of the minister. Bell later said that as his spad wagged his finger Cairns had told him: 'Now you're going to listen to me, big balls'. Bell said he was 'shocked and taken aback at this outburst'. Cairns admitted that he had used 'unsavoury language' to the minister but said that as his finger was pointed at Bell the minister had made a grab for it and in a 'very aggressive' tone of voice told him: 'If you wag your finger at me again, I'll break it'. By this stage Bell was standing up and fellow diners were watching the unfolding scene. The minister demanded that his spad should apologise.

Cairns refused and Bell said that he was fired. Bell rejected the claim that he had threatened physical violence, earnestly telling the inquiry: 'I'll say the allegation that I tried to break a finger or any other bone, or attempted to, is untrue, completely without foundation and has no basis whatsoever in fact. I have never tried to break anybody's finger and never would.' Whatever the truth of what went on in the Park Plaza's breakfast dining room, it is clear that Cairns's behaviour was unacceptable, and probably would have led to disciplinary action in any other walk of life. Cairns later freely admitted that it 'isn't the proudest moment of my working career' and that it was 'not a very savoury incident' in which he had 'made many mistakes'. He conceded that Bell was probably 'right to be annoyed with me'.

Kerr was paying for the breakfast when Cairns approached him and told him that he needed to arrange a flight home because he had just been sacked. But before that could be done, the group had to leave for their meeting with DECC. After squeezing into a taxi, Bell shut down questions about the upcoming meeting and told those present that Cairns would not be attending. While the officials headed into DECC with their minister to meet Rudd, Cairns headed for Heathrow Airport.

After landing in Belfast, Cairns travelled straight to Stormont Castle – the real seat of devolved power. Inside the castle, Cairns informed the two most powerful DUP spads – Timothy Johnston and Richard Bullick – of what had happened in London. During the meeting Johnston phoned Bell – who by now was at a function in the Japanese Embassy – and told him that he could not unilaterally sack his spad because spads were appointed by DUP party officers. This was an inversion of the legal position whereby the appointment of spads – figures who had to be utterly trusted by the minister, given their power within the department for which they were responsible – was meant to be entirely a matter for the minister. The system set up by the DUP gave greater central control to the party leader and meant that spads to other ministers knew that they ultimately owed their jobs to the leader, who was heavily influenced by Johnston – a factor which would soon become highly significant. Advisers were now telling ministers what to do – yet the advisers were barely known to the public and not democratically accountable.

****

The day after the breakfast row, the two protagonists separately met with DUP leader Peter Robinson and Johnston. Sitting in the First Minister's Stormont Castle office, the events of the previous day were rehearsed, first by Bell who told Robinson that his spad had acted defiantly by attempting to command him to follow his instructions in a way which Robinson would not tolerate from his own spads. Having given his side of the story, Bell emerged from Robinson's ground floor room in Stormont Castle and Cairns entered.

Cairns said that he had made clear that the breakfast row had not been an isolated incident, and that there had been previous unpleasant altercations between Bell and DUP members in which Bell had been aggressive. But Robinson had 'dismissed' this, Cairns said. The spad admitted that his behaviour the previous day had been inappropriate. But Bell had previously denied to Robinson that he had done anything wrong. Cairns said that Robinson seemed to look disapprovingly on his voluntary admission of guilt at the first opportunity, viewing it as a sign of weakness. Robinson told the inquiry that in the meeting Cairns had 'raised an issue about Mr Bell's temper' but that 'no other complaints were submitted'. Cairns was told that he was not allowed to talk about what had gone on and that if he did so he would be immediately dismissed.

In a text message immediately after leaving Stormont Castle, Cairns told his friend Emma Little-Pengelly – at that point a DUP spad but who would go on become the DUP MP for South Belfast – that Bell had denied even sacking him when challenged by Johnston. However, Cairns said that Johnston had told Bell that 'he didn't make decisions and especially about his spad. He told him that he would go against the party officers at his peril and that if he didn't like me while his name might legally be at the bottom of an appointment letter they could always get someone else to sign it'. Cairns went on: 'JB [Bell] has come out of this very badly. Firstly because I now owe him nothing and will report his every transgression to TJ [Johnston] who wants him out. Also I've made sure Andrew and Arlene know that he is messing up in their department.' Little-Pengelly replied: 'He is a [expletive censored by the inquiry].' Cairns then told her: 'My goal now is that he was one year max and done. If I get a chance I'm going to film him drunk and talking shit and show it to TJ.' Little-Pengelly endorsed this unorthodox approach to party discipline, telling Cairns: 'You should – but he will rip your head off if he catches you!'

In another message, Little-Pengelly – who was herself close to Robinson – said she was 'shocked' that Robinson 'would take [Bell's] side in any way'. But then, alluding to Bell employing several of Robinson's family, she added: 'Of course he employs the family!' Cairns responded with an intriguing message about Robinson's lobbyist son, Gareth Robinson – who was not employed by Bell but had been lobbying Stormont departments in ways which were beginning to attract attention. Cairns said: 'I laid it on thick about Gareth. That helped a bit.' Little-Pengelly later denounced Bell in another message to Cairns as 'a bully' and nicknamed Bell 'Ding Dong'.

Although Johnston had been advocating for Cairns in the meeting, it was a draining experience for Bell's spad, who felt that Robinson was taking the side of his friend Bell and was not taking seriously the warnings about Bell's temperament and behaviour. Cairns went to his doctor and was medically signed off work with stress. When told about what had gone on, his doctor asked: 'Where on earth do you work? How is this even allowed to happen?' Perhaps as a result of the DUP's strict *omerta* about discussing internal party rows publicly, Cairns said: 'I don't want to say.'

The following day, Cairns exchanged messages with Bullick. Cairns told him he was 'quite upset' that Bell had 'made allegations which are lies', adding: 'He's done that in the past. He is attempting to assassinate my character.' In an indication of how Bell was viewed by one of those closest to Robinson, Bullick replied: 'He would lie without hesitation.'

Two weeks later, Johnston phoned Cairns to say that as a temporary civil servant he could either stay on sick leave for six months – but if he did so there would then be no party job for him – or he could return to work. Cairns said that he was assured by Johnston that there would be mutual apologies and a reconciliation meeting was arranged for the following day. It was a disappointment for Cairns who had expected to be moved to either another spad job or back into DUP headquarters, believing that he and Bell simply could not work together. His hope of moving had been 'shattered', he later told the inquiry, because other spads would not move to work with Bell. During his evidence to the inquiry, Dame Una O'Brien asked him why, having been treated like that, he did not walk away. Becoming momentarily emotional, Cairns responded: 'Well, I guess we've got mortgages to pay and bills to pay and, yes … life.'

Senior civil servant Fiona Hepper briefed Arlene Foster as RHI was designed.

Young DETI official Peter Hutchinson was key to designing the scheme.

Graph 1: Comparison of Northern Ireland and GB RHI non-domestic tariffs from 2012 to 2015 in pence (based on a typical 99kw biomass boiler) *

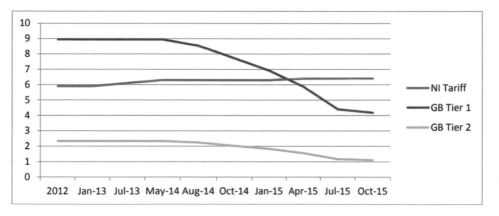

*the 99kw biomass boiler was the main source used in NI non-domestic RHI claims

Source: Department

This chart from the NI Audit Office shows how the tiered GB scheme became less generous – while Stormont's became more lucrative.

Trevor Cooper, DETI's plainspoken director of finance.

DETI's head of energy division at the time when RHI imploded was John Mills.

Arlene Foster pictured with wood pellets at Warmflow Engineering alongside managing director Stuart Cousins in July 2014.

Image: Invest NI.

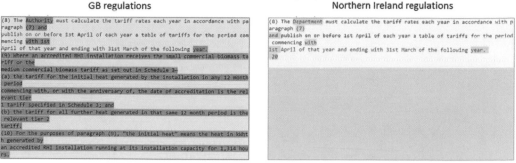

GB regulations	Northern Ireland regulations
(8) The Authority must calculate the tariff rates each year in accordance with paragraph (7) and publish on or before 1st April of each year a table of tariffs for the period commencing with 1st April of that year and ending with 31st March of the following year. (9) Where an accredited RHI installation receives the small commercial biomass tariff or the medium commercial biomass tariff as set out in Schedule 3— (a) the tariff for the initial heat generated by the installation in any 12 month period commencing with, or with the anniversary of, the date of accreditation is the relevant tier 1 tariff specified in Schedule 3; and (b) the tariff for all further heat generated in that same 12 month period is the relevant tier 2 tariff. (10) For the purposes of paragraph (9), "the initial heat" means the heat in kWh generated by an accredited RHI installation running at its installation capacity for 1,314 hours.	(8) The Department must calculate the tariff rates each year in accordance with paragraph (7) and publish on or before 1st April of each year a table of tariffs for the period commencing with 1st April of that year and ending with 31st March of the following year. 20

Using computer comparison software, the author found that the only significant change that Stormont made to the GB RHI legislation was to remove these paragraphs on cost control.

DUP chairman Lord Morrow, Arlene Foster and Moy Park's then chief executive Janet McCollum.   Image: Invest NI.

One of the pieces of marketing in which RHI was literally being marketed as 'cash for ash'.
Image: RHI Inquiry evidence.

Poultry farmer Tom Forgrave was key to opening up the truth about how Moy Park profited from RHI.   Image: Dept of Agriculture.

DUP chief executive Timothy Johnston, left foreground, being questioned by inquiry barrister Donal Lunny, right, standing

DETI official Stuart Wightman was a key figure as RHI ran out of control.

DETI official Seamus Hughes was one of the civil servants briefing the industry to tell it that cost controls were coming – before this information was made public.

Moy Park showed some of its farmers this image of a chicken house, with multiple forms of subsidised green energy and a bag labelled swag

Senior civil servant Andrew McCormick at Stomont's Public Accounts Committee naming Andrew Crawford as the DUP spad allegedly involved in delaying cost controls.

The Stormont Executive in 2016, just months before it fell apart.   Image: NI Executive.

Arlene Foster being interviewed by the author in her Parliament Buildings office on her first day as First Minister, in January 2016.

Janette O'Hagan, the businesswoman who repeatedly attempted to warn DETI about RHI's perverse incentive, but was ignored.

DUP adviser Timothy Johnston has been the power behind the thrones of successive DUP leaders.   Image: DUP.

Former DUP spad Tim Cairns spoke bluntly at the inquiry, admitting a series of failures.

DUP spad Stephen Brimstone was heating his own home with a non-domestic boiler fitted in an outbuilding.

The day after Johnston's phone call, Bell, Cairns and Johnston assembled in Stormont Castle. Johnston claimed that Robinson had been present – a potentially significant point because without his presence Johnston, who was being paid almost £92,000 a year from the public purse to assist Robinson with departmental business, was now engaged in a quasi-human resources role within the DUP. One of the few points on which Bell and Cairns agree is that Robinson was not present, with Cairns saying that he was '100%' sure that Robinson was not even in the building because his police bodyguard's vehicle was not outside. Robinson said that he had asked Johnston to set up the meeting but does not believe he was present for it.

But, having reluctantly come to accept that he was now going to have to return to working with Bell, Cairns was now to be doubly disappointed. Having been, he said, led to believe by Johnston that there would be mutual apologies, there was now no apology from Bell. Bell told the inquiry that 'the supposed issue of my "temper" was never mentioned at the meeting. This allegation is completely new to me'.

Now Johnston turned the meeting to focus on what Cairns had missed in his two weeks away from the department. Cairns told the inquiry that 'I recall NIRO and RHI being discussed. This was a very brief discussion … I was requested to liaise with Andrew Crawford, in the presence of Mr Bell who raised no objections'. Cairns said that Johnston had said RHI cost controls would not be introduced and that he should work with Crawford on developing an alternative. However, Cairns gave two caveats to that evidence. He said that 'I do not believe Timothy was fully appraised of the seriousness of the matter when he made that remark … to be absolutely fair to Mr Johnston, I don't think he knew of what he was speaking'. Then, when asked by inquiry chairman Sir Patrick Coghlin how sure he was that Johnston told him 'tariff controls must not be introduced', Cairns said: 'That's my recollection. I'm not gonna go to the sword on it.'

Cairns said that Bell was nodding and assenting to what Johnston was saying in this part of the meeting with a degree of 'bravado' because he was delighted to have won the argument with Cairns without having to apologise. Johnston told the inquiry:

I don't believe there was any specific reference at this meeting to the RHI scheme but I do recall the suggestion being made by [the First

Minister] that Mr Bell should use Arlene Foster as a reference point if he felt he needed information or advice on DETI matters. I do not believe there was any discussion on the RHI scheme and I did not instruct or suggest at any point to Mr Cairns that tariff controls would be introduced, the details of which I was unfamiliar with at the time.

Johnston's argument that it was Robinson who suggested some working arrangement between Bell and Foster – and presumably their spads – is undermined by the evidence that Robinson was not even at this meeting. For his part, Bell said that 'none of the issues referred to were discussed at the meeting … The sole purpose of the June 2015 meeting was to address Mr Cairns's behaviour'. However, he added that Johnston and Cairns had continued to talk after a point where he had 'disengaged' and was looking at his phone, so on his own evidence he was not paying attention.

In Cairns's mind there was a logic to Johnston having some understanding of RHI because he believed that Johnston and Crawford had been informally working to assist Bell during the time that he had been off work. Whatever went on in Stormont Castle that afternoon, the understanding which Cairns developed at that time was to be crucial in what was to follow. He had what he viewed as two instructions in his mind: the DUP opposed cost controls on the scheme and he was to work with Crawford on how to get something else in their place.

The meeting was on a Friday so the following day did not involve Cairns going back to work at DETI. However, clearly still unhappy at how he felt he had been duped by Johnston, he sent him a text message, reminding him that he had never wanted to be Bell's spad at DETI and that he wanted to record 'my disappointment and annoyance' that at the meeting there was no mention of Bell's temper, something which he warned was 'still an issue'. Johnston replied that it was 'an unfair characterisation of the meeting' and, with a hint of menace, given his huge power, added: 'Believe me there were not to [*sic*] many working to get this resolved so bear that in mind.'

As June came to an end and Cairns returned to his desk in Netherleigh House, there was little trust between himself and Bell. It had been made clear to both minister and spad that the real decision-makers in the DUP were in Stormont Castle and, despite a dysfunctional relationship with the adviser who ought to have been his most trusted political confidante, Bell was left working with a man who he believed did not respect his authority. Right at the point where RHI was moving deeper into the red, it was the DUP's internal arguments on which Bell and Cairns were most focussed. In time, their relationship would improve, but from this point it was a strictly professional marriage of necessity.

****

Just eight working days after Cairns returned to DETI, officials finally submitted their proposal for solving the RHI predicament. It was customary in the Stormont system for ministerial submissions to go first to the spad, who would add any of their own comments before sending it on to the minister for a decision. The submission, which was drafted by Wightman, arrived with Cairns on the evening of 8 July. But although there was now a written communication to the minister setting out that there was a problem with RHI, it omitted some of the key issues of which the officials were by that stage aware.

Inexplicably, the cover of the submission simply referred to the funding as 'AME' – money coming directly from the Treasury. There was no caveat or explanation of what Wightman now knew clearly: there was at best confusion around whether the funding really was AME and at worst it was clear that it probably was not. But it got worse. The submission went on to say that the funding 'does not impact directly on NI departmental budgets'. This submission was central to the huge spike in RHI applications which was to come. Although it was marked 'urgent' by civil servants, they had sat on the issue for months, demonstrating no urgency themselves. However, that was unknown to Bell and Cairns at the time, and what they were presented with was a submission about a scheme, which was hugely over-budget and where officials were asking for an urgent decision. It would take almost two months for Bell to take any decision.

The minister and spad also did not realise that the document sent to them had been significantly watered down the previous night. Wightman had sent a draft of the document to Chris Stewart, McCormick's deputy, and copied it to multiple officials including Trevor Cooper and his boss, Eugene Rooney. It was also copied to Wightman's boss, Mills. Even though Mills was on holiday he kept an eye from afar on what was going on. The draft which he read on his phone included a comment on the financial implications of the situation: 'Forecast RHI expenditure in 2015–16 is £23 million – almost twice current AME allocation of £11.6 million.'

In one of several changes to the document, which made the gravity of the situation less explicit, that was changed to the more anodyne: 'We are currently seeking extra funding as forecast scheme expenditure exceeds previous funding allocations.' Wightman told the inquiry that Mills and Stewart had requested multiple changes to the submission. Mills recalled phoning Wightman from a taxi into central London, suggesting some of the key changes that removed the blunter messages to the minister. Pressed to explain why he had removed important factual information, Mills said that it may have been out of 'caution to not mention specific figures' because the forecasts had risen so rapidly that he did not have confidence in the exact figure. He insisted: 'There was absolutely no intention to conceal or try and make the picture rosier for the minister.'

Wightman said that the first draft was 'my own words' and was 'a bit more up front' but admitted that after requests from his superiors he had agreed to changes which amounted to a 'significant downplaying of the need for concern'. Coghlin said it was clear that all the most senior DETI officials had seen how the document was being reshaped and that 'the end result of this is that the minister gets a submission which has been changed with the knowledge and/or at the direction of the senior members of DETI in such a way that it is false. That's the very difficult situation … that is what is happening here.'

The document also gave a confusing picture of a scheme painted as a great success but which urgently needed to be reined in – while stressing that there was no threat to the departmental budget. Nevertheless, despite the deep inadequacies of the 8 July submission, its central message was understood by Cairns. The submission said: 'Given these budget pressures, we need to urgently implement cost control measures to manage future RHI expenditure.' Cairns knew what that meant. But he recalled what had happened in the meeting with Johnston and forwarded the submission to Crawford, beginning a process which would have disastrous consequences.

The submission did not make its way past Cairns to Bell, but the spad said that they discussed its contents the day after it arrived and then around 30 July. Cairns later said that the minister 'made no significant comments or raised any objections at that time'. The spad said that at this point both he and the minister were still at a 'rank amateur' understanding of the scheme, but that he had briefed Bell in his office and 'what I knew, he knew'.

Two days after the submission, Bell flew to China for two and a half weeks on a family holiday. On his return to Northern Ireland, the minister was briefly back in the department before decamping to his 'summer house' in Portstewart, 60 miles north of Belfast, for several weeks, something which Cairns said impeded decision-making around RHI and other important issues. Bell said that he had left instructions at the department to contact him about anything urgent, yet he was not contacted about RHI.

While Bell was not being spoken to about RHI, Crawford was. Cairns had 'several discussions' with Foster's spad, focussing on the question of cost controls. He said that he also spoke to Johnston about the issue, something Johnston later denied. Few of those discussions – which were mostly by phone or in person – were recorded in any written form. Cairns told the inquiry that the clear message communicated to him in those spad-to-spad discussions was that the party wanted to delay any cut to the tariffs for as long as possible. Based on that, Cairns freely admitted to the inquiry that he had acted to delay changes to the scheme – but said that neither he nor Bell had the slightest interest in the scheme and were only doing so at the request of others in the DUP.

Foster's evidence to the inquiry was that although she knew Cairns had asked for assistance and Crawford had agreed to provide that assistance, there were financial implications to what they were discussing. At no point thereafter did she, as Finance Minister, make any enquiry of Crawford as to what was going on. Foster said: 'I didn't think it was of any issue.' But intriguing new information, not given to the public inquiry, adds to the picture of what DUP ministers knew in this period. On 8 July – hours before the submission went to Cairns – an individual outside of politics met with DUP Social Development Minister, Mervyn Storey.

The meeting was to discuss energy issues in Northern Ireland's public sector social housing stock. In an interview for this book, the individual – who for professional reasons asked not to be named – said that Storey had 'unprompted' raised what he said was a major problem with RHI. That raises two significant questions. Firstly, if Storey was aware of the significance of the RHI problems, how could Bell, as the minister responsible, not have been aware of the importance of RHI and been pressing his spad and officials as to what was being done about the situation? Secondly, if Storey – as a relatively junior DUP minister – was aware of the significant RHI problems, it would be surprising if Foster remained unaware of the significance of the problem. Not only was she the minister who had set up the scheme and therefore had political reason to be concerned, but as Finance Minister she would have known that any financial problems were going to ultimately come to her door.

When asked how he was aware of the major problem in RHI at this early stage and if the issue had been discussed between the DUP ministers, Storey declined to answer and instead responded with a solicitor's letter. Even though there was no suggestion that Storey had acted improperly, the letter – sent in concert with Foster, Johnston, Crawford and Peter Robinson – threatened legal action if 'publication of inaccurate and defamatory material occurs'.

Nine days after the 8 July submission went to Cairns, Bell's private secretary confirmed in an email that Cairns had read it. But as the summer wore on, it became clear to officials that something strange was going on, and they became increasingly concerned about the delay in making a decision about bringing the scheme under control.

On 30 July, Mills emailed Cairns and Stewart after a meeting between the three of them. It is clear from the email that Cairns was kicking back against the request to rein in the scheme. The email also hinted at what was beginning to become clear to officials from Cairns – that the DUP thought that the funding was being paid for by the Treasury and that was a reason not to precipitously intervene. Mills said:

We discussed the need to introduce measure [sic] to manage expenditure on the [RHI]…You made the point that there was virtue in making sure NI was able to make best use of the AME funding available … you rightly said that we would not want to overreact by introducing restrictions too suddenly which took us back to previous underperformance. However both Chris [Stewart] and I emphasised that we have to demonstrate that measures were being taken to ensure proper controls and Chris pointed out that the AME arrangements may have additional caveats.

Twelve days later, Mills emailed Stewart in evident frustration at the lack of movement from the minister or spad. He said that the lack of clearance of the submission was delaying the process of reducing the subsidy. There had been 'no response' from Cairns he said, to an email, despite a reminder from Stewart four days earlier. Responding the same day, Stewart said that he had spoken to Cairns and 'he accepts the need for early control measures', but asked if a more generous cap could be used – a proposal, as would later become clear, which had originated with Crawford. Unknown to officials, that request had been made because it would benefit a huge multinational which was massively benefiting from RHI.

****

But while on the one hand civil servants were putting pressure on Cairns, in an attempt to get a decision out of Bell, even by late July relative serenity continued to surround some senior officials who still believed that they just needed to get more money from London.

In a meeting with the influential Ulster Farmers' Union (UFU) on 22 July, officials faced lobbying for a delay to the introduction of tiering – something the UFU presented as a 'grace period' for those already in the process of installing boilers. UFU policy chief Chris Osborne later recalled at the inquiry that there was no sense of alarm about the situation: 'It was neither urgent nor the opposite really. It seemed to be very sort of calm, very measured in terms of how they were presenting this to us.'

Also at the meeting was Tom Forgrave, a large poultry farmer from Ballymoney who had six RHI boilers and was in the process of installing another four. He had directly contacted Wightman and Hughes more than a week earlier, pressing them to 'give consideration to not rushing through any changes' because 'the proposed date of 1st Oct 15 does not give the poultry industry in NI time to adapt to a new tariff'. He said 'many farmers, myself included' were in the planning process 'to build new poultry sheds for Moy Park', with the cash flow projections on which their bank loans were approved, predicated on the continuance of the existing RHI subsidy, 'alongside the income from the poultry'. He said that if the cost controls were introduced before the sheds were passed by planners, 'it will put in jeopardy the viability of many of these expansion plans'. That sentence ought to have caused alarm within DETI because here was evidence that a business was only able to expand because of the RHI subsidy. There was in that at least the potential for a conflict with EU state aid law.

There were no formal minutes of the UFU meeting. However, a handwritten note survived within DETI and reveals some of what was discussed. The note recorded the words 'budget – over spent'. It then said 'state aid 12%', a reference to a fear that the RHI scheme was so wildly generous that it may be in breach of EU state aid rules. The note also proves the participants discussed that the changes were at that point scheduled for October – even though that was weeks away from being publicly announced, evidence of how the UFU was getting an inside track about the looming changes. Then, highly significantly, the meeting discussed poultry farmers' use of RHI – the single biggest drain on the scheme because of their massive heat requirements. In essence, what DETI officials said at the meeting shows that they were aware of almost every one of the problems with the RHI scheme. And yet they were openly giving warning to the sector they knew had the highest heat demand that it would be reined in within two months. Osborne said that at the meeting 'DETI pointed out that subsidies could be exceeding the cost of biomass fuel'. That shows that Wightman had read the document which had been sent to him six days earlier.

In preparation for the meeting with the farmers, Cathal Ellis at the Department of Agriculture had drawn up at DETI's request a brief paper, which ought to have made Wightman, the recipient, realise why RHI was so popular. Ellis showed, in a simple table, that the cost of wood pellet fuel was significantly less than the subsidy. Wightman told the inquiry that on reading the paper he realised that 'the cost of heat production was lower than the medium biomass tariff'. However, he said that he rationalised it to himself and 'did not appreciate that the fuel cost being lower than the tariff created a perverse incentive to "burn to earn." This is because I knew the tariff had to also cover other costs'. But, explicit as the paper was, DETI did not realise just how much input those with a vested interest in RHI had in its creation. Ellis did not reveal that he had spoken to huge poultry processor Moy Park to discuss what would be a reasonable annual heat requirement for its poultry farmers. Ellis initially did not even disclose his contact with Moy Park to the inquiry but, when pressed about the paper he confirmed that he had spoken to Moy Park manager David Mark and 'would have run the average [heat] figures that we had generated past him'. And those figures were heavily dependent on what had been given to him by Forgrave – who was in the process of installing biomass boilers. When it was put to Ellis that Forgrave had obvious 'vested interests' of which he ought to have been aware, the civil servant said that he 'didn't really have any concerns that he was trying to game the scheme or make things better' for himself.

Ellis seems to have realised that what he was doing was irregular. When his paper was complete, he emailed a copy to DETI and then separately sent a copy to Forgrave, but told the farmer that it was 'probably wise if DETI don't know you've seen final version'. At the inquiry, Ellis said: 'I can't explain why I would've said that'. Ellis, Stormont's foremost expert in green energy, told the inquiry that although he was regularly attending and speaking at events where RHI was being openly marketed as 'cash for ash' he never saw such material because he would have spent much of his time giving talks or 'dashing' through where the trade stands were situated.

Cairns told the inquiry that he recalled a separate meeting around this time between himself, Bell, officials and the UFU – but could not find it recorded in the ministerial diary. He said that the UFU had been lobbying against suddenly reducing RHI payments. The UFU had long been close to the DUP, and the party's policies rarely diverged from those of the farming organisation.

Just 12 days before the UFU meeting, Wightman and Hughes had received an explicit warning about how some farmers were allegedly abusing RHI, a letter which ought to have prompted urgent action. On 10 July – coincidentally, two days after the submission to Bell – major green energy firm Solmatix wrote to Hughes about what it had heard were looming changes to the RHI. The detail set out by the company shows that it had a firm inside track on DETI's thinking – even though there had been no public announcement at this point. Although the letter was asking for a delay in cuts to the scheme, the company was at pains to distance itself from what it said was 'exploitation' by the poultry sector. Informing DETI of the abuse, the letter said: 'We also appreciate that a number of unscrupulous beneficiaries are not only taking full advantage of RHI support, but in many cases, notably within the poultry sector, appear to be actively exploiting it ... it would appear that those exploiting RHI are primarily large suppliers within the agri-sector. It is right that the changes should veto this continued exploitation.' Wightman said that he did not recall the letter. But Hughes told the inquiry that he remembered it and had discussed it with Wightman who had then agreed to set up a meeting with the company for 22 July – the same day as the UFU meeting – at which Hughes said: 'I don't recall any specific discussion on the issue of exploitation'.

However, although Wightman and Hughes later claimed to be ignorant of how RHI was open to abuse, another document suggests that might not be the full story. Five days after the Solmatix and UFU meetings, Wightman wrote the first draft of a formal document which would go to the Department of Finance seeking to regularise the irregular spending on RHI. In that first draft he wrote: 'The introduction of the tiered tariff will reduce the risk of "gaming" and installations being operated over and above the required kilowatt hours just to generate RHI income.' Somehow, at this late stage, it had got through to Wightman and Hughes that RHI was open to abuse. But it had also got through to Arlene Foster's handpicked adviser – and he was now to make a fatal move.

CHAPTER 11
FAMILY FIRST

On the night of July 20, Andrew Crawford sent an email that would give away the game – at least as far as he was concerned. Crawford sat with his iPad at 9pm and typed a 433-word email, which was never expected to go beyond the screen of a fellow DUP spad and so he made explicit what others in Stormont spoke of elliptically. The punch line of the email was an unvarnished articulation of what was a largely unspoken policy around the corridors of Stormont: extract as much money out of the Treasury as possible. Crawford's email was a belated response to the 8 July ministerial submission to Jonathan Bell, which Tim Cairns had forwarded to him. Crawford did not reply immediately but on 20 July the man to whom Cairns had been told to turn for advice responded with remarkable candour.

In setting out his understanding of the issues with RHI, Crawford demonstrated considerable knowledge of the scheme. Foster's spad said that 'the main problem with the non domestic rhi [*sic*] is that DETI have been caught out by the profile of applications. DETI has received a spike in the number of applications over the last number of months as a result of Moy Park suppliers buying biomass boilers ...' He went on: 'I believe that the majority of Moy Park producers who are going to convert to biomass will already have converted.' That sentence did not convey what had actually happened – and Crawford was unusually close to Moy Park. Just a few months earlier, the company had told Seamus Hughes that just 36% of its poultry sheds had converted to biomass and that it expected to get to 60% by the end of the year – there was room for Moy Park alone to drive a spike in applications, even if no one else applied to the scheme. Crawford told the inquiry he was unaware of those figures at that point.

Crawford suggested that Cairns speak directly to Moy Park manager David Mark and offered to 'set up a meeting for you with one of the main biomass installers if you wish'. Cairns contacted neither, telling the inquiry that he thought it would have been 'inappropriate' for him to speak to major beneficiaries of RHI at a time when the department was attempting to bring it under control. Demonstrating further knowledge of what was to come, Crawford told his colleague: 'The word on the street is that there is [*sic*]

going to be changes made in October and you are going to get a massive
spike in applications before this date …'

But it was the penultimate paragraph that exposed Crawford's belief
that it was acceptable to deliberately extract money from the Treasury for a
scheme which was known to be flawed, over budgeted and open to abuse.
He told Cairns:

> I am a little confused over what the problem is for the non-domestic
> scheme. The scheme is being funded from ami [sic] and therefore if
> we go over our 4% target all that will happen is that we will get more
> than our fair share of the UK pot. I would have thought that this is to
> NIs [sic] advantage bearing in mind we are likely to opt out of the cfd
> scheme [another green energy scheme] in a couple of years and may
> not be able to incentivise renewable generation after this date.

He went on: 'I suspect that the problem is that we have only got a guarantee
of funding for the next couple of years and long term we may have to pay for
the scheme out of the NI block [grant].' Then, showing his own knowledge
of the significance of the absence of tiering, he said: 'I think that it is sensible
that deti [sic] introduce a tariff and reduce their [sic] above a certain level
to stop potential "abuse" of the scheme but you need to be careful that they
don't reduce it too much.'

Crawford's argument about Northern Ireland benefiting from an RHI
overspend revealed an element of his thinking that potentially explains
the entire fiasco. It does not prove that he or anyone else in Stormont
had deliberately set the scheme up so that it would be very easy for it to
overspend. But, based on his flawed understanding that the Treasury was
paying the full bill, that would be an entirely logical way of ensuring that
Northern Ireland got 'more than its fair share'. Even if the scheme was not
deliberately set up to take advantage of what seems to have been viewed as
someone else's bank account, once it was running, had he or others in DETI
come to see the potential for such a 'benefit' by facilitating its implosion?
Again, there is no evidence of such deliberate action by Crawford or anyone
else prior to 2015.

But the practices of Stormont whereby many key discussions were never
written down and the inquiry's particular concerns about Crawford's ability

to produce all relevant documentation mean that we will never see the full picture of the spad's involvement in RHI.

In evidence to the inquiry, Crawford linked his thinking about RHI with his thinking about NIRO, which incentivised green electricity generation with payments known as Renewable Obligation Certificates (ROCs). As with RHI, in that scheme the department in which he and Foster had spent seven years had chosen to diverge from what the rest of the UK was doing, had tweaked the scheme to make it more generous in Northern Ireland and had managed to get the rest of the UK to pay most of the bill. Having done that – successfully in their view – and seen an explosion of investment in wind farms across Northern Ireland without having to pay for them, it would be natural to attempt to replicate that 'success' with another green energy subsidy.

In evidence to the inquiry, Crawford explained his email to Cairns by saying that he thought it was

> a perfectly reasonable argument for us [to go] above that 4% figure [more than Northern Ireland's proportionate share]. And, indeed, this is what happened with the ROCs scheme. So, there Northern Ireland went well above ... you know, looking at the total ROCs pot, Northern Ireland had more than its 4% share of that particular pot. And I was just replicating, I suppose, what happened there with coming across to the RHI scheme.

Crawford told the inquiry that he was just seeking to assist his colleague, and 'I never had any belief or understanding that my doing so would ever be construed as attempting to interfere with or set the policy direction that the department would take in relation to the matter'. Cairns had initially expected to have a decision on the 8 July submission by the time of Bell's return from holiday at the end of July. But Crawford's advice suddenly complicated what had seemed a straightforward decision to approve what officials were recommending.

****

It was a time of great industry for the Crawford family. Business was booming and money was being made. While Andrew Crawford was now eight years into his £85,000-a-year role as Arlene Foster's handpicked adviser, back in County Tyrone several of his relatives were turning to poultry to make their money – and RHI was facilitating their expansion plans.

As DETI was working on cutting the subsidy, Crawford's brother James Crawford had returned from working as an engineer in Asia and was constructing two large poultry houses, his cousin Richard Crawford was putting up his own two poultry houses and another cousin, John Crawford, was beginning work on a further two poultry houses – all of them to intensively produce chicken for Moy Park. By this point in July 2015 the spad's cousin Richard had three RHI boilers and was installing three more, his brother James was in the process of deciding to get two RHI boilers and his cousin John had not yet installed RHI boilers – but eventually would do so as well. All three relatives lived within ten miles of the spad's family home in Beragh outside Omagh, part of a rural community where information passed around freely, exchanged at livestock markets, in the village and in churches.

While Crawford was giving advice to Cairns in the summer of 2015, Cairns was oblivious to the Crawford family's major financial interest in the decision now facing DETI. Cairns spoke to Crawford and another DUP spad, Stephen Brimstone, about the 8 July submission to Bell and then on 16 July forwarded it to both of them. Unknown to Cairns, Brimstone was also conflicted, having just weeks earlier decided to install a non-domestic RHI boiler to heat his home. The submission had been sent to them as government advisers, paid handsomely from the public purse – not so that it would be of personal benefit to them or their families. The submission, as Crawford would have known, was confidential and of acute commercial sensitivity. However, he quickly forwarded it to his cousin Richard. For someone either considering or in the process of installing RHI boilers, as Richard was, it was a useful document to have. At the very least – even if, as the Crawfords say, he was already in the process of installing his final three boilers, it made clear that he should rush to get them accredited on the scheme because the subsidy was going to be cut and anyone who missed the deadline would lose out on a huge sum.

Andrew Crawford denied that his intention was to warn his cousin of the looming cuts. He said that he believed his cousin already had installed his boilers but was concerned about a retrospective cut to tariffs, and he was seeking to reassure him on that front. Richard Crawford said that he had installed the boilers 'in or around July 2015' and that the company which installed them had handled the paperwork for the RHI accreditation. However, while it is difficult to prove when Richard installed his boilers, he was only invoiced for them on 2 September – six weeks after he had been sent the ministerial submission. At the inquiry, barrister Joseph Aiken questioned whether a company needing to charge him £132,000 'would hold off billing for a couple of months'. The applications for accreditation to Ofgem indicate that the boilers were operational from 9 September.

Forwarding the July 2015 submission to Richard was not the first time that Andrew Crawford had passed confidential RHI documentation to his cousin. Two years earlier, the spad – at that point working in DETI with Foster – had done something almost identical. On a Saturday afternoon in July 2013 – just over eight months into the scheme – the DUP man forwarded to his cousin a confidential ministerial submission containing the consultation document for phase 2 of the RHI scheme. There was one striking similarity between the documents: they both contained implicit, but fairly obvious, warnings that the subsidy might be cut. The consultation document contained the proposed cost-control mechanism. Although it was subsequently abandoned by DETI, that was not known at the time. By passing the submission to his cousin, Richard had a 16-day advantage over ordinary members of the public, and had there been any sudden move to control the scheme he had been given longer to decide to get on board.

Although Andrew Crawford accepted at the inquiry that he should not have sent either of the confidential documents to his relative, he denied that there had been any benefit to him. He said: 'If I was going out to advantage my cousin – which I wasn't – he'd have installed a biomass boiler two years before that.' The spad told the inquiry that he had been selling cattle for his father at the local livestock market in July 2013 when he had met his cousin. On being told that he was constructing new poultry houses, he said: 'I suspect the debate came up about why he didn't put in a biomass boiler … the scheme was undersubscribed and we were encouraging more people into the scheme.' Crawford said that he thought his cousin had asked for information about RHI and because the submission was fresh in his memory he had sent that to him. The inquiry pressed him on why he would have sent a ministerial submission – written in the slightly peculiar language of bureaucracy – to his farmer cousin, rather than simply sending him a link to the public page on DETI's website, which was marketing the scheme to the public. Crawford accepted that at the time he knew that what he was sending was a confidential government document but that he 'couldn't answer why my conscience didn't stop me doing it; I just can't answer that here today … I shouldn't have sent it through to him. I want to apologise for it. It was wrong'.

Richard installed his first boilers in April 2014. In this period, his powerful Stormont cousin was taking a keen interest in RHI and would continue to do so. Andrew Crawford initially told the inquiry that he did not know at the time that Richard had installed the boilers, but then immediately corrected himself to say: 'I'm not sure when I would've first seen that unit, er, in terms of being heated with biomass'. Just two months later, his brother James got a quote for biomass boilers. After returning to Northern Ireland from India, he had bought a field beside land owned by Andrew Crawford on which to build a poultry unit. The 6 June 2014 quote which James received included two graphs, one for 'RHI income' and the other for 'cumulative savings per annum', which communicated starkly how lucrative RHI would be for him. It told him that the system would have paid for itself before the end of the third year – with 17 more years of huge payments to come.

The farmer was told that he would see savings of more than £300,000 and then an RHI income of £250,000. On the face of it, it was a fairly astounding proposition. James's brother was the spad who had helped design the scheme and who was in the department running it. It might have seemed obvious to at least ask him if the figures were credible or should be treated with caution. The two men certainly were not in any way estranged. Most weekends and during the holidays, Crawford would return from Belfast and stay at the family home – under the same roof as James. When Andrew Crawford was asked at the inquiry if he had any discussion with his brother about these sorts of documents, the DUP man began a lengthy answer that did not address the question. When pulled back to the question, he eventually said: 'I do not recall any discussions, certainly at this time, about this.' But when pressed further he firmed up that 'I do not recall' to an outright denial. Barrister Joseph Aiken asked him: 'How likely is it that you, his brother and the special adviser to the minister who brought the scheme in that he's thinking of participating in, didn't put this document in front of your nose to say, "Andrew, surely that can't be right"?' The former spad replied: 'Well, I'm very clear that he didn't put it in front of my nose. I had no discussion with him about this document; I've no recollection of seeing this document ever before.' Later, he said clearly: 'No, I didn't see the document.' But then he again changed his answer, correcting himself to say: 'Sorry, I've no recollection of seeing it.'

There was another member of the Crawford family who was to benefit from their spad relative's inside track on Stormont's plans. Andrew Crawford discussed the 8 July submission to Bell with his brother-in-law, Wallace Gregg, and then forwarded the submission to him. Crawford knew that Gregg was considering installing biomass boilers at that point but he would ultimately decide against doing so. No email was produced at the public inquiry to show that Crawford forwarded the 8 July submission to his brother James. However, given the pattern with other relatives, he was asked by Aiken: 'Is the reason there's no email … because you just told him? Why would you send it on to your cousin and not tell your brother?' Crawford replied: 'I'd no reason to send it to my brother, because I knew that it would be in place, you know. Did we have a discussion? I don't know whether we'd a discussion about it or not.' Aiken then asked: 'Would it not seem to you highly odd if you sent a government submission, knowing you shouldn't, to your cousin, who's interested in the content, you think – he says he didn't read it – and you wouldn't tell your brother, the same information, who's doing the exact same thing as your cousin?' Crawford replied somewhat uncertainly: 'I had, I suppose; there was no motivation to send it to my brother. Um, in terms; he had new installations just going in from the start. There was no issue in terms of getting them in before any deadline that was proposed.' James – who the Crawfords said installed his boilers in July – would ultimately get two boilers accredited on the scheme before the cut in tariffs.

There was one more family member to benefit from RHI. On 16 and 17 November 2015, the last two days when the lucrative and uncapped 'burn to earn' tariff was available, John Crawford of Augher applied for three 99 kW RHI boilers to be accredited on the RHI. By the time RHI had been reined in – after what others alleged was Andrew Crawford's attempts to delay that happening, something he denied – his relatives had 11 RHI boilers between them. There has never been any suggestion that any of the Crawfords were fraudulently claiming or exploiting RHI. However, given that as poultry farmers they had a high heat demand, it was enormously beneficial to them. Assuming a 50% load factor common for poultry units – and much less than some poultry farmers were claiming for – the 11 boilers could have been expected to pull in more than £6 million between them. Under prolonged and deeply sceptical questioning at the inquiry, Crawford repeatedly insisted that he had not been aware from his family of how lucrative RHI was and denied that the information he had sent his relatives had been financially beneficial to them.

In early 2017, the inquiry had written to Crawford and asked him to state any times where he was aware that anyone involved in RHI – including himself – had broken rules 'including, but not limited to, by means of making premature or unauthorised disclosures' or 'acted in … any way where they had a real or perceived conflict of interest'. He replied to that question by saying: 'I am not aware of any instances.' When Crawford appeared before the inquiry, Aiken told him that the inquiry had obtained a witness statement from Richard Crawford in which he disclosed the July 2013 email Andrew Crawford had forwarded the ministerial submission. When asked why he had not initially disclosed to the inquiry the existence of the communication with his cousin, Andrew Crawford said:

> Because when I done [*sic*] my first statement to the inquiry, in it I said that I didn't have access to my government account and this email came from my government account and I had no recollection of sending this email until I seen [*sic*] it coming back through in terms of the documentation that was produced from the inquiry.

That was not the only instance where the former spad did not immediately make the inquiry aware of information, which was important to its work but highly embarrassing for him.

The inquiry was suspicious about some of Crawford's responses to its requests for documentation. As with all witnesses, Crawford had in early 2017 been served with the first of several formal notices issued under Section 21 of the Inquiries Act, which compelled him to produce all documentation relevant to the inquiry's work.

But in September 2017 the inquiry wrote a stern letter to Crawford after it had found an email from him to his friend Mark Anderson in November 2016. The letter from inquiry solicitor Patrick Butler said that it seemed that the email was relevant to the inquiry's work, had not been disclosed by Crawford and added: 'At the moment, it appears to the inquiry that there has been a prima facie breach of the requirements of [the order for disclosure].' Crawford told the inquiry that he had 'no recollection' of the email to Anderson and said 'it is apparent to me that this email must have been deleted as it did not appear when I performed a search of my emails'. That was the second time that the inquiry had to write to Crawford. Four months earlier, as the inquiry was in its infancy, it had similarly written to Crawford's solicitor 'expressing concern about compliance with section 21 notices requiring the provision of documentation', in particular text messages. Crawford had responded to that by saying that he would only have used his departmental BlackBerry device for text messages about RHI, and it was now in the custody of the department. However, the inquiry then became aware – based on text messages disclosed by other individuals – that Crawford had been using a personal mobile phone to conduct text communications about RHI. In response, Crawford told the inquiry that some text messages may have been deleted but he had found 12 relevant messages 'of which I had no recollection' and belatedly submitted them.

****

But it wasn't just his own family who Crawford put first: it was also that of his party leader, Peter Robinson. When the former spad appeared before the inquiry in April 2018 and was asked about leaking confidential government documents to his relatives, he insisted that his actions had been a thoughtless one-off. Speaking slowly and gravely, Aiken asked him: 'Were you in the habit – and I want you to be very careful and think through what I'm asking you before you answer it – of sending material that you received in the course of your role as special adviser to people outside, whether that be family, friends, anyone else, but outside of the government service?' Crawford replied firmly: 'No, I wasn't. Was I in the habit of leaking consultation documents? No, I wasn't ... I suspect because it was my cousin my guard was down.' Aiken pressed the witness on whether – in light of his statement that he did not remember forwarding the document until it was brought to his attention – he had done so on other occasions but the inquiry had not uncovered it. Dr Crawford said: 'I do not have any recollection; I do not believe that I sent any other communication out ...' Aiken said: 'But, you understand, you didn't remember any of these?' Crawford replied: 'Yes, but ... I don't want to say that it was widespread practice sending out documents; it was not widespread practice sending out documents.'

But that was far from the full story. When back before the inquiry the following month, Crawford admitted that forwarding confidential documents outside Stormont was not a one-off. The former spad was confronted with new evidence recovered from his old government email account, which showed that he had sent confidential information to Gareth Robinson, the lobbyist son of the then First Minister. Crawford admitted that the lobbyist had received preferential treatment because of who his father was. This time, Crawford's intentions were fairly explicit – in a covering email to Robinson Jr, Crawford had made clear that the confidential information was for one of his major corporate clients. The material was particularly striking because of the suggestion that his requests on behalf of paying customers were treated uniquely because his father was the First Minister, a nepotistic approach to politics entirely contrary to the standards by which public officials are bound.

Robinson Jr had long attracted scrutiny not only from journalists and rivals of the DUP but from other Belfast lobbyists who wondered how he operated. A former DUP councillor, he ran Verbatim Communications, a company which only appeared to employ its owner and whose publicly declared accounts suggested it was a modest operation. He had threatened to sue the *News Letter* in 2015 – just a few months after Crawford was forwarding him information – when it revealed that he was working for two energy firms and asked whether he was lobbying a DUP department to pursue policies favourable to those firms. On 20 March 2015, Crawford forwarded an email to Gareth Robinson following a verbal discussion about two of his major renewable energy clients – Gaelectric and Lightsource.

Crawford said he met two senior figures from one of the companies as a result of Robinson Jr's lobbying. The document attached to the email was a Whitehall consultation about UK-wide changes to the energy market and it was not due to be published for three more days, having been sent to

Stormont in confidence. Robinson Jr asked in response to the document: 'Is this for Richard or Patrick?', a reference to Richard Green from Lightsource and Patrick McClughan from Gaelectric, to which Crawford replied: 'It's for Richard.'

Under questioning at the inquiry, Crawford said that he was concerned that 'Northern Ireland companies may miss out' on the consultation. However, company records show that although both companies were operating in Northern Ireland – and were major beneficiaries of the NIRO green electricity subsidy – Gaelectric was headquartered in Dublin and Lightsource was run from London.

More than a year earlier, Crawford had forwarded to Robinson Jr an email which had attached to it a privileged legal document related to the department's judicial review of another Stormont department in relation to planning permission. Crawford told the inquiry:

> I don't have a clear recollection of the sequence of events but I suspect Gareth asked for – and why he asked for that information I can only assume; I don't have 100% knowledge – but was wanting to know about the process in terms of the timelines for the legal case and what not and that is laid out in the body [of the email] …

It was put to Crawford that he could have forwarded the email but deleted the legally sensitive document attached. He accepted that but claimed he had been 'clumsy' in not doing so.

Crawford suggested he may have been asked to send the document by Peter Robinson – something he subsequently denied – and added: 'I can't recall the discussions that I had with Gareth on the particular issue. Obviously, Gareth was Peter's son and because of that I tended to respond to his queries probably quicker than I may have responded to some other PR companies' queries.' The matter of fact tone in which Crawford gave his evidence of preferential treatment for Robinson Jr suggested that he did not think that it was at all remarkable.

DETI was not the only department being lobbied by Robinson Jr. Documents released under an environmental transparency law show that he contacted DUP minister Edwin Poots personally about a planning issue, rather than going through his department. Robinson Jr emailed Poots's private email address. The correspondence was only held by the department and therefore within the knowledge of civil servants who released it because Poots forwarded it to his department.

****

On the day of the 8 July submission to Jonathan Bell, and just over a week before Crawford passed it to his relatives, another issue was troubling senior DUP figures. That day a blog in which loyalist activist Jamie Bryson alleged DUP corruption around the NIRO energy subsidy was immediately brought to the attention of the then Finance Minister, Foster. Crawford, forwarded it to Foster that night and she quickly replied to say: 'That's not good. Is TJ [top DUP spad Timothy Johnston] aware?' Several DUP MLAs were unhappy over the proposal from Bell to soften the blow for some major green energy companies – at the expense of electricity consumers.

Inquiry barrister Donal Lunny said that Bryson's blog was 'to do with, I suppose, what he perceived to be some form of corruption in relation to two companies that were affected by changes to NIRO'. Lunny said that, as with RHI, 'the NIRO involves very large amounts of money'. At the inquiry, chairman Sir Patrick Coghlin was intrigued at how the internet allegations from the young loyalist had gone straight to the top of the DUP – while Crawford said that he had never passed on to Foster much of what he knew about RHI in that period. Coghlin asked: 'What is it about whoever Mr Bryson is ... that [it] had to go to these dizzy levels of government?' Coghlin's bafflement at why Bryson's blog went to the top of the party was understandable and, given the constant swirl of lurid internet allegations, it seemed strange that online claims would be taken seriously by senior DUP figures. However, there was a crucial political context.

The previous week independent TD Mick Wallace had used Dáil privilege to allege that major Belfast law firm Tughans had moved £7 million to an off-shore bank account on the Isle of Man after the biggest property sale in the history of the island of Ireland – the £1.3 billion sale the previous year of property loans held by the Republic of Ireland's 'bad bank' NAMA. Wallace's claim that the £7 million was 'earmarked for a Northern Ireland politician' led the news in Northern Ireland for days. The loans had been sold to US vulture fund Cerberus after a rival bidder pulled out when it realised that leading Belfast businessman Frank Cushnahan had been in line for a £5 million payment as part of the politically sensitive sale. Among Cushnahan's powerful friends was Peter Robinson and on 6 July – two days before the NIRO blog – Bryson had alleged that some of the Isle of Man money was for Robinson. Later that year Bryson would make the allegation to a Stormont committee investigating the affair. Robinson has consistently dismissed the allegations and said that he did nothing wrong. But he was under enormous personal and political pressure in this period, particularly from within his own party. Some senior DUP figures who had long been unhappy either at his centralised style of leadership or the direction of the party saw a chance to further destabilise him. Just two days after tiering was finally introduced in the RHI scheme in November of that year and days after the Fresh Start Agreement with Sinn Féin, Robinson announced that he was stepping down as First Minister and DUP leader, saying that it was time to retire after 'stabilising' Stormont.

****

While Foster said that Crawford did not pass on to her what he was learning about the RHI problem in this period, he was talking to others in their department about the scheme – and his actions raised eyebrows. Sometime in summer 2015 – seemingly in late July – Crawford spoke to mid-ranking Department of Finance official, Michelle Scott, about the scheme. During a brief phone call, which stuck in her mind, the supply officer said that Crawford 'asked why [the department] had an issue with the RHI scheme'. She added: 'To the best of my recollection when Mr Crawford commented that it was fully AME funded, I said we didn't know that it would be fully AME funded but were looking into the situation.' The official informed her boss, Emer Morelli, who passed it up the line to her boss, the budget director, Mike Brennan. All three of them described the contact by Crawford as 'unusual' because he would normally go through more senior officials.

Crawford was decidedly uncertain as to whether he had told Foster, the Finance Minister, about what he said he was describing to Cairns as a looming financial 'tsunami' involving irregular expenditure in the department they had both just left and involving a scheme they had set up. When asked if he told Foster, Crawford said:

Well, er, you know, in terms of, the minister was aware I was speaking to Timothy Cairns on the — on an issue to do with the RHI. You know, I think she's already, you know, it's already appeared in her evidence that she knew, from a meeting at the end of June, that the RHI was becoming an issue … I can't say, at this stage —. I can't say whether I sent her through or made her aware of the problem at this stage.

He added: 'It's something that I should, you know, looking at it now, I should have done. Did I update her verbally on it? I just cannot confirm that one way or the other.' Foster was more emphatic, telling the inquiry that Crawford had definitely not told her about the issue.

The overlap between Crawford's Stormont role and the business activities of his relatives did not stop with passing information to them. The spad told the inquiry of a remarkable coincidence, which brought him into contact with a key RHI beneficiary on 17 July, the day after Crawford received the RHI submission from Cairns. While working in the field adjacent to the construction of his brother's poultry sheds, Crawford said that he saw a vehicle arrive. The occupant was David Robinson of R&S Biomass, one of the biggest biomass boiler installers, who was at his brother's farm to install an RHI boiler. The spad approached Robinson, unaware of his identity, he said, and in a 20-minute conversation was told that the industry was aware of the looming subsidy cuts and as a result orders were flying in at such speed that boiler piping was in short supply. He also informed Crawford that there were allegations of the scheme being abused because it was so generous.

Crawford said that he had then met senior Moy Park managers David Mark and Brian Gibson at his brother's poultry unit less than two weeks later but this had been 'unplanned contact' as they were showing the facility to 'financiers connected to Moy Park' and that they did not discuss RHI. Mark agreed that the conversation had been 'really pleasantries' and that he had no recollection of discussing RHI. Both Mark and Crawford told the inquiry that they had no discussions about RHI in this period. Intriguingly, however, less than three weeks later Mark emailed a Moy Park colleague to say: 'Got this from a contact in Government — have removed names just in case we circulate — can fill you in'. Beneath that comment was a paragraph, which said that DETI were moving 'towards impeding the abuse that has been taking place within the ... poultry sector where they are being blamed for running their system night and day even without poultry present'.

Mark told the inquiry that he could not recall who his 'contact in government' had been. However, precisely the same paragraph he forwarded had been sent the previous day to Crawford. It had originated with boiler installer BS Holdings and had been forwarded to the spad by Howard Hastings, a leading hotelier whose role in tourism brought him into contact with Crawford. Confronted with that at the inquiry, Mark admitted that he could 'see the logic' of his contact having been Crawford – but insisted 'I have no record to show that'. When he subsequently appeared before the inquiry, Crawford insisted that 'I've no knowledge of sending it to Moy Park' but conceded that having been presented with the evidence 'I can only conclude that it came from myself'.

On one reading, the encounter on the farm of James Crawford was an extraordinary coincidence – that senior figures from the company benefiting most from RHI should at this precise moment bump into the man who it would later be alleged was at this point attempting to keep the scheme as lucrative as possible for as long as possible. On another reading, it was entirely natural that Crawford – who came from a rural community, whose family were poultry farmers and who had high-level political interaction with senior Moy Park executives – would rub shoulders with such people as he went about other business. The brief encounter may be irrelevant to RHI. But it is worth recording because what was to follow would suggest that Crawford was now moving to advocate for Moy Park – even though doing so would be at the expense of taxpayers.

CHAPTER 12
IN THE SHADOWS

It quickly became apparent to DETI's senior civil servants that something highly unusual was going on around RHI. The urgent submission to Jonathan Bell had gone on 8 July. A decision had been expected within days but a fortnight later there was no indication of an imminent verdict from their political master – nor any sense of urgency about the money streaming out of the department. On 23 July, DETI Deputy Secretary Chris Stewart spoke to Tim Cairns by phone. The pair had worked together before and had a good relationship so the conversation was relaxed. Stewart was attempting to establish why there was still no decision and rather than finding Cairns apologetic or giving him assurance of a speedy move, the spad was kicking back against the proposals.

In an email to Wightman that day, Stewart relayed that Cairns was 'concerned that the adoption of tariff control legislation in October may lead to a further spike in demand, and suggested that it might be delayed (I countered that we already have a spike in demand, and a well-informed industry will keep demand high until controls are in place).' The spad's suggestion about a spike was drawing on Crawford's email three days earlier, which had said there would be a 'massive spike'. But Cairns's proposal – keeping the unamended tariff for longer – was nonsensical if he was genuinely attempting to limit expenditure. Wightman replied to Stewart that day to say that 'the industry knows that tariff changes are likely to happen in the autumn so installations are already being accelerated to beat the deadline. We reckon that between 60–70% of all poultry houses for instance have already switched to biomass. If we delay the tariff changes, the remaining 30–40% might get through at the current (higher) rates.'

Five days later, Stewart was holding a scheduled update on energy issues with Energy Division Director John Mills when Cairns called in. The spad had been attempting to speak to Stewart about RHI and, seeing that Mills was also there, he spoke to them both. During a detailed discussion about the scheme, Stewart developed the impression that Cairns needed something he could 'sell' to other unnamed DUP members 'as a "do the minimum" approach.' Stewart's view of Cairns was that 'he personally had no objection or was raising no challenge to cost controls … I got the clear impression from Timothy that he wanted to bring this to a conclusion but needed a bit of help'. 'That help came in the form of an email Mills sent to Cairns two days later in which he pressed home the need for an urgent decision. Mills told the inquiry that although the email 'looks like a note to him ... it was intended for him to hand out to others to say "look, we need to be getting on with this". The message referred to the 'urgent need to put appropriate measures in place to ensure proper control of budgets', adding that Cairns had said that it was important to use as much of the available Treasury money as possible and they did not want to 'over-react' to the sudden rise in demand for the scheme – the very points Crawford had been raising. Mills also said in the note that cost controls were 'an important safeguard against over-use' and 'it would be very difficult to justify inaction'.

Mills told the inquiry: 'I think by this stage I was starting to think "this is just deliberate delaying" because the gist of the conversation [from Cairns] was "I need something to convince those I need to convince that we need to proceed" and hence the note that he could then use.' When asked if Cairns told him that was why he needed the note, Mills said: 'He did ... he needed the note to give to others.' Asked by inquiry chairman Sir Patrick Coghlin who those people were, he said: 'The party apparatus is what I took it to be, again using the phrase "the party" meaning in the generality, the political process – other special advisers or whatever political setup was in place.' Mills said that he viewed the intra-DUP machinations as something which was Cairns's responsibility. With something approaching disdain, he added: 'That's a world that I don't inhabit and don't want to inhabit'.

Phone records obtained by the inquiry showed that between the meeting and Mills sending the email Cairns phoned Crawford and they spoke for just under four minutes. Cairns then forwarded Mills's email to Crawford with the comment: 'It's an introduction of tariff controls to stop misuse rather than full reform from 1st Oct. Any thoughts'. Crawford replied the following night. He began by saying: 'I think that you will need to make changes from the 1st October as the system at the moment has no upper limit to the amount of support.' Crawford would come to rely on that sentence, arguing that it showed that he told Cairns to proceed with tiering when officials wanted it, rather than attempting to delay the change. But Crawford's defence is greatly undermined by the rest of that email. He went on to say:

One thing to consider is increasing the number of hours from moving from the higher to lower tariff. Moy Park houses currently run for approximately 6000 hrs for a 99 kW boiler when in their normal production cycle. The current problem is that it pays producers to heat houses when their houses are empty as the rates are attractive and some use boilers for [more] than 6000 hrs per annum. If a Moy Park producer puts in a 199kw boiler he can expect to run for approximately 3000 hours. From these calculations you can see why Moy Park producers will be in a rush to refit their houses before the 1st October. If you increased the step from 1314 to 3000 there will be no incentive for producers to install before the 1 October.

At first glance, it is Crawford's knowledge of the potential for RHI being abused that jumps out of that paragraph. Crawford told the inquiry that by this point 'I knew there was nothing to stop people, effectively, running boilers 24/7 and getting paid for it'. But the really startling element of the paragraph was actually what preceded that. In essence, Crawford was proposing that although tiering should be introduced when the officials wanted it, it should be done in a way that would not make the scheme a penny less lucrative for Moy Park's contract farmers. Crawford's proposal would have seen tiering introduced in name only because many of the heaviest RHI users would have barely, if at all, been worse off even after the scheme was changed in the way he suggested.

Although it sounded technical, his calculation was very simple. A 99 kW boiler running for 6,000 hours produces virtually the same heat as a 199 kW boiler running for 3,000 hours. DETI's plan was to belatedly follow the GB scheme where only the first 1,314 hours were paid at a high tariff. Crawford's plan was a cunning attempt to circumvent that by introducing tiering on paper – but bastardising tiering so that it would do nothing to address the huge sums going to Moy Park's farmers. It was an audacious proposal and the explicit reference to Moy Park left no doubt as to who he thought should be foremost in the minds of DETI in relation to RHI.

Energy expert Keith MacLean, the inquiry's technical assessor, was forensic in deconstructing what he had been attempting to do. MacLean put it to Arlene Foster's long-standing right-hand man that on the basis of fairly simple arithmetic, it seems that what you're proposing is actually a way of maintaining exactly the same income for the poultry industry that they were having before [because your proposal] would mean that they would all get the higher tariff for all of the 3,000 hours, and therefore maintain exactly the high income that was driving the behaviour that you describe that allows them to heat the houses when they're empty.

Crawford argued that 'by doing that, you would stop the rush of people coming in before the changes were taking place'. An incredulous MacLean replied: 'Of course you would – by giving them just as much money as before.'

Crawford then argued that it would at least stop the running of boilers for the entire year. Coghlin said: 'What this is is a sales pitch for Moy Park.' Crawford insisted: 'No, it's not; I don't believe so.' Coghlin then asked him: 'Why 3,000? Because 3,000 is what Moy Park need. Now, unless you have, Dr Crawford, a really helpful reasoned explanation, that is what you have put, in English, in your email.' Crawford said: 'My knowledge at that time, it took the 3,000 hours to heat a house. It's not to heat it when it's empty; it's to heat it when there was a crop in the house.' Spotting that Crawford was now justifying his perverse proposal because it would be good for Moy Park, Coghlin interjected: 'Exactly, but that's what Moy Park need, or want, or told you.'

Crawford said that the message from Cairns had referred to a huge RHI demand from the poultry sector and so he was attempting to find a means of addressing that. An exasperated Coghin said: 'What you're saying here is "there is a special interest here and that is the poultry interest and Moy Park need 3,000 hours"'. As before, Cairns quickly acted as Crawford suggested and enquired about his proposal being implemented. By now officials were suspicious. Their response was rapid and robust. Mills replied on 11 August with a brusque dismissal. He asked what the justification would be for Northern Ireland adopting different tiers to GB and said that 'we would have no basis for 3000 hours, (or indeed any other figure)' and warned that it would be in breach of EU state aid law. He then highlighted the most obvious problem for a department urgently seeking to cut expenditure, pointing out that the new tiering mechanism 'would not address our requirement to bring spending back under control'.

DETI's senior civil servants – by now both exasperated and alarmed – escalated the issue significantly. Stewart passed Mills's dismissal to Cairns. But, lest his colleague's blunt rejection did not sufficiently convey their thinking, Stewart warned the spad that the proposal would 'raise an accounting officer issue for Andrew [McCormick]'. That was a barely veiled threat that McCormick would not be able to justify the scheme as a defensible use of public money. In those circumstances, he had the option of asking Bell for a ministerial direction – effectively asking Bell to order him in writing to implement the pro-Moy-Park proposal. It was a nuclear option, which would trigger formal warning bells in both the Department of Finance and the Northern Ireland Audit Office. McCormick later said that one of his greatest regrets about his role in the scandal was that he did not ask for a ministerial direction. Cairns told the inquiry that if such a request had come, he and Bell would have dropped the issue.

Having received Stewart's warning, Cairns made no effort to argue for his proposal – reinforcing the sense that he was the messenger and Crawford the decision-maker. He again forwarded the officials' response to Crawford with the comment: 'Seems we have no choice but to proceed on the previous sub from early July. Ie. follow GB policy from 1st Oct'. Although there is an element of mystery around what Crawford was doing in this period and why he was doing it, there is no doubt that the impact of his interventions was to delay the scheme being brought under control.

Mills believed that the pro-Moy-Park proposal was just another stalling tactic to eat up another fortnight of officials' time – while across Northern Ireland boilers were being installed as fast as installers could operate. He told the inquiry that it was 'commonly thought' within the department in summer 2015 that Crawford was the individual in the shadows 'pulling the strings' to delay the scheme being made less lucrative. He said that although he did not have 'first hand knowledge' of Crawford's involvement at the time he suspected he was directing Cairns. Mills said the two civil servants immediately above him – Stewart and McCormick – 'felt that [Crawford's] influence was very great in terms of how decisions in DETI [were taken] and that Tim Cairns more or less had to go with Andrew Crawford's suggestions'.

Stewart, a serious and understated senior mandarin, told the inquiry that there had been unmistakable 'resistance' from the DUP as DETI sought to address the scheme's overspend. Stewart said his understanding was that

Cairns was the conduit for resistance emanating from outside DETI, rather than the source of it, with the suggestions he was communicating as 'a result of party considerations'. Stewart said it was not uncommon for a minister to disagree with advice and take time to consider what to do, 'but normally you would know what the concern is'. In this case, he was alarmed because there was 'a lack of rational argument, or counter-argument, coming back … it seemed to me that what we were getting was not rational or reasoned counter-argument, but resistance … I could see no good reason for that happening and that's the aspect of it that's unique'. Expressing bafflement as to what had happened more than two years earlier, Stewart went on: 'The degree of resistance … to proposals that were thought to be modest and proportionate was surprising. I have not encountered a similar phenomenon at any time during my career, which includes serving ministers from five political parties (local and national).' Stewart said that he initially

> put the benign interpretation on it, which was [that] whoever the author was of this resistance or reluctance [was] feeling that officials were being too cautious and were at risk of hobbling a good scheme before it was necessary to do so. As the resistance went on, I found it – and still find it – more and more difficult to have such a benign interpretation of it. But I don't know what the actual reason was for it.

Crawford was clear to the inquiry that he was not pushing to delay the scheme being brought under control: 'I certainly never indicated to Timothy Cairns that he should seek as late a date as possible for the introduction of cost controls.'

McCormick said that documentation revealed by the inquiry 'would suggest that Andrew Crawford was aware of the perverse incentive within the scheme and the excessive use of heat, and of the forthcoming "massive spike" in applications' and had 'detailed knowledge and understanding of the problems with the scheme from the summer of 2015 onwards.' He said that when a year and a half later he publicly named Crawford as the individual believed to have been attempting to delay tiering, he received a phone call from Cairns. He said that Cairns had told him that Crawford had not been the only influence in this period and that DUP MLA William Irwin had also wanted to keep the high tariffs available for longer. He said that Cairns also told him that there was some substance to Bell's allegation about Timothy Johnston having a role in the delay.

At the inquiry, Cairns said that his reference to Irwin had been 'flippant' and along the lines of 'for goodness sake, William Irwin phoned me once on behalf of a constituent – how many DUP people do you want me to name, Andrew?' As a huge dairy farmer and chairman of Stormont's agriculture committee, there was some logic to Irwin receiving queries about RHI, whether from the UFU or individual farmers. But the reference to Johnston was more significant and consistent with what Cairns would later say publicly – that Johnston had 'started the process' that delayed an end to cash for ash. Cairns told the inquiry that during summer 2015 he had on 'at least 10 occasions in meetings and private conversations' attempted to get Stewart and other officials to investigate allegations of RHI abuse which he was receiving. Stewart said that was an exaggeration. However, he accepted that on perhaps two occasions Cairns had raised concerns about possible fraud. Those concerns, he said, 'were clearly serious and needed to be looked into but [were] not in any way specific and not in any way containing any specific information that could be followed up'.

Trevor Cooper, DETI's finance director, said that Claire Hughes, an independent member of the departmental board and a member of the board's audit committee, had told him 'at some point in the autumn of 2015' that she was a claimant under the less lucrative domestic RHI. He said that he recalled her telling him that the installer 'mentioned to her that people may generate heat excessively under the non-domestic scheme' and he believed that 'the poultry sector was mentioned'. Cooper said he reported it to his boss, Eugene Rooney, who asked if the independent board member would put it on the record – which Cooper said she would not.

Hughes, a former bank manager who by this time was working as a professional matchmaker, told the inquiry that she had an air source heat pump installed in her new home in 2008. But it had failed two years later during the big freeze of 2010 and she had replaced it with a new heat pump in February 2011 – it was now eligible for RHI. Hughes told the inquiry that the installer was at her home in January or February 2015 to service the pump. She said that he told her at that point that the scheme was open to abuse and 'there were reports of farmers heating empty sheds and churches being heated when no one was in them'. She said she mentioned that to

Cooper and other board members on 5 June 2015 but denied that she had ever been asked to put it on the record.

****

By late August, civil servants' misinterpretation of another development contributed to a reduction in their sense of urgency. DETI believed that it had suddenly been given extra money by the Treasury. A spreadsheet of its budgets was updated by Stormont's Department of Finance to reflect DETI's forecast for expenditure. However, this administrative update was misinterpreted as a sign that the funding was unlimited after all and they just had to ask for more money. As late as 7 October, that belief persisted. In an email to Crawford that day, Mills clearly viewed the fact – as he believed – that London was paying as significant. He told the Finance Minister's spad that DETI was 'still fighting with your officials on the funding; they will end up forcing closure of the scheme (and it's not even DEL [Stormont's budget]) at this rate'.

The fact that the pot of money for the scheme might have been virtually bottomless ought to have been irrelevant. By now it was known to officials that RHI was seriously flawed. They had received multiple reports of abuse or suspicious behaviour and knew that huge sums were going to individual claimants. They also knew that there may be a conflict with EU state aid law – because the scheme was so wildly generous that it was now an illegal form of state subsidy. Yet their primary concern appears to have been over which pot of taxpayers' money the scheme was funded. As long as DETI itself was not having to pick up the bill, officials appear to have been far less exercised about the fact that public money was being spent in a way that was at best questionable.

But even amid this confusion, Bernie Brankin in DETI's finance division emailed McCormick on 24 August to warn that 'RHI AME is not standard AME. DECC has confirmed that penalties are applied for overspending'. Therefore, even based on the questionable logic that if DETI was not paying for the scheme it was less important to fix it, there was evidence that ought to have caused alarm. Perhaps that reminder from Brankin caused a jolt of fear for those at the top of DETI. The day she sent that message to McCormick, the summer of indecision came to a climax in Netherleigh House. As the civil service and political leadership of the department gathered for a lunchtime meeting of DETI's senior management team, discussion began about RHI.

By this stage Bell had hardly been in the department for a month and a half and he was now late for the meeting. As they waited for the minister, Cairns said that he threw out, as a last half-hearted attempt to secure what he believed his party wanted, a question as to whether 1 October was the latest possible date they could accept. Cairns said that he did so in the expectation that officials would say 'yes'. His motivation, he said, was that it was a defence in case anyone inside the party questioned whether he really had done everything to delay the changes as long as possible. That meant that if a boiler installed complained or if 'Moy Park comes ranting and raving to the party', the DUP could say that it had done everything possible to delay the changes, he said. To the shock of Cairns and McCormick, Mills made 'a strange noise' of contemplation and then after several seconds volunteered a later date. What others at the meeting did not realise was that just that morning Wightman and Hughes had been discussing that it was now going to be difficult to bring in the changes by 1 October and early November was more realistic.

In the formal meeting, Cairns said that Bell expressed no particular view on what was being discussed but turned to him and asked whether others would be happy with the decision – a reference Cairns took to mean Crawford and Johnston. Coghlin said: 'You get the impression that the minister simply sat there while this debate went on until somebody said "right, that's it"'. Over coming days, Cairns communicated the outcome to Johnston and Crawford. He said that Crawford seemed satisfied. Three days after the decision had been taken, phone records show that Cairns phoned Crawford multiple times with one of the calls lasting more than half an hour.

Yet again, minutes of the crucial meeting had not been taken. The closest thing to a contemporaneous record was an email from Mills three days later in which he told McCormick that after a discussion with the minister 'we have revised the position to reflect an implementation date of early November (probably not before the 3rd)'. Even at this stage, formal approval only came – in signatures from Bell and Cairns – nine days after the meeting where the real decision was taken. It had taken eight weeks for Bell to sign what had been presented to him as an 'urgent' need for a decision about a scheme he had been told was over budget. And when the decision finally was taken, it was to delay the changes he had been told were necessary.

Bell said that he had been given insufficient information with which to grasp the urgency of what was before him. Over his weeks of holiday, he said that neither officials nor his spad had attempted to contact him – which they accepted. Cairns said that part of the reluctance in contacting Bell was that he had left instructions for no meetings when he was away in the first three weeks of August. But the spad admitted that he and McCormick 'should have jumped in the ministerial car and gone up [to Bell's "summer house"]' or phoned the minister. Stewart's sense was that the submission had not reached the minister during the entire summer period until the meeting in late August, although Mills believed that it had gone to Bell much earlier. Cairns said that officials had not been candid with him about their concerns about what he was up to. He said:

> I wish they'd come to me and said, 'What are ya playing at?' I mean, on the one hand ... Mr Stewart says, 'Oh, we'd a great rapport, a great working relationship over many years', but yet he didn't feel he could come and say, 'I think you're resisting here in a wholly inappropriate way'. I mean, I would've been very receptive to Mr Stewart saying that.

****

According to Cairns and others, the way summer 2015 unfolded in DETI was only possible because of Bell's remarkable indifference to much of what went on within his department. There is considerable evidence that senior officials almost viewed Cairns as the de facto minister. If they could convince him, then the minister would fall into line with most proposals – and not just on RHI. Bell was a complex, and at times contradictory, character who arguably should never have been elevated to running a Stormont department. Cairns described Bell as 'pretty passive in meetings' and someone who regularly did not bother to fully read his submissions. That, Cairns said, meant that during the weeks when Bell was on holiday he was reluctant to send the 8 July submission to him in the ministerial car – as he said he would have done with another minister – because he believed that Bell would simply have signed the submission without reading it. Instead, he felt that Bell needed to be verbally briefed to satisfy himself that he understood the significance of what he was doing. Bell was contemptuous of that claim, saying that he read submissions 'from cover to cover'. The former social worker said: 'When I got a submission, I read the submissions. I often read them into the early hours of the morning, and my wife … can attest to that.' But Bell's former private secretary, Sean Kerr, lent credence to the claim that was not the case. Kerr said that he was often present when Bell read submissions in the ministerial car and 'I formed the impression that he would read those documents in a summary fashion and rely on the special advisor's guidance … on several occasions the minister remarked directly to me that he had not read all the detail of the submission or annex, but was guided by the special advisor's comments'.

Bell said that his relationship with Cairns, was 'generally good'. He said that

> Timothy and his wife had hosted us for meals in their family home and socially in Belfast and he had been supportive to me at times of family bereavement … while information to the contrary has been given to the inquiry I recall that Timothy frequently expressed support for me to me and on one occasion during this period stated he believed in me as a politician.

Cairns said that those claims of close contact were wildly exaggerated and that after the June 2015 breakfast row in London his relationship with Bell had been strictly professional. Bell said, however, that Cairns on 'many occasions … spoke over me in ministerial meetings, contradicted me and … on one occasion told me he would tell me what to do.' He said:

> My perspective is that Timothy saw himself as working for the other spads as opposed to the minister and felt intimidated by them. An example of this was when he confided in me that Timothy Johnston had told him to get out and canvass for Gavin Robinson – then running for MP in East Belfast – while he was a spad or he wouldn't have a job as spad in the morning.

Cairns was scathing about the man who had been his boss:

Jonathan usually presented a confident manner. During these periods our relationship was good. At other times Jonathan would be emotional, quoting the Bible and wondering about the eternal destiny of his soul. Again, during these periods our relationship was good. Jonathan also exhibited an explosive personality, particularly when he was told that something he wanted may not/would not be possible. During these periods our relationship was strained.

Cairns said that in their early weeks in DETI prior to the London row Bell was 'on a significant high', and often described him as 'top spad'.

On his return to the department, Cairns said that there had been no disagreements between himself and Bell during July and August – although Bell was rarely around in that period. But in November, just as RHI was finally being rectified, Bell and his spad clashed again. Cairns said that Bell 'was concerned that the press office was not delivering enough press coverage' and 'he wanted the press office dismissed'. The press officers were civil servants, and so Cairns and McCormick told him that would not be possible. Cairns said that Bell 'was angry at being told he could not employ a private PR firm to undertake press engagement' and then was 'angry' that his invitation to the BBC Sports Personality of the Year Award had been sent to Foster in error.

However, Cairns said that Bell 'did prepare with great diligence' before his public Assembly appearances. Nevertheless, even after such preparation there were hints of problems with Bell when he appeared in the Assembly, and his public bungling there was one of the reasons why many DUP MLAs were wary of him.

In February 2016, he was challenged during Assembly questions to 'come off the fence' about Brexit. Bell emphatically told a surprised chamber on several occasions that the referendum question had not yet been set, and used that as his reason for not stating whether he supported Brexit. Bell went on to admonish the questioner, Jim Allister QC, that 'as I stand here today, we do not know what the referendum question is'. Allister interjected to correct him, saying: 'we do', but the minister was insistent:

We do not know … we have not been given the terms of the referendum question. Will it simply ask whether we wish to leave the EU? In that case, I imagine that the member will say yes. However, if the question is whether we wish to remain in the EU, I imagine that the answer from the member will be no. In the absence of knowing the exact nature of the question, it is a very, very foolish person who answers it.

Allister, one of Stormont's sharpest intellects, asked the Speaker whether it was right for Bell to 'mislead the house' and highlighted that the previous month Bell had misled the Assembly about unemployment rates. The Traditional Unionist Voice (TUV) leader informed the chamber that the question was set in Section 1 of the European Union Referendum Act 2015. But, even as his DUP colleagues cringed at the obvious gaffe, Bell was unabashed, saying: 'I was referring to the wider question of what the exact implications of a UK exit will be. We will not know what those implications are until David Cameron's negotiations regarding the UK's position within the EU have concluded.'

The evidence of Johnston, who as the key spad to Robinson had the ear of the First Minister perhaps like no one else in Stormont, is particularly intriguing. Johnston said that Bell's

approach to reading, questioning, and engagement was known to me to be very poor during his time as a junior minister in Stormont Castle. I have no first hand knowledge of his work pattern when he moved to DETI but I suspect it did not change … Sammy Wilson as Finance Minister did tell me on one occasion that when he met Mr Bell as part of a monitoring round bi-lateral meeting he was appalled at his lack of preparation.

Johnston said that he had advised Robinson that Bell was 'not a suitable candidate' to replace Foster at DETI and he believed that Richard Bullick, Robinson's other key spad, 'shared my assessment'.

Why then had Robinson gone against the advice of his two trusted lieutenants? He seems to have been influenced by a need for loyalty among his ministers and the fact that Bell also employed some of his family may have endeared him to Robinson. For his part, Robinson told the inquiry that part of the reason was a desire to limit the scale of the reshuffle. He admitted that Bell 'was not the most popular member in the DUP's team and might have been seen as an acquired taste', but that he had 'suitable academic qualifications and worthwhile life-experience in his professional career', as well as experience as a junior minister. But while that was going on within the DUP, publicly the party had lauded Bell. While urging people to elect Bell as an MP just weeks before he became DETI minister, DUP MLA Christopher Stalford had gushingly said: 'I've been about politics a long time … and can honestly say I've very rarely met anyone better with people than Jonny Bell … a good egg … just a big Christian gent.'

However, even though there was enmity between Bell and Cairns, they have consistently agreed that when Cairns worked to delay RHI being dealt with, he had been acting on the instructions of others. Bell said: 'I don't regard Timothy Cairns as having any interest in keeping the tariffs high and it was the pressure exerted on him by the other spads … that led to the more serious detrimental consequences.' Without Bell, the inquiry would never have been established. It was his demand for a judge-led public inquiry which made it difficult for the DUP and Sinn Féin to present a lesser investigation as adequate. The inquiry proved some of what he alleged in his explosive interview with Stephen Nolan – most notably that at least one DUP figure outside his department had played an unseen role in delaying an end to cash for ash. But the inquiry also presented an unflattering image of a lightweight minister who was keen to get the credit for popular decisions but lacked either the interest or the ability to comprehend crucial issues.

During two days of at points excruciating examination when Bell appeared before the inquiry, he was strikingly light on detail, demonstrating one of the weaknesses which his critics identified. On some of the points where he was most dogmatic, he was later proven to be wildly wrong. Repeatedly throughout his evidence he stated that he could not recall the precise details of what happened or that he did not have evidence to back up what he was alleging. In calling for a public inquiry, and in putting his career on the line to speak out in December 2016, Bell performed a major public service. But he was a casualty of the inquiry he had demanded, which again pointed to him not being a details man in that he genuinely appeared not to appreciate how exposed his position had been. By the time Foster left DETI, there was going to be a serious problem with RHI. But Bell's own flaws exacerbated the scale of a problem, which had not been of his making.

CHAPTER 13
THE SPIKE

Few elements of the RHI story sum up Stormont's rank dysfunctionality better than the fact that as one arm of the devolved government was attempting to bring under control a scheme which was bleeding money, another was urging people to join the scheme.

In real-life scenes, which were like something out of the political comedy *The Thick of It*, while DETI was ploddingly working towards the introduction of basic control on RHI spending, the Department of Agriculture was advertising the scheme. Right up until October 2015 – six months after DETI knew RHI was in trouble and four months after it knew that all additional spend was irregular – agriculture officials were pushing RHI to farmers. During the life of the scheme, the Department of Agriculture's educational arm included information about RHI at 58 farmer training events attended by 2,358 people. At some of these, boiler installers were present and selling their wares. Both the private firms and the department were promoting the lucrative nature of the scheme, highlighting factors such as the cost of fuel and the short payback time on investment. When payments on the scheme were later retrospectively slashed, many of those farmers were livid that they had been urged by Stormont to enter the scheme and taken on huge loans only to find the government reneging on its promises.

In evidence of the incoherent nature of the Stormont Executive, the Department of Agriculture was not the only wing of government promoting cash for ash in this period. Even more remarkably, a body for which DETI was itself responsible was more explicitly encouraging potential claimants to beat the deadline for the end of 'burn to earn'. Invest NI, the quango to which much of DETI's budget was allocated, was continuing to advertise RHI. Invest NI technical adviser, John Batch, emailed a company on 21 August 2015 to advise about the need to have a biomass heating system installed 'as soon as possible and hopefully before any changes to RHI are brought into effect by DETI'. Batch said that he had become aware of the looming changes – which at this point had not been publicised – from industry. By this stage, Batch was clearly aware of the RHI riches on offer. Seven months earlier, in response to a heating expert who was attempting to draw his attention to some of the problems with RHI, Batch had said: 'As you know sometime [*sic*] the hotels just see the cash cow called pellets!!'

No one in Invest NI thought to alert their parent department of the problem with a scheme that was so wildly lucrative they were being told that it was leading to firms artificially bending their heat needs to secure the highest subsidy. By contrast, when in October the scheme was about to be made far less generous, Batch emailed Seamus Hughes to pass on a suggestion that RHI was now not lucrative enough to encourage people to install biomass boilers – a suggestion based on a misunderstanding of the changes. But, remarkably, Hughes, the official who spent more of his time working on RHI than anyone else in Stormont, was continuing to promote it while simultaneously trying to rein it in. Hughes said that he gave a presentation on RHI at an event on 29 October – less than three weeks before tiering was implemented – at Greenmount Agricultural College. His presentation included an overview of how the scheme was going to be changed the following month. Hughes and another official also attended an event in Hillsborough on 8 September, to give a presentation 'targeted mainly at a farming audience'. Despite having been promoting the scheme in this way, Hughes would later say to the inquiry that there was an 'unexpected spike' in applications. Even in the story of RHI, the fact that one civil servant was attempting to cut RHI spending while at the same time encouraging spending on the scheme is uniquely farcical.

Part of Hughes's defence is ignorance. He said that DETI believed that it could take 6 to 12 months for a biomass boiler to be installed because that was what he had been told by the UFU. In fact, boilers could be installed in about a fortnight. But even the ignorance defence is difficult for DETI's officials to sustain. They had received multiple warnings that applications would increase sharply ahead of attempts to make the scheme less lucrative. Aside from that being common sense, it was what had happened each time GB had cut its RHI tariffs and by this stage was well understood to anyone with anything more than a basic understanding of how RHI worked.

We know that DETI understood the inevitability of a spike in applications because it was mentioned by officials several times. On 6 July – more than four months before the scheme was changed – Hughes told Ofgem that 'the industry here is now becoming aware that changes are afoot'. Inexplicably, he claimed that 'none of the detail is out there yet' –

despite the detailed briefings by himself and Wightman to individuals in the industry – but said 'it is likely that Ofgem may see an increase in application volumes over the next while'. Several DETI officials later said that they had known there would be a spike, yet had expected it to be modest. But even if the spike in applications was much less than what materialised, it was going to be a significant cost to the taxpayer. With an apparent lack of self-awareness, Hughes later said that the spike may in part have been 'due to the industry being in a strong position to respond to demand'. Part of the reason that the industry was in a strong position to respond to demand was that the department had for months been leaking like a sieve. Now the deluge was to come.

****

Before officials had even brought a formal submission to their minister to outline the problem, word was abroad that it was soon likely to be made less rewarding. In the Ulster Farmers' Union's (UFU) Antrim Road headquarters in Belfast, policy officer Elliott Bell overheard his colleague, Chris Osborne, talking about RHI on 7 July. He immediately emailed him to ask: 'Have you any info on if or when the RHI might be cut for NI?' The UFU man was upfront about why he was asking: 'Currently planning installation of a boiler and want to get in quick before they make changes!' Less than a month later, Osborne emailed Hughes with a somewhat contradictory message. On the one hand, he was lobbying for a 'grace period' for farmers to enter the uncapped scheme if they were in the process of installing boilers. But in the same email he warned Hughes: 'The reason for my email as well is that the rumour mill is starting again from the poultry guys and the UFU would have concerns about any "run" which might occur created by the advent of any grace period.' The surge into the scheme was now so obvious that even the UFU – the body representing the majority of those applying – was warning the department to be careful.

From early summer, it became increasingly clear to officials that information about their thinking was leaking out of the department. From at least June, phone calls were coming in to to ask when tiering was coming. John Mills said that by mid-2015 he 'assumed the leak came from the political side … meaning the spads', based on past experience. The problem became so great that by February 2016, as Stormont moved to shut RHI completely, Mills said that those with a commercial interest in the subsidy seemed to know more about what was to happen than the officials running the scheme. Mills said that throughout the final months of the scheme 'advance knowledge becoming swiftly available to outside interests continued to be a feature of policy development on the RHI until its closure', as well as in another green electricity subsidy where commercially sensitive changes were also being made.

Regardless of whether Mills's cynical instincts about the DUP spads were correct, there was a far more obvious leak – and it was right under his nose. Wightman and Hughes, who were directly beneath Mills in the DETI hierarchy, had been openly discussing the upcoming changes with multiple industry figures. Wightman and Hughes said that they saw their engagement with industry as part of the attempt to expedite the changes, viewing a faster informal consultation as mitigation for the absence of a public consultation on the changes, something which could have been legally challenged. It may also have been the case that past pressure on them to increase uptake had contributed to a freer discourse with commercial interests. After all, the only pressure which ever seemed to come down to them from Foster and Crawford had been to increase RHI applications, while there was never any pressure to implement cost controls.

However, the suggestion from Mills is that DETI had a policy of being as open as possible with industry and that contact with a major player such as Moy Park 'was common across the field on renewable policy'. Even by the time of the inquiry, Mills still maintained that his officials' contact with Moy Park where they discussed the possibility of tiering or a cap on usage 'would be common in developing proposals … I do not regard this type of interaction as premature'. Without any clear direction from Mills as to being cautious not to give companies information, which they could use to exacerbate DETI's problem, Wightman and Hughes seem to have been incapable of coming to the conclusion themselves.

On 19 June, Hughes met Terence McCracken from green energy company Innasol and gave him a detailed overview of the looming cuts. In an email to colleagues three days later, the businessman said that there had been so much 'open dialogue from the official' that 'I was taking notes furiously'. Despite the budgetary crisis, Hughes told him that the scheme was a 'great success'. McCracken came out of the meeting clear that there would be 'a rush to get measures through before the rebanding [subsidy cut]', which would mean a 'short term opportunity for volume [sales] probably up to Nov 15'.

Less than a fortnight later, Wightman updated Fergal Hegarty at Alternative Heat, a major boiler installer in County Down, about what was to happen. Hegarty was a crucial conduit in a bush telegraph within the renewable heat industry where information was being passed around – sometimes originating with him and being disseminated outwards, or sometimes a snippet of information would emerge elsewhere and come to him for circulation. After giving Hegarty far more information than had been given to the minister at that stage, Wightman told Hegarty that he could phone him weekly for an update.

Another key artery for information was Balcas, Northern Ireland's dominant wood pellet company, which was based in Fermanagh. On 1 July, Balcas manager Paula Keelagher updated industry contacts on a conversation which Wightman had with Hegarty. Her email contained detailed information about what was going to happen, including the October date for tiering. She said that Wightman had been open about the fact that in the last seven or eight months DETI had 'overspent on their budget and the reason for this is the operating hours of the boilers in the poultry sector'. Despite being aware of the budget having been exceeded, the Balcas manager then explicitly encouraged entry into the scheme before it was made less profitable: 'This change will only affect new applications after the change comes into force so if any of your clients are considering installing biomass systems we would advise they should move asap to avoid missing out on the best rates from RHI, especially sub 100kW installations'. Balcas later said that the information was never presented to it as confidential.

Later that month, a sales executive in DCI Energy emailed a colleague, forwarding another email from someone, whose name had been removed, who said they had been in a two-hour meeting with Wightman and Hughes. The length of the meeting is striking, given that Wightman and Hughes would tell the inquiry that they were overworked. The email detailed the level at which the cap would be set and the tariffs for each tier, as well as making clear that the 'implementation date mentioned several times was 5th October. This could slip to end of October depending on how long it take [*sic*] the minister to approve ...' It said that a grace period was unlikely because it would 'just leave RHI open to further exploitation (poultry sector)'. Then, in an indication of the individual's confidence that they would be able to obtain future inside information before it was made public – the email added: 'Will let you know when DETI make final confirmation, I should know before public announcement.'

In July, Hegarty actually told Hughes in an email that he was going to spread the news around the industry. In the same email, he admitted the changes were necessary because 'the poultry market was exploiting the scheme'. In early September an email from Connel McMullan, managing director of Alternative Heat and Hegarty's boss, showed that in a briefing with Wightman he had been given detailed information about changes that would not yet be public for several days. In a comment, which suggests he was aware of extreme use of boilers, he said of the coming changes: 'In short the paybacks still work fine but obviously are not just as lucrative as they have been to date with 99kw boilers running for 6 & 7,000 hrs!!!' A boiler running 7,000 hours equates to the heat being used for 80% of the year. When McMullan came before the inquiry he said he had no knowledge of the scheme being abused other than rumours and claimed that his comment about boilers running for up to 7,000 hours a year was 'a joke, basically'.

But while McMullan came before the inquiry, Hegarty did not – because he had left the country. On the day that McMullan appeared before Sir Patrick Coghlin in October 2018, the inquiry was told that Hegarty had left Northern Ireland about a year earlier, around the time that the inquiry was beginning to hear from its first witnesses. By the stage of McMullan's appearance, the potentially important witness was on the other side of the world in Australia and was not planning to return until after the inquiry's hearings were complete at the end of 2018. That day senior counsel to the inquiry David Scoffield QC told Coghlin that it had not even been possible to obtain a written statement from Hegarty despite attempting to contact him through McMullan's company. Scoffield said that Hegarty 'would have been someone that the inquiry was interested in getting evidence from'. McMullan said that he was on 'a sabbatical' to travel the world. Scoffield asked: 'Was his sabbatical in any way related to this inquiry or the possibility that he might be asked to give evidence?' McMullan replied: 'Not in my understanding, no.' When asked if he had discussed that with Hegarty,

McMullan said: 'Em. It's not something that I've discussed with him, no. Em, he is aware of the inquiry and aware of the media stigma that runs with that but … I don't believe it would have any bearing on any decision he would make on that front.'

****

At 10.08am on Friday, 28 August, Wightman formally sent an amended version of the 8 July ministerial submission to Cairns for onward transmission to Bell. The submission was by now familiar and asked the minister to urgently decide to introduce tiering. Given that Bell had verbally agreed to the proposal that Monday and that the only substantive change to the submission was to change the implementation date, it is unclear why it took almost a full working week for the submission to go to the minister. However, Wightman would not be so slow in alerting the industry to what was coming. In fact, those piling into the scheme were told about the decision before Bell had formally taken it – or even received the submission.

At 10.05am – three minutes before the document went to Cairns – Hughes had, on Wightman's instructions, emailed Moy Park. He alerted the poultry processor that, although officials were still waiting the minister's clearance, the changes were now unlikely before late October or early November. Over the remainder of that morning, Hughes and Wightman sent the details to some of those with the most obvious financial interest in the confidential information – a boiler installer, a prospective claimant and the UFU. Wightman was pressed at the inquiry as to why he had done this when the minister had not yet even taken his decision, let alone issued a public statement about it. Struggling to find a coherent explanation for why this behaviour was appropriate, Wightman described it as a form of good manners whereby the officials 'felt there was a courtesy on us'. It did not seem to bother them that what was good manners to those making money out of RHI was bad manners not only to their minister, who had yet to take a decision, but very bad manners to taxpayers who were going to have to pay for their behaviour. Wightman admitted at the inquiry: 'It looks naive now when I look back.' He went on to explain that part of the decision to hand out the information was to stop the phone ringing. Hughes, he said, 'was constantly on the phone, as were some of the more junior staff on the domestic side, fielding these calls. So, it was as much to try to dampen that demand, as well; look, you know, rather than the same person phoning you back three or four times'. But the price of dampening demand on the phone lines into DETI would be to drive demand for RHI boilers across Northern Ireland. Boiler installers would soon be too busy to bother ringing DETI.

Wightman said that he believed that Moy Park was so enormous that it 'could potentially make life difficult for us' if he did not give it a sense of what was coming. Wightman was asked whether – given Moy Park's huge significance to the Northern Ireland economy – DETI felt that it had to let the company get some more chance to get into the scheme before they clamped down on it. Wightman replied: 'I think there was a bit of that … because Moy Park were expanding – and they seen [*sic*] RHI and switching to renewable heat as a big part of their expansion. Of course, they are a major employer in Northern Ireland.' The difficulty with that was that other firms not of that size or without those contacts were not getting the same chance. Even within the poultry-processing sector, the government was now prioritising Moy Park over its few remaining rivals. How could those firms hope to compete when the multinational meat giant was getting such preferential treatment? And if the officials believed it was important to give certain firms inside information, why not just issue a press release at the start of the summer to say that the scheme was soon going to be far less lucrative?

Wightman said that 'we just found ourselves in a difficult situation here in that people are coming back to you saying "well, nothing's out yet; there's been no announcement; are we still on for October?" It's a difficult … you're in a difficult situation there'. Inquiry panel member Dame Una O'Brien interjected to ask: 'Why is it difficult? Why can't you just say: When the minister's decided, there will be an announcement?' Wightman said he now agreed that was what he should have been saying, 'but at that juncture, with everything else that was happening, to be fair, I probably didn't give it as much credence as I should have'.

When Mills was asked why officials had not simply resolved to give the industry no commercially sensitive information before it was agreed by the minister, he said that it was not a message which he recalled ever passing on to Wightman and Hughes. At one point in his evidence, he said: 'I don't think it's particularly possible for me to defend a lot of decisions that were taken in this or any other period on RHI'. Wightman said that with hindsight 'I accept that our engagement was ill judged and naïve and demonstrates a lack of commercial awareness on my part.' But he also told the inquiry: 'I still firmly believe that the industry was receiving information from a source other than Seamus Hughes and myself from early/mid June 2015 given the nature of queries the branch were receiving at that time.' However, when Wightman was interviewed by PwC – before there was a realisation of how big the scandal would become – he gave an extraordinary explanation that undermines his later claims of naivety. Facing questioning around the inadequate response to whistleblower Janette O'Hagan, Wightman offered an inconsistent justification. PwC put to him that Hughes's response to O'Hagan in March 2015 contradicted the suggestion that the department was already looking at tiered tariffs at this time. Wightman said this was because there was a 'tip-off point there … we would never tell anybody that … because of the nature of the scheme and the demand-led aspect of it … we obviously hadn't put anything past the minister at this stage …' Here, when it suited Wightman, he claimed that they had deliberately not been upfront with O'Hagan – who was trying to rein in RHI – in case that tipped off the industry. Yet he would later, along with Hughes, freely hand out commercially sensitive detail about the looming changes to those who – unlike the whistleblower – were making a fortune from RHI.

When DETI Deputy Secretary Chris Stewart was made aware of Wightman's justification of not wanting to 'tip-off' the industry, he thought it was 'ludicrous' for another reason:

> I'm astonished at that suggestion being made because it defies logic – because of the reason given. If the reason given was, you don't want to reveal your hand on something because someone could get a commercial advantage on it, but you think it's OK to tell lies on foot of which someone will make commercial decisions and possibly lose money and who will then come back and say; 'well you know when I heard there were going to be no tariff controls, I immediately went out and bought every 99KW boiler I could find on the face of the planet and got ready to install them and then you introduce these controls and I'm now out a load of money because people won't buy them', is ludicrous.

It is also evident that at the time of Hughes's response to O'Hagan in March 2015 he had already informed others in the industry of the proposed changes. Both Wightman and Hughes admitted that what they had done exacerbated the spike and therefore the huge cost to taxpayers. Their actions meant that potential claimants not receiving information either directly or indirectly from them were at a disadvantage to their competitors. It would not be until 8 September that DETI would issue a press release to say that changes were coming. There had never been any evidence of corruption on the part of Hughes or Wightman and they convincingly highlighted to the inquiry that they had never sought to hide their interactions with industry – which surely any individual acting nefariously would have done. Rather, they used departmental email accounts, recorded notes of some of the interactions and told their boss, Mills, about some of the meetings.

****

It was a frenzied period for boiler installers. From about July, Alan Hegan – a major RHI claimant, a major supplier of wood chip and a boiler installer – was receiving between 50 and 100 phone calls a day. His phone was unable to accept any more voicemail messages due to the level of demand for boilers before the uncapped subsidy ended. He said that 'the whole industry became aware around early July – the phone started ringing off the hook'. He had been due to go on a foreign holiday but he rebooked a later flight, cutting the length of his holiday in order to do more work.

But not everyone saw the spike. Brian Hood, the boiler installer who had been one of the first to spot RHI's potential, said that he never saw any increase in work. However, he did not install in the agricultural sector. He believed that the spike was overwhelmingly driven by agriculture.

The scheme was sufficiently lucrative to allow several enterprising companies to work out a system whereby they installed boilers for other companies for free – and agreed to service them for free for two decades – just so that they could take the RHI payments. One such firm installed 37 boilers in 2015 before the scheme was reined in.

Some of those who managed to get into the uncapped scheme before it ended made a fortune. One business, which was only set up as the spike was starting, would soon be making almost £1,000 a day from taxpayers after it managed to install ten boilers just before tiering. Eco Biomass NI Ltd was only incorporated as a company on 1 September 2015 – seven days before cost controls were publicly announced. Even though the firm – which was set up by 65-year-old Thomas James Spence from Dungannon – only began operating right at the end of the scheme, within 16 months it had the fourth-largest total payment to a single entity on the scheme, pulling in £476,383. The boilers were used to dry wood chip – which could then be used in either the boilers themselves or sold.

In January 2018, at the height of the scandal, Spence spoke to *Ulster Herald* journalist Ryan McAleer and defended his RHI claims – although the scale of the payments was not known at that point. Spence said: 'We're a legitimate business providing to power stations and other farmers and other local people … we simply availed of the opportunity that was there and presented to us. There is nothing illegal about that, there's certainly nothing to be demonised or criminalised about.' Every single one of the Eco Biomass boilers was 99 kW – the maximum capacity boiler for which the 'burn to earn' RHI tariffs could be claimed. By contrast, some individuals chose to install single massive boilers meaning that they received far more modest payments. Sainsbury's Bangor store installed a 630 kW boiler and its Craigavon store installed a 580 kW version – between them, a greater capacity than the ten Eco Biomass boilers combined. The Sainsbury's boilers were also installed at a much earlier stage in the scheme in 2013, meaning that it had a much longer period in which to claim. But Spence's boilers received payments which were almost seven times greater than the two Sainsbury's stores between them. To put the scale of the claims in context, the two Sainsbury's boilers were receiving an RHI payment of just £51 a day, while Spence's ten boilers were bringing in almost £1,000 a day.

But even Spence's late grand foray into RHI was trumped by another late entrant. Dennison Commercials, the Volvo truck and bus dealer in Northern Ireland, managed to install 11 RHI boilers in 19 days after indirectly getting inside information from Stormont. The Ballyclare company had the multiple 99 kW boilers installed at the end of August after the contents of an email, which Hughes had sent to a boiler installer, were sent to it. Hughes had said that it was never DETI's intention to allow 'gaming' of the system by installing multiple smaller boilers to receive higher payments and that it would soon be outlawed. Dennison Commercials had been pondering RHI for some time, and boiler installer FG Renewables used the email to get the company over the line, warning the business that it needed to act urgently or it would lose out. In the first 16 months of the scheme, Dennison claimed more than £340,000 for an installation that had cost it £650,000.

However, having inadvertently tipped off a potential claimant about the looming end of the loophole whereby claimants could 'game' the system with multiple small boilers, DETI then failed to address that problem in its November 2015 legislation. Despite DETI having seven months from the point where it was clear that the scheme was out of control to the point where the scheme was altered, officials said that it had been impossible to agree with Ofgem a suitable way of addressing the problem.

Late in the day, Wightman finally panicked. On 13 November – just five days before the Assembly would pass the reduced tariffs – he emailed Stewart, McCormick and other senior DETI officials. Now aware of the spike, Wightman said that 'uptake has exceeded all expectations'. There had been 800 applications over the last six weeks, he said – off the charts from the hopelessly inaccurate forecast of 150 applications for all of October. This meant that RHI spending could increase to over £30 million in that financial year and to over £40 million the following year – even if both schemes closed in April 2016. Having expected to have about 3% of the GB application numbers, in line with Northern Ireland's size, the Stormont scheme was now running at over 10% of GB applications. In bold and underlined type, Wightman told bosses: 'I feel that in light of this situation regardless of what impact the amendment regulations might bring there is no choice now but to move to close both RHI schemes from 31 March 2016.' He added: 'I am presenting this for your urgent consideration. It will be important for the minister to be aware that further "unpopular" legislative changes are needed early in the New Year.'

In a 13 November email, Wightman said that the delay from 4 November to 17 November had been due to 'the progressing of legal and financial approvals' – a delay which has never been fully explained.

From late August there had been a major political crisis after the police had linked the Provisional IRA, the terror group out of which Sinn Féin had originally grown, to a murder in Belfast. The DUP responded with a series of rolling ministerial resignations, reappointing ministers briefly to take urgent decisions but overwhelmingly leaving departments in the hands of officials for almost two months. Cairns lost his job as a spad and was not in the post from early September until late October. The one exception was Foster who was retained as Finance Minister and made acting First Minister. As Foster's spad, Crawford kept his post. With unintended irony, given the RHI chaos which was unfolding, Foster defended her party's decision to keep her in post by saying: 'I'm not going to put at risk to the people of Northern Ireland the possibility that rogue Sinn Féin or renegade SDLP ministers are going to take decisions that will harm the community in Northern Ireland.'

****

Having got the changes through the department, now officials needed to get them through the Assembly. The first stage was the enterprise committee, which scrutinised DETI's work. On 3 September, Wightman wrote to the committee. It was a misleading piece of correspondence. In explaining the changes, Wightman presented more detail about the move to allow Combined Heat and Power (CHP) plants to apply for RHI than he did about the funding crisis which the legislation was primarily meant to address. The fact that at this late stage DETI was moving to expand RHI at the very point where it was supposedly reining it in was itself astonishing. With the budget seriously overspent and wider concerns about the scheme, allowing CHP plants – effectively small power stations, which under RHI would be claiming many millions of pounds each – was potentially going to undo any savings made by tiering.

Tiering was presented benignly by Wightman as a measure 'to ensure affordability and value for money'. There was no mention of the fact that RHI was now far over budget – giving MLAs less detail than Wightman and Hughes had given to the industry – and no mention of irregular spending. Whatever Wightman's reasons for failing to give the legislature the full information, it meant that there was less scrutiny of his own failures. Wightman also showed limited attention to detail in the letter, misspelling degression in a way which then failed to convey what that GB policy was designed to do. He referred to 'digression' – a temporary departure from the main subject – rather than 'degression', a descent by stages or steps, despite the fact that degression ought to have been familiar to DETI if it had been keeping an eye on events in GB. It is difficult to justify Wightman's failure to give MLAs the full gory picture. He and Hughes were well aware of the real purpose for the legislation. In an email to Ofgem as far back as July, Hughes referred to its purpose being to introduce tiering, with 'other issues' described by him as 'minor'.

Wightman later said that they had tried to 'recoup some lost time' by attempting to get the committee to approve the changes in the first week of November but that the committee clerk 'refused to allow this', pushing it back by a week. However, it is likely that Wightman's – and DETI's – withholding of information from the committee added to the bill for taxpayers. If he had been open about the crisis, it is likely that the committee would have agreed to discuss it immediately. However, Wightman was attempting to have the best of both worlds. He was presenting the changes to the committee as fairly mundane, which meant that they were unlikely to arouse suspicions and hard questions, while then later blaming the committee for delay because it had refused to suddenly be rushed into deciding upon legislation, which he had presented as technical and unexciting. When Wightman's letter came before the committee in September, it triggered no discussion and was nodded through by MLAs.

In a letter to other Executive ministers on 9 November, by which stage DETI knew of the calamitous overspend, Bell himself did nothing to convey the gravity of the situation. The changes were blandly presented as 'primarily to provide for new tariffs for Combined Heat and Power installations and to introduce cost control measures for biomass'. In Bell's defence, his ministerial style suggests that this was not a deliberate attempt on his part to mislead and was another example of where he was prepared to sign what officials put before him. Nevertheless, as a government minister it was his responsibility – and the responsibility of Cairns as his spad – to ensure that he was conveying accurate information to his colleagues. But the culture within Stormont was not one of openness with ministerial colleagues but of attempting to give as little hint of problems as possible – partly because mandatory power-sharing shackled together electoral rivals.

But there was one more chance to give MLAs the full picture. On the morning of 17 November, Wightman and a junior official arrived at the committee to brief it about the legislation. Only five of the committee's 11 members were present for a discussion, which followed consideration of the committee's Christmas card list. Wightman seemed nervous. His hands shook slightly and he fidgeted somewhat as he spoke. What he was telling the committee – both in his letter and verbally – seriously misled the committee to the point of being preposterous.

During an appearance, which was shorter than a television ad break, Wightman led the committee to believe that stalling on the issue could halt investment, when in fact as he knew the critical problem was that further delay would lead to the already vast spike in applications increasing still further. It was unusual that the department was only bringing the request for committee approval on the morning that the legislation was coming to the full Assembly. The committee chairman, Patsy McGlone, began by asking Wightman: 'So, why's it so urgent?' Wightman replied:

> The reason for the urgency was that we were originally aiming for the 4th of November and we've been very open with the industry about that date … so we're keen that there's not a hiatus out there in terms of the industry because I know because we're changing the tariff banding there are a number of installers holding off on new installations. Also in terms of value for money, we're obviously keen to obviously make the changes as soon as possible in terms of affordability of the scheme going forward [*sic*].

Contrary to Wightman's evidence, the original date had not been 4 November but early October. And although he mentioned value for money and budgetary considerations, there was no emphasis given to the seriousness of the situation. Wightman was effectively telling the MLAs that the department was attempting to facilitate turning on the tap of green investment when he knew that they were desperately trying to turn off the tap.

Having been given a misleading impression of the situation, the committee did nothing to probe the glaring holes in his story. Thus, without a single question from anyone other than McGlone, MLAs unanimously nodded the changes through. Wightman's appearance – which ought to have been lengthy and difficult – lasted just two minutes and 13 seconds. Less than an hour later – while the committee was still meeting – the legislation came before the Assembly. McGlone left the committee to head to the Assembly chamber where he was the only MLA other than

Bell to speak briefly on the issue. Within a few minutes, the regulations had been unanimously approved.

Looking back on what happened at the committee that day, McGlone said that he now felt that Wightman had been 'misleading the committee – which is the scrutiny body for the public'. He drew attention to the fact that he had asked Wightman why there was such urgency about the issue. The civil servant knew better than anyone that the real answer was that the scheme was bleeding money. However, McGlone said that he interpreted Wightman's answer to be that it was 'just a wee bit of housekeeping work' and an attempt to help the renewable energy industry by giving it clarity.

He said: 'No member of that committee could have gone out of that room after hearing Mr Wightman's comments and said "there's a problem with this". We're sent by the public to do a job and we try our best. But when you're not provided with information and that is deliberately withheld from you, that's not how any sort of democratic accountability should work.'

But even on the day that the legislation was passed, 13 more boilers would enter the scheme. Based on how they were being used, those boilers alone would be in line for more than £3.1 million of taxpayers' money.

The following day, tiering and a cap were finally introduced. Over the previous ten weeks there had been 982 RHI applications, more than in the entire life of the scheme up to that point – a period of three years.

CHAPTER 14
YOU'RE ON YOUR OWN

On Friday, 13 November 2015, Tim Cairns was taking his children to a church kids' club when his phone rang. It was Arlene Foster, phoning on behalf of a constituent.

It was five days before the RHI cuts were to come before the Assembly. Foster, aware of the looming subsidy reduction, enquired whether it would be possible to delay the scheme being made less financially attractive. The reason, she said, was that one of her constituents, Stephen Harron, wanted to install six RHI boilers and would not be able to get them into the uncapped scheme without further time.

Harron, a salesman for Hegan Biomass, had phoned Foster, who was both his local MLA and, prior to entering politics, had been his solicitor, in an attempt to get what he said were clients' boilers into the uncapped scheme.

With one eye on his children, Cairns phoned Andrew McCormick and passed on the message, asking if it would be possible to delay the change by a week. McCormick said that he thought that would be impossible but that he would check. The senior civil servant said that he recalled Cairns referring to 'a concern that not enough businesses in Fermanagh [Foster's constituency] had been able to apply — there was certainly a reference to Fermanagh'. He said that Cairns had not mentioned Foster on the call, and it was the reference to Fermanagh that meant it was 'clear that the call was on behalf of Arlene Foster'. Neither Cairns nor Foster dispute that the request was made largely as McCormick had said, but disputed his reference to Fermanagh.

McCormick quickly consulted his deputy, Chris Stewart, and that night replied to Cairns that such a delay would cost £52 million over 20 years and that he would refuse to do so unless a ministerial direction was issued from Bell. Cairns passed the information to Foster and waited for what he described as 'instructions'. With the legislation due up in the Assembly in four days' time, there passed a weekend of what McCormick viewed as 'material uncertainty' over whether the changes would now go ahead on time, 'which was a genuine and serious concern'. On Monday, Cairns texted the permanent secretary to say that they were 'back from the brink' and there would be no further delay.

Although the request troubled McCormick, Cairns later said he 'didn't seriously believe' that Foster was asking for an extension but was just going through the motions of asking on behalf of her constituent. Regardless of whether that was her intent, it was particularly odd for Foster to have made any such request because she was the Finance Minister. Common sense would have told her that keeping the uncapped scheme open would increase the bill to taxpayers. However, Foster told the inquiry that she was unaware of the extent of the overspend and had not discussed the issue with Andrew Crawford, who had been aware of the problem for months. Foster said that if she had been aware of the scale of the problem she would not have made the request.

Harron's wife did get a boiler installed on the uncapped scheme – with an installation date of 16 November, the day on which Foster dropped her request for an extension and just one day before the subsidy was cut. Harron himself ultimately installed two 60 kW boilers on 29 February 2016 – right at the end of the tiered scheme.

As with so much in this period, Bell seems to have been an almost incidental figure who was not even aware of the request from Foster. It was Cairns who was the key conduit both for senior DUP figures attempting to influence DETI policy and for mandarins seeking to get a ministerial decision. McCormick later said: 'I have no recollection and I am not aware of any record of Jonathan Bell pressing for early action on the RHI during the period between 3 September and the end of December 2016.'

****

Immediately after the November 2015 changes, demand for RHI dissipated – even though it was still generous. But another problem remained. Hundreds of millions of pounds of public spending had been incurred without proper authorisation. Unless something could be done to regularise that irregular spending, DETI's accounts were going to be qualified for 20 years. That was an unthinkable situation for any public sector body. But for the department which was responsible for the economy and enforced company law in Northern Ireland, it would have been humiliating.

Since the summer, officials had been working on attempting to convince the Department of Finance to grant both prospective approval for future expenditure on the scheme and retrospective authorisation for what had already been spent. The document into which they poured their efforts was called an 'addendum business case'. While securing approval for future spending appeared relatively straightforward after the scheme was made less lucrative, it was clear that DETI was only likely to get retrospective approval for the uncapped scheme if it could be presented in a positive light.

Herein lay a contradiction. For the approval process to mean anything, departments needed to be brutally frank with each other. But being brutally frank about RHI – a scheme which had run out of control and which DETI at least suspected was overcompensating claimants – was unlikely to convince finance officials to approve it as an acceptable use of public money. What DETI now did was construct an absurdly implausible picture of a scheme which – even if it did not fully understand the perverse 'burn to earn' incentive – the department knew was deeply flawed.

Four years earlier, consultants CEPA had told DETI that the entire scheme was likely to lead to a net increase of 37 jobs in Northern Ireland – because new green energy jobs were often replacing what would have been jobs in oil or gas installations. But now DETI appeared to pluck figures from thin air to suit its case. The addendum business case claimed that for every 12 boilers installed, four jobs would be created for the lifetime of the boiler – a figure which equated to about 600 jobs for the almost 1,900 boilers then on the scheme. It was preposterous. But it suited DETI's attempt to justify the huge expenditure which had been incurred and the claim survived as the document went back and forth among DETI's top officials.

The document claimed that for every £74 million of RHI expenditure, £107 million worth of jobs ensued. The inquiry's technical assessor, Keith MacLean, was withering about that claim, saying 'it's difficult to see how that passed the snigger test'.

The plea for retrospective approval also claimed that the 'burn to earn' uncapped RHI 'provides continuous and continuing value for money' and insisted that 'the department could not have reasonably acted sooner' to rein it in. The document, which was primarily written by Wightman but which had input from multiple senior DETI officials, was wildly misleading.

As the summer wore on, the document became a departmental priority because the irregular spending was now a DETI-wide problem. DETI economist Alan Smith was drafted in to assist with the construction of the argument that the expenditure should be approved. The figures which he calculated showed the scheme in a glowing light, with huge economic benefits and a positive return for taxpayers. He had, however, added a major disclaimer to his figures, saying that the estimated employment benefits was 'very much reliant on assumptions' which required further analysis, and added: 'Care should therefore be taken in quantifying the employment benefits because of this degree of uncertainty and whether additionality of jobs has been fully tested.'

That note of caution was stripped out by Wightman. When asked why he had done so, he told the inquiry that it was 'human error'. He said that he had 'no intention or desire to remove the caveat' and he had seemingly done so 'accidentally'. Whatever the reason for that line's removal, it conveniently meant that DETI's flimsy argument appeared somewhat more robust – especially because DETI did not send the document until the last moment, limiting the time for scrutiny.

Senior finance officials had expected the document in August, but did not get it until 27 October. By now the legislation for tiering was on the cusp of being brought before the Assembly. Finance officials felt that they had no real option but to approve the prospective element of the request because by now a refusal to do so – even if there were major problems with it – would lead to the even worse outcome of the uncapped RHI continuing.

It may have been that a lack of political pressure fed into officials going slow. Although Bell insisted that he had been a hands-on minister, there is little evidence of him pressing for the document to be urgently drawn up, or of questioning why that had not happened. And whatever limited implicit political pressure there was to get it to finance officials, it dissipated when Bell resigned from office for most of the period between 10 September and 20 October.

The delay was also at least contributed to by Wightman having other duties. Senior DETI economist Shane Murphy said that Wightman had told him at the time that the delays were partly because 'he was having to also take forward other work'. Trevor Cooper said that Wightman had confirmed to him in a later conversation that he had been instructed by his boss, John Mills, to prioritise another project, Energywise, over RHI. Wightman agreed that he was working on Energywise at the same time. However, he denied that it had been prioritised and said that he was working directly for

Stewart on that project. He said that yet another issue – NIRO – had been prioritised above everything else.

Mills said that he could not have told Wightman to focus on Energywise because he did not manage Wightman's work on that. But he accepted that Wightman had other responsibilities in this period, and that with hindsight actions which he took to increase staffing were 'insufficient'.

Within days of receiving the addendum business case, the Department of Finance granted a conditional and heavily caveated approval for tiering. But on 21 December, DETI was informed that the request for retrospective approval had been rejected.

Wightman was more candid with the inquiry than he had been with his fellow civil servants in the finance department. He told the inquiry: 'I did feel under pressure from senior officials, in preparing the business case, to justify the scheme in its unamended form and for spending to be regularised.' As earlier in the story, individual civil servants – and here a whole department – seemed more concerned about limiting criticism of themselves than they were about presenting the full unvarnished picture to colleagues so that the truth could be established and problems properly addressed. If civil servants could not even be brutally honest with each other behind closed doors, there was less likelihood of them being candid with the public.

The document would have been even more indefensible if those working on it were aware of the widespread rumours that RHI was being abused. Cairns said that during the summer of 2015 he had received generalised rumours of abuse from Crawford and had passed these on to officials. Stewart and McCormick claimed that they had relayed those rumours to Wightman.

Wightman said he had 'no recollection' of McCormick 'directly passing on to me any warnings of possible scheme abuse. I believe I would have remembered because as a Grade 7 I did not have many direct contacts with Dr McCormick'. Wightman said he thought it was 'much later', around September, that he got 'anecdotal claims of basically empty buildings being heated'. However, in his earlier interview with PwC he had referred to such claims almost a year beforehand.

Cooper, who as DETI's finance director was heavily involved in scrutinising the addendum business case, said that although it claimed the scheme was 'continuous and continuing value for money', he knew that

RHI could not be best value for money. He justified allowing that phrase to remain by saying that he was passing on the views of others within DETI. Cooper said that in other conversations with the finance department he was more candid, suggesting that – as with so much of what went on in Stormont – what went down on paper was not necessarily the real story.

****

The day in December 2015 when Stormont's mandarins realised every penny of the 20-year RHI overspend was going to come out of Northern Ireland's budget was 'a day of complete dismay', Stewart later recalled. Despite the false hope of August, when DETI misinterpreted a spreadsheet to assume that the Treasury had simply sent it the extra money which it needed, over the autumn there had been increasing signals that this was not going to be a bottomless pit. But even after reading the 2011 email from Jon Parker in the Treasury, which made clear that there would be penalties for overspending, they expected the penalties to be limited. Parker had speculatively suggested a possible figure of 5%, as well as offsetting any overspend in one year with other underspends. But DETI had never clarified this vague hypothesising in an email from a helpful Treasury official four years earlier. In the rules-based world of the civil service, it was the flimsiest of defences – especially coming *ex post facto*.

By now there was a vast bill to explain to the Treasury. The spike had more than doubled what was already a problem in the spring of 2015. It was an inopportune moment at which to go to the Treasury in the hope of a sympathetic reception.

The level of panic at this point appeared to reinforce the idea that as long as London was footing the bill there was limited urgency – but when the money was coming out of Stormont's budget there was horror. Stewart conceded that was how it could look. But he insisted to the inquiry it was not the reason for the furious activity which happened after the realisation that Stormont was going to have to pay.

He said:

An overspend of the extent that manifested itself was a very serious matter for which we were always going to be, rightly, seriously criticised.

But, whilst it was capable of being borne on the broad back of AME and some DEL [Stormont's main budget], then it was at least feasible to do that. Once it reached the point where it had to be borne entirely from DEL, it's not that it suddenly started to matter, it suddenly became completely unaffordable.

He said that it had been 'a day of complete dismay because we realised that … that money was going to have to be found from other programmes.' When Cairns and Bell were given the bad news, 'there was silence for a few seconds', Cairns recalled. Cairns in particular must have in his mind gone back over his role in the delays.

Now, with panic moving across the Stormont system, Crawford was made aware that the money was coming from Stormont's budget. Senior finance official Mike Brennan emailed Crawford, now the spad in the Department of Finance, on 18 December, noting that 'you asked if there was any update on RHI yesterday'. Brennan told him that the Treasury had informally confirmed that the formal 'settlement letter' 'will state that the NI DEL will have to take the hit on the excess RHI payments'.

Over the preceding weeks, finance officials had in vain attempted to construct arguments as to why Stormont should not have to pay. One of those arguments was that Northern Ireland was now contributing more towards the UK's national renewable heat targets than 3% – its share of the UK population – and therefore it should get more than 3% of the national funding.

Now Brennan told Crawford that the Treasury had come back to dismiss that plea, telling Stormont that the national targets had never factored in Stormont's actual number of installations and had just assumed a 3% figure, so no matter how many green boilers were installed in Northern Ireland anything beyond 3% was not being counted towards the UK's target.

There was one small concession from London. For reasons which are unclear, Stormont was told that the Treasury would not seek to claw back the overspend in the current financial year. But that was outweighed by the message that for the next 20 years the full overspend would come out of Stormont's budget. Brennan told Crawford that 'in light of this we will now have to issue a letter to DETI to advise them to take corrective action immediately'. RHI would have to be shut.

It would have been common for Stormont officials to raise an issue at official level and be knocked back, only for ministers to then get involved. But on this occasion there was no escalation by Stormont ministers to their London counterparts. Perhaps enough was understood about what had gone on with RHI to not invite any external scrutiny. The following month, McCormick said that 'we have advised ministers that nothing would be gained by seeking to re-open this debate with Treasury, particularly in the post 'Fresh Start' [the recent political agreement between the DUP, Sinn Féin and the government which involved extra money for Northern Ireland] context that we find ourselves in with NIO/Treasury. Our stock is low.'

But even though it was by now clear to DETI that it had made a massive blunder, there continued to be a lack of candour by officials. In a ministerial submission on New Year's Eve, Mills referred to a 'change in [Treasury] policy' whereby Stormont would have to pay for the entire overspend. Most readers would have assumed from his description of the situation that fault lay with the Treasury rather than closer to home. Mills later suggested he was referring to the gap between a 5% penalty and a 100% penalty. However, there had never been any formal agreement which the Treasury had broken. Mills still seemed incapable of or unwilling to face up to the enormity of their calamity – and the fact that much of it had been the fault of civil servants, even if he did not fully appreciate the unseen political chicanery.

Among those in DETI's top brass, Mills seems to have consistently been the most optimistic – and therefore, the most naive – about RHI. As late as 27 January 2016, a month after the Treasury had made clear that Stormont would have to pay the full bill, he was still presenting RHI in positive terms.

Mills was irked by an email which McCormick had sent that day to David Sterling, Permanent Secretary of the Department of Finance, in which McCormick had said: 'I also had to say to [Cairns] that a decision not to proceed [with closure] until after the election would mean throwing potentially large amounts of good money after bad.' Mills, to whom the email had been copied, replied brusquely to his boss: 'The RHI is "good" money, just too much of a good thing.'

****

As the scandal which would devastate her reputation was developing unobserved by more than a handful of individuals in Stormont, Foster's political career was ascending fresh heights. Having been promoted to Finance Minister in May 2015 and then acting First Minister during Robinson's period of rolling ministerial resignations that autumn, Robinson's decision to retire led to an immediate expectation that Foster would succeed him as First Minister.

Amid widespread speculation, much of it emanating from DUP sources, that the roles of DUP leader and First Minister would now be split, there was a belief that the capable North Belfast MP and deputy leader Nigel Dodds would become leader while Foster became First Minister. But on 7 December, there was a shock announcement. For reasons which are still not entirely clear, Dodds said that he would not be standing for the leadership. Both crowns would be Foster's. There was still a lingering possibility that Sammy Wilson, the East Antrim MP and a grassroots favourite, would challenge for the top job. But that night Robinson intervened, tweeting to say that Foster's nomination had the support of 'over 75% of those entitled to vote in the electoral college'. The message was clear: Foster was the chosen one and the party did not want a leadership contest.

Ten days later, her coronation as DUP leader was complete and a month after that she formally took over as First Minister on 11 January 2016. Initially, Foster was an incredibly popular leader of unionism. Voters who were tired of Robinson and tired of a series of scandals involving the DUP wanted to believe that there had been fundamental change. Foster – the party's first female leader and someone whose entire political career postdated the Troubles – was happy to accentuate the differences with her predecessor. On her first day in office she invited the *News Letter* and *The Irish News* – publications to which Robinson had latterly refused to speak – to interview her. BBC *Spotlight*, the investigative programme which had repeatedly infuriated Robinson, was invited to interview her and follow the new leader around for her first days in office.

But behind the carefully crafted public image of the new DUP leader, a crisis was unfolding and at its heart would be some of those who owed their positions to Foster. When she became leader, Foster had the power to conduct a ministerial reshuffle, but declined to do so.

In a revealing admission, she told the inquiry that she did not believe Bell was up to the job of running a government department but that she had kept him in post in case there had been a row which could have cost the DUP votes in the Assembly election, then three months hence. Foster said that Bell was 'not a suitable candidate' to be minister and it was 'a great regret of mine that I didn't remove him from the post'. For the DUP – a party which was brilliant at electoral politics – the election was more important than ensuring there was a competent individual in charge of a major government department.

Foster and Bell's relationship was now under huge strain. She said that Bell 'hero-worshipped' Robinson and 'never really accepted my leadership' but that it was said to her by a colleague: 'How much harm can he do in three months?'

At the inquiry, Bell's barrister questioned that evidence, highlighting that Foster had repeatedly endorsed Bell in public. Ronan Lavery QC told how in spring 2015, just as RHI was running out of control, Foster had been a guest speaker at an election event for Bell, 'extolling Jonathan Bell's skills and abilities and detailing why he should be a Member of Parliament for South Belfast. This was in addition to undertaking door to door canvassing with him recommending Jonathan Bell to the electorate of South Belfast'.

Whatever Foster's reasons, by deciding to keep Bell in DETI, it would now be he who would be legally responsible for winding down a scheme which it was now known had to be shut. That decision stood out because at the same time Foster decided not to bring with her Crawford – the man who had been by her side for her entire ministerial career. He was left behind in the Department of Finance and Foster continued with Timothy Johnston and Richard Bullick as her two key spads, along with Stephen Brimstone – even though there was a fourth unfilled spad slot which could have gone to Crawford.

In the ponderous world of Stormont, even though Wightman had in mid-November told his superiors that the scheme would have to be shut, it was only on 31 December that a submission to that effect came to Bell. The minister approved the recommendation and then on 19 January he was given another submission with a date for closure. Bell approved the submission but – in highly unusual circumstances which revealed the power of spads – his approval was overturned by a spad. This incident would add to Bell's growing paranoia.

Cairns said that Johnston had issued an instruction (something Johnston denied) to Bell that nothing on RHI was to be cleared without his approval. However, on Friday the 22nd, neither Bell nor Cairns could contact Johnston, who Cairns said was 'notoriously difficult to reach by telephone; he will often not return calls'. Therefore, he said that Bell had instructed him to email Johnston to say that if he did not reply by a certain time, then two submissions – one on NIRO and the other on RHI closure – were to be cleared. In fact, Johnston had responded before Bell's deadline, but Cairns had not seen the email and so the submissions were approved.

Later that afternoon, Cairns realised that Johnston had replied – and his response was to say that they needed to wait until the following week to discuss the issues properly. Cairns now went back to Bell's private secretary and at a quarter to five on Friday afternoon said: 'Hold the subs on niro and RHI.' Clearance had been rescinded.

The following week, under pressure from officials to take a decision, Cairns said to Stewart and McCormick:

> The Niro and rhi subs are in the hands of DUP party officers and will be dealt with by them. I have recommended officials advice but party officers have requested time to deal with them. I have no idea if they will approve or not. Minister cleared and the subs were then pulled to DUP party officers on Friday afternoon.

In fact, it had not been the party officers, but rather Johnston to whom Cairns was referring. And it was largely a cock-up – if Cairns had seen the email in time, the submission would never have been cleared. But it showed the power of spads to issue instructions which overturned the decision of a government minister. The hugely experienced McCormick and Stewart were perplexed, having never before encountered such a situation.

Foster said she had 'no knowledge of the recall', while Johnston said that it had been partly due to coming on a Friday afternoon when he did not have sufficient time to get Foster's view and also part of a wider attempt to ensure that the scheme was closed rapidly – but in a way that Sinn Féin would support, a crucial consideration to pass legislation.

But although Johnston did not approve the submission that day, he immediately forwarded it to Foster and Crawford, along with Cairns's email message. Even without opening the attached submission, just reading Cairns's brief email would have alerted Foster to alarming facts about the scheme she had set up: 'Keeping it open before Christmas has caused potentially a £27 million overspend … We need to consult and probably close.' Foster later said that she did nothing for five days, until she had been separately told of the budgetary crisis by the Head of the Civil Service.

Cairns is clear that in this period there was no ulterior attempt by his fellow spads to delay closure. But he and everyone else in DETI were baffled. The confusion was exacerbated by the fact that he and Bell, along with McCormick, were flying to the US the following day for a trade mission lasting almost a week. Cairns said that it was 'absolutely and utterly no criticism of Mr Bell in this that he was confused: we all were'.

Bell insisted to the inquiry that he had never been aware of the recall – and that bred in his mind the suspicion about what was going on behind his back. But within one minute of the recall, Cairns forwarded Johnston's email to Bell's personal email address, along with a message to say that he had told the minister's private secretary to 'hold the subs'.

Bell attempted to explain away the significance of that email, claiming that he never used private email accounts for departmental business. His evidence on this issue was so excruciatingly contorted that it defied rational explanation and undermined his credibility as a witness. Appearing before the inquiry, he said: 'I didn't use any form of communication outside the department whatsoever. I just used my official ministerial email address … I never used any communication device outside. I only used the ministerial email and the system.' He went on to say that if his spad had ever used a private email account he would have told him to use the departmental account. Speaking categorically, Bell said: 'It's entirely unusual that it would have been sent to that account. That was just a private account I had, not a ministerial account, and all my ministerial business went through the ministerial account.'

But Bell had already told the inquiry in writing that the only email address which he used for communication about RHI was his Hotmail address. And when later asked in writing to explain the discrepancy he indicated that he did not even have a departmental email address. He told the inquiry: 'My official email address when I was minister was *sean.kerr@ detini.gov.uk*.' Self-evidently, that was the email address of someone else – his private secretary. The civil service said that it could find no record of Bell ever having a departmental email address.

The inquiry then turned up multiple pieces of evidence which prove that Bell had repeatedly used the email address *jonathanbell620@hotmail.com*, including emails to and from his permanent secretary, his private secretary and the First Minister. Referring to Bell's Hotmail account, McCormick told the inquiry: 'It was the only email that I ever used if I was sending things to him.' Bell's nonsensical evidence on this point suggested that, at the most benign reading, he was so unaware of the detail of what was going on within his department that he did not even know his own email address. This was the man in charge of the RHI scheme. What was about to happen in America was to raise further questions about whether Bell was the sort of person who ought to have been in charge of any government department – let alone one facing a vast financial crisis.

CHAPTER 15
GET IT SHUT

On the morning of Wednesday, 27 January, Arlene Foster was in her constituency office in Enniskillen. That in itself was unusual. The Stormont week was structured to keep MLAs free to be in their constituencies on Fridays. Wednesday was a day for Stormont business – especially for someone who just 16 days earlier had become First Minister.

Alongside her was the DUP's most senior backroom figure, Timothy Johnston. That morning, Foster's other key adviser, Richard Bullick, was in Stormont Castle as usual. At 10.40am, he said in an email to Johnston – copied to fellow spads Andrew Crawford and Stephen Brimstone – that the Head of the Civil Service, Sir Malcolm McKibbin, wanted to speak to Foster about RHI that day. Bullick said that Stormont's top mandarin, who was also the permanent secretary of the Office of the First Minister and deputy First Minister (OFMdFM), 'seems very concerned' and observed that it was a 'bit odd he had not been tipped off previously by DETI'. While McKibbin was perhaps only now realising the gravity of the situation, it is clear that those closest to Foster had known for weeks that there was a crisis in the scheme she had launched.

Eleven minutes later, Bullick said that McKibbin 'seems very concerned about spending out of control'. He said that McKibbin 'says [it] will be a huge audit issue and af [Foster] better not implicated'. McKibbin told the inquiry he was sure he did not use the word 'implicated' but would have said 'involved'.

Twenty minutes later, Johnston replied from Enniskillen to say that Foster had now spoken to McKibbin and 'this appears financially messy'. McKibbin had told Foster that he was alarmed about the budgetary problem and that he would be discussing it with DETI and the Department of Finance immediately. The very fact that he phoned her when she was not in Stormont was in itself indicative of the significance of the issue – it could not wait until the following morning.

Now there would unfold a development which was astonishing in its timing. Foster said that later that day a constituent who was well known to her, George Gallagher, arrived in her constituency office. Foster said that over time she had accumulated a 'large file' of constituency casework on behalf of the scrap metal merchant and he was someone who was 'in and out of my office on many, many occasions'. On this occasion, however, she said that as he was leaving he gave her a typed note, 'saying he would "leave it with me"'.

The one-page note was explosive. It had a simple title: 'Facts about green energy and biomass in N.I.' and six numbered points. Throughout, the note referred to 'we' – but without any explanation of who had written it.

It said that the scheme had been taken up by many businesses 'but we also believe it is being seriously abused by many ... the scheme is not being monitored ... many people are availing of the scheme who have had no other means of heating previous to this'. The note went on to spell out what was happening:

> Examples of this are large factories who have had no previous heating have installed three biomass boilers and intend to run them 24/7 all year round. With the intention of collection approx 1.5 million over the next 20 years, approx £1500 per week, paid every 3 months. Another example a local farmer who has no business or need for biomass boilers is aiming to collect 1 million ponds over the next 20 years heating an empty shed. We feel the legislation was never intended to be abused like this [*sic*].

Johnston – who no longer appears to have been with Foster at this point – said that she had phoned him to tell him about the note and he advised her to send it to McKibbin for investigation. Foster did so immediately and McKibbin then passed it to McCormick for DETI to investigate. Even if Cairns's evidence about Johnston having been involved in delaying cost controls the previous year was wrong, Johnston would now have been deeply alarmed – doubly so if it was true that he had played some role in contributing to the overspend. He was among the shrewdest of Stormont's big beasts, a towering power behind the throne of successive DUP ministers, and was adept at spotting both political opportunities and threats. If even McKibbin, who was not a politician and knew little about the scheme, could immediately see that Foster was best not involved in this, Johnston would have been ahead of him in realising the acute political peril now facing his boss.

In passing on the note, it was presented as coming from an anonymous whistleblower, and some in DETI believed that if they had been given Gallagher's name they could have spoken to him to gather further useful information. That aside, the note meant that just at the point where Foster said it was becoming clear to her for the first time that RHI – a scheme she knew would raise questions about her ministerial career – was gravely flawed, there now was within Stormont's system a record of her having acted correctly to pass on whistleblowing concerns as soon as they came to her.

Foster initially told the inquiry that she believed that it was on that day – the 27th – that she had been made aware for the first time of the scale of the RHI problem – even though Crawford had been aware of that a month earlier. When pressed around the issue, Foster then told the inquiry that she had looked at her diary and had seen a meeting with McKibbin on 26 January, and that he might have mentioned RHI at that meeting. For his part, McKibbin said that he believed the phone call to Foster's constituency office had been on the 26th and the note was handed to him on the 27th.

The timing of Gallagher's note was extraordinary. Of all the 108 MLAs, he had gone to Foster – the minister who had been more closely associated with the scheme than anyone else. Of all the times to do so, he gave her the note no more than about 24 hours after Foster said she had first been informed about the gravity of the situation. Gallagher was not called to testify before the inquiry. However, in answer to written questions from Sir Patrick Coghlin's team, he said that he was not a member of the DUP. He said that he had typed the note after hearing rumours. Despite having been specific in the note about what was allegedly going on, Gallagher claimed not to have any specific knowledge of the scheme being abused. He said that he could not remember his conversation with Foster. Even with all that has subsequently emerged, the timing, contents and mystique around the note remain intriguing.

Having received the note, McKibbin sent a thunderous two-page memo to McCormick asking for an investigation and an explanation. But the memo ended with a message which bewildered McCormick. McKibbin said:

Finally in your email last night, into which I was copied, you advised that you had a clear message from your Minister and his Special Adviser that the RHI issue was now a matter for the First Minister and me. I have spoken to the First Minister who has made it quite clear that it is the responsibility of DETI to mitigate costs and to urgently cease accruing further liabilities.

Having experienced, as he saw it, Foster's most senior adviser intervene in his department in an unprecedented way just days earlier to rescind a decision taken by the minister who had legal authority for DETI, now it seemed that Foster and her department were washing their hands of the matter. McCormick was perturbed.

There was added tension because Sterling and McCormick had not only been two of the key figures involved in running the scheme and now in sorting out the mess, but they were two of the permanent secretaries who were shortly expected to apply to be Head of the Civil Service when McKibbin announced his retirement.

Multiple Stormont sources believed that McKibbin was much closer to Sterling, and that may have partly explained why to McCormick it seemed that McKibbin was unfairly dumping the problem in his lap. McCormick later rowed back on that, saying that there had been misunderstandings due to a 'fog of war'.

But Bell was deeply alarmed by what was going on. It seemed to him that a paper trail was being constructed which said that Foster wanted the scheme closed urgently and the responsibility for doing so rested with him. Yet he knew that Foster's top lieutenant had stopped his attempt to do just that the previous week. Festering suspicions within Bell – exacerbated by a wider rift with Foster – now seem to have made him view most subsequent decisions, even benign ones, as part of a conspiracy. Foster and those around her dismissed the idea that there was some shadowy attempt to keep RHI open, with the DUP leader saying: 'It clearly wasn't the case that we wanted to keep the scheme open. We knew of the seriousness of it, and we wanted to close the scheme.'

****

On the night of the 27th, a tumultuous day in which Foster had received allegations of widespread RHI abuse and the Head of the Civil Service was panicking about the scheme, Bell was having a wild night. Three thousand miles west, in the city that never sleeps, Bell was heading up a Stormont trade mission. Having already been in San Francisco for an intense series of meetings with potential investors, he had the evening off in central New York. Cairns, Bell, the minister's Private Secretary Sean Kerr and DETI Press Officer Karen Fullerton went for a drink in the bar of the four-star Fitzpatrick Hotel where they were staying. Then the small Stormont party headed out for dinner to Ruth's Chris Steak House, an upmarket chain famous for steaks served sizzling on 260°C plates. But it was the tempting, 200-strong wine list which caught Bell's attention that night.

Cairns recalled that Bell asked if anyone was having wine. Bell's dining companions declined but the minister 'asked if he ordered a bottle of wine for himself, to take the bad look off it, would we get wine glasses' to which they agreed, Cairns said, before Bell polished off the entire bottle.

But the night was still young and after dinner the group headed to The Irish Pub three blocks away on 7th Avenue. By now Bell was 'clearly intoxicated', Cairns said, but they each had a further drink. At this stage, Bell fell asleep, his pint of Guinness half-drunk. The waitress informed them that if the minister did not awaken then they would have to leave as he was clearly intoxicated, his spad told the inquiry. Bell awakened, finished his pint and ordered another. Cairns said they were 'reluctantly served, but were told if Mr Bell fell asleep we would be asked to leave. He again fell asleep and we were immediately asked to leave'.

The 'unsteady' minister had to be helped back to the hotel. The 15-minute walk back took them past Tiffany & Co beside Trump Tower, and the minister sang the Deep Blue Something hit single 'Breakfast at Tiffany's' 'at full volume', Cairns recalled.

In his closing submission, Bell's QC referred to 'attacks targeted at Mr Bell – he has been accused of … drunkenness'. But he did not deny the accuracy of the claims about his behaviour in New York – nor did Bell himself submit a statement to the inquiry denying what was alleged to have happened.

McCormick, in the language of the senior civil service, referred to the incident euphemistically as 'quite a late night' for the minister. The following morning it was noted that Bell was 'visibly tired at a key meeting', he said, and 'it was my impression that, in consequence the minister was unable to participate fully in the meeting in a constructive way, as I would have hoped'.

Bell, whose party was founded by the vehemently teetotal Ian Paisley who denounced 'the Devil's buttermilk', presented a sober evangelical

Christian image of himself to the public and spoke out against the dangers of alcohol. But according to his adviser the incident in New York was part of a wider pattern of a minister whose actions did not always live up to his words. Cairns said that on one occasion when Bell had overslept to the extent that he missed Assembly business, he furiously told Mr Cairns and his private secretary: 'You two boys have f****d up!' Mr Cairns added: 'When Mr Bell was acting in an aggressive manner he often swore. This is not something I would condemn anyone for as I would often swear myself, however … Jonathan was attempting to portray an evangelical Christian image on the Nolan Show. This was at odds with my experience.'

On another occasion, Cairns said that Bell had pinned DUP MLA Michelle McIlveen against a wall at the party conference and 'berated her for some time until she broke down in tears'. Bell vociferously denied those allegations of inappropriate or violent behaviour and suggested they were later invented by the party in an attempt to undermine him after he spoke out about RHI. He highlighted that the party had been happy to promote him and put him forward as a candidate long after many of the alleged incidents.

The minister 'would be aggressive one minute and your friend the next', Cairns said, but added that even at the end of their time in Stormont 'when he wasn't acting in an aggressive manner he offered me a job in the new company he was setting up to establish trade links with China. He went as far as to offer me a salary of £50,000. This offer was made on the last day before Purdah [the pre-election period]. This highlights his erratic nature'.

McCormick had his own concerns about Bell, particularly around whether he read what was put in front of him. But he said that Bell 'always appeared to respect my role and position, often with relaxed good humour, and I had absolutely no personal experience of his exerting (or attempting to exert) untoward pressure or bullying, as others have alleged'. The trade mission complete, the DETI party flew back to Northern Ireland. But the globe-trotting minister was off again a few days later, heading to Brussels on 2 February and then Canada on 9 February, meaning that he was out of the country for much of the period in which key decisions about RHI were being taken.

****

Initially, DETI officials had proposed a closure date of mid-March. But with the involvement of McKibbin, Foster and Sinn Féin's Martin McGuinness, it was decided that the Executive's urgent procedures should be used for an emergency closure. That required the approval of both Foster and McGuinness. In drafting a request to them, DETI sent a draft submission to the Department of Finance. It explained that 'during the Autumn of 2015 there was an unprecedented surge in applications. This increase relates to one particular technology – biomass and has been attributed to one particular industry's wholesale uptake of the scheme. This is the poultry industry's use of RHI for broiler houses'.

When the document arrived with finance officials, Crawford was unhappy, and on 1 February he asked for the poultry reference to be removed – which it was. DETI Deputy Secretary Chris Stewart was concerned and reinserted the sentence. But the Department of Finance intervened again, and it was removed a second time. Crawford's actions meant that the information now going to other ministers was deliberately incomplete.

When asked why he altered the document, Crawford admitted that what he removed was accurate but said it 'wasn't solely the poultry industry' which had driven the spike. Coghlin asked Crawford to 'think carefully … about any inference that the panel should draw in relation to your removal of this entry, given your family circumstances and your frequent talks to Mr [David] Mark of Moy Park'.

Crawford disputed that he had 'frequent' talks with Mark and said 'it is not in relation to any inference in relation to my family', adding that as a former DETI spad he had a role in encouraging Moy Park's growth. In a potentially Freudian slip, he said that 'singling out Moy Park', before correcting himself to say 'the poultry industry, sorry', was something that was 'unfair'.

Coghlin said it was 'undoubtedly true' that Moy Park had a key role in the spike and asked: 'Why remove a true fact?' Crawford said 'it was the inference that was being created at that time'. Coghlin said: 'It's not an inference. That's what I'm trying to get at with you. The major responsibility for the spike was the poultry industry, and Moy Park in particular. If that was true – and it was – why remove something that was true?' Crawford said: 'My concern was the narrative that it was creating.'

Days later, there was another incident which would later add to what by now were Bell's rampant suspicions about party colleagues. In drafts of an

RHI submission to Bell in early February, officials had referred to 'engaging with OFMdFM' and the Department of Finance before the closure decision had been taken. That was removed at Cairns's request. Stewart was concerned at the change and insisted that the reference to the Department of Finance be reinstated because it was a legal requirement to consult that department before invoking the urgent procedure. Cairns said it had been his own attempt to curry favour with Foster who might not want to be linked to the crisis. But he said that a tracked changes version of the document would have gone to Bell, so it was not done behind his back.

Either that version did not go to Bell, or he did not comprehend the change because at a meeting on 10 February, Stewart said he had mentioned the changes in passing to Bell on the assumption he was aware of them. It was immediately apparent that he was not and was furious.

In his Nolan interview, Bell referred to the incident as a 'cleansing of the record', saying that Stewart had requested to meet him as a whistleblower – although in the interview Bell had suggested this was at a far earlier stage, in 2015, when in fact it had been right at the end of the scheme in 2016, further implying confusion by Bell. He said that Stewart had said 'in a very grave and serious tone' that 'you don't know this, but your special adviser is asking for records to be changed'. Stewart said that was utterly wrong and that their exchange had been coincidental as they chatted while waiting for others to join them for a routine meeting.

Foster said that she was unaware of the change and insisted that it was 'completely meaningless' because Bell had gone on to mention OFMdFM in his Assembly speech anyway. But she admitted that it was 'a very strange episode'.

Stewart later felt that the removal of the reference was because 'there was a desire for the difficult, potentially controversial, decisions that were being made on this matter to be presented as having been made solely by Minister Bell … I think there was a strategy emerging at that point for Jonathan Bell to be front and centre in the decision-making on RHI'. Stewart said that 'an inescapable conclusion' was that the effort was to remove any hint that Foster's spads had been involved.

****

On 5 February, Foster and McGuinness approved for closure on 15 February, with the announcement made public in a press release issued by Bell that evening. But it happened to be a Friday evening – a classic slot in which to bury bad news, although he later said that was not the intention. The industry was furious, having expected RHI to be open until at least the end of March. The following Tuesday, Bell flew back to Belfast from Canada and was immediately summoned to Foster's Parliament Buildings office ahead of his ministerial question time in the Assembly. It was an angry encounter. Bell said that there was an 'abusive' atmosphere, with Foster shouting, telling him that he must delay closure. Foster disputed that, saying that Bell had come into the room 'in a very bad temper'. He stood, she said, 'with his chest pushed out and he was shouting that he wasn't going to be made look foolish'.

Foster, who had observed the backlash against sudden closure and was concerned that it might be defeated in court, later said that Bell 'didn't want to look foolish' by doing a U-turn. Bell said that he was primarily concerned about the cost to taxpayers. Foster said that did not make sense because he had been happy to approve a mid-March closure, and a brief extension beyond 15 February would still see RHI closed before then.

That afternoon, Bell met Robinson. The former First Minister said that Bell felt he was being 'marginalised and alienated'. Robinson said that he advised Bell to have a 'clear the air' meeting with Foster.

That evening, Bell and Foster met again. This time it was a calmer affair. Having realised the opposition to sudden closure, he agreed to the two-week delay, despite being unenthusiastic about it. Bell said that he then spoke to McCormick that evening and was reassured by his acceptance of the delay.

The genesis of the two-week delay was indicative of how many key Stormont decisions were taken on the basis of raw political power. If the DUP and Sinn Féin agreed on anything, they had the numbers – and the discipline – to force it through.

Behind closed doors, the two-week timeframe was plucked out of the air by DUP and Sinn Féin spads, with no analysis of the cost to taxpayers nor any expert input from those running RHI. Foster admitted: 'I don't think there was any science to it.'

The following day, Sinn Féin's powerful 'super spad', Aidan McAteer, texted Johnston to say: 'We should keep any discussion of soft landing for renewable heating scheme out of Executive.' Johnston told the inquiry that it was 'not unusual' for the two parties to deliberately keep issues from being discussed at the Executive to keep them from the smaller parties. He said that McAteer would not have wanted the details 'discussed in front of other Executive parties' because of possible leaks. The Executive was a leaky ship, with all parties guilty when it suited them, but this showed a conscious effort to keep details of a crisis which would impact every minister's budget away from those who on paper made up the power-sharing administration. The real decision-making forum was not the symbolically circular Executive table in Stormont Castle; it was in the back rooms where DUP and Sinn Féin advisers met without notetakers.

Cairns, who was present at the heated meeting between Foster and Bell, said that Foster had been 'up-front and said "this is coming from DFM [deputy First Minister] side … I mean, this is what's required to get it through"'. That is consistent with the fact that senior Sinn Féin MLA Conor Murphy publicly claimed credit for the delay. And fellow Sinn Féin MLA Máirtín Ó Muilleoir was not only both privately taking credit for keeping RHI open for two further weeks but also telling a woman hoping to install a boiler that the party wanted to see as many people like her getting approval as possible. Ó Muilleoir told the inquiry that Sinn Féin felt that 'we're going to try and get a grace period for these ordinary, genuine applicants'.

Those revelations – which came from emails which the inquiry compelled the party to release – undermined Sinn Féin vice president Michelle O'Neill's claim at the height of the scandal in January 2017 that her party 'shut it down straight away' when the problems became clear.

After the emergence of the emails, Sinn Féin then claimed that even though it had helped to delay closure, it had not been aware that RHI was being abused.

Foster told the inquiry that she believed she had told McGuinness, who by that stage was dead, of the abuse allegations – and that even if she had not, that McKibbin would have done so. Sinn Féin reacted furiously. O'Neill told the media that 'any attack on [McGuinness's] integrity in government is spurious' and 'disgraceful'. She said such 'attacks' would be 'robustly challenged' and referred to legal action against a DUP politician.

But incontrovertible evidence then emerged showing that in late January 2016 McKibbin had emailed a copy of the abuse allegations to McGuinness's spads after a meeting in which he briefed the deputy First Minister about the issue. McAteer, McGuinness's key adviser, admitted that was true but insisted that he had never told his boss about the allegations. Regardless of whether that was the case, Sinn Féin clearly knew of the alleged abuse before it decided to delay closure.

Some senior civil servants were alarmed at the delay. DETI Deputy Secretary Eugene Rooney told McCormick that a senior finance official 'has raised whether this announcement is consistent with what the Executive has agreed – he feels it may not be … [he] is also concerned that there will be an additional budget implication … and do we have an estimate?' McCormick replied to say that the delay had been agreed 'through the usual channels' and 'my understanding is that legitimate authority and approval exists for the announcement'.

The two-week delay would let in 298 boilers at an anticipated cost to taxpayers of £91.5 million. Part of the apparent relaxation of Stormont about the two-week extension was the belief that by now RHI had been 'fixed', with abuse or overcompensation no longer possible. But that was wrong. Stormont's own analysis would later say that even after the November 2015 introduction of tiering and a cap of 400,000 kWh per boiler, the scheme was still hugely overcompensating claimants. There also had been no end to 'gaming' the system by installing multiple boilers in one building. The decision to allow the most lucrative tariff to apply to boilers of twice the size meant that it was now possible to install multiple 199 kW boilers and just run each of them up to the cap – meaning that tiering became almost meaningless, because individuals could get paid the top rate for all their heat.

In Stormont's defence, that problem had always existed in GB where RHI was also deeply flawed. Ofgem's inspectors had told it that in the first 18 months of the GB scheme there were multiple problems, including a Herefordshire farmer using eight boilers to heat one building – which had the door open. The GB legislation was deficient to the extent that someone enquired about RHI heating a lake for windsurfing. Another individual in GB successfully used RHI to heat a games room with a large hole in the roof because of a legislative 'duty to accredit', even if the application seemed nonsensical.

In February 2014, energy expert Neil Lawson told an audience at the University of Leeds that the GB RHI was paying 8 p/kWh for the first tier – double the cost of biomass, 'so all the farmers are out there heating their chicken sheds with all the doors open, all their barns with no doors on – it's a crop to them; it's another way of generating income'. Warning that such perverse outcomes were ultimately not in the industry's interest, he told how the previous week he had been informed of a group of farmers in the southwest of England who the previous year had clubbed together to buy 140 biomass boilers at an bulk discount. But, he said, 'they're taking them out; they're throwing them away' to buy better quality boilers. He explained: 'Because the RHI's so generous, they can afford to do that.'

The same month as Lawson's talk, someone at an RHI event told a senior Ofgem manager that they knew 'quite a few people in our local farming community who are saying they're giving up sheep and just raking in the money from the RHI'. Nine months later, an Ofgem manager was told by a Scottish farmer that the GB RHI was so lucrative that he had sold his entire herd to install RHI boilers in the sheds which once housed cows – even though he had no current need for the heat.

CEPA's retrospective analysis was that when the Northern Ireland RHI launched in 2012 the GB scheme was 'much more generous' and 'only at high load factors would the NI scheme be more attractive ... but this then fell rapidly (from c.£11,000 pa at 15% to c.£4,000 in roughly two years) as the [GB] degression mechanism kicked in'.

✳✳✳✳✳✳✳✳✳✳✳

On 18 December 2015, Crawford had been told clearly by a senior finance official that Stormont would have to pay for the RHI overspend. Yet weeks after that – and aware of how Moy Park had massively added to the first spike in applications – he tipped off Moy Park about the fact that RHI would soon be closing.

On 15 January, the new Finance Minister, Mervyn Storey, and his spad, Crawford, met with Moy Park's chief executive, Janet McCollum, at the company's head office outside Portadown. Civil servants were not present and no minutes were taken. Storey said that the meeting had been arranged as an MLA prior to his appointment as Finance Minister.

At the end of the meeting, Crawford told Moy Park that RHI was shutting. Storey said he had 'no specific recollection about this aspect' of the meeting. And, as was frequently the case in his evidence, Crawford told the inquiry: 'I don't have a clear recollection of the meeting' but suggested it was unlikely that he had a clear idea of the RHI closure proposal at that stage – even though he knew the scheme was so far over budget that it would have to be shut.

The meeting took place on a Friday, and on the following Monday senior Moy Park executive Mike Mullen, who had been in the meeting, sent a confidential note to senior colleagues, saying that 'we were unofficially briefed last week that the RHI will soon be closed'. The company immediately tried to get as many of its farmers into the scheme as possible. Moy Park manager Alan Gibson replied to say: 'In absolute confidence. Final push needed on our own farms and contract growers in NI.'

Mullen the following day asked colleagues to 'prepare where we are at, how exposed we are based on some scenario's [*sic*] of what they might do and ideally what are [*sic*] would want them to do'. He ended the message with a clear indication of who the company saw as its most helpful Stormont source: 'Then we could go up and see Mr Crawford!'

Two days later, David Mark told his colleagues: 'I will organise a time with Andrew Crawford.' When asked at the inquiry if Moy Park had then come to lobby him, Crawford said: 'I don't recall.' Mark said to his colleagues that ideally the company would like RHI to stay open until August because 'we would really sweep everything up in this case – but every month [is] a bonus'.

Crawford highlighted that DETI had received a message four days before the Moy Park meeting that the company was pressing its farmers to install boilers before the scheme shut, suggesting that it may have had another source for inside Stormont information.

But regardless of whether Crawford was the first or second source of Moy Park's information, the impact of the leak was that not only did taxpayers now lose more money – but the vast poultry processor again had an unfair advantage over its rivals and anyone else wanting to install boilers.

Defending his interactions with Moy Park, Crawford said he had 'concern about the wider implications for the [poultry] sector' – but insisted there was 'no malice' in his actions.

Astonishingly, less than three weeks after warning Moy Park that RHI was to close, Crawford was giving the impression to fellow DUP spads that he was worried about another spike. He said in an email: 'Should we be making some comment ... that we will be carrying out a full audit [of] the scheme? This might limit another spike in applications before we get approval from the Assembly and will head off inevitable criticism that the scheme is being abused.'

Yet Crawford had already tipped off Moy Park. Was he trying to limit non-Moy-Park entrants, aware that a vast spike of Moy Park plus others would lead to scrutiny? Or was it that at this stage – after seeing the panic from McKibbin and others at the scale of the RHI commitments – Crawford was now panicking, aware that he had given Moy Park a three-week advantage over the public? Or was the thrust of his email actually designed to discourage non-Moy Park applications? After all, the poultry sector had a legitimately huge demand for heat, meaning that an audit process would not necessarily cut the bill to taxpayers – but might frighten unscrupulous applicants out of applying, leaving more of the pot for poultry.

Whatever his thinking, here was Crawford – who had been involved in the scheme from the outset – still playing a key role almost a year after he had left DETI.

Curiously, despite the fact that he had close associations with the Ulster Farmers' Union (UFU), Crawford did not tip it off about closure, according to UFU policy officer Chris Osborne. Was that coincidence, or was it part of a more strategic effort to assist Moy Park in particular, rather than agriculture or even poultry in general?

The final spike is particularly suspicious because there had been negligible uptake after tiering of tariffs in November 2015. When Bell announced the sudden closure of the scheme in February 2016, installers and potential claimants argued that there were a host of businesses planning to enter the scheme only to be left with huge financial liabilities. Understandably, MLAs empathised with their constituents about what appeared to be uncaring government action. But the tiny uptake since November suggests that unless word of the impending closure had leaked out – via Crawford and perhaps others – few of those businesses would have been in a position where they were already in the process of installing boilers. Yet again, the DUP spad had contributed to the bill for taxpayers increasing massively.

It also may have been that there was still a lingering hope from some in the DUP that London would pay more of the bill. On 26 January, McCormick emailed Stewart and Sterling to say that RHI was being dealt with by Foster and McKibbin. 'My impression [is] that the focus is on seeking a better outcome from HMT [Treasury].'

As Stormont moved towards closing RHI, it was boom time for boiler installers. Initially, they were terrified by the threat of closure within ten days because some of them had ordered stock which they feared would be unsellable. But with the two-week delay, and with Moy Park's early warning of the closure, installers struggled to meet demand.

Such was the rush to complete installations before the deadline that installer Alan Hegan phoned his heat meter supplier in Scotland to ask if he could deliver heat meters to the ferry in Stranraer where a passing haulier would collect them, because he could not even wait on a courier. He said that he and other installers were putting up tradesmen from across the Irish border in hotels, with electricians and plumbers working through the night in a bid to beat the deadline – and individuals were willing to pay those additional costs, such was the lucrative nature of the RHI payments, even after the scheme had supposedly been fixed to prevent overcompensation.

Another installer, Neil Elliott, recalled that 'there was desperation to get equipment'. Boiler manufacturers were increasing production to meet the sudden demand. He recalled how some customers were willing to airfreight a boiler from Austria rather than bring it in on a lorry to ensure that they got it in time. 'It was, you know, whatever it cost, [they] didn't care. This was the thing; it was incredible. I mean, we had staff working 24 hours a day to get them installed.' He said that RHI had increased the amount of heat in Northern Ireland rather than simply replacing fossil fuel systems with greener alternatives. He said: 'You know, the idea was to produce 20% heat by renewable sources: it wasn't to add 20% heat onto the current heat load. So, what it's done is now, you've spaces being heated. Now, some of them did need to be heated, but you've added more heat onto the heat load rather than taking away from it.'

CHAPTER 16
LET'S CLAIM IT WAS A SUCCESS

At 4.15pm on 15 February 2016, Jonathan Bell rose from the blue leather benches of the Assembly chamber in Parliament Buildings and began to mislead the Assembly at the request of his civil servants.

Just ten of the 108 MLAs were present as he began to speak with typical self-confidence. Bell was there to ask MLAs to pass legislation which would give him the power to close RHI to new entrants at the end of that month. But even at this late stage, he and DETI found it impossible to admit what they all knew: RHI had been calamitous.

Although Bell's speech to the Assembly referred to 'significant budgetary pressures' and the need to close the scheme for financial reasons, he described it as 'beneficial' and denounced the criticism that 'money has been squandered or investment lost', saying plainly: 'That is not the case.'

It was preposterous – and Bell knew that what he was saying was inaccurate. His spad, Tim Cairns – who over two days of evidence to the inquiry spoke frankly, even where that often meant portraying himself unfavourably – said that Bell's speech had been prepared by officials who, like the minister and his adviser, understood that RHI was a disaster.

Over the preceding weeks, officials had finalised a regulatory impact assessment which had to accompany the legislation. That document, which Mr Bell signed to indicate his endorsement, set out four potential options for the future of RHI.

Even though the scheme was then being closed under urgent procedures due to being vastly over budget and amid allegations of gross abuse, the document set out a far brighter picture. It claimed: 'All four options show that the RHI has a positive impact on the NI economy – i.e. the benefits outweigh the costs. The largest net benefit lies in keeping the scheme open.' Cairns said that he did not recall reading the document, and said it was 'certainly a remarkable paragraph'.

It was Stuart Wightman who prepared the false document. He admitted to the inquiry: 'We should not have been framing the RHI scheme as a success … taking into account the overspend, overcompensation and concerns about gaming or fraud.' However, he highlighted the document was 'shared with and approved by senior officials'. Yet again, DETI seemed institutionally focussed on protecting itself from criticism rather than being honest not just with the public – but with the legislature. As Bell misled the chamber, Cairns, Wightman, Seamus Hughes and John Mills were sitting just feet away in the Assembly box for officials.

Cairns said that the document reflected a similar sentiment to that suffusing Bell's speech and that he had been 'somewhat uncomfortable' about it. He said: 'There kept on being references to how great the scheme [had been] ... of course, the immediate political attack on that is: well, if it's such a great scheme, what are you doing closing it?' He said that the language jarred with the minister and himself because throughout Bell's speech there was 'positivity' when in reality they all knew that there had been a 'cloud of gloom' over DETI because of the scheme. However, he said that although they raised their unhappiness with officials over what Cairns said was 'a bizarre approach that was being taken', with the need for urgency they went along with accepting the speech.

When asked if he and the minister believed what was in the speech, he said: 'No. Absolutely not. No, no, no. You know the budgetary position – you scroll up [in the document] and it's £95 million or whatever it is over five years, just on the page before. There's certainly a disconnect between the two.' He candidly admitted that both he, the minister and officials knew that RHI was 'a disaster'. Inquiry chairman Sir Patrick Coghlin said: 'This is again the creation of a document that you knew to be completely false – just like Mr Bell's signing the letter [to appoint his Spad] that he knew to be completely false and that's what you mean, I think, by "real politics". If you need to do it, you need to do it.' Cairns said: 'You're absolutely right. You know, I think to delay by a day or whatever at this point in time to debate the issues in that, I suppose you've got to pick your fights.' Cairns admitted that what Bell had said was 'crazy' and 'beggars belief'.

During the debate, Sinn Féin's Conor Murphy said: 'I would not like the suggestion that something untoward was going on to hang as a backdrop to or rationale for the decision taken today. There was a clear statement from the most senior officials in the department that they had heard no evidence that any abuse was going on.'

The DUP would later attempt to undermine criticism of Foster's role in the scandal by highlighting that other parties voted to keep RHI open at this stage. Even based on Bell's absurd claims about the scheme being 'very successful' and being 'a positive news story', it ought to have been clear to those parties that the subsidy was now simply unaffordable. But the misleading ministerial speech meant that they were at least able to argue that they had been actively misled.

It was particularly indefensible because the speech was not designed to win over MLAs. As with much Stormont business, a deal had already been done between the DUP and Sinn Féin to vote for the legislation, and they had the numbers to force it through. This wasn't even some ethically elaborate case of the end justifying the means in order to protect the public purse. Rather, this was a straightforward attempt to deflect criticism – and scrutiny – of unjustifiable behaviour.

Bell also presented the decision to delay closure by two weeks as his – even though he later said that it was foisted upon him by Foster. When asked to reconcile that with his later claims, Bell told the inquiry that there are many things which happen in government 'under protest' where 'it's not … politically expedient' to tell the full story.

Though the chamber had been sparsely populated for the debate, when the division bell rang to signal a vote, MLAs piled into the chamber. Foster, who had not attended the debate, came and sat beside Bell as MLAs waited to vote. A smiling and relaxed Bell chatted to his leader with no public hint of the paranoid rage he felt at what had been going on behind the scenes.

The legislation passed and on 29 February the RHI scheme closed to new entrants. By the time it shut, there had been 2,128 applications – the overwhelming majority of which were for biomass boilers.

****

In farcical fashion, Foster and Bell's relationship continued to deteriorate. On 29 February – the last day for RHI applications – London Mayor Boris Johnson visited the Wrightbus factory in Antrim. The celebrity politician was there to announce a £62 million order for Ulster-built Routemaster buses and local politicians were eager to bask in some of the reflected glory.

Bell had not been invited and he was livid. In the end, he just showed up unannounced and was included in photos as Johnson did pull-ups under the chassis of a bus. After the event, Bell demanded that his permanent secretary launch an investigation 'in order to ascertain why he had not been invited to attend the visit'. Bell said that the Secretary of State, Theresa Villiers, had told him that an invitation to him had been issued. McCormick replied in writing to say that he had discussed the issue with the chief executive of Wrightbus and with the Northern Ireland Office, but ultimately advised Mr Bell 'that no further action should be taken'. McCormick told the inquiry that he had been informed – either by Tim Cairns or by Bell – that Bell was 'taking advice from Peter Robinson in this period'.

A week before asking McCormick to investigate the absence of an invitation to the event, Bell had emailed Foster to complain. He said: 'I have major issues with the activities of DUP personnel and the behaviour of DUP SPADS. I am prepared to discuss these with you on a one to one basis at a time that is mutually agreeable to both of us.'

Later that month, Bell emailed Foster, DUP deputy leader Nigel Dodds and DUP chairman Lord Morrow. Bell told them he had been 'extremely hurt by the manner in which I have been treated', and among his concerns he listed RHI, where 'without consultation with me your SPAD advised mine that the scheme was to be kept open ... There has been a number of allegations of fraudulent activity with this scheme and I have been informed that an official has claimed that the scheme was kept open to accommodate a family member'.

Foster forwarded that to Dodds, Timothy Johnston and Richard Bullick with the message: 'I am at the very end of my tether with this individual. He has now put in writing the very serious allegations he has been talking about for sometime [*sic*]. I think he should be asked to provide evidence forthwith ... the very first thing I expect from him is an apology given that he has wilfully ignored my leadership since 3rd March'.

Johnston entered the discussion, saying that 'I think he is running out of road' and 'he is now putting it in writing knowing he is running out of time. He will be unable to substantiate such claims'. Dodds, who had been in written exchanges with Bell that day, then told Foster and Johnston: 'It's interesting that he now decides (after advice??) to pen this lengthy email. Is this his language?? He is on weak ground in not being able to provide corroboration for his allegations so we collectively stand up to him in a coordinated way.'

There was, at least on Dodds's part, a suspicion that Bell was being advised by someone. Bell's closeness to Robinson was well known to all of those on the email but the advice could also be an allusion to a lawyer or perhaps even Ken Cleland. Foster told the inquiry that she had told Bell to come and see her about the issues on 3 March, but he refused 'and instead went to see … Robinson'.

****

Meanwhile, within DETI a postmortem started over how RHI had run out of control. DETI's head of internal audit, Michael Woods, was asked to investigate. Woods said that in a career where he worked on about 500 audits, RHI led to 'the worst opinion I've ever had to give' because in terms of spending public money he found that 'there's just no control there'.

Woods said that even if officials had been right in their belief that the Treasury was funding RHI, 'you don't just spend because the money's there – you spend because it's justified to spend it'. He added: 'I think that was lost. The idea that it was [Treasury funding] almost seemed to people to remove the risk – but we are in charge of public money'. He was shocked by the nature of what he found within Energy Division and was concerned at the way in which the officials running RHI cooperated with him. Woods said it was 'one of the lowest levels of cooperation I've experienced' and led to the department beginning an investigation ahead of potential disciplinary proceedings.

Wightman said he was 'completely astounded' when he heard Woods's criticisms, and said he had been 'entirely open, honest and transparent' with him. He admitted that 'some of the responses were inadequate and of little utility' but defended them by saying that he was 'busy' at the time.

Wightman and Hughes did not provide Woods with a copy of the 'handover note' given to them on joining DETI, which significantly undermined the story which they were telling Woods at that point. Wightman admitted: 'I appreciate that it looks to Mr Woods as if relevant information that should have been disclosed to him was withheld. I accept that the handover note was relevant … if I had recalled its existence, I accept that I should have provided it to him, and indeed I would have done so.' Wightman said that at the time he 'did not recall the handover note'.

In March, Woods's team sent a series of questions to Hughes and Wightman. Among Wightman's responses to the questions were 'don't know' and 'no, haven't asked' – reinforcing the sense those running RHI were ignorant of key aspects of the scheme, even after it had been shut. Woods told the inquiry: 'That is the sort of answer that I have never, never seen. I hesitate to laugh, but I've never seen a response like that from somebody to an audit question.'

Wightman admitted that it might be thought that Hughes's responses were 'unhelpful'. However, he said that they were 'not intended to be our full and final response' and 'identified gaps in our knowledge'. He claimed that 'the candid and unvarnished responses' were 'indicative of an open and transparent approach by officials', and there was 'no attempt to conceal or put any sort of gloss' on their lack of knowledge.

In May, Woods reported that 'the system of risk management, control and governance established by management over the ... scheme' was 'unacceptable' – the lowest possible rating. But despite those scathing findings, Wightman and Hughes remained in post managing the RHI fallout. And, despite what was now known of the multiple failures by DETI officials in this period, just after the scheme was shut Wightman recommended that Hughes should receive a bonus for his RHI work. On a 'Special Bonus Form', Wightman wrote that 'over the last four months, Seamus has performed at a level well above that expected of his grade' in relation to RHI. He said that closure could not have been 'implemented on time without Seamus's involvement'. The bonus was approved.

But by now scrutiny had moved outside the department. The scale of the overspend and the irregular expenditure had been drawn to the attention of the Northern Ireland Audit Office, and it began its own investigation.

As the Audit Office investigated the scheme, it met DETI's audit committee in April 2016. The Comptroller and Auditor General, Kieran Donnelly, told the inquiry that one of his senior staff, Tomas Wilkinson, who was at the meeting recalled a striking comment from Mills. Donnelly told the inquiry that Mills had said that even if the subsidies had been excessively generous, 'the key point was that the money had been available from GB and if the scheme had not been taken up then there would have been a loss of income to Northern Ireland as a whole'. He said that McCormick – who would have been aware of the view the Audit Office would take of such a philosophy – immediately corrected Mills by saying that value for money was critical.

On 5 July, the Audit Office published an 18-page report on the scheme. For the first time, the public heard that RHI had been burn to earn and that the bill could be more than £1 billion.

It was also the first public exposure of the note, which George Gallagher had passed to Foster six months earlier, claiming that a farmer was in line to receive £1m over the next 20 years for heating an empty shed. The Audit Office calculated that the overspend would take £140 million from Stormont's block grant over the next five years, and DETI's accounts were qualified as a result.

By now, there had been a reorganisation of Stormont departments and DETI had been reconstituted as the Department for the Economy (DfE). Just two months earlier, Foster had overseen a remarkable election victory, holding the DUP's all-time record of 38 Assembly seats, while Sinn Féin lost a seat, putting it ten MLAs short of the DUP. Foster removed Bell as minister and appointed the experienced Simon Hamilton to the new department. At the time, it raised eyebrows that despite having the first pick of Stormont departments the DUP had this time – for the first time ever – decided to pick DfE rather than the Department of Finance. Foster said that was because of the importance of the economy, but the decision perhaps also hinted at DUP alarm over what would happen with RHI if another party got to look inside the department.

Responding to the Audit Office report, Hamilton was contrite, saying: 'The potential ongoing costs of this scheme to Northern Ireland taxpayers are incredible and the accusations of fraud will be rigorously investigated.'

Although relations with Bell were privately strained, the DUP presented itself as a 'family' and pretended that all was well. In that vein, there was a closing of ranks where protecting the party was more important than the full truth. After the Audit Office report Hamilton told *Good Morning Ulster*: 'I would point out that whenever those issues were raised with my predecessor [Jonathan Bell] he stepped in very, very quickly – and whenever the full extent of the cost over-run was understood, he moved very quickly to close the scheme down.' If Hamilton had even cursorily investigated what happened in the summer of 2015 then he would have known that one word which could not have been used accurately was 'quickly'.

Senior DUP colleague Sammy Wilson, a green energy sceptic, implicitly denounced Foster and Bell, saying that 'in their manic attempts to show how keen they were to save the planet from global warming, many Assembly members competed with each other to display their green credentials. It was inevitable that the enthusiasm to make sure that Northern Ireland did not fall behind the rest of the UK in promoting RHIs that mistakes would be made'.

When the scandal became a political crisis, Wilson would adopt a very different tone. On *Good Morning Ulster* on 16 December – ten days after the *Spotlight* exposé – Wilson was asked if Foster should apologise for her role in RHI. Incredulous, he replied: 'For what … what role?' and went on to ask: 'What did she do wrong'?

But behind the scenes as the Audit Office report was emerging, something else was going on. By 4 July – the day before the report was published – Stormont had received an embargoed copy. Foster's top spad, Johnston, launched his own investigation. In doing so, he tried to cover his tracks, instructing that documents should only be requested over the phone rather than by email, which would leave a written record.

The spad used private DUP email addresses, rather than departmental accounts, to make the request to his colleagues, meaning that the communication would not have been discoverable unless he or the DUP handed it over. On 4 July, Johnston urgently sought from Hamilton, and his spad, John Robinson, 'all submissions that were put to Arlene on the RHI scheme by DETI'. He went on to say that 'we need this material discreetly today and when asking for it do so by phone call and not email'.

Johnston told the inquiry that he wanted 'to provide an accurate record so that any comments and statements that were publicly issued … were in fact accurate' and said that Foster was aware of his activities.

When asked why he used party email accounts – rather than official government email addresses – Johnston said: 'This was my practice for all of my period as a special advisor … my department and ministers all knew that had always been the case'.

That meant that anything done by the DUP's most powerful backroom figure was off-grid and could not be accessed by the public or the civil service – despite the fact he was being paid £92,000 a year by taxpayers to operate as a temporary civil servant.

The Audit Office report received widespread media coverage. The *Belfast Telegraph* front page that day ran a banner headline: 'Farmer gets £1m of public cash to heat empty shed'. But it was the summer and the Assembly was not in session. Within days the focus turned to the annual Twelfth of July parades and there was a sense that this was just another scandal about government squander – with no one able to be held to account.

In June 2016, just before the Audit Office report, Janette O'Hagan – who had attempted to raise the alarm three years earlier – emailed the Greenvale Hotel in Cookstown. O'Hagan suggested that her energy-efficiency product could save the hotel money, make it more efficient and more comfortable. The hotel's owner, Michael McElhatton, said: 'Can't guarantee you any business [because] we are currently operation [*sic*] on biomass and to be honest the way it operates the more pellets we burn the more RHI we get paid.'

The following month, after the publication of the Audit Office report, O'Hagan emailed Green Party leader Steven Agnew. In the course of her email, she said:

> To give you a bit of an insight, a few weeks ago in early June I had went [*sic*] to Cookstown and called in at three hotels and an office, trying to tell them how I could save them 30% of their heating costs. All four had biomass boilers (apparently it was a 'too good to miss out on scheme') – it was more than 20 degrees outside and all of them had their heating on with the windows open because, as they'll openly tell you themselves, the more that they use, the more they earn and they definitely don't want to start being efficient. One small hotel – that only has 11 bedrooms – told me that he made £5–6k profit last year on their RHI payments (after all pellets had been paid for), so it's easy to see how that will drain the province of millions over the next 20 years.

The RHI list published in March 2017 points to the Greenvale Hotel not running its boiler around the clock. The one 99kw boiler listed for the hotel's parent company, Tobin Ltd, had claimed £34,290 over a 15-month period – indicating that it was running for about half of the total hours in a year.

McElhatton said he had in 2016 spent £90,000 on switching from a diesel boiler to biomass, and the new boiler 'has at all times operated exactly as the old boiler, with thermostatic controls in all rooms for the comfort of guests. There was never any change to how the hotel operated as a result of a different boiler.'

Referring to the claim of unspecified hotels in the area running boilers in June while the windows were open, he said that 'under no circumstances could – or would – this ever have been the case at the Greenvale' and 'the suggestion that guests would be subjected to this sort of environment in any hospitality setting does not ring true'.

The businessman said that Ofgem inspectors had visited the hotel and found that its boiler was operating 'in full compliance of all regulations and completely in the spirit of the scheme'.

By September, the Assembly was back and its powerful Public Accounts Committee (PAC) launched an investigation into RHI, a common step after an Audit Office report. The decision was taken unanimously by the cross-party committee. Its chairman, Ulster Unionist MLA Robin Swann, recalled that there was 'no real political kickback from the DUP until Arlene Foster's name appeared – because until then it looked like it was all the civil service's fault'.

A turning point came in October when the department discovered O'Hagan's emails from 2013. The committee agreed that a cross-party delegation would visit O'Hagan to hear her story. It was a highly unusual move which demonstrated how immediately seriously the MLAs were taking the revelation. She handed over the emails which she had sent to Foster and to the department. However, on the day that MLAs were to meet O'Hagan, the DUP MLA who was meant to attend failed to show up. That would later put the DUP at a disadvantage as it attempted to respond to questions about O'Hagan's emails without a clear picture of what she was saying.

Swann said that throughout the entire process of O'Hagan speaking – without being named – to the BBC in December 2016 and then coming before the inquiry, 'her story never deviated' from what she told MLAs that day. Swann said that at this point, with Foster becoming more closely associated with the scheme, he saw the committee 'start to get slightly political', despite the fact that its role in scrutinising public expenditure is such that MLAs are meant to set aside their party allegiances.

Swann was resolutely apolitical in his role as committee chairman, even tangling with his deputy – SDLP MLA Daniel McCrossan – when McCrossan got into a row with a DUP MLA at the committee. That stood out because the SDLP had by this stage joined the Ulster Unionist Party (UUP) in forming Stormont's first official opposition since 1972.

By the time the scandal erupted with the BBC *Spotlight* programme on 6 December, the committee had held six lengthy evidence sessions. After the sudden explosion of publicity in December there was some criticism of MLAs for not doing enough to uncover the issues themselves. But in truth much of what emerged came through the work of the Audit Office and Swann's committee. What ends up in a television programme or on a newspaper front page often starts its life in a half-empty committee room.

Although the committee hearings were receiving limited publicity, they were being reported by two journalists – David Young of the Press Association, who came up with the phrase 'cash for ash', and BBC NI's Conor Macauley. But, as sometimes happens with important stories, their reports received limited attention.

Alongside the PAC hearings, there was another committee hearing in this period which would be hugely significant. The Assembly Finance Committee was investigating allegations that Sinn Féin had 'coached' the loyalist blogger Jamie Bryson before a major evidence session the previous year.

Sinn Féin's Máirtín Ó Muilleoir, who had been a committee member when Bryson made the allegation but by now was the Finance Minister, was being pressed by Bell, now a member of the committee. Under pressure, Ó Muilleoir spent several minutes attacking Bell over RHI in an attempt to divert from his line of questioning. He said: 'No one did more damage to our finances than Jonathan Bell through the renewable heat incentive, and I am cleaning up his mess.'

Various sources have pointed to this as the moment when Bell became worried that the DUP and Sinn Féin – now in a close Stormont alliance – were going to make him the scapegoat for RHI.

In late October, John Manley of *The Irish News* was interviewing Foster ahead of the DUP conference when he asked about RHI. Few people had made the link between RHI and Foster, who was at the peak of her popularity. Under the front page headline 'Foster washes hands of £1bn subsidies scandal', the paper reported: 'Mrs Foster says she accepts no responsibility for the scheme's shortcomings because 'it was developed by officials in a way that shouldn't have been developed by officials', and said she was not responsible for 'every single jot and tittle' within her department. It was the start of a long pattern of Foster refusing to accept any responsibility for the scheme which, when she believed it was popular, she had proudly presented as her own.

CHAPTER 17
SPOTLIGHT

Conor Spackman woke on the morning of 5 July 2016, turned on his radio and heard something which would lead to him playing a key role in the collapse of Northern Ireland's government six months later.

On *Good Morning Ulster*, BBC Radio Ulster's flagship morning news programme, DUP Economy Minister Simon Hamilton was being questioned about the Audit Office report into RHI. Although he was on holiday, the journalist in Spackman was struck by one phrase from the DUP minister. Explaining how the RHI mess had developed on the watch of successive DUP ministers, Hamilton said: 'It doesn't serve us well to get into the politics of this. It's clear from the mountain of evidence that I have looked at that ministers weren't warned by officials of any issues or risks which subsequently emerged.'

Spackman, a reporter with BBC Northern Ireland's respected *Spotlight* investigative unit, couldn't get the phrase out of his head. He sought out the Audit Office report and immediately realised that this was a huge story.

A few days later, over dinner he told friends: 'You've never seen anything like this in your life.'

Though he did not know it at the time, the 36-year-old reporter, who had arrived at *Spotlight* just ten months earlier, was on to the biggest story of his career.

By September, the *Spotlight* team were closely following the Assembly's Public Accounts Committee (PAC) sessions investigating RHI. Spackman's producer, Richard Newman, watched the first mammoth hearing at which much of the eye-watering detail of what had gone on tumbled out.

Fronting up for the department was Andrew McCormick and it was his unusual contrition which jumped out at the watching journalist. McCormick was verbally clothed in sackcloth and ashes, telling the committee 'there is no good answer to that', 'there is no good explanation', 'we do not understand why' and describing how the department designed the scheme in a way that was 'bizarre'. This was far beyond the normal perfunctory apologies from mandarins.

Spotlight investigations tended to be slow accumulations of material and sources, and there was no rush to air. The following month, the investigation assumed increased political significance when Spackman spoke to a source who told him that a whistleblower had contacted Arlene Foster personally. He obtained the email, something which would become *Spotlight*'s central new revelation.

The team was investigating allegations about DUP spads Stephen Brimstone and Andrew Crawford, but they never featured in the programme. Extensive right of reply questions were sent in writing to Foster in October – the month before Brimstone left his post as Foster's spad.

And queries were also going to senior civil servants, something which discomfited mandarins not used to facing tough media questions. Having received little more than stock responses from officials – who said that it 'would not be appropriate' to talk to *Spotlight* while the PAC was conducting its own inquiry, Spackman visited some of them at their homes in an attempt to understand what had really gone on.

In response, senior civil servants showed greater alacrity in lodging a formal complaint with the BBC than they had done in addressing any of the problems with RHI. The visit to Fiona Hepper's upmarket Cherryvalley home in the leafy East Belfast suburbs led to a particular fightback.

Stormont's most senior civil servants – including the Head of the Civil Service, Sir Malcolm McKibbin – worked on drafts of a letter of complaint which was sent by their press office to BBC NI's controller, Peter Johnston, complaining about 'this incident of intrusion and infringement'. That was unusual because it involved the most senior civil servant and his deputies in what at a glance would have seemed to be a trivial case of a journalist approaching someone and asking them questions.

But it was unusual for a second reason – by taking the complaint to the most senior BBC figure in Northern Ireland, the mandarins were not just going over his head, but over the head of his boss Jeremy Adams, the editor of *Spotlight* who was feared by the powerful and respected by his peers due to his programme's consistently robust investigations.

BBC NI's controller dismissed the complaint, highlighting that the reporter and his producer had been 'acting with proper editorial authority and consistent with relevant BBC guidelines'. He said the claim that they had been involved in 'doorstepping' Hepper was wrong because they did not seek to confront or record the official and did not even have a camera. Rather, he said that they asked Hepper whether she would like to help with their journalistic enquiries.

On 24 November 2016 – less than two weeks before the *Spotlight* programme was aired – there was some intriguing contact between Crawford and Mark Anderson, his friend who was a biomass expert at Ulster University.

Apparently responding to a question from Crawford about written communications between them about RHI, Anderson emailed to say there was 'very little on email :)'. The smiley face suggested that he, and presumably Crawford, were pleased that there was little written record of whatever they had discussed.

At the inquiry, Crawford said that the message was in the context of a discussion about Anderson applying for a new job. Anderson would soon leave his university role to work for a major RHI beneficiary, the wood pellet supplier Balcas.

Although the sender of the email, Anderson, handed it over to the inquiry, the recipient, Crawford, did not. Nor did Crawford hand over other prior emails between the pair. When asked about that, Crawford said that 'from time to time I deleted emails relating to RHI'.

But it was not the only time that Anderson appears to have been concerned about what he had written down about RHI.

Electronic communications which Sir Patrick Coghlin's inquiry compelled revealed that six weeks after the Crawford–Anderson communication about what RHI material was held on email, Anderson sent a message to a public servant.

The 3 January 2017 WhatsApp message – to Chris Johnston, the head of the Environment and Renewable Energy Centre at the Department of Agriculture's Agri-Food and Biosciences Institute – said: 'Some time you have five minutes, will you check your emails from July 15 to September 15 to see if you have anything on the closure of the RHI?'

On 20 July 2017, Anderson sent another WhatsApp message to Johnston which said: 'Please don't put the letters RHI in my emails any more'. The timing of that message alluded to why it had been sent – just three days earlier, the inquiry had written to Anderson and asked him to hand over all material relevant to RHI.

When called before the inquiry, Johnston accepted that he believed the request to be an attempt to prevent material going to the inquiry.

****

Given what several senior DUP figures knew about their role in RHI, when *Spotlight* came to air, they had cause for relief.

Most of what it reported was in journalistic parlance 'old news'. But it was a programme which demonstrated how mistaken journalists can be in the belief that the best journalism has to involve major new revelations. Instead, it was a masterful simplification of a complex story which visually enraged the viewer. Newman, the producer, had the idea of literally burning money to bring home to taxpayers what the scheme meant for them.

And it was that image – filmed in Crawfordsburn Country Park on the shores of Belfast Lough – which gripped viewers. Sitting in the winter dark by a fire, Spackman casually tossed £20 note after £20 note – and then entire bundles of cash – into the fire as he impassively told viewers about the wild incompetence of their representatives.

The programme began with the reporter sitting in a Belfast bar as he delivered his opening piece to camera in the relaxed style of speaking to a friend in the pub:

Did you hear the one about the Renewable Heat Incentive? A government scheme that went hugely over budget. It was supposed to be a green scheme, reducing our reliance on fossil fuels, but as well as being economically disastrous it actually ended up being damaging to the environment. There was a series of extraordinary blunders, and because of those blunders we're likely to spend the next 20 years picking up a tab of hundreds of millions of pounds.

John Simpson, a respected veteran economist who had worked at senior levels in the public sector, told the programme that it may be 'the biggest financial penalty imposed on taxpayers in Northern Ireland that has occurred in my lifetime'.

He described it as a 'heads you win, tails you can't lose, type situation' for boiler owners. Images from a thermal camera were red hot, showing how much heat was being generated – and paid for by viewers – in poultry sheds heated under the scheme.

The half-hour programme ended with a devastating sign-off from Spackman about the anticipated RHI overspend: 'Those ongoing costs are likely to be at least £400 million. That could have paid for the new Omagh

Hospital, the dualling of the A26 at Frosses, the York Street Interchange and the Belfast Rapid Transit System. With £15m left over.'

****

The programme had featured one individual who unwittingly as he set out how disastrous RHI had been was building a trap into which he would himself fall.

Michael Doran, who described himself as 'the foremost authority in Northern Ireland on renewable energy', was chief executive of Action Renewables, a green energy charity which had been set up by Stormont but subsequently became independent of government.

Spotlight had contacted him because of his expertise and he agreed to be filmed explaining the scheme's fundamental flaws. The silver-haired businessman explained: 'What they do is they pay you an amount for the heat that you generate. What's actually happened here is that they've set a rate which is higher than the cost of the fuel in the boiler therefore you're actually incentivised to run the boiler for as many hours as possible.'

An incredulous Spackman asked him: 'In other words, in this scheme the more you burn the more you earn?' The bespeckled and softly spoken Doran replied: 'Basically yes.' When the reporter put to him that it 'sounds like a really fundamental cock up', Doran replied: 'Yes it is.'

But the following month – as Northern Ireland continued to be gripped by the scandal – *The Irish News* revealed that Doran's organisation had processed about 550 RHI applications. That commercial service saw Action Renewables take in almost £400,000.

When asked by the newspaper why no one within the charity relayed concerns about the scheme to DETI, Doran argued that to do so would have been 'ethically improper' because businesses were paying his charity to get them on the scheme. In a change of tone from his interview with *Spotlight*, Doran went on to say: 'The fact that the government created the scheme that some people now think is over incentivised is not our responsibility.'

Those comments led to a complaint to the Charity Commission that Action Renewables had been acting improperly. But, after speaking to Doran and other trustees, the commission received assurances which led it to reject the complaint.

However, more than a year later Doran appeared before the RHI Inquiry. During a day of devastating evidence, he emerged as someone who knew far more about the flaws in RHI than he had publicly suggested until that point.

Pressed by inquiry counsel Donal Lunny, he accepted it was 'possible' he had given evidence to the Charity Commission which was the opposite of what he had given under oath to the inquiry. Coghlin said it seemed an 'inescapable inference you were misleading the charity commissioners'. Doran paused before saying: 'It would appear from this document, yes.'

The inquiry also revealed how Action Renewables not only knew about RHI's perverse incentive and kept quiet – the charity actually explained to a business how RHI could be abused and informed it that to deliberately run boilers just to get public money 'is not wrong'. Those comments were made in reports which were funded by taxpayers and commissioned by Invest NI in an attempt to encourage energy efficiency.

The inquiry was suspicious of the fact that Action Renewables initially did not hand over the reports when ordered to do so by the inquiry and only produced them two days before Doran's appearance.

In one report drawn up for a company, Action Renewables said that RHI payments 'artificially encourage larger biomass systems to be installed … these systems are operated longer than necessary, generating more heat and making more significant returns on investment … whilst this philosophy is not wrong, it is not considered the most cost-effective, due to higher capital outlay'.

Confronted with that, Doran accepted it was 'incorrect' and said such a philosophy 'is not only wrong; it's possibly also illegal', but insisted he had not been recommending it. Although the reports never suggested businesses should abuse the scheme, they showed a detailed understanding of how eye-wateringly lucrative RHI was. On one occasion, the charity set out considerable detail of how to 'maximise return from the RHI' as opposed to using the most efficient heater. In another report, it calculated that RHI was so generous it would see payback in just 1.7 years – with the high payments to go on for another 18.3 years.

****

Five thousand miles away, Arlene Foster was asleep when *Spotlight* went out. Two days into an exhausting trip to deepen links with China, the First Minister and her team were pleased with how things were going.

That day she had held talks in Shanghai with Chinese Vice Premier Madam Liu Yangdong, the most powerful woman in the Chinese state, as well as having taken part in a series of meetings with Communist Party officials and businesses.

Unusually, the First Minister was the only politician on the trip. Two days before they were due to travel, Stormont Castle announced that Martin McGuinness was pulling out of the trip 'due to unforeseen personal circumstances', an allusion to the illness which within four months would take his life.

The deputy First Minister's place was taken by McKibbin, and a small group including Foster's private secretary, her spad Richard Bullick, a Stormont press officer and a photographer travelled with her.

Foster was enjoying the trip. She was at the height of her powers – almost a year into office as First Minister, on the back of a remarkable DUP election victory and jointly at the helm of what was then the most united Stormont Executive since the 1998 Good Friday Agreement.

She had a packed diary, with the windows for reflection or consultation with party colleagues back in Belfast largely limited to long periods of travel between three Chinese cities.

As the trip wore on, Foster and Bullick would be seen deep in conversation away from the others, but they kept up appearances and the trip went on as though nothing was amiss.

Although the DUP knew that the programme was coming and had carefully prepared written responses to *Spotlight*'s questions in advance of leaving Northern Ireland, Bullick did not see the broadcast.

The following morning at breakfast – just a couple of hours after the programme had gone out in Northern Ireland – one of Foster's departmental press officers, Leona Edgar, approached the only journalist on the trip, UTV's deputy political editor Tracey Magee, to ask her if she intended to question the First Minister about *Spotlight*.

The journalist asked if there had been much new material in the programme and Edgar said that she did not believe so – a not unreasonable response, given that much of the meat of the programme had already been published.

The issue was dropped until later that day when UTV's newsdesk rang Magee, who by then was in Shenyang. 'You've got to get her,' they told her. 'But there's nothing new,' Magee protested. 'I know, but the shit has hit the fan here and we have to get her,' came the response.

Unusually for a foreign trip, Magee and her cameraman were embedded with Foster's party, in part due to Chinese sensitivities about filming by a Western television crew. But in travelling from Shenyang to Beijing, the UTV team became separated from the others, arriving late at night at the Chinese government-approved hotel in central Beijing where Foster was staying.

Foster and Bullick – in contact with colleagues in Belfast, but focussed on that day's meetings – mulled over whether to agree to the interview. Having declined to do a detailed sit-down interview for *Spotlight*, Foster knew that at some point she was going to have to address the allegations. Declining a second interview would not look good.

By the time the journalists arrived at the five-star China World Hotel, which boasts that it offers 'a grandeur worthy of royalty', the interview had been approved. But time was running out. UTV's main 6pm news was looming and getting film back to Belfast was not straightforward due to China's internet firewall.

As soon as the UTV team arrived at the hotel, they abandoned their luggage and took Foster to a vacant area in front of the entrance. About 1am Foster, wrapped up against the winter cold of the Chinese capital, stood in a vacant piece of land amid the skyscrapers which dominate the skyline of the Chinese capital's central business district. She faced four questions about her RHI role.

Outside the glare of the television lighting, most of the others present on the trip stood in the dimly lit open space, observing the First Minister's first public reaction to what had erupted at home. Dressed all in black, Foster was a confident interviewee. But at the end of the brief interview, her answer to one obvious question would come to encapsulate how the public viewed her response to the scandal.

Magee asked: 'Do you regret how you handled the matter? Could you have done more?'

Unperturbed, Foster said that she had spoken to her former permanent secretary that day and he had told her that while she was minister he did not understand the problems with RHI 'and therefore wasn't in a position to advise me of the difficulties of [sic] the scheme'. Then she added: 'So there really isn't anything more, with hindsight, that I could have done, given the advice that was given to me at the time.'

Foster still gave no signs of being tense or alarmed by what was going on. But the following day, the final day of the trip, the full scale of the crisis back at home began to dawn on some of those in the travelling party.

The group had some free time, and that afternoon Magee tuned in to *The Nolan Show* where the whistleblower was speaking publicly for the first time. Foster was not listening to the broadcast – but Bullick was. Both he and Magee grasped the significance of what was now unfolding. Some of the civil servants could also comprehend that RHI was moving from a financial crisis to a political crisis.

Foster was in the immediate line of fire and it was impossible to fight back against Janette O'Hagan, the woman whose warnings should have prevented the scandal. Still speaking anonymously, the businesswoman told Nolan how she had simply gone online to check the RHI tariffs and told him: 'I swear it took me five minutes to realise it was set up wrong, Stephen, when I compared it with the UK one. So all these people saying they didn't know … it took just five minutes of a normal person looking online to realise that it wasn't right and there was [sic] opportunities for fraud there.'

It was the second day of Nolan's coverage in the wake of the *Spotlight* broadcast on the Tuesday night. His team had been on to the scandal as well, digging around in the final weeks of the *Spotlight* investigation, and therefore immediately grasped the significance of the whistleblower going to Foster directly.

Nolan – whose programme was part breaking news, part phone-in – cut through the complexity of the story to explain in graphic terms how the money had been squandered and what that meant for others who depended on public money.

From the morning after *Spotlight*, he was hearing from people who couldn't afford to heat their own homes who were livid at what they had watched. An elderly woman was interviewed live from her bed where she was wrapped in a blanket because she couldn't afford to turn on the heating.

On the other side of the world in a luxury hotel, Foster was vulnerable. But the DUP leader, perhaps insulated from reality by the extended honeymoon she had enjoyed since becoming First Minister, was slow to grasp the threat which the story posed to her.

Back at Stormont the following Monday – six days after *Spotlight* – Foster knew she had to address the issue publicly after a weekend of revelations about DUP links to RHI boilers. That represented the emergence of a narrative of DUP links to claimants – something which would prove calamitous for the party.

That Monday morning Foster agreed to give a 12-minute interview to BBC NI's political editor, Mark Devenport. When asked if the public was owed an apology, Foster ducked the question, saying that 'the implementation of the scheme is something I do regret', before shifting to highlight the failures of many others involved in RHI.

Devenport pressed her on whether she owed the whistleblower an apology. Slightly irritated, Foster corrected him for using the phrase 'claw some of this back' in relation to the overspend, noting 'you don't claw back something if you haven't spent it'. She was less keen to directly answer his question but offered no apology, with the First Minister again shifting focus to 'my officials' who she said failed the whistleblower.

It was a sign of the pressure on the DUP that during the interview Foster performed a rapid U-turn, abandoning the stance of the minister responsible for RHI, Simon Hamilton, just four days earlier when he had said that 'the Data Protection Act prevents, even if I wanted to, me from putting these names [of RHI claimants] into the public domain'. Foster, seemingly influenced by the fact that DUP-linked names on the list had started to leak out, said it was now her desire to see all the names published.

The interview also confirmed a fact which had been widely rumoured among political journalists and at Stormont, but which had not yet been reported – that Stephen Brimstone had an RHI boiler. Brimstone had suddenly left his job as one of Foster's spads about a fortnight earlier. It was claimed at the time that he was leaving the £92,000 job to which he had been reappointed just six months earlier to pursue unspecified private sector endeavours.

When asked by Devenport if Brimstone had an RHI boiler, Foster's answer was somewhat vague: 'Yes, as far as I understand Stephen was a claimant.' In fact, Brimstone had gone to Foster almost a year earlier, within days of her becoming First Minister, and told her that he had a boiler.

That conversation in her Parliament Buildings' office was brief because, Brimstone later recounted, Foster simply asked him: 'Are you happy everything's OK with it?' and when he said that he was 'that was the end of the matter'. Foster did not ask him to make a written declaration of interest, and over coming weeks he was sent correspondence about what was becoming increasingly urgent attempts to close RHI.

When asked about keeping a written record, Brimstone told the inquiry 'that wasn't the way we worked … other than a letter of resignation or a letter of appointment – that was the sorts of things that you put in writing to each other [*sic*].'

As Christmas approached, there was a belief among senior DUP figures – and some in Sinn Féin – that the story would blow over. They could not have been more wrong.

FIRE, AND BRIMSTONE'S PROBLEM

For seven years, Stephen Brimstone was getting headaches. When the weather was cold and he crossed the yard from his home to work in an outbuilding, as with most garages or sheds, there was no permanent heating.

Brimstone wanted to have the building – which resembled a very generously sized garage – heated, so he used both an electric heater and a portable oil-fired heater. But the oil heater emitted fumes which hurt Brimstone's head whenever he went to the shed to repair a tractor or check on sheep from his father-in-law's nearby farm which might be temporarily residing in a corner of the building.

For seven years, the DUP spad put up with the headaches. But in late 2014, Brimstone began to consider a solution: he would install an RHI boiler in his shed. By the summer of the following year – as RHI was running out of control and others in the DUP were involved in delaying it being reined in – Brimstone settled on what he would do.

The 36-year-old party loyalist decided that he would install a wood pellet boiler in the shed, use it to heat the shed when he needed it, and run most of the heat via an underground pipe to his large detached home in the countryside outside Ballymena.

A welcome bonus of his decision was that as well as curing his sore head it meant that it moved him on to the lucrative non-domestic RHI scheme. That meant that as Brimstone stood in the shower each morning he could do so in the knowledge that the more heat he used, the more he earned.

The vast bulk of the heat from Brimstone's boiler was going to heat his house and there was a domestic RHI scheme he could have entered. But its terms were far less lucrative, involving set payments for seven years – not the unlimited 20-year 'cash for ash' payments under the non-domestic scheme.

Although it would seem strange to the average person that a tiny use of heat in an outbuilding would allow someone to get paid under a non-domestic scheme for heating their home, Brimstone believed that was within the letter of the law which his party colleagues had brought through the Assembly.

He had encountered RHI through his work as spad to the Social Development Minister. Using his Stormont connections, Brimstone asked fellow spad Andrew Crawford for some help. In November 2014, Crawford asked a DETI official for the phone number of Stuart Wightman, the key RHI official, and passed the number to Brimstone.

Brimstone did not call Wightman for about three months, but eventually phoned in February 2015. Wightman remembered the call because it was unusual. The spad, who gave his name but did not identify himself as a senior Stormont figure, began by saying: 'I believe you're the man to talk to about RHI.'

It was only after the call that Wightman worked out the identity of the man to whom he had spoken. Even in the fairly anonymous world of spads, Brimstone, whose name was in itself memorable, had a degree of public notoriety. Three years earlier, BBC *Spotlight* had broadcast an investigation which centred on a whistleblower, the DUP councillor Jenny Palmer. Palmer, who was a DUP representative on the board of the Housing Executive, the public sector social housing body, said that she had been put under inappropriate pressure by Brimstone to change her vote on the board. The vote related to a request by Brimstone's minister, Nelson McCausland, to extend a maintenance contract for the controversial firm Red Sky.

The £8 million-a-year contract had been terminated amid allegations of over-charging and Palmer was concerned about its activities. But Brimstone, she said, told her how to vote, adding bluntly: 'The party comes first. You do what you're told.'

The DUP denied that some of its senior figures had links to the firm and Brimstone said that Palmer's account of their conversation was inaccurate. However, a lengthy Assembly committee inquiry process – during which there were farcical scenes as Brimstone either refused to answer multiple questions or repeatedly said he could not remember what had happened – found Palmer to have been a credible witness while it described Brimstone as 'deliberately evasive in his answers to the point of obstructing the committee', a finding with which DUP members of the committee disagreed.

In August, six months after he had called the civil servant for advice, Brimstone's 32 kW boiler was installed. But there was another factor which made the Stormont adviser's situation highly unusual – he had removed an existing domestic wood pellet boiler in order to install one which would be eligible for RHI.

The Fermanagh-born spad had put in a biomass boiler in 2007 and received a £3,000 government grant to do so. Biomass boilers are expected to have a life expectancy of between 15 and 20 years but Brimstone said that his became costly to maintain after just eight years and it was that – rather than a desire to make money – which led him to scrap it.

Whatever Brimstone's motivation and whatever the letter of the law said, if the regulations allowed someone to use a non-domestic boiler to heat their home when they had very little other need for heat, there were obvious deficiencies in how the scheme was set up.

In June 2015 he agreed to the installation of a boiler at a cost of about £15,500, writing on his application form that the shed was 'used for both machinery and at times animal pens for out farm livestock (namely sheep) that require close monitoring and heat during lambing season'.

Brimstone described the shed as a 'non-domestic' building, save for 'one small area ... used at times for storage of firewood'.

Denzil Cluff, who checked the boiler on behalf of the installer, recalled that among other things the shed held several domestic items – a ride-on lawn mower, a canoe and a 'substantial amount of firewood'.

Around that time, and for reasons which remain unclear, Brimstone became involved in discussions between the two main DUP spads dealing with RHI – Crawford and Cairns. The 8 July ministerial submission to Jonathan Bell was forwarded to him by Cairns. That document made clear that RHI could not be afforded and would have to be urgently reined in by the autumn. Brimstone, by this stage just three weeks away from having his boiler installed, emailed back to say that it was 'hard to argue with what's being suggested'.

The following month Brimstone's parents-in-law, major farmers John and Lilian Anderson, would install two RHI boilers which between them would attract payments of more than £85,000 in their first year and a half of operation. Brimstone's brother Aaron, who ran a go-karting business in County Fermanagh, installed a boiler in January 2016, the month before RHI was shut for good. At the public inquiry, Brimstone said that he had not played any role in his relatives' applications.

Over many months from the summer of 2015 onwards, Brimstone would intermittently go on to be involved in internal discussions about how to handle the RHI problem without ever formally declaring a very obvious financial interest. At no time in 2015 did he even informally say to others that he had an RHI boiler. By early 2016 he spoke to the First Minister about it but she did not tell him to provide any sort of written record of his potential conflict of interest.

Confronted with that at the public inquiry in 2018, Brimstone admitted that he should have immediately declared an interest and then taken no part in the discussions. 'I thoroughly regret not putting my hands up and withdrawing myself,' he said.

****

On the morning of 10 May 2016, senior Ofgem manager Edmund Ward opened his post to find an anonymous letter which raised his eyebrows in the Milbank office where he was based. Even without any special knowledge of Ulster politics, it was clear from the letter that there was an allegation of fraud against a senior political figure.

Ward, a mild-mannered specialist who headed up the teams responsible for technical decisions relating to RHI, immediately scanned the letter and forwarded it to colleague Teri Clifton in Glasgow, Ofgem's head of operations responsible for administering the Northern Ireland scheme.

Who sent the letter remains a mystery, but whoever it was had an intimate knowledge of Brimstone's heating arrangements. The allegation was that Brimstone was heating his home with a boiler receiving subsidy under the non-domestic RHI when he should have been on the domestic scheme. He was doing so, the letter said, by telling Ofgem that the boiler was installed in an agricultural shed. The typed letter alleged that Brimstone's activities amounted to 'total fraud ... in keeping with the mindset of our political elite'.

The letter went on to question whether Brimstone had any agricultural business of his own – something which seemed significant if his justification for having a non-domestic boiler was that he had a sideline as a farmer. Showing detailed knowledge of the spad's arrangements, the individual said that Brimstone had a flock number but told Ofgem to ask him whether he had any sheep and alleged that on his form for EU farm subsidy there was no mention of him owning any land. In blunt language, the letter writer said: 'The shed is no more agricultural than he is! He is using the pellet boiler to heat his mansion home at the TAX PAYERS [*sic*] expense! This is a total fraud!'

What would become Case 335 for Ofgem's counter-fraud team would expose Brimstone to deeply uncomfortable public scrutiny, and by the time the investigation was complete he would no longer be working for Foster. It would also reveal multiple concerns about both the poor drafting of the RHI regulations and Ofgem's enforcement of them.

On receiving the letter, Clifton immediately used her power to halt payments to Brimstone and asked for an audit of his installation. However, under Ofgem's sluggish processes it took six weeks for his premises to be inspected. And remarkably, even though this was a targeted inspection about a detailed allegation of fraud, Brimstone was phoned before the audit to alert him to the date of the inspection.

The DUP adviser was unhappy that the audit was to be on a day when he was on a foreign holiday, meaning that it was his father-in-law who showed the inspector around.

The auditor's report included the observation that he 'could find no evidence of the building described as agricultural workshop/storage being used as a workshop or for animal pens as described'. That, he said, constituted non-compliance. In simple terms, it meant that the auditor believed that Brimstone was breaking the rules.

The auditor reported that inside the shed he had found a tractor, shelving, tools and some fencing posts – but also children's toys. There was 'no sign of animals having been there or any adaption for that purpose'. He gave the site an overall assurance rating of 'weak' because it was in breach of the rules but said those 'moderate issues with eligibility ... can be rectified within a reasonable timescale'.

In Glasgow, Clifton was unsettled by the auditor's report. She did not feel that it provided the 'definitive evidence' she had hoped for as to whether he was a legitimate claimant or a fraudster.

On 3 August, she emailed a colleague to discuss what she termed 'our special case'. She was acutely aware of Brimstone's position as an adviser to the First Minister but later told the inquiry that he had been subject to the same rules and processes as any other member of the public.

Eventually Ofgem wrote to Brimstone asking for explanations and was satisfied with his responses. On 23 September 2016, it informed him that his situation was acceptable and payments resumed.

But within three weeks – perhaps another indication that the person making the allegations was either close to Brimstone or had access to some of his RHI information – a second note making similar allegations was sent to the DUP's political nemesis, Traditional Unionist Voice (TUV) leader Jim Allister. The MLA passed on the note, which bore similarities to the May letter, to the Northern Ireland Audit Office, the Police Service of Northern Ireland (PSNI) and Ofgem – unaware that Ofgem had already investigated the issue.

The Audit Office forwarded the note to the DUP-run Department for the Economy and asked it to investigate. Two days after that letter from the Audit Office, the DUP spad in the department, John Robinson, went and directly told Brimstone that there had been an allegation that his RHI boiler was fraudulent. That was potentially significant because although Brimstone knew that he had been audited, he did not know that it was because of an allegation against him.

Despite the timing of that conversation with Brimstone, Robinson told the inquiry that he was unaware of the letter from the Audit Office at that point and that instead he had received an entirely different briefing from his permanent secretary in relation to the first Ofgem investigation of Brimstone.

On Robinson's evidence, that seemingly quite anodyne news – that a complaint had been investigated but dismissed – led him to immediately send a text message to Timothy Johnston, the DUP's most senior backroom figure, to say: 'I need a [sic] urgent word with you before your next meeting. It's RHI and Stephen.' Robinson then travelled that day to Stormont Castle and told Johnston that Brimstone had been investigated.

Brimstone then joined the two spads and, according to Robinson, was told that he had been investigated and cleared – something he knew anyway by that stage because Ofgem had written to him. Robinson said he did not tell Brimstone that he was still being investigated because to do so would have been inappropriate.

Less than a fortnight later, on the morning of 24 October, Johnston emailed his senior spad colleague Richard Bullick to say that Robinson was 'in possession of more material about sb [Brimstone] and his rhi [sic] application. We are both of the view this is not good, now involves the Auditor General and will not end well'. Bullick replied almost immediately to say 'oh dear' and said he would call.

Three weeks later, Brimstone resigned from his £92,000-a-year job as a spad, just six months after being reappointed by Foster. Brimstone has always said that his resignation, just three weeks before the BBC *Spotlight* programme, had nothing to do with RHI.

He later told the inquiry that he had not wanted to return as a spad after the May 2016 election and only reluctantly was 'talked into' continuing in the well-paid job for a 'short period'.

Because of the fact he was choosing to resign, rather than being made redundant by his minister, Brimstone did not get the lucrative golden handshake common for Stormont spads who lost their jobs. Since that point Brimstone has been working as a self-employed IT consultant.

Like Brimstone, Foster insisted that there had been no link between RHI and her spad's departure. But although Brimstone did not ultimately feature in the *Spotlight* programme, rumours about him and the impending *Spotlight* had been swirling around Belfast for weeks.

On 14 October 2016, the PSNI also got involved. Having been passed the allegations by Allister, police asked Ofgem to assist its investigation. Three days later, Ofgem's Samantha Turnbull emailed Ofgem's head of counter fraud and Clifton to ask: 'Given the political sensitivities [*sic*] how would [*sic*] like us to proceed with the DC Adams?'

Turnbull wanted to show police the auditor's report into Brimstone's boiler. However, others in Ofgem were less keen for that to happen. Turnbull was given legal advice from an Ofgem lawyer that 'whilst we should strive to assist them [the police] with their investigation, we should only do so if we are convinced that they have good reasons to be investigating him'.

Rather than sharing the audit report, she was instead advised to confirm that Ofgem had investigated the issue and 'concluded there isn't any cause for concern'. Detective Constable Adams subsequently agreed there did not seem to be any criminal issue and the case was closed.

****

On 23 January 2017, seven weeks after the *Spotlight* exposé which had turned RHI into a huge political scandal, Allister got to his feet in the Assembly.

By that stage, it was clear that Stormont was collapsing and there was an air of chaos. It was the penultimate sitting of the Assembly before dissolution and an election. MLAs did not know it at the time, but the Assembly would not sit for debates of any sort for more than two years.

Allister, a formidable criminal QC, was loathed and feared by many in the DUP. As he got to his feet from his customary seat by the main doors of the chamber, the TUV leader began with a joke at his own expense, assuring the Speaker that he would be 'much easier to control' than the last contributor, veteran socialist Eamonn McCann. The Assembly laughed, but Allister was there on serious business. The Assembly was debating emergency legislation to retrospectively slash RHI payments.

More than half an hour into his speech, Allister – in whose North Antrim constituency Brimstone lived – turned to the former spad. Speaking under Assembly privilege, meaning that Brimstone could not sue him for defamation, Allister told the story of a farmer who had come to him in distress the previous week. He told the MLAs: 'Interestingly enough, this farmer was introduced to the scheme by the then DUP special adviser Stephen Brimstone, no less.'

Allister said that the farmer, who had invested heavily in RHI boilers based on the cast-iron guarantees given to him, had been audited and found to be bona fide. 'When that person asks "What's going to happen to the fact that I am relying on this promised return to pay off my bank? What am I to say to my bank manager, Mr Allister?" I do not have an answer for him.'

Allister then turned to 'others' who 'saw this as a quick buck … or as a means to heat their house'. Knowing what was likely to come, the DUP minister Simon Hamilton nervously twiddled with a paperclip as he listened from his front bench seat.

Allister then brought into the public domain that Brimstone was claiming to heat his home under the non-domestic scheme. 'Did he claim that he had a few sheep and was a sheep farmer? Does he have sheep?' Lowering his voice, he said gravely: 'One thing is for sure: he is heating his own house. Is that right? Is that how things should be under this scheme?'

Allister said that what he was doing was 'scandalous' and a 'rip-off', telling MLAs that Brimstone had taken out a relatively young boiler in order to enter RHI.

Although the story immediately led to front-page coverage in Northern Ireland's daily newspapers, Brimstone reacted to Allister's allegations with silence. The DUP was evasive about someone who had been one of its most powerful Stormont figures until just a couple of months earlier. When faced with questions about Brimstone, the party refused to say if he was even a member and then said it was 'not privy' to details of his situation, as he was now a 'private citizen'.

****

Unknown to the public, Ofgem had already decided to conduct a second – and this time unannounced – inspection of Brimstone's boiler. On the morning of 30 March 2017 Brimstone found an investigator sent by Ofgem standing at the gated entrance to his home.

Inside the 'agricultural shed', the auditor found a vintage tractor which was part of a restoration project, a large pile of logs for Brimstone's home, children's toys, a workshop area and – perhaps because this time, unlike the earlier inspection, it was lambing season – some soiled wood shavings.

As with the initial inspection, Ofgem asked Brimstone follow-up questions. On 4 July 2017 – seven months after the *Spotlight* programme – Ofgem's chief operating officer, Sarah Cox, met senior colleagues to discuss Brimstone's case. They were there to finally decide on what should be done about Brimstone, and Cox's presence reflected how significant this case had become.

During the discussion she challenged the view of Clifton and Ofgem's internal lawyers that Brimstone was acting within the law, pressing them about the value for money of what was happening and whether Ofgem was protecting taxpayers' money. In response, they admitted that the former spad's arrangement may not have been within the spirit of the law but said that he was acting within the letter of the regulations and therefore there was nothing they could do.

At the conclusion of the meeting, even the presence of Ofgem's chief operating officer was insufficient for a decision to be taken and instead she took the issue to the very top – to chief executive Dermot Nolan. Whatever the nature of their discussions, the case was settled in Brimstone's favour and his payments kept flowing.

After more than two years of internal debate and investigation, Ofgem ultimately came to give Brimstone a completely clean bill of health. He had not broken the rules in any way, Ofgem said, and that view was endorsed by the public inquiry which conducted its own substantial investigation into his situation. That concluded with inquiry counsel Joseph Aiken stating that not only was Brimstone in compliance with the law but the evidence of how he was using the boiler was in keeping with the average heat use for a house, with the boiler running for an average of about four hours a day.

But the case exposed yet another glaring loophole in the regulations which Foster had put to the Assembly. Ultimately, Ofgem came to logically interpret the rules in a fairly remarkable way. Aiken set out how Ofgem effectively believed that under the rules if in a hypothetical situation Brimstone had allowed a local farmer to bring his sheep to Brimstone's shed for one day in the year and that was its only non-domestic use, even though it was carried out by a third party, it would still be entirely acceptable for him to claim for heating his home for the rest of the year.

Under that interpretation, it is likely that many of those who applied to the less lucrative domestic scheme could have found creative ways of getting on to the 20-year non-domestic RHI – and, in the eyes of Ofgem, acted entirely legally.

Although the inquiry and Ofgem both agreed that Brimstone did nothing to break the letter of the law, that did not save him from rigorous questioning. He insisted that he had not thought it odd that he was able to claim a non-domestic subsidy to heat his home. Dame Una O'Brien put it to him that 'the clue is in the name – it's a non-domestic Renewable Heat Incentive scheme'.

She asked him: 'When it became apparent to you that it was possible to do this – you know, admittedly, within the rules – did it never occur to you to say 'Hmm, I wonder if this was really ever intended ... Did it occur to you to say 'This is a bit odd'?'

Mr Brimstone paused before saying: 'It didn't, and probably my understanding of the scheme – limited as it was ... was that up until July 2015, mid-July 2015, I wasn't aware that there was a differentiation for example on the tariff between the GB scheme and the Northern Ireland [burn to earn] scheme.'

CHAPTER 19
THINGS FALL APART

From the night of 6 December 2016 when *Spotlight* seared RHI into the public consciousness, events began to move faster than Stormont veterans had ever experienced or anticipated. Relentless coverage of the scandal on BBC Radio Ulster's biggest programme – *The Nolan Show* – involved two damaging elements. Investigative reporting, with the hidden help of Jonathan Bell and others, was daily revealing new elements of the scandal while the programme's phone-in gave voice to the public's anger.

It was Nolan who had first broadcast an interview with Janette O'Hagan – then known simply as 'the whistleblower' – two days after *Spotlight*. Attempting to undermine that story, the DUP had the following week released what it said was the sole correspondence between O'Hagan and Foster, an email which did not raise concern about RHI. In a statement, DUP deputy leader Nigel Dodds 'called on opposition parties and sections of the media to retract allegations against First Minister Arlene Foster'. He said that the email 'nails the myth that Mrs Foster as DETI minister failed to follow up on "whistleblower" concerns about RHI' and said that Foster was 'now owed an apology'.

There were two problems with that. Firstly, the email was not the only contact with Foster – there had been a second explicit warning of abuse. Bizarrely, Foster had already conceded this to BBC *Spotlight*. Secondly, in releasing the email the DUP had blacked out O'Hagan's name and email address. But it was quickly possible to piece together her identity based on other information in the email – which quickly happened online.

It was a disastrous attempt to quash the story. The DUP had not been sufficiently brave to approach O'Hagan directly but had got senior civil servant Brendan McCann to acquire the email. The businesswoman, who was seeking to protect both her young family and her business from being embroiled in a political argument, emailed McCann in dismay to remind him that 'at no point did you ask for my consent nor did anyone from the DUP and it is really unfair to say publicly that you/they did'. She said that what the party had done 'makes me out as a liar and I can tell you that I have not and will never lie about what happened'.

Pressed at the inquiry about how her party had so shabbily treated O'Hagan, Foster distanced herself from the incident, saying that she did not think that she was involved in discussions about releasing the email. However, Andrew McCormick told the inquiry that there had been a discussion in Stormont Castle with Foster, his own minister Simon Hamilton and the DUP spads in which 'the First Minister wanted to release the email publicly'.

McCormick insisted that the civil service had operated on 'a factual and apolitical basis' but said he appreciated how to O'Hagan the distinction between officials and the DUP would 'appear at best to be blurred'.

The incident appears to have been down to DUP and civil service desperation and sloppiness rather than a deliberate attempt to unmask a whistleblower – there was no benefit to them in saying what they did unless they believed it to be correct. But it added to the public perception that the DUP was attempting to hide what had gone on.

The DUP faced a second difficulty in that the *News Letter*, the editorially pro-Union newspaper read by many of its rural supporters, devoted significant resources to the story. The paper had once been very close to the DUP, and there was a time when the DUP hierarchy could phone the then editor to have uncomfortable stories pulled or altered with the threat that government newspaper advertising controlled by DUP ministers might otherwise be pulled. But those days had long gone by the time the scandal broke and the newspaper now ran front page after front page revealing more and more of the scale of what had gone on – while editorials argued for a public inquiry.

There was an immediate and unique public appetite for the story, which grew with every emerging morsel of information. The *News Letter* was receiving reports that it had sold out in republican parts of Northern Ireland and website records were being broken. Those stories were replicated across the media landscape. By 20 December, the BBC NI website's main RHI article – an online report of a vote of no-confidence in Foster over the scandal – was read 870,000 times, a staggering figure, given that Northern Ireland's population is just 1.8 million and there is generally limited interest in Stormont politics outside Northern Ireland.

Four days after *Spotlight*, it emerged that a Free Presbyterian Church – the denomination closely tied to the DUP – had an RHI boiler. Hebron Free Presbyterian Church in Ballymoney was in line to receive £270,000 from the subsidy. One of the church's elders was DUP MLA Mervyn Storey, who had been the DUP Finance Minister when the boiler was installed. Storey said he had 'nothing to do with it' and 'didn't even give [a fellow elder] any advice in relation to it'.

It later emerged that the church, a building which many of the public would expect only to be heated for services, had in fact installed two RHI boilers – one of them during the October spike in applications before the scheme was made less lucrative – for which it had been receiving huge payments. The boilers had between them brought it almost £60,000 in less than two years.

That same day, the front page of *The Irish News* revealed that Andrew Crawford's brother was on the scheme. Crawford did not volunteer that between them his relatives had 11 RHI boilers. But even without that full transparency, the story added to a public perception that those close to the DUP had got into the scheme.

Within ten days of *Spotlight*, what prior to the programme would have seemed preposterous – that Foster, a popular and politically secure leader, could be out of office within months – had become plausible. The DUP denounced the BBC's coverage, shooting the messenger by claiming that the corporation was biased against unionism – while not legally challenging the facts which were being reported.

DUP MP Gregory Campbell went further. Appearing on *The Nolan Show* January, he warned Nolan on air – as the presenter was stating that he was 'digging' into the RHI scandal – that 'digging works both ways'. When pressed on the comment, he denied that it was a threat. Two years later, Campbell revealed that he had made a series of complaints about the BBC – and Nolan's production company in particular – to the National Audit Office. As a result of Nolan's RHI coverage, the DUP would begin a boycott of his programme which at the time of writing has been going on for more than two and a half years.

It was more difficult for the DUP to accuse the unionist *News Letter* of bias. Several DUP spads heavily involved in RHI were among the senior party figures to privately acknowledge to the paper that its coverage was fair. But some of their colleagues had other ideas.

On 31 December, the *News Letter* front page revealed that just seven months into the scheme, Foster's department had been warned about buildings being needlessly heated, with windows opened, to collect subsidies. Brian Haslett, a DUP employee in Foster's constituency office, tweeted approvingly of that day's *Belfast Telegraph* front page – which had no mention of RHI at all, describing it as 'a front page with REAL issues. Rather than the bias tripe from Newsletter's [*sic*] @SJAMcBride'. He then added: '#Boycott'. Mr Haslett's message was 'liked' by ex-DUP MLA Ian McCrea, then DUP MLAs Phillip Logan and Gary Middleton, and DUP Mid and East Antrim councillor Paul Reid.

But, rather than become a more pliant organ, the *News Letter* reported the boycott threat and drew support from readers and DUP members. The party said that Haslett's views 'do not reflect the party's position'.

Inadvertently, the boycott call drew attention to the paper's coverage and suggested that if some of those close to Mrs Foster wanted the story suppressed, then it must be worth reading.

But there was also a cottage industry of rumour – much of it wildly inaccurate. Some of the accurate stories read like April Fools' Day efforts. The wife of former Ulster Unionist MLA Neil Somerville was using an RHI boiler for a 'horse solarium', the party confirmed – adding that her claims were entirely legitimate.

In January a source told the *News Letter* that police had become suspicious of a building in South Armagh because during a frosty spell the building's roof remained unfrozen while ice covered surrounding structures. Officers, who suspected that it was a cannabis factory, reported their suspicions to their superiors, who requested and obtained a search warrant to inspect the premises. However, when police entered the shed they found that it was almost entirely empty – but that the heating was running, with the owner admitting that he was making money from it.

In the early hours of 6 January, there was a major fire at a shed in the countryside near Enniskillen. Inside the 20m x 12m building, eight biomass boilers had been drying woodchip for a company, Corby Biomass Systems.

Even at this stage, there was more bungling from the department. As late as early January – almost a year after RHI had been shut – it was continuing to use public money to advertise the scheme on Google. Later that month, it sent letters to all RHI recipients to warn them that they were going to be named, prominently advising them to phone a helpline number which did not work.

****

When the RHI crisis struck Stormont's Executive, it was more united than any power-sharing administration which had preceded it. In Assembly elections seven months earlier, the DUP and Sinn Féin had confirmed their dominant positions within unionism and nationalism respectively. In response, the smaller parties – the Ulster Unionists, the SDLP and the Alliance Party – chose not to re-enter government but to instead form Stormont's first official opposition since 1972.

Unused to facing such organised opposition, the DUP and Sinn Féin realised that they would have to prove that they could govern coherently – and set about doing so with gusto.

The referendum vote for Brexit in June strained the Executive, whose parties were on opposite sides of the argument. But even that was taken in the stride of the new administration. It was, after all, not unusual for there to be such fundamental disagreements among Stormont's governing parties – the DUP and Sinn Féin did not even agree on whether Northern Ireland should exist.

In September, the two parties appointed their first ever joint spokesman for what would be a joint DUP–Sinn Féin message. To do so, they secretly changed the law, using prerogative powers which they exercised on behalf of the Queen in order to ensure that they could appoint leading journalist David Gordon as their spin doctor without advertising the £75,400-a-year post.

Gordon drafted the first joint Foster–McGuinness newspaper article which was published just two weeks before the RHI scandal broke. In words which would soon prove to be worthless, the ministers said: 'Imagine if we had followed the example of others and decided the challenges of government were just too daunting. That would have opened the door to years of direct rule – Conservative ministers ruling over us without a mandate. Rest assured, this Executive is not going to abandon you to that. We are in this for the long haul.'

Therefore, when the RHI storm came in December there was an expectation that these two pragmatic parties had invested so much in their relationship that they would ensure it was not destroyed after just a few months.

Within days of *Spotlight*, Sinn Féin's left-wing rival People Before Profit was organising 'Foster must go' street protests. It was obvious that Sinn

Féin was not. People Before Profit's Foyle MLA, the erudite socialist veteran Eamonn McCann, blasted Sinn Féin's inaction: 'The DUP is up to its oxters in ordure. Sinn Féin holds its nose and props them up … it's up to the rest of us.'

On Wednesday, 14 December – just over a week after *Spotlight* and the day on which Jonathan Bell was recording his explosive TV interview – the Executive met. One source present at the meeting recalled it as 'positive', with a 'collective spirit' and 'no ill will at all – far from it'. Another source who was there said that the clear view was that 'all was well' and there was 'a route map' to getting out of the crisis.

After the Executive met, there was a smaller gathering of Foster, Martin McGuinness and some of their key advisers. At that meeting they discussed setting up a limited inquiry into the scandal, with a view that this would put a lid on the story. A public inquiry wasn't on the menu. They agreed to ask David Sterling – one of those implicated in RHI and who therefore had a conflict of interest – to lead the search for an independent investigator.

Those events contradict later unionist fears that Sinn Féin always wanted to pull down Stormont and did so at the first opportunity. But they also undermine Sinn Féin's later claims of taking a principled stand when it was made aware of RHI. Both parties' instinctive reaction was to keep Stormont together, even if that was at the expense of getting to the truth.

Bell's interview, in which he alleged shady behaviour at the heart of Stormont, would blow that strategy apart. His demand for a public inquiry led by a judge instantly showed up Sinn Féin's desire for a tamer probe.

By Friday afternoon, less than 24 hours after Bell's interview, Sinn Féin had shifted its position. The seriously ill McGuinness, who was in London for medical tests, phoned Foster to tell her that she should step aside as First Minister. Foster, a determined character who detested retreat, immediately refused. Within half an hour, a Sinn Féin press release revealed the phone call. It had taken just ten days for their apparently firm partnership to fall apart.

But even now, McGuinness was only calling for something far short of a public inquiry. Foster's stepping aside was envisaged as a few weeks while an 'initial assessment' was carried out. There was precedent for such a move. Peter Robinson had cannily stepped aside as First Minister in 2010 amid a scandal about his MP wife Iris's affair and financial dealings with property developers. Doing so took the heat out of the crisis and, after a lawyer provided legal advice which Mr Robinson said cleared him but which has never been published, he returned to office. But with McGuinness having made the call public it was now difficult for Foster to back down.

Nevertheless, Sinn Féin was not yet ready to topple Stormont. Three days later, the Assembly met to hear a personal statement from Foster about RHI and then to debate an SDLP motion of no confidence in her. The sitting immediately descended into farce. The DUP Speaker of the Assembly, Robin Newton, had already seen his authority diminished over allegations separate to RHI. Before Foster even got to her feet, the hapless Newton faced repeated points of order from across the chamber, challenging him over why Foster was being allowed to speak as First Minister.

McGuinness had initially consented to Foster's statement as First Minister, something only possible in her joint office if McGuinness agreed. But over the weekend he had withdrawn that consent after a meeting of Sinn Féin's leadership, including leader Gerry Adams, in his home city of Londonderry – a further indication of his weakened physical state.

Newton allowed the statement to continue regardless. Amid chaotic scenes in which the veteran SDLP MLA Alex Attwood was almost shouting at the Speaker – who lacked the authority to expel him from the chamber – Newton lost control and had to suspend the sitting. Eventually, opposition MLAs walked out, leaving Foster to address empty benches.

Her speech had largely been written by Richard Bullick. Over the weekend, he had been in contact with McCormick to discuss what Foster could say. The DUP wanted to put the maximum distance between itself and the scandal. But that was undermined by McCormick telling Bullick that Crawford had been 'decisive' in delaying cost controls.

In the early hours of 19 December, Bullick was still corresponding with McCormick who advised him that his warnings 'should be a show-stopper' about what it was then proposed for Foster to say because 'the investigation will find too much that will [show] that JB [Jonathan Bell] had a point re last summer'.

Bullick defended what he had written but McCormick replied: 'The draft is all true, but misses the fact that AC's [Crawford's] influence was decisive. I fear that saying "Jonathan Bell should have stood up to him" won't be enough. It's not what it is. It's what it looks like.'

To the keen observer, Foster's speech ultimately alluded to some of what McCormick had told Bullick – but did not make it explicit. Bullick and Foster defended that opacity, saying that they had been given no evidence that Crawford had delayed the changes in 2015.

But Foster knew much more than she was letting on in public. The previous week, former DUP spad Tim Cairns had phoned Bullick, who was in Foster's Stormont Castle office, to say that he thought the party's strategy was misguided. Foster and Timothy Johnston were present so Bullick put Cairns onto speakerphone. During a lengthy call, Cairns said that he was clear that he had acted to delay cost controls after liaising with Crawford at Johnston's request.

Cairns said that at the point he mentioned Johnston the senior spad 'clearly became uncomfortable and the conversation was quickly brought to an end'. That night Bullick phoned him to say that Johnston 'was uncomfortable with my discussion of the June 2015 meeting, as up until that point he was adamant that he had played no role in RHI. However, my revelation had undermined his position'.

Johnston rejected that claim. Cairns said: 'I do not believe that Mrs Foster, either in her Nolan interview … or in her statement, fully expressed the view I had stated to her in the speaker phone call.'

Initially, Foster told the inquiry that she had no memory of the call. Then, after Cairns's evidence, her memory improved and she firmly rejected key elements of his story. She said that Cairns's comment about Johnston 'was not news to me, so it wasn't anything noteworthy' because she had been aware that Johnston had asked Cairns to seek assistance from Crawford in summer 2015 – but not to delay cost controls.

On paper, the Assembly speech which Bullick had written had a modicum of humility, including the line that RHI was 'the deepest political regret of my time in this house'. But that was lost amid Foster's defiant delivery and lengthy sections in which she attacked opponents. She denounced 'trial by television' and described the attempt to remove her as a 'coup d'état more worthy of a Carry On Film'.

But amid the public theatre in the Assembly chamber, Sinn Féin's John O'Dowd criticised the SDLP no-confidence motion as 'fatally flawed and premature' and his party did not vote for it – a symbolic decision because the DUP had already deployed its veto to ensure that the motion would not pass.

Then, days before Christmas, the DUP Communities Minister Paul Givan axed a £55,000 bursary scheme, Líofa, which provided small grants for those from disadvantaged communities who wanted to learn the Irish language. A message conveying the news said it was due to 'efficiency savings' and added: 'Happy Christmas and happy new year'.

In Stormont terms, it was an inconsequential sum of money and the DUP's lack of enthusiasm for the Irish language was well known. But the timing and the tone of the move was disastrous. To nationalists, it seemed that the DUP – having overseen a scheme which was squandering hundreds of millions of pounds – was now seeking to cut funding largely accessed by nationalists. And it seemed to them that far from showing contrition over what had been revealed, the DUP was arrogantly flaunting its power. Givan – who after an outcry reinstated the fund, but too late to undo the political damage – insisted that the row had been unintentional rather than a cynical attempt to take the focus off RHI.

On the day of Foster's Assembly speech, McGuinness had insisted that Sinn Féin was not going to topple Stormont. But the backlash over that day's events and then the Líofa decision piled pressure on a party which was not used to being out of touch with its base.

For weeks after *Spotlight*, Sinn Féin had been publicly floundering over how to handle the scandal. In early December, Sinn Féin's then deputy leader, Mary Lou McDonald, called for a 'public inquiry as a matter of urgency' – perhaps her instinctive reaction as an opposition politician in Dublin, without fully realising that as one of the two main ruling parties in Stormont such an inquiry could be embarrassing for Sinn Féin. Former Stormont minister Conor Murphy said a public inquiry should be one of the options considered.

However, by late December Sinn Féin had consciously taken a public inquiry off the table. While it was prepared to look tough – by calling for Foster to quit, a symbolic gesture which would humble her but not get to the truth – it was unwilling to actually be tough by doing everything necessary to uncover the heart of the scandal. A party spokesman said it believed that holding those responsible to account could 'be best achieved by an independent, time-framed, robust and transparent investigation undertaken by an independent judicial figure from outside this jurisdiction … it is Sinn Féin's view that a statutory public inquiry could drag on for years at a significant cost to the tax payers and adding to the cost of this scandal'.

It was precisely because a public inquiry would rigorously drill into what had happened that it would be expensive and time-consuming. The reverse was true of what Sinn Féin was proposing. An investigation done on the cheap, at break-neck speed, without the power to compel evidence or witnesses, without the ability to take evidence on oath and probably behind closed doors would almost certainly fail to peel back the secrecy which Sinn Féin knew was at the heart of how it and the DUP ran Stormont.

As much as Sinn Féin wanted to shore up its own credentials for keeping the DUP in check, the party was unenthusiastic about a forensic examination of how Stormont operated on its watch.

By 2 January, Sinn Féin's stance moved again, with party chairman Declan Kearney backing a public inquiry. Writing in the party's newspaper, *An Phoblacht*, Kearney called for a 'comprehensive, independent public inquiry'. But, after that was reported, the party claimed that it had been an error, blaming it on a 'typo'. However, that night Kearney re-released his original article calling for a public inquiry, emailing it to the *News Letter* from his personal email address with the message: 'Please share this important information widely'.

But the following morning the hapless Sinn Féin chairman – who seemed unable to grasp the crucial difference between a public inquiry and an investigation with few powers – returned to arguing against a public inquiry. He blamed 'some sections of the media and juvenile journalists' for focussing on Sinn Féin's multiple positions on the issue. As late as early January, the independent Justice Minister, Claire Sugden, echoed the DUP and Sinn Féin opposition to a full public inquiry, claiming that it could take a long time and 'let people off the hook'.

But by 9 January, Foster performed a U-turn, saying that she could now accept a full public inquiry under the Inquiries Act. The following day, in a final act of desperation, she called for that inquiry to be established. Foster – the person seen to be at the heart of the scandal – was now calling for the most rigorous investigation possible, while Sinn Féin continued to oppose that.

With McGuinness now seriously ill, Adams – who had largely left Stormont and focussed on southern politics – had moved north to take a central role. On the afternoon of Saturday, 7 January, hundreds of republicans packed an upstairs room in the Felons' Club in West Belfast.

Adams addressed the crowd, spelling out what was a final warning to Foster that she must resign or Sinn Féin would take action. After a month in which Sinn Féin had been seen as weak and ineffectual, there was a strongly anti-Stormont mood in the room. A call to 'bring the institutions down now' was cheered by an audience which included senior Provisional IRA figures.

Things were moving fast now. Two days later, a tiny group of journalists was called at short notice to McGuinness's office in Parliament Buildings. There they witnessed his final major political act, his resignation as deputy First Minister, bringing to an end almost a decade of unbroken devolution – the longest period of local rule since 1972. In doing so, it was clear that this was a calculated abandonment of Sinn Féin's strategy under the former IRA commander's leadership and potentially the valedictory act of his political career.

But aside from the politics, McGuinness's gaunt appearance and audible physical weakness were in themselves shocking. By refusing to confirm that he would even be a candidate in the election which he was triggering, the public could read between the lines as to the severity of his condition.

Once seen as an IRA hawk, he had morphed into Sinn Féin's most accommodating senior figure since ascending to office as Stormont's Education Minister in 1999. He was no push around, but he was a pragmatist. Since taking over as deputy First Minister with Ian Paisley in 2007, his overt strategy had been to accept all manner of perceived or actual slights by the DUP, or crises for the sake of 'the process'. In that time, the Stormont institutions were to him sacrosanct. Now they were not.

His dramatic departure from office gave the imprimatur of the dove in Sinn Féin leadership to a strategy which had come to view the very presence of devolved government in Northern Ireland as a bargaining chip.

Foster's hubris had contributed to tearing down the institutions which gave her political power. By refusing to either stand aside or even show contrition, she had fuelled public anger, putting pressure on Sinn Féin to act. Having toppled Stormont in such circumstances, it would be difficult to restore it – even when both leaderships later wanted to compromise to do so.

****

If Arlene Foster was listening to BBC Radio 4 to get away from the local news on Saturday, 14 January, she would not have liked what she heard.

Comedians on *The News Quiz* were regaling an English studio audience with tales of the RHI scandal. To guffaws, they told how 'concerns were first raised when a farmer in County Antrim was spotted turning the door knob to his cow shed wearing oven gloves'.

Stormont was now a national laughing stock. The scandal was everywhere – even places Northern Irish politics seldom featured. If Foster had ventured into Belfast's stylish Cathedral Quarter, she ran the risk of stumbling across a huge – and vicious – piece of art on the wall of a car park which had appeared in reference to RHI, depicting her as a hideous green reptilian creature.

Foster's tactics became increasingly out of touch with the public mood. On 12 January, she suggested that there was some sort of misogynistic undertone to the media coverage because she was, in her words, a 'strong female leader' while DUP MLA Tom Buchanan said of the scandal: 'Of course this has all been hyped up by the media for their own advantage'.

But by 17 January, as the prospect of facing the electorate in a snap election loomed, there was a markedly different tone from former DUP minister Edwin Poots. The party veteran said: 'We owe the public an apology for devising a scheme that was not fit for purpose'.

Twelve days earlier, David McIlveen – who until recently had been a DUP MLA – came out to accuse Foster of being personally responsible for RHI turning into an 'omnishambles'. In an unusual public assault on the leadership from a DUP member, McIlveen said that Foster had 'seriously misjudged the public anger' and her lack of humility had turned the RHI problem into a political crisis, leaving her 'deeply damaged'. As Stormont lurched towards collapse, DUP big beast Sammy Wilson dismissed the criticism, claiming that Foster had handled the RHI crisis 'magnificently'.

CHAPTER 20
A BROWN ENVELOPE

On the afternoon of Thursday, 19 January 2017, I was late arriving in the newsroom. Writing about RHI had gone late into the previous night and that morning there had been another Stormont committee hearing.

On my desk was a large brown envelope, inside which were printouts of several emails. The communication, which was addressed to me by hand and delivered by Royal Mail, was anonymous, but its contents were extraordinary. After skimming through the emails, I walked a few feet to the deputy editor's office and told him that we had a huge story that had to run the following day. The emails showed that some renewable energy firms had been given detailed inside information about the plan to rein in cash for ash four months before the subsidy was cut – and that the information had come from the two officials running the scheme: Stuart Wightman and Seamus Hughes.

It added a new layer of complexity to the story. Aside from Jonathan Bell's allegations of political skulduggery in delaying closure of RHI, here was firm proof that civil servants had been alerting the industry to the looming changes – and evidence that those firms immediately acted to pile into the scheme.

After quickly establishing that the emails were genuine, I asked the Department for the Economy for a comment and the story ran on the *News Letter*'s front page the following morning under the headline 'RHI firms given inside track on end of scheme'.

Although I had no clue as to where the emails had originated, it struck me that they were uniquely helpful to the DUP, diverting focus from a party which for five weeks had been unable to shift the spotlight from itself. But whoever was helped by the information was not my concern.

The story had been turned around rapidly – within about six hours from the emails arriving on my desk to being on the front page – partly due to an expectation that they may have been sent to other media outlets. In order to act so quickly, we had not published the names of any of those involved in the correspondence. There was insufficient time to give them a reasonable period of time in which to respond.

But the following morning I went back to the department with a series of questions for Wightman and Hughes, informing them that we would be naming them. Meanwhile, I set about trying to track down the various industry individuals involved in the exchanges – Paula Keelagher at pellet manufacturer Balcas (who replied through a PR firm), Fergal Hegarty at Alternative Heat (who never responded) and others, one of whom had worked for a company no longer operating in Northern Ireland.

The department's immediate response was to warn that it may go to the High Court to seek an emergency injunction preventing publication of the names – an exceptionally rare move, particularly for a government department. It then said that Andrew McCormick wanted to brief me in person, but that was cancelled after McCormick's minister, Simon Hamilton, said he was unhappy with it.

Over several days, the department argued vigorously against the officials being named – something it said would undermine their right to a fair disciplinary process. There was one difficulty in advancing that argument. The day before the brown envelope arrived, McCormick had named – based on hearsay – Andrew Crawford as the individual who he had been told delayed cost controls in 2015. Having been prepared to name a spad based on uncorroborated second-hand accounts, the civil service was now threatening to use public money to block the naming of civil servants – not based on hearsay, but based on documentary evidence that they had contributed to the spike.

The only way in which the emergence of the names could be prejudicial to the officials' right to a fair disciplinary hearing would be if the department was open to being influenced by the *News Letter*'s coverage, something which in itself would be alarming.

By the following Wednesday, having taken legal advice and given everyone in the emails ample opportunity to explain their position, the *News Letter* told the department that we would be publishing the names the following morning. At about 7pm that night I was on my way home from the office, stuck in heavy traffic, when the department's senior press officer phoned to say that McCormick wanted to speak to me. 'I know you are probably going to publish now, but he wants to make a final appeal not to name them,' she said. Some minutes later, on speakerphone as I drove home along Belfast's Ormeau Road, he appealed for Wightman and Hughes not to be named. Although he made a firm appeal not to name the officials, it was along strikingly different lines to those advanced by the department in the

Arlene Foster's key adviser, Andrew Crawford.

Inside what Stephen Brimstone described as an 'agricultural shed', Ofgem's inspector found children's toys and a wood pile. Image: RHI Inquiry evidence.

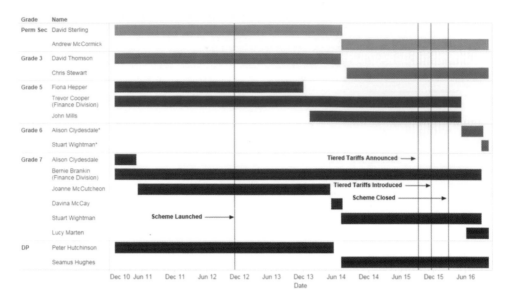

All DETI's key staff working on RHI were replaced in a short space of time, as shown in this staff turnover chart from a PWC report for DETI.   Image: RHI Inquiry evidence.

FACTS ABOUT GREEN ENERGY AND BIOMASS IN N.I.

1. In the last few years a big push has been made to encourage businesses to use renewable energy sources to heat their business. In the last few years a government backed scheme, where the business owner installs a biomass boiler can receive payments for up to 20 years for the heat produced.
2. This scheme has been taken up by many businesses in N. Ireland, but we also believe it is being seriously abused by many, who are not working within the intended guidelines.
3. Where we believe the problems are arising is that the scheme is not being monitored and is very much left to the installer to vet whether you are a suitable business to enter this scheme.
4. Many people are availing of the scheme who have had no other means of heating previous to this, or if they presently have a heating system there is no comparison made between the cost of the current heating and the heating generated by the new system.
5. Examples of this are large factories who have had no previous heating have installed three biomass boilers and intend to run them 24/7 all year round. With the intention of collection approx 1.5 million over the next 20 years, approx £1500 per week, paid every 3 months.
6. Another example a local farmer who has no business or need for biomass boilers is aiming to collect 1 million ponds over the next 20 years heating an empty shed.

We feel the legislation was never intended to be abused like this.

George Gallagher's note hand-delivered to Arlene Foster in January 2016 alleging widespread RHI abuse.   Image: RHI Inquiry evidence.

BBC Spotlight reporter Conor Spackman's programme featured images of him casually tossing cash into a camp fire as he recounted the RHI disaster.   Image: BBC.

Arlene Foster being interviewed by UTV's Tracey Magee in Beijing on 7 December 2016, the night after *Spotlight*.

Three days after BBC *Spotlight* in December 2016, cartoonist Brian John Spencer captured the absurdity at the heart of the RHI scheme.

Prior to being interviewed by Stephen Nolan, Jonathan Bell bent down and was prayed over in the studio.

Unseen by TV viewers, DUP spads Timothy Johnston and Richard Bullick, Stormont press secretary David Gordon and DUP press officer Clive McFarland were in Stephen Nolan's eyeline as he interviewed Foster.

This image of the Stormont Assembly at 11.48am on 19 December 2016 captures the bizarre scene as the other parties left Arlene Foster to just address DUP MLAs.

The Pride of Northern Ireland | FRIDAY, JANUARY 20, 2017 | £1.10 (UK £1.90) | facebook.com/belfastnewsletter | @News_Letter | newsletter.co.uk

News Letter

Since 1737

McGUINNESS QUITS POLITICS

SEE PAGES 6 AND 7

EMAILS LEAKED TO THE NEWS LETTER SHED ALARMING LIGHT ON 'SPIKE' IN APPLICATIONS

RHI firms given inside track on end of scheme

By Sam McBride
Political Editor
s.mcbride@newsletter.co.uk

Emails leaked to the News Letter show that some renewable energy firms had detailed inside information about the plan to rein in the 'cash for ash' scheme four months before cost controls were implemented.

In correspondence which sheds alarming new light on why there was a massive spike in applications to the Renewable Heat Incentive (RHI) scheme, several firms were sharing technical and financial information weeks before the huge influx of applications.

The emails between individuals in the renewable energy industry cite discussions with Department of Enterprise, Trade and Investment (DETI) officials as the source of the information and include the suggestion that clients considering wood pellet boilers should "move asap" to "avoid missing out on the best rates from RHI".

Until now, it has been believed that the spike came in the period between 8 September 2015 (when the plan to introduce cost controls was publicly announced) and 18 November (when cost controls were implemented).

In that period almost as many applications were received as had been made in the previous almost three years of the scheme.

On that basis, the Northern Ireland Audit Office calculated that those applications will cost taxpayers £480 million.

However, the correspondence seen by this newspaper points to the potential for the spike actually beginning much earlier, with some in the industry aware of the looming changes a full ten weeks before they were made public – and 20 weeks before critical flaws were rectified.

A 1 July 2015 email referred to an "update" from DETI officials about "proposed changes to RHI tariffs...with a proposed implementation in early October".

TURN TO PAGE 2 →

One email said that if the introduction of cost controls was delayed it would "leave RHI open to further exploitation [in the] poultry sector"

The January 2017 *News Letter* front page that was based on leaked emails, which, unknown to the author, had been leaked by DUP spad John Robinson, left.

RHI THE FACTS

- Costs have been capped – no future overspend
- A public inquiry is being set up
- A full inspection of all sites to be carried out
- All RHI recipients will be named

The Renewable Heat Incentive scheme has been used as a political football in recent months. Behind all of the spin here are the facts ...

1 Arlene Foster has been vindicated
by an independent senior civil servant.

2 All parties in the Assembly voted for
the flawed scheme.

3 At all times Arlene followed Civil Service advice
including that there was no need for cost controls called 'tiering'

4 There was no overspend or warning of an overspend
during Arlene's time as Minister.

5 Arlene Foster took Ministerial responsibility
and apologised for what went wrong from the start.

 DUP
www.mydup.com

ACTION TO SORT THE PROBLEM OUT
KEY QUESTIONS ANSWERED

Q: What about the potential overspend?

A. The Assembly has passed cost control measures to address the potential overspend. From April there will be little or no further cost to the Northern Ireland budget. The DUP's plan to seek to reduce the cost to zero has been introduced. This has been done by legislating to return the scheme to its original intention. While others spent their time making headlines, we worked for a solution.

Q: How will we get to the truth of this?

A. A full public inquiry has been set up. The DUP has been calling for an inquiry to be set up since mid-December. A full public inquiry is now being set up and will get to the truth of what happened. This should have taken place before an election was even called.

Q: Will all those benefiting from the RHI scheme be named?

A. The Economy Minister has ordered the full list of all those who benefited from the scheme to be published. The DUP wants the the full list of RHI recipients to be published as soon as possible. The Minister has ordered that this take place.

PUBLISHED AND PROMOTED BY NAME SURNAME ADDRESS · PRINTED BY PRINTER NAME AND ADDRESS

 DUP
www.mydup.com

This 2016 DUP election leaflet was deeply misleading.

Pictured on the first day when the RHI Inquiry met in public in September 2017 are chairman Sir Patrick Coghlin, centre, Dame Una O'Brien and Dr Keith MacLean.

Arlene Foster being sworn in at the beginning of her evidence to the RHI Inquiry.

Former DUP minister Jonathan Bell, left, arriving with his lawyer at Parliament Buildings in September 2018 to give evidence to the public inquiry.

official statements and made clear that the contact between officials and the industry had been unknown to him until very recently.

The following morning, the *News Letter*'s front page named the officials, making clear that we were not alleging corruption – or even necessarily wrongdoing of any sort – by Wightman or Hughes. The minister, Hamilton, had approved the department's response to the *News Letter*, which had argued for the officials not to be named, something it said would cause an 'irreversible … interference with their rights to privacy'. And his department had spent public money on legal advice around seeking an injunction against the newspaper.

What neither McCormick nor I understood at that point was that Hamilton himself had authorised his spad, John Robinson, to leak the emails. Many weeks earlier, Crawford had been sent the emails by David Robinson – the major boiler installer who had installed his brother's boilers. Then, the day after Bell's explosive interview – which named Crawford as a spad who delayed cost controls – he forwarded the emails to John Robinson.

Robinson, who had been the DUP's chief spin doctor before becoming a spad, had initially made no mention to the inquiry of his role in leaking the emails. Both in writing and then when appearing before the inquiry, he was asked if there was any other relevant information and he did not mention his role. But after Hamilton admitted to the situation, Robinson told the inquiry that there was a desire to use the emails to take the focus off the DUP. On 23 December, Foster's senior spad Richard Bullick asked Robinson why he had not yet sent the emails to the media. Bullick volunteered to bring envelopes to Robinson to facilitate the leak. Robinson said he 'wasn't convinced' that they should be leaked, and 'as a means of delaying this course of action further, I did not print the emails'. He then sent the emails anonymously to McCormick. But, despite being paid a spad salary of about £85,000 a year, he did not pay for sufficient postage, meaning that the envelope did not get to him until 5 January. McCormick, unaware of the source, informed Robinson and Hamilton of the troubling new information.

But, having done so, Robinson then did not follow through on sending them to journalists as Bullick had instructed. Robinson claimed that the emails 'were almost forgotten about' – remarkable, given how desperate the DUP was in this period for anything which would distract from its role in the scandal.

Bullick recalled waiting over Christmas for the story to appear, and by early January he was surprised at the lack of media coverage. He said that it was only during the inquiry that it became clear to him that Robinson had not sent the material to the media until far later. So why had he delayed? His reasons may have been far more about protecting himself than protecting the DUP – or even Crawford.

Two days before the emails arrived with me and with the BBC, the Press Association had outed Robinson's father-in-law as an RHI beneficiary. There was no suggestion that there was anything improper in this, but it was still front page news for two reasons. First, Robinson was the key adviser in the department seeking to cut the RHI bill – yet he had a conflict of interest which he had not declared to the department. After the revelation, he accepted that and recused himself from any role in RHI, the key issue with which the department was grappling – but still retained his full salary. The second problem for Robinson was that the day before his father-in-law's claim was revealed he had faced an accusation from Bell that he had an inappropriate role in RHI. Speaking under Assembly privilege, Bell, who by now had been suspended by the DUP, said he had been told that he would not be allowed to rein in RHI because of Robinson and his brother-in-law Timothy Johnston's 'extensive interests in the poultry industry'.

The DUP branded that 'outrageous, untrue and unfounded', adding that 'John Robinson has no personal interest in the poultry industry. His family home farm have chicken houses but are not part of the RHI scheme and never have been recipients or applicants'.

DUP members who had defended Robinson on the basis of what was – at best – a misleading statement were livid when they read about his father-in-law's status as an RHI beneficiary, and he was under acute internal pressure. In that context, having decided not to leak the emails to the media when it suited the party or Crawford, he now sent them to the media at the point where he was in peril.

There may have been another reason for his timing. The day before the envelope arrived on my desk, McCormick had alluded to the emails during a meeting of the Public Accounts Committee. Robinson might have hoped that the mandarin would say more about the emails in public, but McCormick was circumspect and there was little coverage of what he had said on the issue.

Bullick, who said that from December he had believed that the DUP's media response was 'inadequate', told the inquiry that the emails had 'in due course' secured significant coverage but added:

> This however was too late to save the Assembly from an election in which the DUP would lose 10 seats and since which 20 months later no Executive has been re-established. With the benefit of hindsight I regret not speaking to Sam McBride directly myself in December 2016 about matters in relation to the RHI as I believe that a proper understanding of what occurred would have led to more favourable coverage for the DUP.

Hamilton told the inquiry that when Robinson showed him the emails in December he could see that 'this is pretty explosive', but he feared that handing them to McCormick would see the issue 'get bogged down in a process'. Under pressure to explain why he had acted surreptitiously with his own chief official, Hamilton said: 'I accept that this is highly unorthodox.' But he argued that his actions needed to be seen in a context 'where we ... the party – are being assailed on all sides ... and there isn't much to fire back, there isn't much to combat some of these allegations with'. Hamilton said that it was 'not my proudest moment' and was 'one of many things that I regret around this period'. McCormick told the inquiry that what had happened was 'self-evidently astonishing'.

Several weeks later, a second anonymous brown envelope containing printouts of emails arrived on my desk. This time, the emails showed how the Ulster Farmers' Union (UFU) had lobbied to delay cost controls. Remarkably, given how the emails obviously shifted the focus from the DUP to the UFU, it had been the UFU's chief executive, Wesley Aston, who had forwarded the emails to Crawford at the start of January. Crawford had done favours for the UFU in government, and the UFU could generally rely on him to argue farmers' case within Stormont. Robinson and Hamilton had also – almost certainly knowingly – played a part in shifting the focus from themselves to farmers. Journalists and others had made multiple Freedom of Information (FoI) requests for RHI material. The DUP, a party which routinely flouted FoI legislation, simply ignored many of the requests, which were never answered until Hamilton left office. But one of my FoI requests was answered. It showed that the UFU had been lobbying to delay cost controls and also showed that civil servants had shown the organisation how lucrative RHI was for poultry farmers. The DUP now seemed willing to even push its friends under in an attempt to deflect blame for what had happened.

****

On the day that the first set of leaked emails arrived at the *News Letter*, Crawford resigned as a spad. The previous day, McCormick had appeared before the Assembly's Public Accounts Committee where he publicly confirmed that DETI had faced 'political pressure' against cost controls in 2015 – and then named Crawford as the individual he had been told was behind that pressure.

With Bell sitting in the public gallery behind him, the mandarin said that it was a 'not unreasonable inference' that some in 'political class' urged RHI claimants to pile in, although he stressed he had no evidence of this. Facing intense criticism, the following day Crawford announced his resignation as spad. In a statement published by the DUP press office, he said: 'In light of the allegations made at the Public Accounts Committee yesterday I believe it is appropriate that I step back from my position in government and resign as a special adviser. I am conscious I have become the focus of the story.' But although he gave the public the impression that he was resigning because of the RHI allegations, Crawford cleverly told the civil service something slightly different – that he was resigning to campaign for the DUP in the forthcoming election. That made him eligible for a £34,000 golden handshake, which would not have been payable if he had quit over RHI. The day before McCormick named Crawford, the spad enquired as to how much he would be paid if he resigned. On the day that he was named by McCormick, Crawford texted his friend who worked in the biomass industry, Mark Anderson, to say: 'I've been destroyed'. Anderson replied: 'Time to leak an email?'

Hours after McCormick named him, Crawford met Johnston and Foster in the DUP leader's Fermanagh home and he offered his resignation which she accepted. He said that Foster told him 'it was possible or likely that John Robinson was also going to resign from his role as adviser'. In the end, Robinson, who was Johnston's brother-in-law, did not resign and went on to return to his old job as the DUP's chief spin doctor. Crawford would later form the view that senior party figures sacrificed him to protect others in the party by quietly acquiescing in McCormick naming him. Although there seemed an element of self-pity in his view and a failure to face up to the damage which his behaviour would do to the party if it was to all have emerged, Crawford's paranoia may have been at least partially justified. He drew particular attention to how when allegations were aimed at the powerful Johnston, senior DUP figures were 'quick to defend him ... in a way that they did not defend me ... It may have been the case that I was viewed as expendable whereas Timothy Johnston was not'.

Johnston – who had been close to Crawford – had taken a particular interest in Crawfords's relatives' RHI applications. Just three days after *Spotlight*, he had got a copy of the list of claimants through Robinson. That day, Robinson asked McCormick to bring the list of names to Parliament Buildings, justifying the request on the grounds that Hamilton was considering releasing the names – even though the night before Hamilton had been on TV saying that he was not planning to do so.

McCormick brought the list to Stormont and left it in the minister's room and moved next door with Robinson. McCormick later said that leaving the list unattended was part of a deliberate 'charade' to 'create a fig leaf of respectability' for him as a civil servant that he was not openly handing such sensitive information to a DUP figure outside his department – even though he knew that Johnston was looking at the names next door.

Three days later, Foster was asked by the BBC's Mark Devenport if she was aware that Crawford's brother James was a claimant. Although Crawford had been her spad for many years and although her key adviser had viewed the entire list, she said of Crawford's brother: 'I wasn't aware of that because of course I wasn't privy to who had applied into the scheme.' That same day, Johnston spoke to McCormick about the list, telling him that he should look up details of a Richard Crawford and a John Crawford. Pressed around that, Johnston told the inquiry: 'I certainly don't recall asking particularly for that gentleman.' But, asked why McCormick would invent such a claim, he then said it was 'very possible' that he asked McCormick to check out several DUP-linked individuals, including Crawford.

Inquiry barrister Donal Lunny asked him whether his actions that day were part of a strategy to direct McCormick towards material which he knew would be damaging for Crawford because he realised that McCormick was soon going to be giving evidence in public.

Johnston said: 'Certainly not. Andrew Crawford has been a long-standing friend of mine for many years, and I think in the way that his name came out was very difficult for him.' McCormick privately discussed with the Executive's Press Secretary, David Gordon, the fact that John Crawford got into RHI on the final day of 'burn to earn' left the DUP dangerously exposed to criticism.

After Foster's speech to the Assembly, Crawford became increasingly concerned that he was being set up to be the DUP's sacrificial lamb. On 28 December, Robinson texted Bullick to say: 'Andrew Crawford called. He's very angry. Can't leave the house. Family being treated as thieves. Says AF [Arlene Foster] statement to the Assembly hung him out to dry. Says he told Cairns in an email in July to close on 1 October.' But a sceptical Bullick responded by saying that he had not been aware of the email, 'but, if true, why did TC [Timothy Cairns] want it kept open? Makes no sense'. But even after publicly quitting as a spad, the DUP did not sever ties with Crawford. Instead, it gave him a post advising on its most critical policy area – Brexit.

****

Although the DUP, Sinn Féin and the civil service had known for a year that there was a vast overspend, it was only after *Spotlight* that ministers pledged to halve RHI's losses. Then, as the public fury intensified, Foster pledged to bring forward changes, which would mean slashing payments to a level that there would be no overspend at all. The shift from initial inaction to fevered attempts at clawing back money was a demonstration of how public anger was driving politicians who feared the electoral consequences.

In December, the DUP and Sinn Féin had discussed ideas for dealing with the huge RHI overspend – from shutting the scheme entirely and buying out claimants' contracts to the more legally challenging option of retrospectively slashing the subsidy. As the scandal intensified and Stormont lurched towards collapse, the DUP settled on the retrospective cuts. But time was running out. The Assembly would have to use emergency powers to rush through legislation with limited scrutiny before devolution collapsed.

Now Sinn Féin's position became fascinating. On paper, the party's Finance Minister, Máirtín Ó Muilleoir – the most powerful Stormont minister after Foster and McGuinness – had a key role in signing off on Hamilton's plan to cut costs. But he lingered over the decision for weeks, alarming his officials who feared that the legislation might not be passed before Stormont collapsed. Unknown to the public, Ó Muilleoir was in constant contact with unseen – and therefore publicly unaccountable – senior republican figures about the complex legal question facing him, even though they were neither legal nor energy experts. In an insight into where real power lay within Sinn Féin, the minister did not seem able to take the decision based on the advice of his civil servants and his own party-appointed spad.

The revelation only emerged at the inquiry because of its power to compel the release of internal Sinn Féin emails and text messages. It added weight to the belief of the DUP and others that Sinn Féin's Stormont operation was so ultra-centralised that even its ministers were operating in an environment in which they were being effectively overseen by unseen republicans.

On 18 December, three days after Bell spoke out, Ó Muilleoir met Hamilton in Belfast City Hall to discuss RHI. No minutes were taken of the ministerial meeting – just the way the DUP and Sinn Féin liked it. Three days later, Mr Ó Muilleoir emailed senior republican Padraic Wilson to provide a detailed summary of the meeting. Wilson, a former 'officer commanding' of the IRA prisoners in the Maze Prison, had been caught in possession of a bomb and after his release from jail had been given crucial roles by the IRA. Sinn Féin denied that the IRA still existed in any form. However, just over a year earlier, a major security assessment for the government said that the IRA Army Council remained intact and that IRA members believed that it controlled Sinn Féin. Ó Muilleoir told Wilson: 'It's up to [Hamilton's department] to come up with a solution … that gives us a certain distance from the DUP attempts to say we were all in this together.'

By 4 January, Ó Muilleoir was emailing other Sinn Féin figures, including Ted Howell. When asked by the inquiry who Howell was, Ó Muilleoir described him as 'the former chair and chair of every negotiation Sinn Féin's been involved in around these institutions and political processes since 1997' and a member of Sinn Féin's *ard chomhairle* [executive] who was 'brought back from retirement at the request of Martin McGuinness to

chair a crisis committee to deal with the crisis' over RHI. What Ó Muilleoir
did not tell the inquiry was that Howell was another figure trusted by the
IRA leadership. Howell had acted as a go-between on behalf of the IRA
when the terror group was beginning to make connections with senior US
figures in the early 1990s. The veteran journalist Ed Moloney, author of *A
Secret History of the IRA*, described Howell as '[Gerry] Adams's most trusted
advisor and counsellor' but also 'a highly secretive figure' who was 'arguably
one of the most influential figures in the Provisionals'.

Another individual being updated by the Finance Minister was Martin
Lynch. Lynch and Wilson were described by Panorama's John Ware as 'two
of the IRA's most senior representatives' in 2003 when they had a key role in
handling the Scappaticci informer affair for the IRA.

Within two days of his email to Howell, Ó Muilleoir wrote a letter to
Hamilton criticising his approach – and released the letter publicly. A draft
of the letter had been circulated among the group of senior republicans.

On 16 January, Ó Muilleoir wrote again to the unseen figures to say:
'I will shortly sign off a submission from officials agreeing that the interim
solution of Simon Hamilton stacks up.' But he then received a text message
from Howell three days later to tell him that 'the hole in our case is "what is
the SF cure?"' if it rejected Hamilton's plan. Ó Muilleoir replied in detail to
Howell setting out his preferred approach.

By 23 January, the Assembly was sitting for the penultimate time before
dissolution. Hamilton brought his retrospective subsidy cut legislation to
the Assembly – but without Ó Muilleoir having signed off on the business
case, a highly irregular situation. Hamilton told the Assembly it was 'deeply
troubling' that the business case had not been approved and challenged Ó
Muilleoir as to why that was the case. Ó Muilleoir told the Assembly that the
reason was down to the lack of EU state aid approval. He made no mention
of the off-grid role of senior republicans. He also assured the Assembly
that his decision would be 'politics-free' – just weeks after suggesting to
the IRA veteran Wilson that his strategy was heavily influenced by political
considerations.

Ó Muilleoir's refusal to sign off on the business case was repeatedly
mentioned during the Assembly debate and it raised the possibility that the
legislation would fall. If all the opposition MLAs voted against Hamilton's
legislation – and Sinn Féin abstained – then it would not pass. Going into

an election, that would have left the DUP unable to argue that it had at least fixed the problem. However, in the end every MLA outside the DUP abstained, leaving the DUP to pass the legislation on an oral vote – a highly unusual situation.

The following day, Ó Muilleoir emailed Howell again to tell him 'there is now no further reason for me to delay holding up [*sic*] this business plan ... would you be content if I were to sign off the business plan on Wednesday afternoon?' Here was the Finance Minister – one of Stormont's most powerful democratically accountable figures – asking an unelected and entirely unseen republican with long links to the IRA whether he was 'content' for the minister to take a complex decision worth hundreds of millions of pounds, even after the legislation had been agreed by the legislature. By this stage, the minister had clear advice from his officials that he should approve the subsidy cut as the only possible solution available. Ó Muilleoir insisted that he was not requesting permission and was simply informing Howell of what he would be doing, acting as 'a courtesy ... giving him his place'.

But just three days earlier, Ó Muilleoir's behaviour had caused such concern for his most senior civil servant, David Sterling, that he expressed alarm about the situation. In a text message to McCormick, Sterling said that his minister had been 'unforthcoming' and added: 'I can't say whether the "will" is there and wonder whether he knows himself. He may be acting under instruction.' Even after asking if Howell was content, Ó Muilleoir did not immediately get a green light. Instead, Howell summoned him to a meeting with 'the usual suspects' at Sinn Féin headquarters on the Falls Road. Within three minutes, the minister's spad agreed that they would attend. The meeting, of course, was not minuted so we do not know what was discussed, but the minister belatedly approved the business case.

****

With Sinn Féin having collapsed Stormont, an election campaign now began – and the DUP was desperate to move the focus from RHI. Unable to fight the election on her record in government, Foster explicitly made it the most tribal contest in years. When asked about RHI, Foster repeatedly talked about Gerry Adams's 'radical republican agenda'. In McGuinness's resignation letter he had not just demanded that Foster step aside over RHI but had also revived a list of mostly forgotten Sinn Féin demands, including an insistence that there should be an Irish language act. At the launch of the DUP campaign, Foster used a phrase which some saw as a gaffe but which may well have been a deliberate attempt to take the focus off RHI. Asked by veteran *Belfast Telegraph* political correspondent Noel McAdam if she would agree to Irish language legislation, Foster visibly bristled and said to loud cheers from her candidates: 'I will never accede to an Irish language act … if you feed a crocodile it will keep coming back and looking for more.'

Sinn Féin was delighted at the remark. Hours later, Gerry Adams beamed as he dismissed Foster's animalistic analogy, simply saying: 'See you later, alligator.' Sinn Féin activists donned crocodile suits to campaign. But many nationalists – who had until then not been pressing for Irish language legislation – saw it as an example of Foster's arrogance and her disdain for those who cherished the language.

Two weeks later, as Foster launched the DUP's manifesto, she mentioned Sinn Féin 32 times, with a further 12 mentions of Gerry Adams and five references to republicans in the 20-minute speech. But there was no talk of RHI – and no chance to raise it because Foster, blaming a sore throat, took no questions from the media. Less than a year after a positive campaign in which Foster's face adorned all DUP literature and the party's candidates were described as 'Arlene's candidates', now the party was reduced to simply stopping Sinn Féin and giving Foster as little media exposure as possible.

The DUP's one attempt to tackle RHI head-on was wildly inaccurate. The party produced a leaflet which claimed to 'go behind all the spin' – but it was a poor piece of propaganda. It claimed that there would be 'no future overspend' when Hamilton had admitted that there was still an overspend of about £2 million a year. It also claimed that 'Arlene Foster has been vindicated by an independent senior civil servant', a claim which infuriated McCormick, to whom it referred, because he was in no position to 'vindicate' her. He felt that the party was selectively quoting him when it suited – while distancing itself from other things which he had said.

The election result was seismic. Although the DUP vote held up, nationalist turnout soared, propelling Sinn Féin to a position of unprecedented power. What had been a ten-seat gap between the parties became just one seat as the DUP lost ten MLAs. The election was the first since the cut in MLAs from 108 to 90, but even allowing for that it was a disastrous result for Foster. More significantly, the outcome presented a fundamentally altered political reality: unionism was no longer a majority in the Stormont chamber for the first time since the creation of Northern Ireland almost a century earlier. At the time of writing, more than two years later, the DUP and Sinn Féin have been unable to agree to return to Stormont.

Former DUP minister Edwin Poots bluntly accepted that his party had played a part in enraging a previously apathetic section of nationalism, driving them to vote for Sinn Féin. He said: 'Unfortunately nationalists and republicans turned out in a way they haven't done for a long time. We made a contribution to that. We have managed to get nationalists and republicans angry and that has led to them winning more seats as well and that's something that we have to reflect on.'

The election ended Bell's hopes of a continued political career. Standing as an independent candidate in his Strangford constituency after being suspended by the DUP, he pulled in just 3.8% of the vote – down from more than 10% of the vote which he had secured under the DUP banner the year before and well short of the 16.6% quota needed to win one of the five seats. It was a disappointing result for a candidate who had been given an exceptionally high profile after his Nolan interview and who had paid for large 'time for the truth' billboards as part of his re-election campaign. Bell quickly returned to his former life as a social worker, adopting a low public profile. The DUP had been reluctant to publish the full list of RHI claimants. That fed the narrative that there was a darker truth than mere incompetence. By the time the party decided that it was in its interests to publish the list rather than have individual names leak out one by one, it faced a legal challenge from some claimants, slowing the process. Eventually, most of the claimants were named – and the scale of their payments made public – on 24 May 2017, almost two months after the election. But, for reasons which have never been fully explained by the department, the names of those claiming for 48 boilers were not made public.

The list showed that one farmer had been paid almost £660,000 from RHI in less than four years. Paul Hobson, a Dungannon poultry farmer who supplied Moy Park, installed his first biomass boiler just eight months after RHI launched in late 2012 and went on to put in a further 12 boilers. The scale of Hobson's income showed how eye-wateringly lucrative the scheme was, even for those who like him are using it for a legitimate purpose. In an interview with the author, he freely answered every question and explained that the total installation cost had been £380,000. Over the period covered by the figures Hobson said that he had spent £426,000 on wood pellets, £75,000 on electricity to run the system, £12,000 on boiler servicing, £10,000 on parts and £57,000 on interest payments for the loans which financed the investment. That meant that in less than four years Mr Hobson had made about £80,000 in profit.

Three months before the list was published, Crawford texted his friend Mark Anderson again to ask if he knew details about the inspection of boilers which Stormont was planning. Anderson replied to say that no one would be able to meet the department's terms for the inspections contract – something subsequently borne out by events. That delayed any attempt to quickly identify fraudsters. Anderson added bluntly: 'And if someone does farmers are f****d hi [*sic*]'.

CHAPTER 21
NO HIDING PLACE

Having spent weeks arguing against a public inquiry, Sinn Féin's U-turn was so abrupt that it caught the party's chairman, Declan Kearney, embarrassingly off-guard. On the morning of 19 January, Kearney had been, yet again, on the radio arguing in defence of his party's refusal to support a public inquiry. Just before 4pm that afternoon, the Sinn Féin Finance Minister, Máirtín Ó Muilleoir, suddenly announced that he was setting up a public inquiry under the Inquiries Act. He said that the about-turn was because it was clear that with Stormont being dissolved the following week there was no alternative route to investigate the scandal. Yet that had been clear for some time. What would also have featured in Sinn Féin thinking was that the DUP, which had initially also bitterly opposed a public inquiry, had in the preceding days swung to supporting such a move, and the Economy Minister, Simon Hamilton, was exploring setting up the inquiry himself.

It would have been politically damaging for Sinn Féin if the party most responsible for RHI moved ahead to launch the most rigorous inquiry possible while Sinn Féin opposed it. Sinn Féin had long been opposed to the Inquiries Act 2005 because it argued that an inquiry under that legislation was inadequate for investigating controversial Troubles incidents – and especially the murder of the solicitor, Pat Finucane, for which republicans had long campaigned. But it was difficult to see that as the real reason for the party's aversion to an RHI public inquiry. If Sinn Féin was arguing that the Inquiries Act did not go far enough, clearly its preference for a less rigorous form of investigation would be even less likely to get to the truth. And when the party ultimately did its U-turn to set up the public inquiry, far from there being any major backlash from within republicanism, there was a sense of relief that the party's embarrassing flip-flopping was at an end.

The following week, Ó Muilleoir announced that the inquiry would be chaired by Sir Patrick Coghlin, a recently retired judge from Northern Ireland's Court of Appeal who had been nominated for the role by the Lord Chief Justice. Ó Muilleoir told the Assembly: 'Rest assured, every stone will be turned and there will be no dark corners where the light won't be shone.'

The minister probably did not envisage at this point that the unflinching pursuit of the truth would involve his own actions being scrutinised in painful detail.

Having decided to instigate the inquiry, Ó Muilleoir now set it up with the most sweeping terms imaginable. Despite the terms of reference stretching to four pages, Ó Muilleoir gave Coghlin the power to add to his remit if he felt it appropriate.

Ó Muilleoir pledged that the inquiry would be 'free of ministerial control or interference', stressing that after his signature to establish the inquiry 'it will now progress entirely in the hands of the chairman. Sir Patrick Coghlin will … have absolute control over the scope and execution of the inquiry'. But in doing so, there was an irony. In setting up the inquiry into the absence of RHI cost controls, Ó Muilleoir had set up the inquiry without any cost controls. The inquiry was entirely open-ended, both in time and expense, although Coghlin had been told that both should be 'reasonable'. The minister had done so for a noble reason – to prevent outside interference. That would prove wise, given how deeply the inquiry would delve into politicians and civil servants. But it would have been shrewd to find some mechanism to protect the public purse, perhaps through an independent figure such as the comptroller and auditor general having to sign off on spending beyond a certain figure. Initially, an indicative budget of just over £4 million was set aside for the inquiry, but from the outset that always appeared an optimistic figure for such a task involving so many lawyers.

Having given Coghlin a vast remit, Ó Muilleoir had a hopelessly optimistic view of when he would conclude his work. Stressing that the timeframe would be a matter for Coghlin, the minister told MLAs: 'I would think it appropriate for us to have a report six months after the inquiry starts.' The inquiry would not even begin its public hearings within that timeframe – and to anyone with a passing knowledge of the complexity of RHI or the nature of public inquiries, there was never any prospect of it concluding within six months.

Ó Muilleoir was not the only person to be overly optimistic about how long the process would take. Coghlin himself told a senior civil servant in March that he hoped to begin evidence sessions in 'the second half of May'. The first witnesses would in fact not be called to give evidence until the final days of November.

In more than four decades at the bar or on the bench, the Cambridge-educated Coghlin had developed a reputation for independence. Displaying a robust – sometimes even abrupt – manner in court, Coghlin was not the sort of figure who was going to sit back quietly while a witness spent hours obfuscating. Before being promoted to the Court of Appeal, Coghlin had also played a part in a trial which caused alarm across the UK media. In 2000, *The Irish News* had published a scathing review of Goodfellas Pizzeria in West Belfast, savaging every aspect of the establishment. The restaurant sued for libel and Coghlin was the trial judge. There was shock across the UK media when the jury found that the review had been defamatory and awarded £25,000 to the restaurant. The media argued that the law had been misinterpreted to an extent that if the finding was to stand it would jeopardise all reviews.

It was a measure of the significance of the case for the media as a whole that *The Times* flew its critic Giles Coren to Belfast to review the restaurant. Coren described the pollo marsala caustically: 'It is revolting. It is ill-conceived, incompetent, indescribably awful. A dish so cruel I weep not only for the animal that died to make it, but also for the mushrooms.'

The Court of Appeal quashed the verdict, finding that Coghlin had misdirected the jury – although it was also critical of the arguments advanced by the paper's lawyers. One individual familiar with the case described it as 'not his [Coghlin's] finest hour'. By the time of his appointment, that case had been forgotten by all but a few journalists, lawyers and those involved. The way in which Coghlin would handle the RHI Inquiry would ensure that it would be that, not the libel action, which would define his career.

In his first public comments at the start of March, Coghlin reinforced his refusal to be cowed by outside influences, saying: 'When I agreed to take on this complex task I was promised complete independence, and I will insist upon it.' He set out how the inquiry would be an 'inquisitorial process, designed to establish the facts … not an adversarial trial' and without any power to determine criminal or civil liability. But if any of the prospective witnesses thought that meant they would get an easy ride, they were to be disappointed.

As chairman, Coghlin was ultimately the inquisitor-in-chief. But before witnesses ever arrived before him, they had faced prolonged written questioning by the inquiry's team of lawyers. For those who were then called to give oral evidence, most of the questioning was conducted by one of a three-strong team of inquiry barristers. That team was headed by David Scoffield QC, one of Belfast's sharpest legal minds. Scoffield, a former pupil of Attorney General John Larkin, had acted for and against Stormont departments and had seen the devolved administration from both sides.

With impeccable manners and none of the overt aggression of a hostile courtroom cross-examination, Scoffield forensically probed witnesses. But he could be diplomatically brutal. At one point, summing up the evidence that Jonathan Bell was a minister uninterested in detail, Scoffield referred to 'what might be described as a limited relationship that Mr Bell had with the paperwork that was placed before him'. Scoffield was supported by Joseph Aiken, who had also acted as junior counsel to Sir Anthony Hart's public inquiry into historical institutional abuse in Northern Ireland, which had just reported a few months earlier, and Donal Lunny, who could be acerbic in dealing with some of the less forthcoming witnesses.

There were two other veterans of the Hart inquiry: Andrew Browne, a Stormont civil servant who would reprise his role as secretary to the inquiry; and Patrick Butler, who as solicitor to the inquiry would be at its epicentre. Butler was virtually unseen, choosing to not attend any of the inquiry hearings until its final days. But it was he who was in the background pulling together myriad strings of the investigation, quizzing witnesses through lengthy letters and issuing hundreds of notices under the powerful Section 21 of the Inquiries Act 2005, which allowed him to demand that individuals or organisations hand over every scrap of RHI-related material.

Coghlin appointed Dame Una O'Brien, a former permanent secretary of Whitehall's Department of Health, as an inquiry panel member. And he brought in Dr Keith MacLean, a veteran of the UK energy industry, as the inquiry's technical assessor. As the inquiry wore on, and MacLean acted as a de facto inquiry panel member, there was an attempt to elevate him to that role but it was not possible without a Stormont minister in place. It was a formidable trio. Coghlin understood the law and had decades of experience of cross-examination, O'Brien knew how the world of bureaucracy ought to operate and MacLean was relentlessly observant about mathematical and technical details. During inquiry hearings, Coghlin, O'Brien and MacLean sat looking down on proceedings and frequently interjected to take on the questioning of a witness themselves.

Coghlin decided to hold his public hearings in Stormont's Senate Chamber – which prior to the collapse of devolution was used as an Assembly committee room, saving public money. Holding the hearings in the Senate Chamber had two other benefits – the inquiry could avail of the Assembly's Hansard staff to produce a daily transcript, and it was equipped for live online broadcasts. An old-school judge, Coghlin was initially unsure about live-streaming proceedings online. It was not how things were done in court and it removed an element of the control which a judge has whereby he can rule that something said in court which is prejudicial or inappropriate must not be reported. But central to a public inquiry is the principle that its proceedings should overwhelmingly be public. The most damaging situation would have been the expenditure of a huge sum on an inquiry which did not command public confidence.

In the end, Coghlin decided that hearings would be streamed online – but with a five-minute delay, giving him some control in an extreme situation. That decision made the inquiry a televised experience – and an unnerving one for many of those giving evidence. A witness would arrive in the west car park at Parliament Buildings and have the option of going in a back door, although some, including Bell, opted to walk in the front door, in view of the cameras. From there, they were escorted to a disused filing room in the basement which had been cleared out for use as the witness room sparsely furnished with a desk, a chair and a choice of tea or coffee. Having generally conferred with their lawyers the previous day, the witness was then brought up to the chamber to be sworn in and questioned. That process could be protracted. Andrew Crawford spent eight days giving evidence.

One witness described the experience as 'very lonely' because after being sworn in a witness was not allowed to discuss their evidence with anyone – even their lawyer. During the lunch break, 'I couldn't eat,' he said, even though food was offered. Sources close to the inquiry indicated at the time the five-minute delay was announced that a particular concern was that Jonathan Bell might start making wild accusations, which would otherwise be defamatory but would be protected by the absolute privilege afforded to witnesses. There had been rumours in January that Bell was on the verge of using Assembly privilege to name at least one senior DUP figure who was alleged to have had an affair with another politician. In the event, Bell did not do so but it caused considerable distress to those involved. In the end, the

five-minute delay was never interrupted because Coghlin never felt the need
to intervene in that way. Perhaps the closest which it came to being activated
was during Bell's evidence. While still a minister, around the time that RHI
was being shut in early 2016, Bell had compiled a dossier of allegations about
some of his colleagues. He had submitted its contents to the inquiry.

Referring to the document, Scoffield told Bell: 'I don't want to get into
any detail about that.' But Bell then told the inquiry that it was his spad, Tim
Cairns, who had told him the allegations, going on to say that he had told
him 'inappropriately, in garish and lurid detail, the sexual misbehaviour of
two DUP ministers'. Scoffield interjected to say: 'I don't want to get into that
detail' but Bell continued to dwell on the point and said 'I want to put on
the record' the source of the lurid claims. Coghlin interrupted him firmly,
saying: 'No, no, no, Mr Bell. I'm sorry, this inquiry is not some form of
media record for people making allegations and counter-allegations.'

The following morning, on what was the second and final day of Bell's
evidence, Coghlin opened proceedings with a caution that the inquiry 'is
not a media platform' and there was 'no open invitation' to witnesses to use
the hearings as a platform for 'publishing or referring to material ... for
reasons that are irrelevant to the purposes of the inquiry'.

The following week, Cairns told the inquiry that Bell had prepared the
dossier on senior DUP members' private lives and that Bell claimed it would
'end several people's careers'. The former spad said:

> Mr Bell had lost the protection of [Peter] Robinson and he became
> paranoid about the DUP in general and senior members of the party
> in particular. On a daily basis he would recount stories about party
> members and their indiscretions. It was clear to me that someone was
> feeding Jonathan gossip ... On one occasion Mr Bell was asked to come
> to Stormont Castle for a meeting with Mrs Foster. Mr Bell refused and
> spent the evening with Peter Robinson, refusing to attend.

Cairns said that Bell did not say who was feeding him the stories about
DUP members' private lives. But he insisted that, contrary to Bell's claim, it
was not coming from him.

****

But although the inquiry was relentless in some of the avenues it explored, there were those following proceedings closely who were discreetly critical of the avenues not being explored – and of the haste with which the process began to move from late spring 2018. About a month before the inquiry broke for the summer holidays in 2018, there was a sudden and obvious urgency about proceedings. Where before relatively junior witnesses had been brought back for days on end, now there was a stated desired to move things briskly and deal with any further matters in writing.

BBC NI's agriculture and environment correspondent, Conor Macauley, who had been covering RHI since early 2016, sat through almost every day of the inquiry. He too detected a sudden quickening in the inquiry's pace. 'The way it came to a close was a bit dissatisfying. After summer 2018, they seemed to rattle through it very quickly. It felt that there was an acceleration which to my mind didn't serve the public interest as it could have done,' he said.

Though Sir Patrick would bristle at the suggestion, there was a concern from one well-placed source that the inquiry was being cleverly managed by others. Senior civil servants and politicians had the power to at least influence some elements of the inquiry, even if they could not control it.

The decision to hold hearings in Parliament Buildings meant that use of the building was at the discretion of the Assembly authorities. That brought into play civil servants, but also politicians because the financial and management affairs of the Assembly were overseen by the Assembly Commission, a body on which the DUP and Sinn Féin had between them a majority.

From autumn 2018, there were rumours that the Assembly authorities were putting pressure on the inquiry to vacate the Senate Chamber. At that point, Coghlin announced that the inquiry would be dispensing with its sitting pattern of two weeks of oral hearings followed by a week off in which investigative work continued in the background. From now on, he said, the inquiry would sit every week.

One of the legal representatives at the inquiry said: 'From early summer, decisions seemed to have been taken that the inquiry would not be sitting in public session from Halloween, come what may. From early September, it was becoming more and more apparent that a clock was running down, for good or ill.'

That pace meant that some potentially significant witnesses were not called at all – although they all provided written evidence in response to the inquiry's questions. Peter Robinson, the architect of the DUP's system of governing which the inquiry was tearing apart and the former First Minister whose key spad, Timothy Johnston, was alleged to have delayed cost controls, was not called to give oral evidence at all. George Gallagher, the whistleblower whose allegation of empty sheds being heated had arrived with Foster on the very day she said she was first told of the crisis, was not called. Only one Sinn Féin member, Máirtín Ó Muilleoir, was called for half a day – and it initially appeared that he would not be called at all. The situation exemplified the tension between keeping the inquiry to a reasonable time-frame and budget, while getting to the bottom of a saga, which was uniquely complex to investigate because much of the evidence was hidden because it had not been recorded within DETI.

A spokesman for the inquiry said: 'No pressure has been exerted from any quarter on the inquiry to foreshorten its hearings, curtail proceedings or complete its work.' He added: 'The perception that the inquiry quickened its pace during hearings in 2018 reflects the fact that as more witness statements were received and more witnesses had given their oral evidence the inquiry's knowledge base grew and it was possible to refine and focus the questions ...' But no one could credibly accuse the inquiry of being a cover-up. From the outset, Coghlin pressed for transparency. Many tens of thousands of pages of witness statements and evidence were published on the inquiry website. It was this openness which was Coghlin's bulwark against any accusation of protecting the powerful. And the inquiry rigorously interrogated those from all quarters, whether politicians, advisers, civil servants, boiler installers or those with other links to the scheme. It was every bit as thorough with the man who called for the inquiry, Bell, and with the man who set it up, Ó Muilleoir, as it was with those politicians' target, Foster.

Without Bell, the inquiry would never have happened. But the picture of Bell which emerged from the inquiry was horrendously unflattering. On the evidence of senior civil servants and others, Cairns was almost acting as the *de facto* DETI minister in some key areas, while Bell as the *de jure* minister nodded along but took limited interest in the detail of RHI. When he appeared before the inquiry, Bell did nothing to dispel that view. The man entrusted by Robinson with running a major department spent two days giving evidence which was frequently anecdotal or involved hearsay, and was repeatedly imprecise about key details. He did not refuse to answer any question, but many of his responses wandered far away from what he had been asked, and when he was brought back to the question he was hazy as to what had happened or said he could not remember. But the inquiry had through its own work established that some of Bell's key allegations had a basis in fact. And in the inquiry's final weeks of evidence it unearthed something which breathed life into one of his biggest allegations – that the DUP's most powerful backroom figure, Timothy Johnston, had been behind the attempt to delay cost controls.

Initially, Bell's claims about Johnston had appeared weak, with no corroborating evidence. Then Cairns – who disputed much of Bell's evidence and was still a DUP member – told the inquiry that in summer 2015 Johnston had told him that tariff controls should not be put on the scheme and that he should work with Crawford on the issue. That direction, Cairns said, was why he had attempted to implement Crawford's suggestions. Johnston consistently denied those claims and said that he had no knowledge of RHI at the point where it was running out of control.

But late on the night of Wednesday, 5 October 2018 – just hours before Johnston returned to the inquiry for his final day of evidence – there was a major development. Cairns's lawyer met inquiry barrister Donal Lunny at the law courts in Belfast and handed over new evidence. Among it was an email which Cairns had sent to Johnston, using their dup.org.uk email addresses. The communication significantly undermined Johnston's story. On 17 August 2015, Cairns had emailed Johnston about another issue. Cairns went on to say: 'We also need to get a catch up on renewable heat. If we are to deviate from GB policy, it will require a ministerial direction [the nuclear option for a minister].' The implication of the email seemed clear: someone had prior to this point suggested they should 'deviate from GB policy' and Johnston was at least aware of it. The lynchpin of the modern DUP, who until that point had spoken with a clarity and authority which demonstrated why he had been the power behind the throne of successive DUP leaders, struggled to explain the email.

Under sustained questioning, Lunny put it to him that the email 'seems to assume a degree of knowledge' about the issue, with the language being 'cryptic' to the uninitiated. Johnston said Cairns may have assumed he had more knowledge than he had. When asked if he read the email, Johnston initially said that he 'probably skimmed it'. Coghlin put it to him that 'it's not a long email ... so skimming it means you probably read it?' Johnston said: 'Yes, I think if you're pushing me – I can't be absolutely 100% certain.' Coghlin asked why Johnston had not instantly phoned or gone down the corridor to ask 'what on earth are you telling me about 'deviation' for? I haven't said anything about this. You must have got the wrong person'. Johnston replied: 'I certainly ... have no sense that I did do that ... I have no sense that at the time I paid a lot of attention to it.' Johnston, by now the DUP's chief executive, said that he had forgotten about the email. Lunny put it to him there may have been other occasions where RHI was mentioned. Johnston said: 'I can't rule that out. I can't rule that out.' But he was 'absolutely clear' that he did not oppose cost controls, something he said he would remember.

Several weeks later, Cairns explained why it emerged so late in proceedings. The email, he said, was 'stored on the server owned and controlled by the DUP and/or its agents' and as someone no longer employed by the party, he did not have access to its systems. Cairns said that when the inquiry began he was 'concerned' at not having access to his DUP email account, and had attempted to access it but was unable to do so. The former spad said that he had read DUP chairman Lord Morrow's statement to the inquiry which said that DUP staff had searched party accounts, leading him to wrongly assume 'that my account, which belonged to the party, had been searched'. But then, in October 2018, his solicitor advised him to attempt to access his old email account, and at that point he said he had been reminded that there had been 'default email passwords' and by using those he 'gained access to the account'. It was not clear whether the emails remained on the DUP server or whether Cairns's phone had retained copies of them locally, which he was now able to access – regardless of whether the party had wiped them.

****

It was not the only occasion in the summer of 2015 that Johnston had been informed about significant RHI developments. Another email – which Johnston gave to the inquiry – showed that Crawford had in August 2015 forwarded to him an email alleging poultry farmers' 'abuse' of RHI. Later that month, in another email which Johnston also handed to the inquiry, Cairns had forwarded to him a message to Crawford that they had 'no choice' but to proceed with cutting the subsidy. The inquiry had already separately asked Johnston why it was that he had only provided it with one side of text message conversations with his colleague Richard Bullick, while Bullick had handed over both sides of the exchanges. When asked if he had deleted messages or altered them, Johnston said that he had not. He said that his phone was set to automatically delete text messages after 30 days but that he had paid for software to recover as many messages as possible.

****

In the 97 years from the creation of Northern Ireland, the RHI Inquiry was the most forensic examination of how Stormont governed, turning over rocks which in some cases had lain undisturbed for decades. Unlike the Republic of Ireland, where there had been major public inquiries into political scandals, there had never been anything comparable north of the border. Lord Saville's public inquiry into the events of Bloody Sunday had been a mammoth undertaking, but it had been a discrete investigation into the events of a single day of the Troubles rather than into the governance of Northern Ireland. It was a brutal experience for the DUP and the Northern Ireland Civil Service in particular. But, like painful surgery, the inquiry's work exposed multiple governance deficiencies which, if left untreated, would only become more dangerous. A government as systemically dysfunctional as that exposed by the inquiry was always going to implode at some point, no matter how much spin or money or blind eyes were deployed.

The powerful elite, which under devolution had come to dominate Stormont, could scarcely have imagined that they would ever face such scrutiny. Many senior DUP and Sinn Féin figures kept key communications off-grid, using private phones, non-departmental email accounts and modern forms of communication such as WhatsApp which – even in the event of a major scandal where they were questioned – they could expect would never see the light of day. It was Coghlin's willingness to use the sweeping powers of compulsion at his disposal which led to him seizing a vast volume of 'private' communications about government business.

Four days after the establishment of the public inquiry in January 2017 and amid publicity about its sweeping powers to compel private documentation, former DUP spad John Robinson sent a text message to Crawford which said: 'Ok. Will delete everything else?' When asked what he was deleting, Robinson told the inquiry that Crawford had sent him new contact details and he was deleting his old email address and phone number. When asked if he was deleting messages, he said: 'No, nothing of that nature at all.'

The inquiry ultimately amassed 1.5 million pages of evidence. The private emails and messages provided an unprecedented insight into how the modern DUP and Sinn Féin – parties which value privacy and discipline – governed. Without that private information, which had been kept off government servers and out of departmental filing systems, most of those parties' senior figures would have emerged with their true roles in the scandal unrevealed. That was a lesson for a weak civil service which had allowed ministers and spads to use private forms of communication and evade record-keeping. Even if some of them did not care about the truth being recorded, pure self-interest ought to have caused them to realise that if they were the only ones whose actions were recorded then when something went wrong, ministers and spads could wash their hands of it – leaving it in the laps of officials.

Overall, the BBC's Macauley was impressed by the inquiry's diligence. But what will be its impact? 'If it changed the system of government to be more accountable and more transparent, that would be public money well spent. But if the report sits on a shelf and becomes just well-meaning words, people will feel cheated.' At the time of writing, more than two years after Coghlin's appointment, he was finalising his report. From the outset, Patrick Butler, as solicitor to the inquiry, had been its beating heart. But as the inquiry drew to a close he made a move which – although entirely within the rules – raised eyebrows in Stormont among some of those who heard of it.

In summer 2019, as the inquiry was finalising its report and preparing right of reply letters to those it would criticise, Butler took up a high-level post advising the department most centrally involved in RHI – the Department for the Economy (DfE). For half of the week he was working in the inquiry and for the remainder he was in Stormont, acting as a senior legal adviser to DfE. The move was not announced by the inquiry but was confirmed by it in response to questions after a source contacted the author. As with several members of the inquiry's staff, Butler was a civil servant – working as a lawyer in the Departmental Solicitor's Office (DSO) – who had been seconded to the inquiry for its duration.

The inquiry said that Butler had been a staff member of the DSO throughout, in the same manner as with the public inquiry into historical institutional abuse, and

> the inquiry chairman and the departmental solicitor were aware of this from the outset and were satisfied that robust measures were put in place to address any possible concerns about an actual, or perceived, conflict of interest. Ethical walls have been put in place to avoid any such conflict. Patrick Butler has not worked on any RHI-related work in his new role with the DSO.

The Department of Finance, within which the DSO sits, said that Butler had been appointed 'on a temporary and part-time basis, to a legal advisory post which deals with DfE' but that the role was 'completely separate from RHI and energy related matters. This is a temporary appointment which was filled internally and was offered to lawyers in the Departmental Solicitor's Office, the Crown Solicitor's Office and the Department of Justice. Robust mechanisms have been put in place to avoid any potential or perceived conflict of interest'.

But even without being involved in anything RHI-related, the idea that a critical figure in the multi-million-pound inquiry investigating a departmental disaster would move to work for that department before the inquiry had even finished was problematic, at least in public relations terms. One civil servant said: 'In terms of how it's perceived, it doesn't look good. There's a lot of talk about it within the civil service.'

An inquiry of this scale was never going to be cheap. As well as paying the bill for the inquiry staff, taxpayers funded the vast majority of the lawyers working for those who gave evidence to the inquiry. Even those who had long left government had their legal costs covered by Stormont departments or public bodies, under the principle that if they incurred legal costs as part of their work then those should be paid by their employer. Lawyers funded in this way quickly racked up huge bills. Senior counsel were paid £200 an hour, junior counsel or a solicitor advocate were paid £100 an hour, a solicitor (partner) was paid £146 an hour, a solicitor (assistant) was paid £130 an hour and a paralegal or trainee solicitor was paid £65 an hour.

By the end of the inquiry's hearings, four Stormont departments and other public bodies had spent £5.6 million on legal representation for those coming before the inquiry who were linked to departments. In fact, the cost of the inquiry to Stormont was much higher because the Department of Finance said it had made no record – or even estimate – of the vast amounts of time required by serving civil servants to respond to inquiry questions. By May 2019, Ofgem had spent £2.2 million on the inquiry, made up of legal fees, travel, staff to search through 1.5 million documents and examining material disclosed to it by the inquiry. With the inquiry itself costing in the region of £6 million, and allowing for other smaller public sector costs, the entire inquiry process cost taxpayers more than £14 million. It was a lot of money, on top of what had already been wasted on RHI. But it was only through the laboriously detailed work of the inquiry that one of the major revelations emerged – that many of those who seemed to be making a fortune from RHI were not necessarily in fact the ultimate beneficiaries.

CHAPTER 22
TOO BIG TO FAIL

What if RHI was not an accident? Ever since the scandal broke, there has been a widespread belief, based on flimsy evidence, that the scheme was deliberately designed without cost controls to enrich individuals close to the DUP. But what if that was at most a mere side benefit? What if the real reason either for stripping out cost controls at the outset, or for delaying their introduction, was not to funnel a few hundred thousand pounds to those with boilers but to divert hundreds of millions of pounds to a multinational corporation?

In Stormont, which consciously did not keep records of many even mildly embarrassing issues, an obviously improper decision would be kept off every departmental filing system. Word of mouth would be used. Phone calls in corridors or quickly deleted text messages on private phones would convey the truth not recorded for the public – or the courts – to see. As with so many elements of this story, the official record, which ought to be a bulwark against outlandish allegations, was so distorted under the DUP and Sinn Féin that the absence of something from departmental papers is almost meaningless in attempting to disprove a concern.

****

If you live in the UK or Ireland and eat chicken, you've almost certainly eaten gargantuan quantities of Moy Park chicken – even though it is unlikely to have been labelled as such. An industrial behemoth, which at any one time has about 40 million chickens and kills six million of them every week, it grew from a small family farm in the County Tyrone village of Moygashel to a position of unrivalled domination within Northern Ireland's agri-food industry.

As a monopsony, Moy Park had by the time of RHI come to be the only significant buyer of poultry in Northern Ireland, having swallowed up or put out of business every major rival. Its customers included each of the ten largest supermarkets in the UK – including Tesco, Sainsbury's, M&S, Waitrose, Morrisons, Aldi and Lidl – as well as major retailers in continental Europe, including Carrefour and Picard, and an exclusive licence to make

Jamie Oliver branded, ready-to-cook poultry meals in the UK. Even if you avoided all of those and instead went for some basic sustenance in McDonalds or KFC, there is a good chance that you would be sinking your teeth into a product Moy Park made.

The company, which also had plants in GB, estimated that it was the second-largest poultry producer in the entire UK and that it supplied 50% of the entire UK 'chilled fresh coated market' – items such as chicken nuggets. It now turns over £1.5 billion every year. The company has expanded rapidly and that expansion was facilitated by RHI, making huge profits for its owners many thousands of miles away. The company had been owned by Chicago-based OSI group and then was sold to Brazil's Marfrig in 2008 in a $680 million deal. But within just seven years, Moy Park's valuation more than doubled. In September 2015 – as Moy Park's farmers were piling into RHI, the company was sold to another Brazilian meat giant, JBS. Less than a year later, bribery charges – unconnected to the Moy Park sale – would begin to be levelled at senior JBS figures in a massive scandal which would shake Brazilian society.

Described by Forbes as 'the beast of Brazilian beef, beating out competitors Marfrig and Bertin thanks to government favors', JBS was engaged in corruption on an industrial scale. Moy Park has always said that it had no role in the scandal. Then, two years after it bought Moy Park, JBS sold it – but to a company which is 78% owned by JBS, Pilgrim's Pride, for about $1 billion.

In 2013, the year after RHI's launch, Foster and Crawford travelled to Brazil on a trade mission. One of the major engagements was with Marfrig. Briefing notes obtained by the author show that on the night of 23 May, Foster had been due to dine with Marfrig executives at the Michelin starred Mani Manioca, one of Sao Paulo's hippest restaurants. According to Foster's briefing material, she was to conduct the key meeting – unusually – without her civil servants. It was the only event on the entire trade mission where one of Foster's officials or an official from the British consulate did not accompany the minister. Only Crawford and Invest NI chief executive Alastair Hamilton, a former DUP spad, were to be present. The unusual situation was justified on the basis that it was 'to ensure that the two Marfrig representatives aren't overwhelmed'.

The purpose of the meeting was 'to further discuss Marfrig's presence in Northern Ireland'. The following year, Brazil hosted the football World Cup and Marfrig was a major sponsor and decided that Moy Park's logo would be prominently displayed on advertising hoardings at the tournament amid rumours that it was planning to float the company on the stock market.

When asked questions about the meeting, Foster and Crawford replied with a solicitor's letter which did not answer the questions but threatened to sue for libel. The letter also said that the meeting had been shifted from dinner to breakfast and that the DUP figures 'did not meet with Marfrig executives without officials present in order to ensure there was no minute of the meeting'. The letter added that a translator had been present, although it would not be the role of a translator to record a civil service minute of what transpired.

The year after Foster travelled to Brazil, Marfrig chief executive Sergio Rial said the company had 'ongoing, positive engagement with the Northern Ireland Executive and have experienced a very pro-business attitude'. It was quite an understatement. With Northern Ireland slow to emerge from the global recession, and Stormont desperate for good news, Moy Park knew that it had the devolved administration at its mercy. In a 2014 interview with *Farmers Weekly*, Moy Park director of agriculture Alan Gibson suggested that the company's financial clout meant that Stormont had to help it get around environmental laws. When asked how the company could get around environmental legislation which on paper meant that it could not expand, Gibson said: 'It won't be a roadblock to Moy Park expanding in [Northern] Ireland, though. Everybody politically within Northern Ireland understands; a core part of the country's economy is the agri-food sector … the expansion and intention to build 400 houses is a great incentive [to Stormont] to find a solution.'

Invest NI was offering payments of £9.5 million to Moy Park towards the cost of its expansion, having already given it £5 million in 2010 to upgrade its Ballymena plant. Invest NI decided that farmers could only get public funds from a £35 million Stormont loan scheme to help the poultry industry if they had a contract with Moy Park. But RHI was one of several government measures about to turbocharge Moy Park's profitability without anywhere appearing on a government document as a direct subsidy.

Moy Park was being bought and sold by some of the world's biggest industrial food companies. They wanted to expand and squeeze more profit out of their new acquisition. But they had a problem. Northern Ireland, with a far larger agricultural sector than the rest of the UK, was already in breach of EU environmental directives, including the Nitrates Directive, which protects water quality. Poultry litter – containing everything from chicken dung to feathers and birds, which die in the crammed houses – was loaded with nitrates and spreading it on fields was polluting rivers. Expansion was out of the question.

Moy Park came up with a plan. It would build an incinerator to burn the poultry litter. But it was immediately controversial. The proposed site of the incinerator was beside Lough Neagh, the largest freshwater lake in the British Isles, which supplied almost half of Northern Ireland's drinking water and the plan provoked widespread opposition. The proposal was put forward by a company called Rose Energy. But Moy Park was its majority shareholder – and the main beneficiary if the incinerator got approval. In August 2010, the then DUP Environment Minister, Edwin Poots, announced his intention to give it planning permission. However, the following year Poots was replaced by the SDLP's Alex Attwood and he rejected the application.

The DUP had been stridently in favour of the plan and some of that had been seen publicly. At one point, Sinn Féin tabled an Assembly motion calling for a public inquiry into the proposal. Even though the motion would just have led to a debate in the Assembly and would not in itself have instigated such an inquiry, the DUP used the nuclear option at its disposal – the petition of concern veto mechanism – to block it. But behind the scenes some senior DUP figures were leaning heavily on public servants in an attempt to clear the way for what Moy Park wanted. In 2009, celebrity chef Michael Deane was a member of the board of the Northern Ireland Tourist Board, and he spoke out forcefully against the proposed incinerator. The restaurateur said he was concerned about the impact on tourism and the effect of emissions on farmland:

This is a beautiful location, every bit as vital to our tourism offering as the Lake District is to the north of England or Loch Ness to Scotland. There would be a public outcry if an incinerator was even considered in those areas. This proposal should be flatly rejected by the Planning Department or at the very least a public inquiry should be granted. I will give whatever support I can to ensure that this monster is never built in this location.

But Crawford was furious. In an interview for this book, Alan Clarke, who at that point was chief executive of the Northern Ireland Tourist Board, has spoken for the first time about what went on. He said that 'Andrew went mad'. Crawford, he said, had told Howard Hastings, who was chairman of the tourist board, 'to rein Michael in'. Crawford was 'right over the Tourist Board making any comment on the planning application – which is our right to do as the Tourist Board because we're there to look after tourism', Clarke said. The tourist board was legally an 'arm's length body' but in dealing with Crawford, Clarke said that it had been 'arms' length with an arm round your neck'.

Crawford's links to Moy Park manifested themselves in myriad situations. Clarke recalled how when in early 2014 it was announced that the Irish Open would the following year be coming to Royal County Down it was Crawford who informed him that Moy Park would be sponsoring it. 'Moy Park sponsorship came out of thin air on that one', he said. 'Normally you would go chasing the sponsor. They came chasing us ... Andrew said "Moy Park will want to sponsor this."' When contacted for this book, Crawford declined to answer questions about this and other episodes. Instead he replied with a solicitor's letter which claimed that what had been put to him was 'replete with inaccuracies and defamatory content'. The letter did not specify anything which was actually inaccurate but threatened that 'in the event that publication of inaccurate and defamatory material occurs our clients are fully prepared to issue appropriate legal proceedings'.

A DUP source who at a senior level worked with Crawford over many years described the spad as having been 'so, so close' to Moy Park. The political figure said: 'Moy Park certainly cultivated that relationship – dinners, lunches, etc. But I don't believe for a second that Crawford was paid by them.' The DUP source also said: 'Andrew Crawford was unusually interested in RHI. He was all over it like a rash.'

Crawford set out to the inquiry some of his links – as well as his family's financial link – to the firm. He met Moy Park's chief executive about once a year but had 'more frequent contact' with four other senior figures – Alan Gibson, his successor as agriculture director, Brian Gibson (described by Crawford as a neighbour and a family friend), the senior manager who managed the poultry house expansion, David Mark, and Mike Mullan, Moy Park's executive director for human resources.

At the heart of government thanks to Foster, Crawford was consistently working on behalf of Moy Park's interests. When asked to explain why he had removed a reference to the poultry industry – essentially synonymous with Moy Park – from a crucial Stormont document in early 2016, Crawford's answer to the inquiry was potentially revelatory. The former spad said that he was 'very conscious at this time that this was going to become a very public debate' and that 'this was the first time that it was going to other ministers in the Northern Ireland Executive' and he was 'concerned' that singling out Moy Park or the poultry industry was 'unfair'.

Even at that late stage, when Stormont knew it was having to pay for what had been a disastrous scheme – something which might have caused someone in Crawford's position to have felt angry at how aggressively Moy Park had taken advantage of RHI – he was instead seeking to protect the company. The consequence of his action was that the paper, which went to other ministers in the Executive, did not give the full picture.

Having failed to secure the incinerator, Moy Park turned its focus elsewhere and Stormont bent over backwards to help. Investigative journalism by the website Source Material in the wake of the RHI scandal uncovered how in tandem with RHI, Foster's department had used another green energy subsidy, the NIRO, to facilitate Moy Park using Anaerobic Digester (AD) plants which used poultry litter to create electricity.

In 2012, Stormont set up the Agri-Food Strategy Board to create a 'strategic action plan' for farming and was chaired by Tony O'Neill, a senior director at Moy Park. Two years later, by which time he had left Moy Park, O'Neill set out forthrightly that the industry expected Stormont to do as told: 'We will be suitably demanding and critical if they are not doing exactly what we ask them to do.'

The following year Stormont created what it described as 'a dedicated team of officials' to help Moy Park expand despite its environmental problem. By 2015, as the rest of the UK was cutting subsidies for AD plants, O'Neill's committee successfully lobbied to lock payments at the top level. By the following year they were four times higher than anywhere else in the UK.

A policy, which was presented to the public as evidence of Stormont's commitment to the environment, was actually designed with the poultry industry specifically in mind, according to documents unearthed by Source Material journalist Marcus Leroux. The subsidy was 'an indication that government is highly supportive of sustainable solutions for poultry litter', according to speaking notes prepared for a senior civil servant.

At the same time, Stormont ministers approved a £12 million loan scheme 'supporting the NI poultry industry in developing sustainable treatment solutions to comply with the Nitrates and Water Framework Directives'. That taxpayers' money went to build two giant biogas digesters, one specifically designed to deal with Moy Park's poultry waste. Moy Park was by now so deeply intertwined with Stormont that a briefing document of the Department of Agriculture's top official considered the idea that AD plants for Moy Park should be classified as 'strategic assets' and fully funded by the government along a model used for the army's Challenger tank. A hugely profitable multinational company shovelling money to its shareholders in Brazil and the USA was now being talked about in the same breath as the defence of the country. The answer drafted to that question was enlightening. It said: 'The Challenger tank was procured by the MoD which is not bound by EU procurement rules around State Aid'. The significance of that was that it showed that Stormont was not saying that it would be either wrong or undesirable to treat a multinational company in the same terms as the defence of the nation; rather, it was prevented from doing so by EU state aid law. Given the later suspicion that RHI had been used to circumvent state aid law, that is potentially significant.

Stormont was so desperate to help Moy Park expand that it contradicted its own stance – and that of Moy Park – to do so.

A major problem with AD plants is that the sludge left at the end of the process is spread on fields and contains just as much ammonia as the untreated litter. In 2008, when Moy Park was still pushing the incinerator, it admitted that poultry litter 'does not lend itself well to the process of anaerobic digestion' which 'does not remove the nitrates and phosphates which is essential to comply with [EU law]'. Stormont agreed, saying that the use of AD 'does not address the fundamental issue of excess nutrients in the manure, as it requires land spreading of the digestate'. Yet once the choice became between protecting the environment or allowing Moy Park to expand, Stormont immediately decided that the company's growth was paramount.

Source Material calculations showed that Moy Park's lobbying helped unlock subsidy payments for biogas which are likely to ultimately hit £830 million, although much of that money will go to other companies. The payments are funded by charges added to household energy bills across the UK. Just as with RHI, Northern Ireland received far more than its 'fair share' of the UK pot. Essentially, GB consumers were paying a charge on their electricity bills to facilitate the expansion of Moy Park in Northern Ireland. Moy Park's extraordinary influence at Stomornt in dealing with poultry litter is potentially crucial to understanding cash for ash. That is because, as with AD plans, the RHI scheme involved Moy Park benefiting – and GB paying. It involved Stormont consciously making its scheme more generous than that in GB, in the belief that doing so unlocked 'free money'. And it involved two of the central characters involved in RHI: Foster and Crawford.

****

By the time RHI was shut, 943 of the 1,526 poultry houses owned by Moy Park's farmers were heated under the scheme. About half of all RHI boilers were linked to Moy Park. No single entity came close to benefiting as handsomely from RHI. Even those allegedly heating empty sheds to pocket the subsidy were bringing in sums which were dwarfed by the legal gains for Moy Park.

The company operates a complex – and secretive – pricing structure, making it difficult to comprehend how RHI payments to farmers benefit its shareholders. That mystique ended on 22 June 2018 – the day that major Moy Park farmer Tom Forgrave gave evidence to the RHI Inquiry. Until that point the public perception was that poultry farmers – who on the published list of RHI payments occupied many of the top positions – had greedily milked the public purse. Forgrave's evidence was that while the money seemed to be going to the farmer, much of it ended up with Moy Park. At considerable personal risk, given Moy Park's dominant position and his dependence on the company, Forgrave pulled back the curtain on what had gone on.

Forgrave's evidence showed that RHI had allowed Moy Park to improve the quality of its product while slashing the proportion of what it paid farmers to heat poultry sheds – in the knowledge that they had a separate income. In essence, RHI was a backdoor subsidy to Moy Park. Forgrave said that prior to RHI, Moy Park set chicken prices in a way which effectively covered all its farmers' production costs. However, he said that after RHI the company – despite gaining significantly – no longer covered all heating costs. Farmers instead found RHI making up the significant shortfall in their income. Forgrave then went on to set out how Moy Park's 'clever business model' had the effect of driving poultry farmers into RHI. He said:

> As more hot water systems went live, the performance and welfare continued to improve and at almost every quarterly monthly meeting [with the company] a further 50% of the total financial savings brought about by improved performance was removed from the price paid to the farmer. This continued each and every quarter to the point where any financial benefits to the grower [farmer] due to improved performance had been eroded to zero.

He added: 'As of present day, all financial benefits derived from any improvements in performance achieved from the move to hot water heating have been removed from the growers [farmers] and they remain on the same margin that they were on in 2013, with only a small inflationary-linked increase.' He said that the switch from problematic 'wet' heating provided by gas burners to 'dry' heat from indirect hot water heating fuelled by biomass boilers was 'one of the biggest changes implemented in the poultry industry in the last 30 years' and was enthusiastically promoted by the company.

The system the company had in place meant that after it had successfully encouraged a critical mass of its farmers to switch to the new heating system, the others either had to follow suit or would find themselves at a serious competitive disadvantage. Forgrave – who received £750,000 in subsidy during the first three years of the scheme – said there was tension between farmers and Moy Park because the company had set an acceptable figure for heat usage which was far short of what was required to maintain poultry sheds to optimal standards for bird welfare. He said that farmers then had to decide whether to make up the heat shortfall out of their own pocket or see conditions for their birds deteriorate.

A week later, senior Moy Park manager David Mark, who was one of the company's key figures involved in the rollout of hot water heating systems fuelled by RHI boilers, gave evidence to the inquiry. Mark had a particular reason to be *au fait* with RHI – he was heating his home with an RHI boiler for which he received payments under the non-domestic scheme. Even though the boiler was mainly heating a domestic property, he secured the subsidy because he rented several rooms in his home to guests on Airbnb. The boiler – registered in the name of his wife, Joy – was installed at the height of the spike, just before cost controls, and they claimed £9,236 in the first 16 months. Mark was deeply reluctant to accept that Moy Park had benefited from RHI. However, he eventually admitted that the subsidy had what he described as 'a minor part to play' in improving its efficiency. Detailed scrutiny by the inquiry of heating figures showed that Moy Park paid its farmers considerably less for heat than what its internal documentation described as reasonable.

Mark described in a document heat usage of between 1,800 kWh and 2,000 kWh per thousand birds as legitimate – and elsewhere Mark suggested to a bank that a poultry farmer could use 5,000 kWh and it would be reasonable. However, Moy Park only paid its farmers for about 1,400 kWh of heat per thousand birds – a lucrative financial benefit to the company.

Mark insisted that he was motivated not by attempting to enrich Moy Park, but 'trying to guard against' wasteful use of heat by setting the heat allowance at a lower level. Initially, Mark denied that he had ever seen RHI as a 'safety net' for Moy Park's suppliers. However, barrister Donal Lunny showed him a document where he had used that precise phrase, saying that if a Moy Park farmer was struggling, 'the £20k RHI is a big safety net' in what would otherwise have been an 'unrecoverable disaster'. Mark then insisted that was 'in a different context'.

Like Mark, Moy Park's chief executive at the time of RHI, Janet McCollum, was doggedly unwilling to accept that the company benefited financially from RHI. In her written evidence, she said: 'Moy Park has not indirectly earned any RHI scheme tariff income.' But, under forensic scrutiny by the inquiry, McCollum eventually admitted that the corporation indirectly made money from RHI. She acknowledged that RHI not only helped Moy Park's rapid expansion by funding better heating systems for poultry houses but also helped make up for a shortfall between the fuel allowance which the company was prepared to pay to its farmers and the cost of the fuel which they required to raise chickens. However, the trained accountant, who had previously been Moy Park's chief finance officer, insisted that she was ignorant of that fact at the time when the company was reaping the financial reward.

What the inquiry did not hear was that the lucrative nature of RHI for poultry was widespread knowledge long before the scheme was shut. In November 2014, an article with the title 'The poultry farm nest egg' appeared on the website of Celtic Green Energy, a Welsh-based renewable energy company.

Highlighting that Moy Park's GB operation was increasing the number of its biomass boilers from 68 to 86, the article said that while 'Moy Park enjoys promoting the fact that they will be saving around 18,500 tonnes of CO_2 per year thanks to these new biomass boilers ... the government have this sweet little earner for companies that use renewable fuels, known as the renewable heat incentive (RHI) scheme. This scheme is worth BIG BUCKS especially if you have 86 biomass boilers installed!' It said that because poultry farms require heat all year round they 'can earn an incredible return'. It calculated that even on the GB scheme – with tiering – Moy Park's 86 boilers would likely be earning over £1 million a year through RHI payments.

The boiler installation company was openly attempting to persuade poultry farmers to realise how lucrative the GB RHI was at that point. Is it really credible that Moy Park did not realise how valuable RHI was to its business, and did not realise that the Stormont RHI was uncapped and therefore far more beneficial than even the GB scheme?

By the time McCollum gave evidence to the inquiry she had been replaced at the head of the company. Intriguingly, after her evidence, the new chief executive, Chris Kirke, submitted a written statement to the inquiry in which he contradicted what she had said. He claimed that 'the RHI scheme did not of itself provide any enhanced financial benefits to Moy Park'. However, even in rebutting the claim of financial gain from RHI, Kirke admitted such gain, saying that 'the RHI scheme certainly stepped up hot water heating installations' – something with myriad benefits to Moy Park. He insisted that the availability of RHI and Moy Park's massive expansion had been, in the words of RHI Inquiry barrister Donal Lunny, 'a happy coincidence'.

Moy Park's credibility is undermined by its lack of candour when the story first broke. In December 2016 the company told the BBC: 'Moy Park derives no financial benefit from poultry farmers participating in the RHI scheme.' The company also said at that point that it had nothing to do with lending by banks to Moy Park's farmers, something it said was 'between the lender and borrower alone and have nothing to do with Moy Park'. It was an attempt to put the greatest possible distance between the company and a scandal which at that point was on course to topple devolution. But it was wildly misleading. Moy Park manager David Mark was working closely with banks, right down to the banks passing details of individual loan applications to him for advice before deciding on whether to lend money. In March 2014, Mark gave a presentation to Danske Bank in which he set out Moy Park's payback calculation for its farmers who entered RHI.

****

Moy Park was willing to offer gifts to Stormont ministers it was seeking to influence. In December 2016 as the cash for ash scandal raged on newspaper front pages and across society, DUP minister Simon Hamilton was desperately attempting to find a way to slash Stormont's RHI bill. Several of the options were obviously going to cost Moy Park. Hamilton recalled that he had been told by his private secretary that Moy Park had contacted him to offer him a free turkey. Hamilton told the inquiry that he was 'aghast' because he 'thought this to be inappropriate in the circumstances'. He turned down the turkey.

On 30 November 2016 – just a week before BBC *Spotlight* and weeks before the turkey offer – during a visit to Moy Park Hamilton had met McCollum and Mullan. He said he was 'surprised [that] RHI was raised at all and especially in the context of Moy Park seeking a new RHI scheme … I was aghast at them raising the issue at all and especially in the way they did'. Hamilton said that Mullan then contacted his constituency office – rather than his department – in January 2017 as he prepared to move to retrospectively slash RHI rates. Hamilton felt the request for a discussion about RHI was 'inappropriate'. But while Hamilton thought that Moy Park's free Christmas turkey offer to him was inappropriate, not all of his party colleagues took the same view. In December 2012 – just over a month after Foster had opened RHI – she accepted a free turkey from Moy Park. Foster properly declared the gift internally in DETI, describing it as a 14-kg turkey worth £65.

Then in December 2015 – just after the poultry-driven rush, which had crippled the scheme – Moy Park approached DETI again. A source with knowledge of what happened recounted how Jonathan Bell had been offered a small, medium or large turkey. But the minister asked his private secretary, Sean Kerr, to phone the company back and ask: 'Do you have anything bigger?' Kerr made the call and Moy Park gladly offered a larger bird which Bell used to feed his extended family. A departmental source said that Kerr had told colleagues that Bell was 'a greedy f****r'.

Bell and Kerr each declined to comment on the incident. The department said it had no record of Bell making any declarations of interest, declarations of hospitality or any other declarations during his time as minister.

When asked why as a hard-nosed company known for its efficiency Moy Park spent money on giving free turkeys to DUP ministers taking decisions which had major implications for Moy Park's profitability, and to set out what other gifts Moy Park offered to DUP politicians or civil servants, the company declined to comment. Foster and Crawford similarly declined to comment on what gifts of hospitality they had accepted from Moy Park.

When asked a series of questions about RHI during the writing of this book, a PR company acting for Moy Park said that as the inquiry was still ongoing it was 'precluded from providing any additional information'. However, senior counsel to the inquiry David Scoffield made clear on day 58 of the inquiry's hearings that once a witness had completed their oral evidence and been released from their oath 'there's nothing to stop [them] from talking about [their] evidence in the inquiry'.

It is, of course, common for many businesses to send gifts at Christmas, and only the most venal of ministers would be influenced by a few mouthfuls of free turkey when they came to decide on the expenditure of hundreds of millions of pounds. But if there was any benefit whatsoever to Moy Park from such gifts, it was a good investment. Buried in a JBS market update in the fourth quarter of 2016 – a full year after most Moy Park farmers had entered RHI – was the revelation that Moy Park had become significantly more profitable. Although its overall revenue had fallen slightly, the profit (before tax or interest payments) which it was making on that revenue had risen from 7.9% at the end of 2015 to 9.8% a year later. There was no mention of RHI – just an oblique reference to 'an improvement in operational efficiencies and an enhanced focus on cost control'.

There are at least four ways in which Moy Park benefited from RHI:

1. The company had a modest benefit from two of its own boilers, rushed into service after it was tipped off by Crawford about closure.

2. The cost of its farmers' heating was heavily subsidised by taxpayers, allowing it to cut the percentage of heating for which it had to pay.

3. RHI paid for a more expensive 'dry heat' system which reduced ammonia and reduced the hock burn on the chickens' legs from where they were crowded together in sheds deep in their own wet faeces. Aside from considerations for the birds, that meant that they were in better condition and more of each carcass could be sold.

4. RHI was a cost-free means of improving Moy Park's image, both by improving bird welfare and enhancing the environmental credentials of a company which in many of its operations damaged the environment. Those benefits would then be marketed by the company for financial gain, helping it to charge a premium as a green company, such as in its deal with environmentally conscious celebrity chef Jamie Oliver.

In May 2015, just as DETI was realising the RHI problem, the company sought to raise £100 million to help finance its expansion. A 276-page document compiled for potential investors provides unique insight into its operations. In Moy Park's own words, its business model 'gives us significant control' – it supplies farmers with everything from the chicks themselves to their feed and the exact conditions for their housing. It said: 'We intend to continue to improve our operational and agricultural efficiency by implementing measures such as improvements to the feed conversion ratio (the measure of an animal's efficiency in converting feed mass into increased body mass) … [and] controlling costs of production.'

RHI improved the feed conversion ratio – it took less food to produce each kilogram of chicken. Is it possible that a company managing its budgets so meticulously could not have realised that RHI was a huge benefit? If, as the company claims, it did not realise that it was benefiting, why did its senior management spend so much effort to rush through boiler applications before RHI shut?

The company was also alive to the potential for it being scrutinised by anti-monopoly regulators because 'the production of fresh chicken in the UK is a relatively concentrated industry in which we estimate ourselves to be the second largest producer, with 26% of UK production'. It said that 'any attempt on our part to expand our production of fresh poultry, particularly through the acquisition of other fresh poultry producers in the UK, may attract the scrutiny of UK and European competition and antitrust regulators'. Here the company was showing awareness of not just state aid law, but of the potential implications of its dominant market position. The company said that 'increasing the number of farms providing poultry to us is critical to increasing production' and that

> if we are unable to increase the number of farms supplying us with poultry at a high enough rate, we may not be able to increase our production at the same rate as competitors. This may cause us to lose market share and may have a material adverse effect on our business, our results of operations and our financial condition.

Even if RHI had no other benefit to Moy Park, it was critical to mitigating this self-identified threat to the company. RHI persuaded farmers to expand where otherwise they would have been cautious. Putting up another huge poultry shed was suddenly more attractive to farmers because of the RHI profit on offer. Sean McNaughton was one such poultry farmer. He admitted that 'the tariffs promised by RHI were a very important factor in deciding to proceed with both the new biomass boiler and the poultry shed, as in the absence of the tariff the financial calculations would almost certainly have led to us not going down this path'. Another farmer who was deciding between putting up another poultry house or installing biomass in his existing houses decided on the latter because he calculated that he would make more money from biomass – both in direct RHI payments and indirect financial benefits from healthier birds – than by expanding his business.

****

Poultry sheds require huge quantities of heat. Day-old chicks are crammed into vast sheds where they will die if they do not receive the warmth which in nature they would get in the nest. From the outset, Stormont's scheme was designed on paper to be less generous than that in GB. The rationale was that differing fuel prices meant that people in Northern Ireland required less subsidy to shift to green energy. For that reason, the tariffs were significantly lower in Northern Ireland. Had it not been for the removal of cost controls, it would therefore have been more attractive for Moy Park to expand in GB with a more generous payment scheme. Stormont was desperate to secure the expansion on its side of the Irish Sea and, as demonstrated by the Challenger tank analogy, discussed the company as a strategic asset.

Cathal Ellis, the green energy expert at the Department of Agriculture, met Moy Park in September 2014. Moy Park told Ellis that the cost of a biomass hot water system was £30,000 per house and they were expecting an RHI income of £10,000 a year – meaning that in crude terms the boiler would be paid off in three years, with 17 more years of payments to come. Ellis repeatedly used poultry and mushroom-growing examples in the slides of his presentations to farmers, explaining to them how lucrative RHI could be.

There is considerable circumstantial evidence that RHI was used to provide a backdoor subsidy to Moy Park. It is also clear that from at least 2014 Stormont officials knew of a looming rush into RHI from Moy Park's farmers. By 2015 at the latest, Crawford was aware that RHI was wildly lucrative for poultry farmers, yet he was working in the shadows to keep payments high for Moy Park's farmers. In that period DETI officials were giving crucial RHI information to Moy Park before even giving it to their minister. Crawford then tipped off Moy Park in January 2016 that RHI was to be shut, giving the company weeks of a head start on others and allowing it to rush through yet more boilers. But all of that came after RHI was established. Could it have been the case that the scheme had been deliberately set up without cost controls to facilitate one company?

At first glance, the fact that Moy Park did not immediately pile into the scheme when it was opened suggests that it took some time to realise how beneficial it was, undermining that theory. However, that may not be the case. Even though the company wanted to build new poultry houses, it could only do so with planning permission and environmental consents which were tied to its inability to adequately dispose of its chicken dung mountain.

One senior civil servant said that until the middle of 2014 Moy Park was not in a position to expand. Therefore, the delay in entering the scheme may not have been because Moy Park was ignorant of RHI's benefits from an early stage.

But whatever the genesis of the scheme, it soon became clear to most of those involved that it was strategically significant to the poultry industry. By May 2015, as RHI was running way beyond budget, DETI's Stuart Wightman told colleagues that closing RHI 'should be a very last resort as it would be very damaging for the local renewable heating and poultry industry ... the performance of the NI RHI is a success story'. That comment is one of many which make it difficult for Stormont to argue that it was unaware of what was really going on. Here Wightman was presenting RHI not as a scheme which helped the poultry industry cut its carbon emissions – that would not in itself have been 'very damaging'. Rather, it was presented as crucial to the industry – and therefore Moy Park. But one very senior civil servant's words – spoken on the understanding that they would never be made public – undermine the benign view that RHI was an accident which Moy Park belatedly began to exploit.

Prior to RHI becoming the scandal which toppled Stormont, David Thomson, who was second in command in DETI until he retired in June 2014, spoke candidly about the significance of poultry to RHI. In an interview with PwC, he said: 'It was a very important scheme because we then tied it into all this poultry stuff and it became a very critical element of that ...' Thomson knew what he was talking about because he was DETI's point man on the attempts to help Moy Park solve its poultry litter problem. Thomson set out how the situation had arisen because Moy Park had persuaded Stormont that it could massively expand in Northern Ireland – if it got sufficient government support. Drumming on the desk with his fingers, he said:

This all goes back to ... one of the big supermarket chains said that they were going to stop sourcing poultry from outside the UK and that from a certain date ... the trouble is we didn't have the capacity, alright? Moy Park came to Invest NI and the department and said this is a wonderful opportunity for us. The minister got very excited about it, quite rightly, because [of] great export opportunities but also great employment opportunities ...

The veteran civil servant went on:

There were two or three problems with it. One was [that] banks weren't lending so again one of the things we spent a lot of time doing with [the Department of Finance] was trying to get a lending scheme because banks said there is no value in a chicken house. The value is actually on the income generated, not in the ground. The second was poultry litter where we were in default [of environmental regulations] … and the third was costs and hey the RHI was a wonderful way to help that so this was part of – I don't think it was written down as a formal poultry strategy but everybody in the department knew along with Invest NI [*sic*] gave Moy Park a very substantial grant assistance from my knowledge so it was all part which was why we were encouraging all this and to see as what you see in the press now and you can see the maps of you know of blobs of where this money went [an allusion to RHI claims clustered around Moy Park's abattoirs].

Moy Park employed more than 5,000 people in Northern Ireland, and its expansion would increase that to 6,000. That was Stormont's justification for the huge direct subsidies which it got from taxpayers. But government subsidy to private companies is constrained by EU state aid laws which aim to provide a fair playing field for companies, something which is distorted if a government is propping up or unfairly supporting chosen firms. Stormont was acutely aware of the state aid rules. It wanted to do everything it could to help Moy Park without crossing the line into illegal state aid. But even if many in Stormont were well-intentioned, no one observing Moy Park's entwined relationship with government could deny that it had an unfair advantage over its few remaining rivals. Insofar as officials or politicians ever questioned the preferential relationship, they justified it on pragmatic grounds – if they didn't keep the company happy, it could move jobs elsewhere. But how was another poultry firm to compete in a situation where Moy Park was not only financially benefiting from taxpayers subsidising its heating bills, but where the government gave it the inside track ahead of its competitors?

From Stormont's perspective, Moy Park was too big to fail – or too big to be lost to Northern Ireland. And it knew it. In a February 2016 meeting with Andrew McCormick, the company lobbied to see an RHI-type scheme kept open. DETI's note of the meeting said that Moy Park 'feared competitive disadvantage with GB … Moy Park believed in NI but, ultimately, had to go wherever made best sense for the company'. Although that was on one level a statement of basic capitalist principles, it also reads as a quasi-threat: if you don't keep us happy, we might move jobs. But in tolerating that argument, Stormont adopted a tunnel vision which obscured the perverse nature of what government was prepared to do to placate the firm. When asked about the Moy Park relationship, one senior DUP source did not defend it as such, but said bluntly: 'Do you think this wasn't happening with other big companies?' In a globalised capitalist world, it is perhaps inevitable that governments would be tempted to bend or break rules to secure jobs in their region. Yet, aside from the question of fairness, for capitalism to function efficiently it requires free markets in which the strongest survive and the weakest fail – not the crony capitalism whereby a company's size or political connections buys it preferential treatment.

It was not just Moy Park which was, at best, treading a fine line with EU state aid law. In January 2017, Elaine Shaw, who was speaking on behalf of mushroom growers, told MLAs that 90% of mushroom farmers in Northern Ireland had installed biomass RHI boilers, and went on to say: 'This investment reduced our growing costs by 4%, which was a substantial margin. That has been critical to allow our growers to remain competitive and compete with the Polish mushrooms that are being imported.' Here was *prima facie* evidence that RHI was distorting the pan-European mushroom market. In defending RHI claimants' court challenge to the subsidy cut, the Department for the Economy's QC cited those comments as demonstrating 'the potential for market distortion through state aid' and that the scheme was never envisaged as a way to 'allow producers to drop their prices'. He added: 'There are other sectors – poultry, other industrial sectors which may be enjoying a similar advantage'. Having tolerated that for years, Stormont was now about to pull the rug from under those who had entered the scheme it had promoted to them.

CHAPTER 23
EVEN THE WINNERS LOSE

Barney McGuckian was always looking for ways to improve his animal feed business. Every year the north Antrim man went on a study trip, mostly to continental Europe, in an attempt to see how the feed mill in Cloughmills, which he ran with his brother Liam could become more competitive.

On the 2014 trip, a powerful DUP figure who was completely unknown to him was present. It was Andrew Crawford. McGuckian had recently heard about RHI and was exploring the possibility of applying to the scheme for a massive heat plant. Crawford, whose brother-in-law, Wallace Gregg, was from Cloughmills, got chatting to the businessman and, in McGuckian's words, 'made it a lot easier for us to get in the door' to the department. Crawford put him in touch with DETI's Stuart Wightman who met him to discuss the possibility of the McGuckians building a combined heat and power (CHP) plant – a mini-power station, generating electricity, but also utilising the heat for the manufacture of wood pellets. McGuckian never met Crawford again. The next time he saw him was on television where he was facing allegations about his role in the RHI scandal.

At the point he met Crawford, CHP plants were ineligible for RHI. But that was to change in November 2015. At the point where RHI was at last being reined in, it was also expanded. It was an absurd decision, given the scale of the overspend. CHP plants are huge and involve enormous subsidy claims. But, perhaps based on the the continued belief that London at least might be paying, DETI pressed ahead with expansion at the point where the entire scheme ought to have been shut. However, a cruel fate was to befall the McGuckians and their business partner Colin Newell. Having consulted DETI at every stage and taken its advice about the plant's design, they pressed ahead with their plans. The installation, which would never have been on the 'cash for ash' tariffs and would have been paid at a lower rate than similar plants in England, was actively encouraged by civil servants and promoted in government literature, which led them to invest half a million pounds in getting it to the verge of construction.

In September 2016, three months before the *Spotlight* exposé, DUP Economy Minister Simon Hamilton wrote to them to say that 'subject to satisfying all Ofgem's eligibility criteria' they would be 'entitled to the CHP tariff', and went on to refer to 'the current RHI CHP tariff of 3.5 pence per kwh'. In December, after the scandal erupted, having believed that they had been given preliminary accreditation, they were told in writing by a senior departmental official that they were 'the operator of an accredited installation under the [RHI] scheme'. But the following month, after Stormont retrospectively capped and tiered all tariffs, a huge problem was discovered. When officials went to the European Commission to ask for state aid approval, they were told that they had never applied for approval for the 2015 changes – of which CHP had been part.

It was an extraordinarily basic failure by DETI, which meant that the 2015 RHI changes had never been lawful so CHP plants were ineligible. But when the error was discovered in 2017, civil servants sought to wash their hands of the implications of their disastrous mistake.

Having been treated shabbily by government, the three businessmen found themselves financially punished – while those responsible for the error escaped any censure. The Department for the Economy (DfE) said that was because it could not conduct disciplinary investigations while the public inquiry was ongoing. The three men challenged DfE's decision in court and at the time of writing are awaiting the outcome. But they were angry for a second reason. Even after discovering the huge error in 2016, civil servants could have belatedly applied for state aid approval. But – by now under huge pressure to cut the RHI bill to taxpayers – they chose not to do so. A Stormont memo showed that around this time Moy Park privately expressed concerns to civil servants about the McGuckian proposal.

Senior Moy Park officials met Stormont's Department of Finance in January 2017. A senior finance official, Emer Morelli, took a note of the conversation. Setting out three 'key issues' raised by Moy Park, she said: 'The Moy Park team expressed a concern that one of the large combined heat and power plants with preliminary accreditation may not met [*sic*] the eligibility criteria due [*sic*] planning permission being granted 25 days after the scheme closed.' When asked about that, Moy Park – which by now knew that there was a limited RHI pot and if the McGuckians entered the scheme it would take tens of millions of pounds – insisted that it had not lobbied against the plant and said its meeting was to 'offer insight and suggestions to secure the NI RHI scheme within budget'. The McGuckian plant – one of two CHP installations at an advanced stage of design – could have cost the department between £60 million and £75 million over 20 years. The McGuckians said that they were so dismayed at their experience of officialdom and politicians that they would never again get involved with any Stormont scheme. It would be a sentiment shared by many of those who had trusted Stormont's assurances about RHI.

****

The final substantive act of devolved government before it collapsed in January 2017 was to pass legislation which retrospectively moved every RHI claimant to the November 2015 tariffs. In effect, it extended tiering and a cap to everyone for a temporary period until a long-term solution could be found. Unsurprisingly, many claimants reacted with anger because they had been promised – in legislation, in the words of Arlene Foster in the Assembly, in Foster's letter to the banks, in government literature and in innumerable other ways – that the tariffs were set in stone. That certainty was at the heart of the scheme – rates might fall for future entrants, but for those who got in on time, the payments were locked in. Some claimants had taken on enormous loans, sometimes at high interest with finance houses because they could not get bank loans and sometimes secured against the farm which had been in their family for generations. And some claimants had used the lucrative RHI income as leverage to borrow for wider expansion of their business.

A group of boiler owners – ultimately about half of those on the scheme – came together to form the Renewable Heat Association of Northern Ireland (RHANI) to lobby Stormont. They brought in Andrew Trimble, who in a previous career had worked in Whitehall and the British Embassy in Washington, as chief executive. With military-like discipline, Trimble set about fighting back against the public perception that every claimant was a crook.

Alongside that PR offensive, the group launched a judicial review of the changes. During that high court challenge in October 2017, Stormont's lawyer made an argument that had far-reaching implications for anyone trusting a government promise. Tony McGleenan QC said that although government told RHI claimants that the subsidies were unchangeable for 20 years, boiler owners should have realised that might be wrong. He effectively said that despite the multiple assurances – including in statute – the users, many of whom were farmers, should have been more careful in accepting at face value what they were told. The lawyer argued that the fact the tariffs – which government described at the time as 'certain', 'guaranteed', 'reliable' and 'long-term' – were contained in secondary, rather than primary, legislation should have alerted claimants to the possibility of change. When asked by the judge, Mr McGleenan clarified that the possibility of such a change extended to any other piece of secondary legislation. Mr Justice Colton comprehensively rejected RHANI's argument that they had a legitimate expectation of the payments continuing, that the legislation which retrospectively altered their payments was *ultra vires* and that there had been an interference with their human right to property. Stormont's actions were proportionate and in the wider public interest, he ruled.

During the hearing, an argument was made by DfE which alarmed some of the claimants. Where normally government departments attempt to play down the scale of a crisis, DfE was now playing up the scale of RHI. It was only going to win in court if it could prove that it faced a financially devastating situation to which the retrospective cuts had been a proportionate response. Until then, the figure for what was known as the RHI 'overspend' was put by the department at £500 million, a fairly crude extrapolation from the Audit Office report's expectations of what the scheme would cost for the next few years. The very fact that it was the 'overspend' which so concerned everyone was in itself an allusion to the fact that this was the part of the expenditure which really exercised Stormont. The total bill was estimated to be about £1.2 billion, but because most of it was coming from London it was the overspend which Stormont put its energy into tackling.

In court, Stormont's QC introduced new information. He told the judge that the worst-case scenario was that the overspend – if the old scheme was reinstated – could be as much as £700 million. For their part, the boiler owners claimed – with an accountancy report to back them up – that the overspend could be as little as £60 million. Both figures seemed exaggerated, with a figure somewhere in the middle more likely.

Northern Ireland's comptroller and auditor general, Kieran Donnelly, was surprised that when he sent a draft of his July 2016 report – on which the £500 million figure was based – the department was not defensive, and accepted it readily. But DfE's figure was based on a series of improbable assumptions. It assumed that no boiler would drop out of the scheme, even though boilers being run heavily were unlikely to last 20 years and some firms would close or no longer require heat. It also assumed that the CHP plants would be built – a drain of up to £100 million – even though that was only possible if the department lost a separate court challenge. It made no allowance for even a single boiler being removed from the scheme due to fraud. And it assumed that the GB scheme – from whose budget Northern Ireland received just under 3% – would not continue to grow, even though it remained open and was scheduled to do so until at least 2021. As it expanded, Stormont would receive an increasing pot of RHI money, thus cutting the overspend.

As time went on, there was increasing evidence that DfE's figures for the overspend – even if reasonable at the time – were incorrect. RHI boilers have dropped out of the scheme. Eight boilers were destroyed in a fire in Fermanagh and other companies have gone bankrupt.

The department did not publicise the fact that the overspend for 2016–17 was £26.7 million. That figure – for the final year of the 'burn to earn' scheme – was 17.5% lower than Stormont had expected. Yet despite the actual overspend falling from what had been anticipated when the department calculated a total £500 million overspend, rather than cutting the estimate for the total overspend, it hiked it to £700 million. There was little obvious logic for the increase, which was not explained in open court.

When asked to explain the apparent contradiction, the department said that a major reason for the larger figure was a change in how it calculated inflation over future years. Yet, because the Stormont scheme was based on a percentage of the GB scheme, even that explanation made little sense. An inflationary increase in the NI scheme would be offset by an inflationary increase in the total pot from which Stormont's share was derived. For all those reasons, even if the tariffs had not been retrospectively cut, the overspend would not have been £700 million.

Mr Justice Colton said that his court was not best placed to resolve the true cost of the overspend, but he lent towards DfE's figure, saying that although it represented the worst-case scenario it was reasonable for the department to approach the issue in that way. At the time of writing, that verdict is before the Court of Appeal.

But while aggrieved claimants' recourse to the courts was understandable and perhaps inevitable, their tactics were problematic for two reasons. Firstly, although many of them now accepted that the scheme which they had entered in good faith was fundamentally flawed, they sought the reinstatement of that scheme in its entirety. While in law that was the necessary step to take, they could have made clear that it would be the basis for a voluntary negotiation with the department. Even the introduction of a simple cap on usage would have prevented the most extreme payments. Far from weakening their case, that would surely have shown them to be reasonable people who were not blind to the scale of the problem.

Secondly, in taking the court challenge, RHANI painted a bleak picture about the impact of the 2017 regulations which had introduced tiering and a cap. The situation was not only unfair in principle, they argued, but disastrous in financial terms. That would become a problem in March 2019 when Westminster – acting on the advice of DfE because devolution had not returned – acted to implement a long-term solution which was far worse for claimants. The earning potential of a typical 99 kW boiler had been more than £55,000 a year under the original scheme. In 2017, that had been cut to just over £13,000. But in 2019 that was slashed to just over £2,000 a year – a 96% cut. On the day the legislation passed, Tom Forgrave, who had ten boilers and who was a director of RHANI, said that for himself and other claimants 'it's going to be hell'.

Forgrave was one of the most articulate and knowledgeable voices for claimants. As a poultry farmer, he was also among those with the highest legitimate heat usage. But, when confronted with the scale of the 2019 cuts, not everyone with a biomass boiler agreed with the wisdom of their approach to the initial reductions. An individual in the biomass industry said that many claimants – especially those with more modest heat needs – had been content with the 2017 regulations. He said it had been a mistake for RHANI to attempt to reinstate what had been a flawed scheme which even many claimants did not want to see restored. If it did succeed in restarting 'cash for ash', the level of public scrutiny and anger at claimants – perhaps even boycotts of companies not voluntarily accepting lower payments – would potentially undo any financial benefit.

The 2019 RHI cuts also exposed the department further because it was saying that not only was the original scheme flawed, but even after introducing what it billed at the time as cost controls in November 2015, the scheme had been wildly overgenerous. That meant that those who had entered RHI in the belief that it had been fixed – and accepting the department's guarantee that they could invest with confidence – now found themselves in difficulty. Most of those individuals had only been in the scheme for three years and still had major loan repayments to make. Thomas Douglas was one such individual. The 56-year-old poultry farmer from Dungannon had been told about RHI by Moy Park and gone to a Stormont event where it was promoted. He eventually installed a single 199 kW boiler in February 2016, just five days before the scheme was shut, and received £16,200 in the first year. He said that the hot water heating system, which the biomass boiler powered not only improved the birds' welfare but also reduced both the volume of litter and its ammonia level – a key benefit. Even when those on the 'cash for ash' tariff had their payments cut, he had no fear about that happening to him because he had entered the scheme after cost controls and was devastated by the 2019 changes.

In implementing the 2019 cuts, the department said that it would not make sense for anyone with an RHI boiler to revert to fossil fuels because wood pellets were the cheapest form of fuel. However, Douglas disputed that, saying that in the near future he believed it may be 'not feasible to run' and he would revert to gas. 'Their figures are all wrong,' he said, pointing to payments of up to £3,120 a year from RHI while his bank loans – which in May 2019 stretched for another six and a half years – stood at £11,000 a year. And he was one of the cautious claimants, taking his bank loan over ten years. Believing Stormont's pledge that the subsidy was immutable, others spread their loan over five years, with mammoth annual repayments. He said: 'It's put serious stress on people. They're wondering where they're going to find the money to meet their bank commitments. And it's brought in a great mistrust of any government scheme – how can we trust them?'

DfE argued – and its argument was echoed by Northern Ireland Secretary of State Karen Bradley when she brought the change to the Commons – that its hands were tied by the EU and under state aid law it could only allow an average rate of return of 12% or would face EU fines.

Figures set out up by RHANI – and not disputed by the department – showed comparative payments of £19,000 a year for GB claimants with a 99 kW boiler installed before July 2014, £12,000 for someone entering the GB scheme in 2019 and £20,000 for someone entering the Republic of Ireland's scheme which was launched in spring 2019.

If, as Stormont claimed, anything beyond £2,100 a year in Northern Ireland represented illegal state aid, then what about those other schemes? In fact, while the burn to earn tariffs had clearly been a breach of state aid law – especially because they were effectively subsidising one company in particular, Moy Park – the 2019 cuts meant that Northern Ireland was at a state aid disadvantage. Moy Park now faced a state aid incentive to expand in GB or the Irish Republic where its heating bills would be subsidised heavily while in Northern Ireland they would not.

And while the department centred all of its arguments around the rate of return, that was a figure which could be altered up or down by the department. In effect, the 12% figure was almost meaningless – virtually any figure could be claimed to be 12%, depending on which costs were allowed to form part of the equation. Stormont had, for instance, claimed that its initial scheme – offering payments of up to £56,000 – represented a 12% return. It then argued that the 2017 cuts – offering payments of up to £13,000 – represented 12%. So there was scepticism about the claim that the 2019 rates – offering payments of little over £2,000 a year – somehow were the only way to offer a 12% return. In getting to its 2019 figure, the department stripped out multiple expenses involved in installing an RHI boiler. Yet the Republic of Ireland scheme, which also got state aid approval, allowed for all sorts of other costs, recognising that a boiler sitting on its own was not much use without the concrete on which it sat, the building in which it was housed, a pellet bin to store fuel and the pipework to deliver the heat and so on.

DfE admitted that its cuts were so deep that it would now be massively underspending on its allocation from the Treasury – allowing it to re-open a new form of RHI at some future point. The re-opening of RHI was an outcome for which Moy Park had lobbied. Both Jonathan Bell and Simon Hamilton had tentatively raised the possibility with Whitehall in 2016, only to be firmly told that it would be unthinkable with the scale of the existing overspend.

Although DfE overstated the scale of the overspend, whatever its precise sum, it was a huge figure. And with time the evidence of RHI's flaws mounted. In June 2017, auditors found that ten RHI boilers were running for almost all of the year except for the time required to service them. The boilers were being used for 90% or more of the 8,760 hours in a year and in each case getting at least £50,000 per boiler. For comparison, if a boiler ran for every minute of the year – with no maintenance or cleaning – it would have made a notional £56,371 in subsidy. Ten percent of claimants accounted for more than 40% of the scheme expenditure. Yet by that stage just two claimants had been put out of the scheme, with DfE attempting to recover what they had been paid. And the inspection of boilers was so shockingly slow that the chance of catching a fraudster red-handed quickly receded to the point where only the most obtuse crooks would ever be caught in the act of heating empty sheds.

Extraordinarily, the department could not be sure that all the boilers for which it was paying even existed. No one from DETI or Ofgem had ever visited more than a tiny handful of sites. A claimant simply logged on to Ofgem's website, uploaded their details and submitted a photo of the boiler. Even if Ofgem had queries, they were overwhelmingly dealt with by email. Once approved, the claimant just submitted meter readings and the cash flowed. The department only tendered for a full audit in early 2017, at the height of the public outcry. But it was immediately clear to Andrew Crawford's biomass expert friend Mark Anderson that no company would be able to meet the terms of the contract. He was right, and further months were lost.

By October 2018 – more than a year and a half after Foster passed to officials allegations of widespread abuse – the department said that just 190 of the 2,128 installations had been inspected and inspections were by that stage being undertaken at a rate of 10–15 boilers per week. There were complexities in ensuring that audits were robust and legally sound. Nevertheless, it is difficult to avoid the conclusion that if huge sums were coming out of civil servants' personal bank accounts there would have been greater alacrity.

One of the consequences of the delay in auditing boilers was that the most lurid allegations could neither be proven nor disproven. Was a farmer heating an empty shed around the clock? Clearly it was possible – the tariff made it lucrative to do so and the lack of inspections meant that if it was happening it was unlikely to be discovered. There was another possible explanation. Poultry sheds have to be heated when empty – for one or two days – in order to bring them up to the temperature necessary to receive day-old chicks. Doing so was not fraudulent, but if observed by someone unaware of the poultry cycle and combined with knowledge of RHI's flaws could have seemed so. However, there is evidence that at least some poultry farmers became greedy. In June 2015, Moy Park's despatch manager, Gareth Patton, asked senior colleagues for guidance due to changes he was noticing after many farmers switched to biomass. He was concerned because catchers, the workers who enter poultry houses to grab chickens and load them into crates for slaughter, were struggling to work in the heat they now found in poultry houses. The catchers had been asking him what temperature they were expected to work under 'because it seems to be the norm that when they arrive the heating system is still fully on. They are currently going through approximately four changes of tops a night'. He told senior Moy Park staff: 'My teams are telling me that they are going into houses where the temperature is as high as 28/29 degrees and the biomass is still on and the fans are not!'

****

Given the sea of rumour and allegations, which have swirled around RHI, the most convincing thing about Fred Maxwell's story was the openness of the man who told it. The major RHI claimant agreed to be interviewed and then walked into a newspaper office to hand over financial documentation behind his payments.

The Clogher Valley poultry farmer grew his business to become Northern Ireland's largest producer of chickens. Maxwell installed the first of his ten biomass boilers in July 2013. Sitting in the *News Letter*'s office in September 2017 – six months after the first RHI cuts took effect – the industrial scale farmer estimated that by that stage his total investment in the boilers and their running costs was about £2.1 million – mounting by £4,000 each week for fresh wood chip. He had received more than £900,000 in subsidy by February 2017.

Three of his boilers were used to dry wood for the other boilers. But they had not been accredited by Ofgem, a decision he said was 'scandalous' because Stormont encouraged him to install the drying facility and Stormont's Greenmount Agricultural College had used it as a positive example of burning locally sourced timber. The middle-aged farmer said: 'The loans were all done based on the RHI income and the farm income – once one of those goes, the other has to prop it up because banks have to be paid. They won't take no for an answer. They have to get their money.' Maxwell's wife, Amanda, argued passionately for audits to identify fraudulent claims: 'We're not doing this for any crook – they make me sick, just thinking about them. They need to hook them out and make them pay their money back.'

At the height of the scandal, Maxwell faced unfounded allegations from the blogger Jamie Bryson that he was 'a large DUP donor' and that he had close relationships with senior DUP spads who advised him on how to maximise RHI returns. Bryson, who had DUP sources aware that he would publish material which journalists would not report due to libel concerns, reported a suggestion that 'there was an agreement that some of the profits creamed from the RHI scheme would be funnelled back into the party as 'donations'. There was never a shred of evidence for that. Mrs Maxwell vehemently said that it was 'absolute nonsense', adding: 'I wouldn't give them DUP dopes one penny; never have, never will. They couldn't run a tap … I've never been to a DUP meeting in my life – would I waste my night?'

With the inaccurate allegation that they had been part of some DUP inner circle benefiting from RHI, and with the public perception that every RHI claimant was a swindler, she said that they faced social stigma. She likened it to being in a room full of innocent people where everyone knows that one of them is a rapist, leading to everyone facing suspicion until the innocent men in the room are cleared. Her husband phlegmatically said: 'Dirt sticks and no matter what ever happens, this is with us for the rest of our lives because that's what people think.'

The Maxwells were among five RHI claimants, most of whom were farmers, who I spoke to in September 2017. All said that they were facing extreme hardship and mental trauma – in some cases because they had used the promise of the lucrative RHI funding to fund business expansion with huge loans. One man broke down as he spoke of his debt being like a 'ball and chain' which had him working 100 hours a week.

Another man told how he was initially turned down for a loan but he had 'really pushed' the bank and took his borrowings to the limit. 'I wish I'd never gone anywhere near it,' he said. Dismissing the erroneous perception that most of those on the RHI scheme had some link to the DUP, he said 'I'm not in the DUP or any party – I think they're all useless'. Breaking down, he said: 'It's a nightmare. I've borrowed £350,000 over 10 years. Next month I've an £8,000 payment to make. I'm working night and day to pay that. I'm spending no time with my family. I could strangle the civil servants because they aren't accountable – I've done nothing wrong but I'm the one who's paying.' Like most claimants, he had still not been audited but said: 'I wish they would come out and audit because this is putting my head away.'

A boiler installer said that he did not have a boiler, but his father was a claimant and

> on current levels he cannot repay his loans … he collapsed one day and was in hospital for three weeks. The stress is palpable. You've got the financial stress and then the emotional stress because they don't feel able to speak to anybody. I know someone who went to his GP who, in his view, was less than sympathetic. There is an underlying sentiment that other services have taken a hit and RHI is responsible, which I don't believe is the case.

Claimants had on their side a considerable moral argument because in September 2016, three months before BBC *Spotlight*, DfE's top civil servant, Andrew McCormick, endorsed what most claimants had done as normal human behaviour. At the Public Accounts Committee, DUP MLA Trevor Clarke asked him: 'If you needed 280 kW of heat, would you go for three burners or one? Would you go for three on the basis that you would get 5·9p per kWh or for one at 1·5p per kWh?' McCormick replied: 'Obviously, you would go for the one that is more lucrative.' Clarke asked: 'What would you have done wrong?' McCormick replied: 'Nothing.'

David Kernoghan, a farmer in Broughshane, installed five boilers – four 99 kW units to heat poultry sheds and a smaller 35 kWh boiler for an office and his house. While building two new poultry sheds in summer 2013, RHI had been suggested to him by his electrician – who specialised in poultry houses and saw what was going on elsewhere. But Kernoghan was wary about the large investment and the 'hassle' of the extensive plumbing. Eventually, he came to the view that 'if I didn't do it, I knew I could be put out of business because there are very tight margins in poultry'. When his first units were installed in July 2014, he said that Moy Park was 'not pushing' biomass and to him seemed 'not overly interested' in what he was doing. 'Moy Park are a hard firm – but they're professional. I like working with them. I want to do business, they want to do business and I'm happy.' He said that politicians and civil servants 'don't seem to realise the damage they've done to Northern Ireland – and they don't seem to care'. Though bruised by his experience and left distrustful of government promises, Kernoghan had at least paid off the cost of his boilers. Others were not in that position.

Alan Hegan was heavily involved in RHI – as a claimant, a boiler installer and a biomass fuel supplier. But by 2018, he said that his boiler installation business had 'all but collapsed'. Although he did some work in England for a period and continued to service boilers in Northern Ireland, he said that his company was heading for possible closure. A similar company ceased trading the previous week, he told the RHI Inquiry in October 2018.

He said: 'There's not one biomass boiler that has been installed in Northern Ireland in the last two years.' Hegan said that Stormont's decision to break its promise meant that confidence in government had been 'shattered'. He said that the industry would not recover and he did not know how lucrative Stormont would have to make a green energy scheme to persuade people to take a risk.

Hegan also said that he could not accept that the department responsible for energy did not know that the cost of biomass fuel was less than what it was paying in subsidy. In forthright testimony, he said: 'This was not a secret. Everybody was widely aware of this – but this was accepted.' He highlighted that tariffs in GB – where there were cost controls to stop unlimited burning – were also higher than the cost of fuel to speed uptake. Dismissing Stormont's argument that those who knew that the subsidy was higher than the cost of fuel did not alert it to that fact in a 'conspiracy of silence', he said:

> I say that's a similar argument to saying [major gas suppliers] Firmus and Phoenix Natural Gas have a conspiracy of silence that they're not telling the department what price natural gas is … there's no conspiracy

of silence as to the price of pellets ... it's the equivalent of saying 'we don't know what price diesel is; we don't know what price petrol is'.

He said that he would have seemed 'a fool' if he had pointed out to civil servants what price biomass fuel was, adding: 'It would be like me ringing up the department at the minute and saying "do you know what price mains gas is?" He added: 'It is my steadfast opinion that DETI was aware but chose to ignore the issues, in their quest to roll out the programme.'

CHAPTER 24
FREE MONEY

Two decades before RHI was conceived, the Northern Ireland Civil Service identified the moral hazard that would contribute to the destruction of devolution in 2017. In 1992, as the Troubles continued to rage but what would become the peace process was getting quietly under way, a civil servant in Stormont's Department of Finance performed a detailed analysis of public spending in Northern Ireland. His confidential assessment, which went to Stormont's top mandarins, calculated that the previous year government spending in Northern Ireland was close to 43% higher than the average in the rest of the UK, and that in several areas of expenditure Northern Ireland was receiving 'between three and four times' more than the UK as a whole. The only area he could identify in which Northern Ireland received less money was roads and transport.

To this day Northern Ireland remains enormously dependent on GB in financial terms, receiving about £10 billion more per year from the Treasury than is raised locally in taxation. The 1992 civil service analysis was striking because it did not major on the Troubles as the reason for increased public spending, an argument still being used – and with some legitimacy – by many local politicians more than 20 years after the Troubles ended.

The author of the paper probed the strength of Stormont's argument that Northern Ireland either deserved the money which it received or ought to be receiving even more. He said that while the higher spending had not been the subject of 'direct controversy', there was 'a common perception in Whitehall that NI is very generously funded, if not actually over-funded'. He set out what 'at least at a superficial level' explained Northern Ireland's increased dependence on the taxpayer – proportionately higher social security spending because of higher unemployment and lower incomes, higher agriculture expenditure because of a larger agricultural sector, higher health spending 'because of higher levels of morbidity', higher education spending because of a relatively young population 'and so on'. But he said there was a dichotomy between the 'apparent wealth' of Northern Ireland's public sector and the difficulty which they found each year in funding public services.

The Department of Finance official then raised a question, which is crucial in understanding RHI: is higher public spending always necessarily a good thing? He wondered whether having a large pot of money which had to be spent could lead to undesirable behaviour. He raised what he said was a controversial question – the degree to which the 'need' for public expenditure is dependent upon that money being available. He said that there was the potential for moral hazard 'where the existence of public expenditure gives rise to a "need" to absorb it by encouraging undesirable changes in the behaviour of individuals or organisations …' He said that if this was the case it would 'call into question the general assumption that securing a larger share of available public expenditure in the UK for NI is a desirable objective'.

****

In February 2016, as RHI was about to be shut and MLAs were beginning to ask awkward questions, senior DETI official John Mills spoke the unspeakable. Appearing before the Assembly committee which scrutinised DETI, he was asked why cost controls had not been introduced earlier. The official, a veteran of the Northern Ireland Civil Service (although ironically he was English), replied candidly: 'At that point, the Northern Ireland scheme was under performing and we were not using up what you might say was free money in terms of AME [Treasury money] to bring it in. So the minister decided that the priority should be on the introduction of the domestic RHI scheme so resources were devoted to that.'

As already recounted, Mills later retracted his claim about Arlene Foster having consciously decided to delay cost controls. But the rationale in his mind for that decision – whoever took it – was that it was a legitimate and unsurprising policy objective to keep open a deeply flawed scheme in order to use up 'free money' from London. It was a perfect exemplar of the perverse outcome which the Department of Finance official had identified some 24 years earlier. But Mills was not some rogue official operating to radically different values than his colleagues and his political masters. While he expressed the philosophy in cruder terms that was common, the idea that one of Stormont's overriding goals was to spend as much of London's money as possible was deeply engrained across the devolved political and administrative apparatus.

In some circumstances, there was nothing wrong with such a view. If the national government in Westminster wanted Stormont to contribute to a national effort – in this case, cutting carbon emissions to stave off EU fines – then the financial incentive to do so was a legitimate carrot. But that benign hypothesis was not what was happening with RHI. Stormont had decided not to copy the GB scheme, which would have seen a fair distribution of funding across the UK, and instead created a far more generous scheme. Despite repeated warnings, it ignored the problem until the budget had been broken and it began to fear that it might impact its own funding.

Foster's spad, Andrew Crawford, had been personally given allegations that RHI was being abused, yet after having been warned he said that he could not see what the problem was because London was paying. In his own words, 'I would have thought that this is to NIs [*sic*] advantage'.

DETI Permanent Secretary Andrew McCormick was not aware of that email when it was sent in mid-2015. But he was not oblivious to the philosophy behind it. Mandarins knew that ministers wanted to get as much money into Northern Ireland as possible. In a note to the Head of the Civil Service in February 2016, as he sought to defend himself in the face of awkward questions about what had unfolded, McCormick said that if it had been known earlier that London was not paying the full bill, 'DETI may have recommended to ministers that we should move straight to suspension, rather than to introduce tariff controls'. He said that 'had the [funding] position been clarified earlier, we might have had an opportunity to introduce cost controls at an earlier stage'.

Just prior to the scandal erupting in December 2016, McCormick went further, telling the Public Accounts Committee that civil servants agreed in mid-2015 to delay cost controls 'because that was the view that was wanted [by the DUP]. It was a determined view, partly driven by the thought that it would maximise our take on funds from London. That was definitely part of the thinking. That was wrong and not acceptable, but ...' That indicates that there was a looser approach to money coming directly from the Treasury. And yet Stormont's bible on public spending, the voluminous *Managing Public Money*, was clear that the same principles should apply to the use of all taxpayers' money. It said that as accounting officers, the permanent secretaries of Stormont's departments had to ensure value for money 'judged for the public sector as a whole, not just for the accounting officer's organisation'.

McCormick's predecessor at DETI, David Sterling, told the inquiry that although as an accounting officer he was required to treat the spending of public money with the same diligence, 'if there's an opportunity to draw down money which will give an economic benefit in Northern Ireland, the realpolitik here is that we draw down the maximum amount that we can because we will get an economic impact from that'. He said that 'if it [RHI] had been constructed differently, we might have been incentivised in a different way and indeed more strongly to go for the cheaper option'.

Sterling, by then Head of the Civil Service, insisted that the desire to get the most money into Northern Ireland would not lead to departments compromising value for money but added that 'you're not obliged to choose the cheapest option on all occasions – there are other factors'. He added:

> When you are in a devolved administration, you will seek to maximise the amount of resource you can get from the Treasury – it might generate some surprise but it shouldn't. That's the way in which we operate ... Part of the reason for that is that you obviously want to maximise the resource available for the local economy and for public services but on top of that there's an expectation – ministers and politicians – that we will again draw down the maximum amount that is available.

David Scoffield QC asked if he would have thought 'the more money we can get from England, the better ... so let's fill our boots'. Sterling replied: 'I wouldn't be that cynical.' But while Sterling either wasn't that cynical – or was too shrewd to put it in those terms – Crawford did not have any such compunction and clearly saw overspending not as an error but as a perfectly acceptable policy. That is clear from his 2015 email. However, McCormick told the inquiry that the spad had at one point used that precise phrase.

McCormick said that in late October 2016, just over a month before the scandal erupted, he and Crawford were present at corporate dinner organised by the food industry. He recalled how a 'very relaxed ... smiling Andrew Crawford' had set out what his thinking had been. McCormick told the inquiry: 'He said "I thought this was AME [Treasury funding, rather than from Stormont's budget] and we could fill our boots."'

In earlier oral evidence to the inquiry, Crawford had been asked about the conversation and said that he could not recall what had been said. But after McCormick's evidence he told it in writing that he believed it could not have been at the October 2016 dinner because he did not believe he attended the event.

Crawford, who by then had completed his oral evidence, told the inquiry in writing that McCormick's evidence was false. Pointing out that the civil servant had been asked about the conversation on several occasions and had initially not used the phrase 'fill our boots', Crawford said: 'This statement is not true. At no time did I make this or any similar comment'. He said he thought McCormick gave the 'unfounded and untruthful' evidence in an attempt 'to deflect any criticism of his role' in RHI and 'this has resulted in a great deal of negative publicity towards myself'.

The inquiry then put to him a YouTube video, which showed him at the dinner. At that point, Crawford conceded that 'it appears I did in fact attend the 2016 NIFDA dinner'. However, he said he did not believe that he had 'any detailed conversation' with McCormick that night about RHI and he was 'absolutely clear' he never said 'we could fill our boots'.

Crawford's vehemence in rebutting McCormick's evidence was striking because the allegation was that he had simply been cruder and more direct in expressing a view which was in the mid-2015 email which he did not dispute. As Foster's right-hand man, Crawford believed that it was good for Northern Ireland to overspend – even though, on his own evidence, he had by that stage been told by a boiler installer of allegations of serious RHI abuse. The obvious question was: if Foster's handpicked adviser had that view, did Foster? She insisted that she did not, and that all taxpayers' money had to be spent diligently. But the DUP had a deep streak of Ulster nationalism which wanted to extract as much from London as possible. It was one of the few areas on which the DUP and Sinn Féin, as nationalistic parties of different hues, enthusiastically agreed.

If the policy was to get as much money as possible into Northern Ireland, then the Stormont system would effectively be on the side of claimants, rather than taxpayers. Why not make the scheme super generous? Why clamp down on that generosity when it became obvious across Northern Ireland? If the policy was to get as much money into Northern Ireland as possible, why would officials and spads not be openly giving warning to the industry that it would soon be less lucrative, enabling them to pile in before that happened?

As late as January 2017 – after *Spotlight*, after the open knowledge of widespread abuse and the extreme generosity of RHI – the business case drawn up by civil servants for their political masters contained a curious objective. Alongside obvious goals such as ending the perverse incentive to waste heat, the document referred to maximising Northern Ireland's spending power. Thus, even at that late stage, the policy was being shaped by how to spend as much of London's money as possible – not by simply asking: what is necessary to incentivise claimants and provide value for money for taxpayers?

There was and is an inherent difficulty in public spending in Northern Ireland, which made RHI more likely. Being so heavily dependent on the Exchequer, Stormont politicians are invariably spending other people's money. Their voters know that much of it is not really their cash, and therefore tax and spend arguments are not a feature of political life. Ensuring value for money in the use of taxpayers' money is seen by the Treasury as the responsibility of the devolved institutions. There is a logic in allowing Stormont to take its own decisions and make its own mistakes – there is after all no point in devolution if the key decisions are still being taken in London. But there is a problem if Stormont is spending other people's money without consequences. And it is naive to rely on devolved institutions to be the watchdog for value for money when there may be a consensus in those institutions that milking the maximum sum from the Treasury teat is not an error but a policy.

****

Under devolution, the Northern Ireland Civil Service grew servile to its political masters to the point of sycophancy – although there were honourable exceptions within its ranks. The civil service was a venerable organisation which had once effectively run Northern Ireland for its first half-century when policy in the *de facto* one-party state glided along at the pace set by mandarins. It had then helped to keep Northern Ireland functioning through 30 years of the Troubles when to be a senior civil servant was to have a target on one's head. It produced men of the calibre of Sir Ken Bloomfield, the erudite Head of the Civil Service whose family narrowly escaped death when the IRA bombed their house, and Maurice Hayes, a proud Catholic Irishman of formidable intellect who courageously saw it as his duty to serve the community and seek to find a way out of those murderous decades. However, while some were drawn to the world of bureaucracy out of a belief in public service, others viewed it as a cushy career with salaries and pensions on a par with the rest of the UK – but in reality much higher because of the lower cost of living in Northern Ireland. With a huge workforce, powerful unions and a focus on constitutional politics, stories of lazy or incompetent civil servants being allowed to draw salaries for years abounded.

In the first 89 years of the Northern Ireland Civil Service, none of its most senior figures – the permanent secretaries – had even been seriously disciplined or demoted. With no culture of being held to account, some officials acted in ways which suggested they thought that even a massive crisis would only ever lead to political heads rolling. That changed in 2010 when Paul Priestly, a high-flying permanent secretary, was demoted after it was proven that he had written a letter sent in someone else's name which attacked MLAs who had grilled him during an appearance before the Public Accounts Committee. But even what the committee described as 'utterly disgraceful' conduct did not see Priestly sacked. Rather, he was shuffled sideways to another well-paid senior post in Stormont's Strategic Investment Board which oversaw some of the most expensive public sector projects.

The failure to effectively oversee civil servants under decades of direct rule was not corrected by devolution. With ministers often focussed on tribal disputes, there was little evidence of ministers putting real effort into rewarding the good civil servants and rooting out the incompetent. While nominally it was the role of the Assembly to scrutinise how ministers were running their departments, the Assembly was controlled by the Executive's two dominant parties who would cut deals in party rooms to protect one or the other. In the short term, that suited the DUP and Sinn Féin, who had reason to believe that the public were motivated to vote based on who seemed a competent tribal champion, not who provided good government. By taking expedient shortcuts they were building their administration on sand.

But while politicians' attempts to evade embarrassing scrutiny are unsurprising, it was the approach of civil servants which shocked a swathe of the public. The head of the Northern Ireland Civil Service, David Sterling, told the inquiry that he saw his role 'first and foremost to help ministers do that which they want done ... I would always advise staff: "You don't say no to a minister"". Sterling was referring to the principle that ministers had a democratic mandate for their policies which should not be overridden by unelected bureaucrats. But plenty of officials seem to have more literally believed that 'you don't say no to a minister' even if what they wanted involved rule-breaking or law-breaking. Too many civil servants failed to speak truth to power and remind ministers or spads that they had no mandate for bad behaviour.

It was their devastating mix of weakness and incompetence that, at the very least, facilitated the scandal. In March 2019, Lord Alderdice, the former leader of the Alliance Party and a former Speaker of the Assembly, spoke for many when in a House of Lords debate on the future of RHI he said: 'When I was growing up, I had a relatively implicit trust in both the competence and the integrity of the Northern Ireland Civil Service. That has been shattered and blown apart repeatedly over the last number of years, as a combination of incompetence and a lack of integrity has been demonstrated over and over again.'

It was clear that inadequate resources had been allocated to energy division, despite requests for additional staff. But that did not explain most of the individual failings – from Fiona Hepper's and John Mills's misleading ministerial submissions through to Stuart Wightman's astonishingly misleading evidence to MLAs. Bad practice had become acceptable at every level. From the very top, where Sir Malcolm McKibbin tolerated Sinn Féin circumventing the law, to lowly officials who knew that their superiors did not want them to take minutes of potentially embarrassing decisions, the organisation was broken. Unable to prove they had acted properly because of the culture of verbal government, some officials came to regret that they had set aside good practice. DETI's plainspoken finance director Trevor Cooper said: 'You know, one of my greatest regrets in this is not putting a hell of a lot more down in writing.'

The claim of inadequate resources is undermined by where Stormont chose to focus its staff. As departments desperately sought to spin their failures as successes, the Executive employed more than 160 staff in its press offices – more than all the newspaper journalists in Belfast, more press officers than the Scottish government, more than double those in the Welsh government and more than the press officers in the Irish government, all of which were far larger. It also directed enormous resources into secrecy, battling to reject

Freedom of Information requests. In 2014, Peter Robinson and Martin McGuinness's department was surprisingly open about why it was so closed, arguing to the author that it should be allowed to withhold information if releasing it might cost the First Minister and deputy First Minister votes – an argument thrown out on appeal to the Information Commissioner.

The resources that Stormont could find for such frivolous activities undermines the narrative from some officials that the civil service was under-resourced. Rather, priority was given to actions which were in the interests of politicians but not in the wider public interest. A Whitehall official well placed to compare the situations in London and Belfast pithily said: 'There are some hugely impressive people in the NI Civil Service who care deeply about Northern Ireland. But the idea that it is under-resourced is just nonsense. It is incredibly well resourced. In truth, there are lots of people doing not very much.'

An individual with significant professional qualifications who met a senior civil servant to discuss an energy proposal, which they believed was self-evidently beneficial to Northern Ireland – and in which they did not have a commercial interest – said that he had been surprised at the official's response. Rather than debate the proposal's merits, the senior civil servant asked how it would impact on farmers, adding: 'The farmers must have their subsidy.' The individual, who was from outside government, said that it was made clear that this was not necessarily the view of the official but that he knew it was what his minister was going to ask.

Northern Ireland's Comptroller and Auditor General, Kieran Donnelly, – whose June 2016 report into RHI first exposed it to public scrutiny – told the inquiry that many of the practices which led to RHI had become embedded within the civil service. He said:

> It is clear to me that value for money is not front and centre in the mindset of too many civil servants … every public official should treat taxpayers' money exactly the same as they treat their own money – it doesn't matter where that money comes from … I think that needs to be ingrained in the mindset of a whole generation of civil servants.

Even amid the unfolding crisis in December 2016, the civil service seemed to carry on as if nothing was amiss – to an extent which was almost comical. In the weeks after *Spotlight*, Hepper, one of the key officials involved in setting up RHI who was responsible for key errors but who had been promoted, was advertised to deliver a civil service workshop on good policy, drawing on what was described as her 'unique perspective' in the field. Sterling would be promoted to Head of the Civil Service, while Wightman would also be among those involved in RHI who were promoted.

More than three years after RHI was finally shut, not a single official involved had been disciplined. In late 2016, a 'fact-finding' exercise had been commissioned as the first step to possible disciplinary action, but that was put on hold until the public inquiry completed. Already by that stage, some of those involved in RHI had retired or left the civil service, making discipline impossible.

The early weeks of the inquiry were spent dissecting how the scheme had been approved by multiple layers of civil servants in two departments as well as a minister and her spad, none of whom said that they spotted any of the basic problems. Dame Una O'Brien said at the inquiry that it appeared to her that officials were simply 'hoovering up assurances from others as a way of saving themselves from having to look at the detail'. Essentially, civil servant E appeared to think that because civil servants A, B, C and D had already looked at or were to look at the proposal then it must be fine. In that sense, having multiple layers of scrutiny potentially made the process more dangerous than if one or two people knew they were fully responsible.

****

But even in a battered organisation whose myriad deficiencies had been exposed in humiliating fashion, there were glimpses of leadership and the sort of personal responsibility which was lacking in many political figures who came before the inquiry. Even before the scandal had properly erupted in December 2016, McCormick had been publicly penitent. On the final day of the inquiry's hearings, he spoke bluntly about his own role. Pausing at the end of his evidence, he said:

We bear shame. I said ... in January '17 shame on us for all that we missed ... I personally bear shame; I feel ashamed personally for not doing better at the meeting on the 24th of August [when he agreed to delay cost controls] ... I should have stood up; I should have asked for a [ministerial] direction that day, and that's my responsibility.

Becoming briefly emotional, McCormick said that while 'it's certainly done me personal damage', the scandal had undermined devolution – something in which he said he was a passionate believer. But, in a recognition that many of the practices exposed by RHI were indefensible, he said that the inquiry report 'can be a new foundation' for a new Stormont.

CHAPTER 25

THE SPECIAL WORLD OF SPADS

In proportion to its size, Stormont had more special advisers than any other legislature in the UK or Ireland. Paid almost double the salary of an MLA, and in some cases more than ministers, spads were often the real power running Northern Ireland – yet with less accountability than their counterparts in other systems of government. While expedient in the short term, RHI exposed how in that system thrived bad behaviour – nepotism, laziness, greed and an arrogant disregard for rules.

The inquiry forced the DUP to admit that even the way in which it appointed spads was sometimes unlawful, while Sinn Féin put in place a system to circumvent the law. In the words of former DUP spad Tim Cairns, politics can be a 'grubby world' and spads were often the dispensable and deniable firewall between a minister and controversial decisions.

Many spads operated as quasi-gods in the Stormont system. DETI Deputy Secretary Chris Stewart, a vastly experienced civil servant, said: 'I can think of few, if any, instances of officials challenging spads in any way in terms of their activities.' Cairns's minister, Jonathan Bell, claimed that the spad had said to him at one point 'ministers come and go, but spads remain'. Looking at Stormont over almost a decade since its restoration in 2007, that was largely true – especially for the DUP. At the top of the DUP spad tree were two figures who were there for the entire time: Timothy Johnston and Richard Bullick. Curiously, Johnston initially denied to the inquiry that there was any DUP spad hierarchy. But, after that evidence was challenged by witness after witness, he changed his evidence, accepting that he had been one of the most powerful advisers.

Johnston was always kept close to the DUP leader – and always stayed close. Intellectually sharp, politically shrewd and willing to be ruthless, he has been the beating heart of the DUP for about 15 years. Though he had never been elected nor had any ambition to enter electoral politics, he wielded power far beyond that of most elected politicians. When Johnston arrived in the DUP from PwC in 2002, the other key adviser to Peter Robinson was Richard Bullick. Although Bullick remained a key aide up until he left for a public affairs job after the collapse of Stormont in 2017, it was Johnston who quickly became Robinson's chosen emissary. Whereas Bullick was the strategic brain of the party – and unusually for a senior political figure had almost no enemies – Johnston was the internal enforcer. The young accountant could be brutal with colleagues and had the authority to tell them what to do. Unlike Bullick, who had a languid and light-hearted style, Johnston was a bundle of energy. He would stride into a room, perhaps filled with party colleagues or civil servants, and briskly announce: 'Right, clear the room' so that he, Bullick and the leader could talk candidly. Even his many internal enemies never accused Johnston of laziness. Johnston's power extended through patronage. His future brother-in-law, John Robinson, went straight from university to succeed him as the DUP's director of communications in 2007 when Johnston first moved into Stormont as a spad. Robinson (no relative of Peter) had not even finished his exams when at the age of 22 was offered the job of chief spin doctor for Northern Ireland's largest political party. When asked at the public inquiry how he got the job, Robinson could not recall whether the post had been advertised or even whether he had submitted an application form. While Johnston would highlight that as an adviser he had no power to appoint anyone, the fact that Peter Robinson trusted his judgment and that he was one of a tiny handful of aides who had the leader's ear meant that if Johnston was against an appointment it made it much less likely to happen.

But it would be misleadingly simplistic to paint Johnston as some sort of swaggering bully who just whipped DUP politicians into line. His relationship with colleagues was more complex and more codependent than that. One shrewd Stormont observer, who has watched the most senior DUP figures at close quarters over many years even though he is not a DUP member, says: 'An awful lot of MLAs do trust Timothy. He's sorted problems for them with the media or elsewhere and they would have a bond with him.' And although Johnston was the most powerful backroom figure in a party that was frequently facing allegations of financial or other impropriety, even his internal enemies did not believe that he was corrupt. Behind closed doors, Johnston, who for most of his time as a spad drove an old car and lived in a terraced house in Portadown before building a large house in the County Armagh countryside, would be heard bemoaning that 'there's too much sleaze in this party'.

But there was a fundamental difficulty in how Johnston – and to a lesser extent, other spads – were operating. They were being paid by taxpayers up to £92,000 a year as temporary senior civil servants. Yet Johnston's role extended far beyond departmental business. In effect, the DUP was having the salary of its de facto chief executive – a role to which he was formally appointed after Stormont collapsed in 2017 – funded by the taxpayer. That gave the party an advantage on its rivals, who had to fundraise in an attempt to pay their staff far more modest salaries.

When Cairns appeared before the inquiry, he spoke freely, providing an unprecedented window into the kitchen cabinet of powerful aides around the DUP leader. He said that Johnston wielded far more authority than even senior elected DUP politicians up to the rank of deputy leader Nigel Dodds. Real power within the party, he said, resided with a tiny handful of spads. Cairns set out a situation in which he said Johnston was essentially acting as the DUP chief executive who was involved in everything from discipline to choosing more junior spads. He said: 'Mr Johnston's influence was seen in the party from top to bottom.'

Cairns, whose family was steeped in the DUP, said:

He controlled all party matters and was viewed as being the most senior DUP employee by elected representatives and staff. I believe that Mr Johnston in running party matters while a spad was operating outside of what he was permitted to do. This would obviously be problematic for the DUP if the media were to get hold of the story.

During the writing of this book, a large brown envelope was handed into reception at the *News Letter*'s office, marked for the attention of the author. The envelope was bulging with printouts of internal DUP emails stretching over years. An unsigned handwritten note showed that whoever was behind the leak was aware of this book being written and wanted to draw attention to the centrality of Johnston's role in the DUP. The scores of emails were described as a 'small sample' of what the individual or individuals behind the leak said was available.

The emails show a figure who was involved in the biggest DUP decisions and the smallest. He was the one to whom DUP associations went to seek clearance for election literature. He gave detailed instructions to the specialist designer contracted by the DUP to design its posters and manifesto as to how his work should be improved, advising him on everything from the white space in his designs to the colour of the text. The first draft of the manifesto went to him. He was involved in advising on Facebook and Twitter advertising. He was involved in decisions about newspaper advertising. Quotations for the purchase of DUP equipment were sent to him. He directed the party conference schedule. Requests for holiday leave went to him. Even the party rule book was approved by Johnston.

In a July 2013 email to party headquarters staff, Johnston said: 'I apologise for the late notice of holiday leave. Offices will close tomorrow at 3pm ... I would ask that staff make themselves available on Tuesday unless they are booked to be on pre-approved leave and/or are out of the country.' In October of that year, Johnston sent a lengthy email to DUP headquarters staff 'to again clarify staff responsibilities'. The spad, who was funded by the taxpayer to solely work at Stormont, told staff that 'above all else our priority is the forthcoming European election and the poll to the new councils. Election preparation from now on will place a greater burden on all our time. We are in the business of winning elections and that must be reflected in our time priorities'. He then said that John Robinson would 'have overall responsibility for [party] conference preparation' and told various staff what they would be doing over coming months. He added: 'I am instigating a new staff meeting which I will chair every Friday afternoon commencing next week at 3pm in Dundela [DUP headquarters] for a max of an hour. I expect all HQ staff ... to be present.'

On another occasion, Johnston made clear to the DUP's team of handsomely paid spads that they should make a financial donation to the party's election campaign, asking them 'if you are agreeable to contribute £500 to the party centrally'. He was heavily involved in esoteric details such as the design of DUP candidates' posters, describing a proposal for colour on the back of posters as 'bonkers'.

Elsewhere, in a message to the party press office the taxpayer-funded temporary civil servant suggested that they needed to organise party members or sympathisers to phone BBC Radio Ulster's *Talkback* phone-in programme. On 7 May 2014, he said:

I'm struck by the number of supportive questions that TUV have managed to get through to Jim [Allister] on his Talkback slot. Many of them appear to be detailed and it suggests they have been placed. We need to start work on questions we want submitted for DD [Diane Dodds] appearance on Tue 20th May and who will phone in.

That evidence was not made available to the inquiry. However, in response to similar allegations from Cairns, Peter Robinson told the inquiry:

If his allegation is intended to suggest that Mr Johnston was running the operation and functioning of the party then it is palpably absurd. Mr Johnston was fully employed as my special advisor working hours well beyond what would be expected. The idea that in addition he was moonlighting as a DUP manager involved in all the party's business is risible. If, on the other hand, it is intended to convey the fact that his role as a special advisor to the First minister required his regular and frequent involvement in aligning the position of the party in the Assembly with the party in the country then, of course, that would be accurate. However, that was part of his remit as a special advisor and not contrary to it.

It is unclear how a role which encompassed suggesting planted calls to a BBC radio programme, approval of party staff leave, quotations for the party's purchase of equipment or approving the party rule book meets with Robinson's description of his spad's activities – nor why taxpayers should have been funding such a party role. While the DUP got at least one free part-time party manager, Sinn Féin got a small fortune. The party operated a rule that all its elected or unelected staff received the same 'average industrial wage'. In a court case in 2016, former Sinn Féin MLA Phil Flanagan revealed that they were allowed to retain £24,000 a year. That meant that for a Sinn Féin spad being paid £92,000 a year, £68,000 gross was the party's, enough to employ almost three other individuals on its average wage. The justification for such high spad salaries was that it was necessary to retain exceptional talent. Yet in Sinn Féin's case that was demonstrably not true – all of its staff had to be prepared to work for £24,000. But by paying them huge salaries, the party was receiving a backdoor subsidy from taxpayers.

When Johnston was asked why he was acting in a party management function – and in an explicit election function during purdah – when he was paid by taxpayers, he did not answer the question. Robinson was asked if he accepted that Johnston's role extended far beyond what taxpayers ought to have been funding. He did not answer the question. Rather, both men responded with a solicitor's letter which threatened to sue.

****

Special advisers have long existed in many guises, but the role as it is now known was created in Whitehall in the 1970s. Under Margaret Thatcher, the power of the roles increased, and under Tony Blair a powerful network of spads almost became an alternative to the senior civil servants who traditionally advised and assisted ministers. But in London, spads increasingly became synonymous with scandal – often involving poisonous, deniable briefings against party colleagues. Thus, by the time devolution was restored in 2007, there was not the excuse of ignorance about the difficulties and dangers of powerful but unaccountable political advisers.

It was not that there was no value in having spads. One former veteran spad said that the role was democratically important in giving the minister a trusted pair of eyes and ears within the department, while also reminding officials that it was the minister who had a democratic mandate for their policies and ensuring that they were implemented. But the only defence of the salaries, power and lack of accountability for spads was if ministers took full responsibility for what they did. Foster's response to RHI demonstrated the opposite.

Setting out what to many people appeared a semantic distinction to accepting blame, Foster admitted that some of Crawford's activities had been wrong, yet said that she was 'not responsible'. She said: 'If he had committed a criminal offence as a special adviser, I wouldn't think that the panel would be asking me to be responsible for that. I am accountable, perhaps, for what my special adviser does, but I'm not responsible for it.' There was some logic to what Foster said. But she was not the best person to set out such a defence, given that she had shown little inclination to be either accountable or responsible for what had gone on with RHI until forced to confront the issue.

Looked at as a principle, and not in relation to RHI specifically, there were inherent difficulties in a situation where a spad was not able to be held accountable for their actions and the minister who appointed him refused to take responsibility. There was in this a very dangerous perverse incentive for ministers to use spads as deniable conduits for anything questionable or controversial. The spad would know that the worst that might happen to them would be that they might have to quit – but they would have the comfort of a bumper salary and quite possibly a large golden handshake. The minister would meanwhile be able to evade censure for what otherwise – had they acted alone – may have cost them their job.

Andrew McCormick told the inquiry that after the 2016 Assembly election – Arlene Foster's first as leader – he and the other permanent secretaries in DUP departments were called into Stormont Castle for a meeting at which a rank structure for DUP spads was set out. What until then had been implicit – that Johnston was the central figure – was now made explicit, at least verbally. As ever, nothing was written down to record the truth of what was going on. McCormick said that Bullick and Johnston were the only spads present at the meeting, and most of the talking was done by Foster and Johnston.

> They made it clear that there would be strong degree of control from the First Minister's office – for example press comments would normally be subject to clearance by Timothy Johnston; copies of first day briefs for all the DUP ministers had to be provided (promptly) to the First Minister's office. The clear message was that Richard Bullick and Timothy Johnston as the First Minister's senior spads had in effect a role as 'primus inter pares' to speak with her authority and backing on any difficult issue that required resolution. While this post-dated the main events in relation to the RHI Scheme, it was not presented as a new arrangement, though clearly it was an implicit correction of the disorder that had applied in DETI in the previous few months under Jonathan Bell.

****

There was one point where issues with spads threatened to derail the DUP and Sinn Féin's Stormont arrangement. In 2011, the Sinn Féin Culture Minister, Carál Ní Chuilín, caused outrage when she appointed Mary McArdle to be her spad. McArdle was a convicted murderer, having played a key role in the IRA killing of 22-year-old schoolteacher Mary Travers, who had been shot in the head as she left Mass with her family in 1984. Ann Travers, the slain teacher's articulate and unimpeachable sister, led the charge against what had happened. She said: 'She's now [McArdle] in the position in which she is paid by the taxpayer – of which my mum is one. I am absolutely horrified that she has been given such a position.'

The TUV leader Jim Allister, the most vocal opponent of the entire Stormont system, brought forward a private member's bill to bar those with serious criminal convictions from acting as spads unless they had shown contrition for their actions and assisted the investigation of all others connected with the crime. Under enormous public pressure, the legislation was supported by the unionist DUP, UUP and TUV, and the centrist Alliance Party. Crucially, the nationalist SDLP abstained, allowing the law to pass. But it was opposed by the Greens and viscerally opposed by Sinn Féin which denounced it as 'sectarian, anti-equality and anti-Good Friday Agreement'. Yet after the legislation passed, Sinn Féin appeared to accept that it had lost the argument in the legislature and now had to obey the law. The party removed its spads who had serious criminal convictions and replaced them with party colleagues. For many people, the issue was then forgotten.

However, unknown to the public, Sinn Féin immediately put in place a parallel system to circumvent the law. It appointed Aidan McAteer, whose criminal conviction for IRA activity would have barred him from being a spad, to a role where he was effectively a 'super spad' – senior not only to the party's spads but also in a role where he 'managed' Sinn Féin's ministers.

Former Sinn Féin minister Máirtín Ó Muilleoir openly told the inquiry that his party did not agree with the law, so had worked to nullify it by appointing McAteer and others to de facto spad posts. He said: 'I don't think there would have been any difference in Mr McAteer's role pre and post the 2013 act in terms of how he would have behaved and done his job every day.' In doing so, Sinn Féin was confident that the DUP would go along with it, since, in the words of the then Head of the Civil Service, Sir Malcolm McKibbin, they viewed McAteer as a 'pragmatist' with whom they had a 'constructive' relationship.

The approval of civil servants was also necessary for the system of unofficial spads to operate since they worked out of Stormont departments, daily meeting officials. McKibbin said that he reconciled himself to the arrangement because 'whether or not Aidan McAteer had been in the building or not, and whether I had ever seen him, he could've exercised that same function from party headquarters'. Sinn Féin's actions meant that its key advisers were even less accountable than the DUP's. Since its unofficial spads were not registered on paper as departmental advisers, they were no longer bound by the limited checks that did exist, including a code of conduct.

But while Sinn Féin was deliberately working to evade a law which it had always opposed, the DUP was breaking the same law – despite having voted for it in the Assembly. The terms of the Civil Service (Special Advisers) Act (Northern Ireland) 2013 stated that all spad appointments 'shall be subject to the terms of the code' for appointing spads. The code required the minister to be the decision-maker on his or her spad, after considering several candidates. But Bell told the inquiry that he did not consider a number of candidates, and it was the DUP leadership which allocated Cairns as his adviser. When confronted with the letter of appointment signed by him – in which he claimed that he was the decision-maker and he had considered a pool of candidates – Bell admitted that it had been a 'false' declaration.

Despite their many areas of dispute, Cairns agreed with Bell that he had been appointed outside the rules. He said that 'whilst there is an official procedure, the Democratic Unionist Party exercised an unofficial procedure which took precedence'. Cairns said that he did not apply for the role or go through any formal process. Instead, he said that the then First Minister Peter Robinson approached him at a DUP executive meeting and took him into another room with Johnston, where he was informed that there would be a vacancy for a spad to Bell 'and would I move from my position in the party to become a special adviser in his office' four days later. Bell was not even in the room. Both the DUP and Sinn Féin quite literally saw themselves as being above the law. And, as with many of their other excesses, they were only able to circumvent the law because civil servants acquiesced in the process.

****

Throughout almost a decade in government, some of the DUP and Sinn Féin's most senior figures shunned departmental email addresses in favour of private email accounts. The First Minister and his spads down would forward sensitive government documents – some relating to decisions worth hundreds of millions of pounds – to Hotmail accounts, Gmail addresses or email servers run by their party. Their explanation for this was that it was incidental: a minor issue explained by the convenience of using an existing email account. But, given how instinctively secretive the DUP and Sinn Féin were, it would be entirely in keeping with their wider thinking for the decision to have been conscious and strategic. Keeping their emails – the life blood of modern government business – off government servers removed control of that information from the department to themselves or their party. The significance of that became apparent during the inquiry when questions about why some DUP spads had not handed over certain emails or text messages were being put to them, rather than to civil servants in their former departments. These two ultra-centralised parties would not have wanted the threat of their sensitive government communications lying in the hands of others.

In approving the practice, civil servants were allowing the official record to be corrupted. In writing this book, the author submitted a Freedom of Information request to DfE for material about Moy Park in Crawford's private email account. DfE refused the request, saying "the department does not have direct access to Dr Crawford's private email account and access is, therefore, a matter for Dr Crawford". Having allowed a DUP spad to retain control of his government communications, it then pleaded an inability to get control of the information. The problem for the department – and the attraction for political figures – was obvious.

Whatever the motive, their decision to use private communication systems for government work further lessened scrutiny of their actions in government – even though Stormont was already one of the least scrutinised democratic governments in the world. At one point, there were only two MLAs out of 108 who were not members of governing parties.

But the practices adopted by many DUP and Sinn Féin ministers and spads had implications which were profounder still. In rejecting secure government communication systems in favour of basic free email accounts or party-run systems, they were leaving Stormont wide open to attack from commercial interests or a foreign power.

The private secretary to Jonathan Bell told the inquiry how he believed that the only email address the DETI minister ever used for government business was a Hotmail account. Bell was asked how he ensured private departmental information was secured in his Hotmail account. Alluding to an alarmingly simplistic understanding of cyber-security, he responded: 'My private email account is password protected. Access to my email account can only be made with the knowledge of my password.' That was the same account to which Bell handed the password to BBC journalists in December 2016.

The Sinn Féin Finance Minister Máirtín Ó Muilleoir routinely used *mairtin@newbelfast.com* (his personal website) rather than his official departmental email. When asked by the inquiry about its security, he said with a degree of pomposity: 'In terms of security I was and am confident the email account, the only email attached to a secure and stand-alone domain, is best-in-class.' Ó Muilleoir's use of a private email account for government business was in keeping with how most Sinn Féin ministers and spads operated. Yet it was contrary to the standards the party demanded of others. In December 2016, Sinn Féin's press office issued a statement which described as 'shocking and extremely concerning' that the Taoiseach, Tánaiste and other Irish government ministers had been using private unencrypted email accounts for government business. In a statement reeking with hypocrisy, Sinn Féin said at the time: 'No minister should be using any private unsecured email accounts for any official business whatsoever.'

First Minister Peter Robinson and many other ministers also used non-departmental email accounts to transact departmental business. Crawford said that his government-issued iPad had 'no security settings on it' – a fairly obvious clue as to why it should not be used for confidential material – and he therefore could not access his departmental emails on it. Instead, he forwarded emails from his secure government email account to his personal Hotmail account and read them on the unsecured iPad. He told the inquiry: 'I would have got the iPad … when I was travelling with the minister to places where there was not a secure network. So there would've been places where you're advised not to use the government phone. And, you know, for that reason I would've had the iPad that I could access information …'

But it was not just Stormont's political elite that set aside security protocols – civil servants, from the highest grades down, were also doing it. Civil servants got around Stormont's IT security rules by forwarding information from their secure BlackBerry devices to personal email accounts so they could view them on their home computers. McCormick said that it was common for confidential emails to be sent outside the government system because it was 'expedient'. He said:

> It's not good practice. It's not secure in that sense, and we — It is relatively easy to work without it. I used my personal account at times, simply because it gave me access to a much larger screen at home to work on, so it's just expedient in a context where nothing was … We weren't dealing with high state secrets, so it was not regarded as good practice but also not a great harm, either.

What ministers and officials were doing was contrary to Stormont security protocols, which deliberately locked down access to such information outside the office to secure devices. The civil service's security policy said that 'the transfer or storage of data is only permitted on Ironkeys [encrypted USB pens] issued through IT Assist or on encrypted hard drives, and not on any other device'. It said that 'any breach of this policy will be viewed as a security incident and dealt with as such, possibly leading to disciplinary action'. Yet, despite the fact that this policy was disregarded across the department, DETI's 2015–16 resource accounts said that a security risk overview report to the Head of the Civil Service was completed in July 2015 'with no significant issues identified'.

Stormont's amateurish approach to data security was particularly significant not just because it was handling an annual budget of around £20 billion but because it was increasingly interacting with foreign governments and companies. Ministers and officials regularly travelled to China – a state accused by the British government of being responsible for sophisticated state-sponsored cyberspying – to negotiate lucrative financial investments.

Professor Anthony Glees, director of the University of Buckingham's Centre for Security and Intelligence Studies and a member of advisory board of the Oxford Intelligence Group, said that what had been going on was 'totally astonishing' and that it 'certainly affects our national security given the important role that Northern Ireland politics and politicians now play in our national life'. He said: 'Just as we should not allow criminals to make laws – as MPs or peers – so we should not allow people who are careless with the security of official communications to help determine the security boundaries in the UK as a whole.' Professor Glees said that the 'reckless way' in which communications relating to China had been conducted 'gives rise to the gravest concern'. He said that

> any Northern Ireland links with China, even if they appear to be wholly about the economy and not politics, are always going to have national security implications for the whole of the UK. One can only assume that GCHQ and MI5 either did not know what [Stormont figures] were doing, or, if they did, felt that Northern Ireland was a 'special case' and that they ought to be reluctant to interfere in any way. For them, as for all of us I suppose, peace in Northern Ireland is the number one consideration.

Pointing to Hilary Clinton's use of a private email server – and the hacking of her emails by Russia – he said that standard private sector electronic communications, whether by email or services such as WhatsApp, do not have the safeguards which are built into government communication systems.

CHAPTER 26

MINISTER FOR PHOTO OPPORTUNITIES

O ver 20 years, Arlene Foster crafted an image of competence, likeability and attention to detail. One story – RHI – blew that away, exposing how the woman who rose to become Northern Ireland's first female First Minister had managed to do so because of a lack of scrutiny of her record. Her response to the scandal was consistently disastrous, escalating a crisis Sinn Féin had been prepared to assist in de-escalating. Yet through the inherent tribalism of Northern Ireland politics and a quirk of electoral arithmetic, the DUP leader would go on to wield more influence on a national stage than any of her predecessors – while at home her power was ebbing away. After the March 2017 Assembly election, whereby unionism was shaken by the scale of the DUP's losses to Sinn Féin, Foster was under significant internal pressure. But, just six weeks after the Stormont election, Prime Minister Theresa May called a snap general election. Foster was largely kept out of the campaign limelight, with the DUP's Westminster leader, Nigel Dodds, to the fore. Unionism responded by voting for the DUP in record numbers, delivering it ten of Northern Ireland's 18 House of Commons seats. By contrast, May's disastrous election result saw her dependent on the DUP. From clinging on as DUP leader in March, by June, Foster was triumphantly walking in and out of Downing Street where she was feted by a Prime Minister who was by now clinging to office. It was an astonishing turnaround and in some ways it masked the extent to which Foster's inadequacies had been exposed over the preceding seven months. But while on the surface it was Foster who was holding inordinate influence over the British Government as it negotiated Brexit, her internally weakened position meant that it was her MPs who increasingly took matters into their own hands.

Foster had long been a mould-breaker. As a female politician, she had worked hard to break through in a culture antipathetic to women taking leadership roles. As a member of David Trimble's Ulster Unionist Party (UUP), she had been one of those who had been vocally opposed to the direction of the party after it endorsed the Good Friday Agreement in 1998.

She moved to the DUP in 2003, but her move was overshadowed by UUP MP Jeffrey Donaldson also defecting that day. But Foster would quickly leapfrog Donaldson, the man who from a young age had been seen as the future leader of unionism. As an Anglican, Foster stood out somewhat in the DUP, a party still dominated by the Free Presbyterian Church, which viewed the Church of Ireland as dangerously liberal.

Foster had also suffered more personal trauma than most politicians. Brought up on the Fermanagh border with the Irish Republic, her Protestant family were isolated and vulnerable in an area where the IRA was systematically targeting many rural Protestants. As an eight-year-old girl in 1979, she was in the kitchen when IRA gunshots rang out while her father, an off-duty policeman, was outside closing his few animals in for the night. She later recalled: 'I didn't know what they were until my father came in on all fours crawling, with blood coming from his head.' After distress flares were fired into the air to alert the police, Foster hid in her bedroom for seven minutes, waiting for help. Her father survived that murder attempt but the family had to move further from the border. Then eight years later her school bus was bombed by the IRA. TV footage from the time shows a composed Foster being interviewed afterwards, despite the fact that the girl sitting beside her had been gravely injured.

On joining the DUP, Foster's career was fast-tracked by a party keen to promote a female Anglican ex-Ulster Unionist – exactly the sort of person to convince Ulster Unionist voters to similarly make the switch to Ian Paisley's party. Foster immediately entered the Executive as Environment Minister when devolution was restored in 2007, and then a year later was made DETI minister. It was viewed as a straightforward posting and Foster was seen as one of Stormont's most successful ministers. Rarely involved in scandal and well-liked by many in the business community, she was the epitome of the modern DUP. Foster was trusted by Robinson to the extent that when he had to step aside as First Minister during a scandal in 2010, she was chosen to be acting First Minister. When Robinson announced his retirement in 2015 and DUP deputy leader Nigel Dodds said that he would not be standing, Foster was the obvious alternative. For a year she was wildly popular within unionism. But RHI would cause her entire ministerial career to be reassessed.

****

Although the permanent secretary was the most senior civil servant in DETI, there was at the top of the department another powerful triumvirate: Foster; Andrew Crawford; and Foster's private secretary, Glynis Aiken. 'They were very close', one individual who observed them closely recalls. People would sometimes ask of Foster and Aiken 'are you sisters?'

Aiken ran a tight diary for her minister. On a typical day Foster would be collected by her ministerial driver before 7am to attend a business breakfast in Belfast; then driven to a company, which was announcing new jobs for a brief discussion and a photo; then brought to DETI's Netherleigh House headquarters for meetings with officials; then up to Stormont Castle for an Executive meeting; back to Netherleigh for more meetings; out to a tourism dinner before making the long journey back to Fermanagh late at night – often working on departmental papers in the back of the ministerial Škoda. Foster was doing so many hours that Aiken had to arrange for her driver to be put up in a hotel in Fivemiletown, a few miles from the minister's Brookeborough bungalow.

Aiken's organisational skills were such that despite packing so much into the diary, Foster was known for never being late. At events, Aiken would bustle in with the minister who would work the room. Crawford was a shyer member of the team, always staying in the wings. Aiken had been the gatekeeper to Foster since she first became a minister in 2007, showing what one close observer described as unusual loyalty to her political boss. And that loyalty was reciprocated for years, with Foster bringing her private secretary with her as she moved between three departments over seven and a half years. But when her big move came and Foster was made First Minister, she did not bring either Aiken or Crawford with her to Stormont Castle, instead retaining Robinson's aides. In what one Stormont source said was a significant disappointment to both Aiken and Crawford, Foster decided that the triumvirate, which had been crucial to her ministerial career, would be broken up and she would slot into Stormont Castle's existing team.

But behind the public image of professionalism, Foster had a fierce temper – and hated admitting mistakes. RHI was just one example of where a retrospective assessment of her career showed flaws and a lack of attention to detail, which had been missed at the time because people, including the author, were not looking sufficiently closely. Foster told the inquiry that although she was Energy Minister for almost seven years she did not find renewable heat an interesting topic. She said that she had 'favoured parts' of DETI such as tourism. She found energy 'very complex' and said of renewable heat: 'I think it would be unfair to say I found it interesting … I didn't find it interesting.'

David Ford, who as leader of the centrist Alliance Party served as Justice Minister, spending six years around the same Executive table as Foster, said that when she was Environment Minister she 'struck me as a good minister'. However, he added: 'My impression was that when she went to DETI she did all the glad-handing and the junkets but really there was a sense that there was nothing of substance in DETI – most of its work was done by Invest NI and it seemed that she got into that culture of "there's nothing to do here".' That view was shared by one of those who saw Foster at close quarters over six years. Alan Clarke was the longest-serving chief executive of the Northern Ireland Tourist Board (NITB), spending 13 years in the role, during which he worked under direct rule Labour ministers and then the Ulster unionist Sir Reg Empey and the DUP's Nigel Dodds prior to Foster. Prompted by the RHI scandal to speak publicly for the first time about his experience, Clarke set out multiple concerns about Foster's role in how Stormont had evolved under devolution.

Clarke said that working under Dodds was 'absolutely fine'. But with Foster and Crawford, something changed. Although he did not have a bad relationship with the minister, her spad acted in ways that alarmed him – and he held Foster responsible for what Crawford was doing. Crawford, he said, 'wouldn't have liked you going to the minister' so Clarke asked for a regular 'issues meeting' with Foster to ensure that he was getting to brief her in person. The meetings were revealing as to the minister's priorities, he said. 'Half that meeting would have been going through next week's diary "where am I going, PR-wise", rather than issues.' Civil servants would have said that she was really difficult to engage on strategy. She had no real interest in strategic direction or strategic thought. It was more 'where's the next photograph coming and how can I get in that?'

Foster had long been lampooned by opponents as the 'minister for photo opportunities', such was the volume of PR photos of her which DETI sent to newsdesks. Many of the events Foster attended would not have been considered sufficiently newsworthy for newspapers to send a photographer, so DETI used public funds to hire photographers to follow her around at many of her engagements and send the images to the media. The scale of Foster's photographic spin was such that someone set up a website called *Arlene Foster Holding Things* on which they mocked photo after photo of her standing holding everything from giant numbers to a gilet.

While Foster kept her hands clean and did not act inappropriately towards him, Clarke said that 'Andrew was her shark; she was personable and all the rest of it but Andrew was the one who kicked people and he used her power, if you like, to have his power – and she knew that'.

Criticism of Crawford's aggressive manner is common, but little of it is on the record. In a small place like Northern Ireland where the DUP is the dominant party in the Stormont system, business figures or civil servants are reluctant to be publicly critical of someone so close to the party leader. But Clarke, who is retired and now lives in Scotland, has no such concerns – and his claims are backed up by documentation seen by the author. Clarke said that the spad 'would threaten you' and although he could not do much to Clarke personally, he could make things very difficult for the tourist board. 'So what he threatened us with was "if you step out of line, I'll do an inquiry on you", which he eventually did just before I left.' He said that Crawford seemed to have created 'a culture of fear' within DETI. Clarke said that he had said to senior civil servants in DETI 'he's an employee of you guys, he's a departmental employee … you guys need to be hauling him in. But I might as well have talked to the wall'. By contrast, Clarke said that senior DUP spad Richard Bullick was 'always very affable, smiling and no bother' and Crawford's predecessor, Wallace Thompson, 'wouldn't have been nearly as interfering as Andrew Crawford'.

In a 'confidential file note' Clarke made of a meeting with Foster on 22 July 2013, he recorded how after they discussed the Northern Ireland events strategy, the minister had asked Aiken, DETI official Lorraine Fleming and NITB official Susie McCullough to leave the room. The exclusion of Aiken was particularly significant, because it is the role of the private secretary to record a minute of meetings in which the minister is involved. With Clarke, Foster, Crawford, David Sterling and David Thomson left in the room, 'the minister raised the Museum of Free Derry project'. Clarke wrote:

Both the spad and she [Foster] described it as a Sinn Féin project, that it had little or no tourism benefits. I explained the background to the project, in terms of the Western Perspective, the combination of the Apprentice Boys and the Museum of Free Derry and public realm space between. It was explained that the Museum of Free Derry had gone through all requisite board approval ... again the minister and the spad described this as a Sinn Féin project and considered that, while the Apprentice Boys had 'history', the Museum of Free Derry had not.

About a month later, BBC business correspondent Julian O'Neill had – from reading tourist board minutes – picked up on the board's concern at Stormont's pressure to cut advertising spending. He made inquiries and filed a report which said that the board had lobbied Foster to urge a rethink because the cuts may lead to it losing its targets for visitor numbers. On 30 August 2013, Clarke recorded another 'file note' to say that Crawford had phoned him the previous evening at about 7pm.

He was extremely aggressive that we had not copied in himself when we issued the statement to [BBC journalist] Julian O'Neill, which I accepted re the DETI press office, but [he] kept asking why this had not been done and was it either incompetence or were we deliberately attempting to undermine the minister. I repeatedly said that we never had any intention to undermine the minister. He also cited that [*sic*] Duffy Rafferty [advertising agency] in the conversation and had they been involved in the issue – I clarified that they definitely had not. He said he would come back to this later due to the substantial money we were paying them. He said he was off to see the minister re this issue, that she was already angry about it and that he would 'deal with this'. I clarified that Julian O'Neill had said that he would put in an FoI request if he was not given the information and that we had tried to control the situation. He said that any FoI request could be put on the long finger and that Julian O'Neill had phoned him five times the previous week which he had ignored.

Significantly, another 'file note' prepared by Clarke appears to implicate David Sterling – now the head of the Northern Ireland Civil Service – in the fallout from that incident. Clarke had explained to Sterling that the issue had not been leaked to the BBC, as Crawford seemed to believe to have happened, but had been picked up by the journalist after reading the minutes of a NITB board meeting. Clarke's note of their conversation on 30 August 2013 said: 'David said he felt that this was more a cock up than conspiracy [and] that he would speak to the [NITB] chairman regarding … the nature of our board minutes.' When asked about Clarke's comments, Sterling said he did not remember the conversation or the issue 'so I cannot comment in detail'. He added: 'I would however refute any suggestion that I was involved in any moves to "water down" the minutes of the Northern Ireland Tourist Board (NITB) either generally or specifically. The minutes of NITB board meetings were a matter for the board. The department had no role in their scrutiny or approval.'

A 29 August note by Clarke said that in a voicemail from Crawford the previous day at 5.09pm the spad had said:

Alan I understand that you folks have went [sic] and briefed the media against the department and against the minister … you haven't cc'd myself in but that's no surprise; you never do that. A very cross minister on the phone, she [sic] looking an answer from me which I can't answer and I need to answer the questions as soon as possible.

Crawford, the note said, had gone on to demand that Clarke contact him as 'a matter of urgency' because the minister may give an interview in which 'I suspect she will not be very complimentary about the NITB', adding: 'I expect a response back very quickly.' Clarke said that he was 'not remotely nationalist' – and had striven to be politically neutral in his role – but had been accused by Crawford of being 'SDLP, nationalist, whatever else' because some of what the NITB was doing did not meet with his approval.

At a valedictory media lunch just before his retirement, Clarke spoke about what he said had always been a 'very difficult relationship' with Tourism Ireland, the cross-border body responsible for promoting the island of Ireland abroad. He told the press that Tourism Ireland was not doing enough to promote Northern Ireland. But although he said that Foster also shared his view, Crawford was 'hopping mad' because it showed that 'Andrew couldn't control me'. When Clarke's comments were put to Foster and Crawford, they declined to directly comment on them but responded with a joint solicitor's letter which threatened to sue the author and the publisher 'in the event that publication of inaccurate and defamatory material occurs'.

****

At the heart of Foster's disastrous response to the RHI scandal when it erupted was her failure to accept personal responsibility – despite having wanted to take personal credit for the scheme when she thought it was a success. That contrasted with how some officials – and even some political figures, such as Tim Cairns – had freely admitted their individual failures. One such official was Elaine Dolan, who was head of the internal audit in Foster's department when RHI was designed. She accepted that an auditor working under her had not done enough to query what officials were telling him. Although the auditor was not one of her staff, with the work having been subcontracted to accountants ASM, and although his report had not come to her directly but had been checked by another individual, Dolan accepted ultimate responsibility. Dame Una O'Brien thanked her for 'taking responsibility ... they're perhaps words we hear too infrequently so far in this inquiry'.

By contrast, Foster was keen to apportion blame to others whom she said had failed her, but insisted that she did nothing wrong. At the start of her evidence, David Scoffield QC began by asking 'a question with which many of the public may be concerned, and it's this: are there any of the mistakes or errors in relation to the RHI scheme, which you've identified for which you bear any measure of personal responsibility?' In a rambling answer which did not answer the question, Foster was prepared to say that 'the way in which the RHI scheme has brought it to this place is a matter of deep regret for me, politically and personally'. She went on to say enigmatically: 'There will be known unknowns and unknown unknowns but certainly there seems to be a lot of unknown unknowns.' Scoffield asked her again as to whether she felt she bore any personal responsibility. He said that she seemed to be saying that with hindsight there were several things she would do differently but at the time she did not do anything which was wrong. Foster replied: 'That's correct. Yes, that is my position.' Pressed by the inquiry's technical adviser, Dr Keith MacLean, to say if there were any things which she could have done or should have done, Foster said: 'None that spring to mind at present.'

During her evidence, she spoke with remarkable imprecision about key moments in the story, repeatedly using phrases such as 'I don't remember', 'I can't recall' and 'I don't think I have any clear recollection' about important meetings which went unminuted. The scandal also exposed a lack of candour by the DUP leader. On the night of the Nolan interview on 15 December 2016, she was asked in writing if she had 'any knowledge or concerns that any members or associates of the DUP or members of their family have benefited from the RHI scheme'. She responded that she had no knowledge of who was a claimant, saying 'I have no knowledge of who is on the list'. Yet it is now clear that she was at least aware of her spad Stephen Brimstone being on the list, as well as being aware of Crawford's relatives. The scandal also exposed Foster as frequently incapable of striking the right tone. Where a cannier politician would have presented contrition, Foster – even when attempting to do so, at the advice of those around her – managed to sound bullish and aggressive. In September 2018, after the inquiry had exposed myriad DUP secrets and dysfunctionalities, DUP MLA Paul Frew candidly accepted that it had damaged the DUP. Striking a very different tone to that of Foster and other party colleagues, the North Antrim MLA told BBC politics programme *The View* that the inquiry's revelations did not reflect well on the DUP, and he was 'very concerned' but he believed that at the end of the inquiry there would be 'better government – and that's a good thing'.

CHAPTER 27

THE LEGACY

Since 1921, when Northern Ireland was pragmatically carved out of the rest of the island of Ireland – as Britain's attempt to solve 'the Irish question' – Irish republicans have argued that it could not work and would not work. Only Irish reunification would solve the ills of the states on both sides of the border, they argued. In at least one respect, they were wrong – the new northern state would survive for 100 years, despite their expectations and efforts, often involving violence, to the contrary.

Despite the fact that the one metric used to determine Northern Ireland's borders had been the number of Protestants who would be within the new UK region, even radically changed demographics, which had brought the Catholic–Protestant split almost level, had not led to any great surge in support for Irish unity. On the contrary, by 2016, with Northern Ireland still constitutionally within the UK but with an increased Irish dimension and enforced power-sharing between unionists and nationalists, polls had consistently shown record levels of support for the constitutional status quo.

That was shaken in June 2016 when the UK voted to leave the EU, despite the fact that Northern Ireland voted to remain. Nationalists were discombobulated by a sense that they were not in control of their destiny. The plebiscite demonstrated how forces in England could alter the course of life in Northern Ireland in a way which had practical and psychological implications for them. But although Sinn Féin responded to Brexit by renewing its call for an Irish unity referendum, it did not seem to contemplate toppling Stormont. Despite being on opposite sides of the Brexit argument, Arlene Foster and Martin McGuinness were able to write a joint letter to the Prime Minister setting out their practical priorities for the Brexit process. It was against that backdrop that the RHI scandal emerged. The revelations in December 2016 were met with dismay and anger from unionists and nationalists alike. But over time the narrative shifted subtly in a way which could have constitutional implications for years to come.

For decades, unionists in Northern Ireland looked south and scoffed at what they saw as an endemically corrupt political establishment. From brown envelopes for councillors corruptly nodding through planning applications, to the crooked Taoiseach Charlie Haughey, it was a society most unionists looked on with a disdain and reinforced their constitutional preference to remain British.

But with a booming southern economy and with the Republic perceived as a place with a modern outlook, RHI has contributed to at least a partial reversal of that image: now it is Northern Ireland that to many people looks shady. Cash for ash was not the first Stormont scandal. There had been Red Sky, NAMA, SIF, expenses and myriad others. Though there are many honourable DUP members, far too many of the scandals involved DUP figures. Together, they had sapped public confidence in a system where there seemed to be a culture of impunity – although conversely voters generally did not seem to punish those whose conduct angered them.

Often a profound issue is understood through an anecdote. For many people, their vague sense that Stormont was broken came to be encapsulated in the story of RHI. Some people would take from the tale that those running the system were so incompetent that they could not understand why people were piling into a scheme that paid more for heat than the cost of the fuel to generate that heat. For others, they assumed – as the public often do, and often unfairly – that there was a darker truth and corruption had to be involved. Regardless of which camp an individual fell into, their view of Stormont was severely tarnished. RHI became the prism through which ordinary people came to understand the scale and the nature of the dysfunctionality among their rulers. That in itself was powerful, because most politics never makes its way beyond the bubble of people who follow the minutiae of political debate.

Everything in life is interlinked, and RHI did not happen in a vacuum but in conjunction with Brexit, the DUP's Líofa decision, McGuinness's mortal illness and the collapse of Stormont. What the scandal revealed embarrassed the DUP, the civil service and, to a lesser extent, Sinn Féin. But it was unionism that was acutely vulnerable. RHI revealed a system that was freewheelingly dysfunctional. Almost three years after the scandal erupted into a political crisis, the question for unionism is whether it can confine the fallout from this to Arlene Foster, or to the DUP, or to the civil service, or to the devolved Stormont system – or whether it persuades some people that Northern Ireland itself is unsustainable as an entity.

The scandal revealed critical deficiencies in four areas, which have constitutional implications. Firstly, the civil service was shown to be populated by generalists, who were hopelessly out of their depth in dealing with RHI. That use of generalists was not in itself an accident or failure; it was by design. Some of that is tied to the size of Northern Ireland and whether a region of 1.8 million people can sustain the expertise necessary for running a devolved government with the powers of Stormont. If not, the entire devolution settlement may have to be reassessed, with knock-on implications for public support for the constitutional status quo.

Secondly, the scale of the incompetence within the Northern Ireland Civil Service has led to the first-ever calls from a senior politician, Arlene Foster, for consideration to be given to ending its historic independence from Whitehall and subsuming it into the Home Civil Service, with power residing in London. Such a development is unlikely to happen, not least because it would seem to nationalists to be a move against the spirit of devolution, but the very fact that it is being raised demonstrates how old certainties have been shaken by RHI. However, civil servants can be wily creatures able to find alternative means of achieving the same goal. In January 2018, there was surprise when it was announced that Sue Gray, the right-hand aide to the Cabinet Secretary, was moving to Belfast – not to take over as head of the Stormont civil service, but as permanent secretary in the Department of Finance. It was a curious move for a figure described in London as 'the most powerful civil servant you've never heard of'. There had been dismay at a senior level in Whitehall as mandarins read reports of what was emerging from the RHI Inquiry. Whether by accident or design, Gray's move to Belfast meant that Whitehall had the heart of the Northern Ireland Civil Service a figure it trusted – and someone who immediately set about reforming Stormont's bureaucracy.

Thirdly, although the scandal has been largely missed in the rest of the UK, it has revealed a crudely grasping attitude of some senior figures in Stormont, which has the potential to undermine support for Northern Ireland on the British mainland. The unedifying picture of a greedy culture of 'get whatever we can, regardless of the consequences' undermines the image unionist politicians, such as Foster, have sought to portray of deep care for the entire Union. The scandal is likely to have immediate implications for the next time Stormont's politicians go to the Treasury with a begging bowl asking for more money. And at some point, if middle England realises it is paying for these sorts of scandals, there will be a day of reckoning.

Fourthly, the timing of the scandal undermined unionism. At a point when Brexit had already angered many nationalists, and the centenary of Northern Ireland was around the corner, RHI – made in a unionist ministry and disastrously dealt with by the leader of unionism – was calamitous for the ideology of which she was the leader. The snap election called, as a result of Foster's refusal to stand aside, saw unionism lose its Stormont majority for the first time in almost 100 years. But perhaps, more significant than that, it breathed life into the narrative that Stormont can never work and only Irish unity is the answer – even though there is still no hint of a majority for removing the Irish border. The timing of the scandal came just four years before Northern Ireland's centenary – a rare moment at which even those with scant interest in politics are more likely to reflect on the constitutional question. In 2021, when allegiances will be pondered, and in some cases reassessed, RHI will be fresh in the memory. Prior to Brexit and RHI, polling pointed to the likelihood that many Catholic voters might think: one hundred years on, our position has been transformed, we feel comfortable and treated fairly within Northern Ireland.

Now, amid an increasingly tribalised political landscape, the uncertainty of Brexit and the RHI Inquiry's revelation of incompetence across a swathe of the machinery of government, there is an acute danger for unionism that in 2021 a section of Catholics who could have been persuaded of the Union's merits instead say: we gave this 100 years and it is just a failed state. In that regard, what senior DUP figures such as Foster have done with RHI has been recklessly detrimental to that which they say they cherish above all else: the Union. Regardless of Northern Ireland's constitutional future, it will have to be governed – and in all likelihood even a united Ireland would involve a regional Stormont administration. Therefore, irrespective of constitutional aspiration, it should be in the interests of both unionism and nationalism to rectify the faults exposed by RHI. This scandal saw huge sums of public money squandered, brought down a government, involved reprehensible behaviour by some of those charged with serving the people of Northern Ireland, caused financial pain for individuals and trashed Northern Ireland's reputation. But it also exposed to the light practices which will be difficult to continue if devolution is restored. If the scale of this scandal convinces all sides of the imperative to change – and if Stormont can be reformed as an open, responsive and competent institution – then cash for ash may be remembered as the darkness just before the dawn of a new age.

But above all, the six-week period in December 2016 and January 2017 showed the power of public opinion in a democracy. Whether what has happened leads to lasting change or there is a reversion to the old ways will depend as much on the public as on politicians. If voters in Northern Ireland care more about constitutional or tribal disputes than good government or integrity in public life, it is quite logical for politicians to act in line with those wishes. In a democracy, the politicians tend to be reflective of society even if many people like to think otherwise. After decades of constitutional politics, RHI involved sustained cross-community public fury about a financial scandal, contributing to the collapse of devolution. On 6 December 2016, the day of *Spotlight*, anyone suggesting that RHI could lead to Stormont falling within 34 days would have been looked upon as a melodramatic and deluded fool. In time, RHI may be viewed as a warning to the leaders of unionism that if they do not learn from what has happened and change their ways, there is the potential for a far greater collapse: that of Northern Ireland itself.

KEY PLAYERS

Jonathan Bell. Foster's successor as DETI minister, in post until May 2016.

Stephen Brimstone. DUP special adviser to First Minister Arlene Foster. Removed a domestic biomass boiler to install a non-domestic boiler in his garage – which heated his home and allowed him to claim RHI.

Tim Cairns. Bell's spad who admits he tried to delay RHI being reined in, but he says on the orders of others in the DUP.

Sir Patrick Coghlin. Retired Northern Ireland Court of Appeal judge who chaired the public inquiry into the scandal.

Andrew Crawford. Foster's special adviser (spad) throughout her time as DETI minister and Finance Minister.

DETI. Stormont's Department for Enterprise, Trade and Investment (Renamed the Department for the Economy, DfE, in May 2016), which set up and oversaw the RHI scheme.

Arlene Foster. DETI minister from 2008 to May 2015, then Finance Minister until January 2016, then First Minister until January 2017.

Fiona Hepper. Head of DETI's energy division when RHI was being set up and for its first year. Left in November 2013.

Seamus Hughes. Immediately beneath Wightman in DETI's energy division. Succeeded Hutchinson, arriving in June 2014 and a key figure as RHI fell apart.

Peter Hutchinson. The mid-ranking DETI official under Hepper most involved in designing and overseeing RHI until he left in May 2014.

Timothy Johnston. Special adviser to every DUP First Minister and the party's most powerful backroom figure.

Dr Keith MacLean. Energy expert appointed by Coghlin to act as the inquiry's technical assessor, a role in which he quizzed witnesses.

Andrew McCormick. As permanent secretary, DETI's top official from July 2014, arriving just months before RHI ran out of control.

Joanne McCutcheon. Hutchinson's boss. The only key player not to give evidence to the RHI Inquiry.

John Mills. Succeeded Fiona Hepper as DETI's head of energy division in January 2014.

Dame Una O'Brien. Former permanent secretary of Whitehall's Department of Health, appointed by Coghlin to assist him as a panel member at the inquiry.

Ofgem. The Office of Gas and Electricity Markets, the GB energy regulator, which also runs some government schemes and was contracted to run RHI day to day by accrediting applications and making payments.

Janette O'Hagan. A businesswoman who saw RHI's perverse incentive and tried to warn DETI. Sometimes referred to as the first whistleblower, but saw herself as a 'concerned citizen'.

Chris Stewart. From August 2014, directly beneath McCormick as deputy secretary (head of policy group) at DETI.

Stuart Wightman. Worked under Mills, having replaced McCutcheon as head of energy division's energy efficiency branch in June 2014, about eight months before it began to run out of control.

ABBREVIATIONS

AME – Annually Managed Expenditure, money which is funded directly from the Treasury in London and is effectively limitless.

DEL – Departmental Expenditure Limits, the budget allocated to each Stormont department.

CEPA - Cambridge Economic Policy Associates, an economic consultancy.

CHP – Combined Heat and Power plants, mini electricity stations which utilise the heat which would otherwise be a by-product of generating electricity.

DECC – Department of Energy and Climate Change, the Whitehall department which ran the GB RHI scheme.

DETI – Department of Enterprise, Trade and Investment, the Stormont department which set up and oversaw Northern Ireland's RHI scheme.

DfE – The Department for the Economy, the department which replaced DETI in May 2016 as part of a reorganisation of devolved departments.

FoI – Freedom of Information, the law which allows members of the public to ask for government documentation, subject to certain exemptions.

kW – kilowatt, a unit of energy. In biomass boilers, the higher the kilowatt number of the boiler, the more energy it can use and the more heat it can produce.

kWh – kilowatt-hour, a unit of energy (in the same way that distance can be expressed in feet, metres or miles, energy can be expressed as calories, therms, kilowatt-hours, etc).

MLA – Member of the Legislative Assembly, Stormont's equivalent of MPs.

MW – Megawatt, equivalent to 1,000 kilowatts

NIRO – the Northern Ireland Renewables Obligation, another public subsidy used to encourage wind turbines, anaerobic digestors and other technologies.

Ofgem – Office of Gas and Electricity Markets, the GB energy regulator which also runs some government schemes and was paid by Stormont to handle accreditations, payments and inspections under its RHI scheme.

PAC – the Assembly's Public Accounts Committee, a cross-party group of MLAs which scrutinises public spending.

RHANI – The Renewable Heat Association of Northern Ireland, the group set up to represent RHI boiler owners in early 2017.

UFU – the Ulster Farmers' Union, the representative body for farmers in Northern Ireland.

TRIM – Stormont's data management system into which all significant documentation ought to be saved.

TIMELINE

2008

Stormont decides to opt out of an RHI scheme being developed by Westminster.

2012

June: Ofgem warn the officials in Arlene Foster's Department of Enterprise, Trade and Investment (DETI) designing RHI that their scheme was seriously flawed.

November: Rather than delay the scheme to fix the problems, DETI presses ahead and launches RHI.

2013

August: Businesswoman Janette O'Hagan warns DETI officials and Arlene Foster about RHI's perverse incentive.

2014

May: O'Hagan again attempts to raise the alarm, offering to provide proof of abuse.

March: O'Hagan yet again seeks to raise the alarm, pleading with DETI to listen to her.

December: DETI consciously chooses to delay introducing cost controls and instead expands RHI to domestic properties.

2015

March: It becomes clear to DETI that RHI is running beyond budget.

June: New DETI minister Jonathan Bell is told about the problem for the first time.

July: A submission goes to Bell arguing for urgent cost controls. No decision is taken until September – and then it is for further delay.

July: Arlene Foster's adviser Andrew Crawford forwards to relatives a confidential ministerial submission revealing the looming cost controls.

September–November: A huge spike in applications sees the number of RHI claimants double in the final few weeks before cost controls.

November: A basic form of cost control is finally implemented.

2016

January: Crawford tips off poultry giant Moy Park that RHI is to shut for good, giving it weeks to pile into the scheme, driving a second spike in applications.

January: A whistleblower gives Foster a note alleging systemic abuse of RHI to the extent that a farmer is in line to get £1 million for heating an empty shed.

February: After rows between Foster and Bell, RHI is finally shut – but only after closure is again delayed.

July: The Northern Ireland Audit Office reports on 'serious systemic failings' projected to cost taxpayers hundreds of millions of pounds.

September: Stormont's Public Accounts Committee begins public hearings as it launches an inquiry into the scheme.

December: A BBC *Spotlight* exposé of what happened triggers a political crisis. Nine days later, Bell does an unprecedented televised interview with Stephen Nolan in which he alleges senior DUP figures stopped him shutting the scheme.

Deputy First Minister Martin McGuinness calls on Arlene Foster to step aside as First Minister so that the allegations can be investigated.

2017

January: After Foster refuses to stand aside, McGuinness resigns, ejecting her from office and triggering a snap Assembly election.

After weeks arguing against a public inquiry into the scandal, Sinn Féin's Finance Minister sets up a public inquiry under Sir Patrick Coghlin.

MLAs pass legislation to retrospectively slash RHI payments.

March: After an Assembly election in which the DUP loses 10 seats and unionism loses its Stormont majority for the first time, devolution cannot be restored.

November: Public hearings of the RHI inquiry begin.

2018

December: The public inquiry concludes its public hearings, but its investigations continue.

2019

March: In the absence of devolution, Westminster passes legislation which involves punitive retrospective tariffs for RHI claimants.

ACKNOWLEDGEMENTS

I am grateful to my editor at the *News Letter*, Alistair Bushe, deputy editor Ben Lowry and news editor Rod McMurray for their unstinting support for my work on this story, facing down the inevitable threats.

My thanks also go to Stephen Walker who has been a deep well of wisdom on book publishing and the process of writing. His advice has made this project far smoother than otherwise would have been the case, as has the support of my publisher, Conor Graham of Merrion Press. This book would be very different without Conor's immediate and sustained belief in the importance of the subject, his patience with my relaxed journalistic interpretation of deadlines, his willingness to accept a manuscript which is 40% longer than planned and his commitment to excellence.

My longsuffering wife, Anna, not only toiled through every chapter spotting errors and inconsistencies but put up with losing me for unreasonably long portions of the last two and a half years because she appreciated the significance of these issues.

But the people who have contributed most to this story have been you, the readers. From the earliest reports in the *News Letter* in 2016, it was the online – and then print – figures which gave my editor confidence that we were reporting an important story which deserved significant resources. In turn, readers fed through hundreds of pieces of information which prompted further investigation and more stories.

Often the public can feel helpless to effect change when reading newspapers or watching news programmes. But with online analytical tools which like never before pinpoint the stories with which the public engages, RHI demonstrates the part which can be played by ordinary people in encouraging investigative journalism. Outside of the BBC, news is a commercial business and if no one is reading important stories it becomes harder and harder to justify them. If you click on clickbait, expect to get more of it. If you click on serious journalism, or buy a newspaper, or subscribe to an investigative news outlet, then you are likely to get more of it. So thank you for buying this book.

INDEX

abuse and potential for fraud, 96, 123, 139, 140, 142, 163, 208–9, 211–12, 217, 220, 229, 231, 240–2, 314; due to higher subsidy payments, 67, 70, 71, 158, 230, 234; and reports of heating empty buildings, 154–5, 162, 190, 200

accountability and discipline within the Civil Service, 326–7, 329

accountability for spads, 336–9

Action Renewables, 59, 73, 230, 231

AD (Anaerobic Digester) plants, 292, 293

Adams, Gerry, 256–7, 268, 269, 270

Adams, Jeremy, 227

addendum business case document for future and retrospective expenditure, 187–9, 190

AEA Technology consultants, 25, 45

AECOM Pöyry consultants, 21–2

Agnew, Steven, 60, 222

Aiken, Glynis, 115–16, 346, 348

Aiken, Joseph, 115, 118, 145, 146–7, 148, 149–50, 246, 276

air source heat pumps, 24, 100, 103–4, 162

Alderdice, Lord, 327

Alexander, Ian, 43

Allister, Jim, 167, 168, 242, 243–4, 335, 338

Alternative Heat Ltd, 174, 260

AME (Annually Managed Expenditure), 35–7, 38, 53, 116, 117, 133, 136, 153, 163, 192, 321, 323

Anderson, John and Lilian, 239

Anderson, Mark, 45, 149, 228, 264, 272, 314

applications for the RHI, 74–6, 89, 91, 92–3, 106, 119, 141; and court appeals by aggrieved claimants, 308–11; and the rapid installation of boilers, 160, 171; and spike in demand before the introduction of tariff rates, 8, 133, 141–2, 156, 161, 171–2, 176–7, 179, 181, 185, 191, 205, 211–12, 213, 216, 249, 260

Arlene Foster Holding Things (website), 348

Arthur Cox (law firm), 39

'assurance statements,' 120

Aston, Wesley, 263

Attwood, Alex, 69, 70, 253, 290

audits, 199, 212, 219; and delays in, 314, 316, 317; for non-compliance, 241, 243, 244, 245–6, 313–14, 316 (*see also* Northern Ireland Audit Office, the)

Avis, Keith, 56, 57

Balcas Ltd, 174, 228, 260

banks and loan support for RHI, the, 67–8, 69

Barker, Greg, 72, 75

Barnett Formula, the, 116

Batch, John, 96, 170–1

BBC broadcast interviews, 1–8, 12–15, 18

Belfast News Letter (newspaper), 68, 150, 194, 248, 249–50, 256, 259, 260–1

Belfast Telegraph, The (newspaper), 222, 250

belief in maximising Treasury funding to Ulster, the, 31–2, 34, 36, 46, 52–3, 109, 111, 116, 136, 141, 142, 157, 191, 321–2, 323, 324–5

Bell, Elliott, 172; and claims to the Assembly that RHI was a success, 215, 216

Bell, Jonathan, 1–7, 80, 94, 139, 141, 156, 160, 168–9, 186, 189, 192, 220–1, 224, 239, 253, 262, 264, 271, 299, 331, 337, 339; and blame for RHI, 14, 15, 68, 202; and the closure of RHI, 212, 214, 216; and delays to tariff controls, 8–10, 14, 15, 16–18, 131–2; and interview for *The Nolan Show*, 1–7, 206, 252; and perceptions of misleading, 167–8, 183, 214, 215; and questions about secret recordings, 11–12; and relations with Arlene Foster, 14, 15, 68, 132, 195–6, 202, 207, 216–18; and relations with Timothy Cairns, 125–8, 129–30, 131, 132–3, 165–7, 169, 204, 331, 339; and sense of responsibility about RHI, 135–6, 156, 164–5, 183, 187, 189, 276; and suspicions of colleagues, 202,

'A monumental work of solid reportage, measured, elegant and thorough. This is a story of political ineptitude and waste. That Stormont sought to use a scheme for saving the environment as an opportunity for the lavish squandering of money and energy speaks of ignorance and cynicism. Sam McBride, throughout this story, has been one of the journalists who stayed with it and explained it best through his articles and broadcasts. Now that work coalesces into an exemplary work of journalism. If politicians had maintained their standards with a similar responsibility, this book would not have needed to be written.'

Malachi O'Doherty, journalist and author

'The RHI scandal played a significant role in bringing Northern Ireland's experiment in devolution to its knees. Future historians will ask how did this happen? Sam McBride's book will be their first port of call. He has been at the heart of the journalistic coverage of this crisis and it shows in every page.'

**Lord Bew, historian and Emeritus Professor of
Irish politics at Queen's University, Belfast**

'This is one of the most important books in the history of Northern Ireland. To devastating effect, it sets out the path of RHI, a scandal that highlights profound problems with how we are governed in the 21st century.'

Ben Lowry, deputy editor, News Letter

'Superbly researched and explained with clarity and precision, *Burned* tells the tale of a grossly mismanaged green energy scheme which brought down Northern Ireland's power sharing government, tarnishing its internationally-acclaimed reputation for partnership and peace-making. The sorry saga of incompetence, groupthink, buck-passing and failure to pay heed to warnings unfolds like a slow motion car crash. Sam McBride's book should be required reading for those working in the public and private sectors far beyond Northern Ireland as a manual on how not to run major projects and how not to govern a society.'

Mark Devenport, political journalist and broadcaster

'This book is essential reading for anyone who wants to understand how the Stormont institutions were brought down by a scandal of enormous proportions. It clearly, coldly and comprehensively sets out a series of astonishing events involving incredible sums of public money and deserves to be studied by all those interested in our political process.'

Noel Doran, editor, The Irish News

'As Brexit dominates politics in Westminster and Dublin, Sam McBride's lucid and compelling account of the nightmarish reality of devolution in Northern Ireland shows us that there will be no easy solutions in Belfast. This triumph of investigative journalism from one of the UK's most important reporters spares nobody. Anybody who wishes to understand how the DUP and Sinn Féin's great experiment failed should read it – not that they will want you to.'

Patrick Maguire, political correspondent, New Statesman

'An intriguing forensic examination of the RHI scandal which brought down Stormont. It should be an essential textbook for politicians , advisers and the civil service. Sam McBride's book clearly points out this must never happen again if faith in politics is to be restored.'

Ken Reid, UTV Political Editor

'Unlike the RHI legislation she introduced, I hope Arlene Foster actually reads this. Sam McBride brilliantly untangles the facts about RHI to reveal a jaw-dropping and occasionally hilarious omnishambles. The author has taken the fiendishly complex RHI scandal and made it both comprehensible and shocking. If I were a civil servant, or a DUP spad or worked at Moy Park I would demand that all copies of this book were burnt in a 99kw wood pellet boiler.'

Tim McGarry, comedian

'One of Belfast's most authoritative journalists has produced a fascinating and detailed account of one of the city's most controversial episodes.'

David McKittrick, journalist and author

'One of the most important books on Northern Ireland politics since the Good Friday Agreement; and certainly the most important on the Assembly and the function — and dysfunction — of devolution. Disturbingly revelatory.'

Alex Kane, columnist and commentator